CW01475867

FATEFUL HOURS

VOLKER ULLRICH is a historian and journalist whose previous books include biographies of Bismarck and Napoleon, as well as a major study of Imperial Germany, *The Nervous Superpower, 1871–1918*. Ullrich was for many years editor of the historical section of *Die Zeit*. His two-volume biography of Adolf Hitler was an international bestseller.

JEFFERSON CHASE is a writer, translator and journalist based in Berlin. He has translated more than fifty German texts into English, including *The Writers' Castle* by Uwe Neumahr, also available from Pushkin.

FATEFUL HOURS

The Collapse of the Weimar Republic

Volker Ullrich

Translated from the German by Jefferson Chase

PUSHKIN PRESS

Pushkin Press
Somerset House, Strand
London WC2R 1LA

Original text © Verlag C.H. Beck oHG, München 2024
English translation © 2025 Jefferson Chase

Fateful Hours was first published as *Schicksalsstunden einer
Demokratie* by C.H. Beck in Munich, 2024

First published by Pushkin Press in 2025

SBN 13: 978-1-80533-279-4

GOETHE
INSTITUT

The translation of this work was supported in part
by a grant from the Goethe-Institut.

A CIP catalogue record for this title is available from the British Library

The authorised representative in the EEA is
eucomply OÜ, Pärnu mnt. 139b-14, 11317, Tallinn, Estonia,
hello@eucompliancepartner.com, +33757690241

Offset by Tetragon, London
Printed and bound in the United Kingdom by Clays Ltd, Elcograf S.p.A.

Pushkin Press is committed to a sustainable future for our
business, our readers and our planet. This book is made from
paper from forests that support responsible forestry.

MIX
Paper | Supporting
responsible forestry
FSC
www.fsc.org
FSC® C018072

www.pushkinpress.com

1 3 5 7 9 8 6 4 2

Contents

Preface

Democracies are fragile. They can flip into dictatorships. Liberties that seemed won for all time can be squandered.

With the end of the Cold War, our awareness of the threats to democracy diminished. Francis Fukuyama's thesis about the "end of history" held that the future would no longer see any serious challenges to liberal democracy. In his view, there was simply no longer any alternative. Although few observers may have advanced this view as radically as he did, Fukuyama's faith in the triumph of democracy became the hallmark of an entire epoch. The only remaining question seemed to be how long it would take for the ideology to spread to the entire world and how stubbornly those dictatorships opposed to progress would resist.

Little remains of this certainty. Democracy is under internal and external pressure across the globe. Authoritarian states like China and Russia vie for power with the Western democracies on the world stage and attack them from within. In the United States, Donald Trump's first presidency provided a preview of what his second term in office might bring. This time, he is better prepared, less constrained by advisers, and more determined to push his agenda through. The future of American democracy has never been so uncertain since the declaration of independence almost 250 years ago. But also in almost all European countries, right-wing populism is on the rise. In Germany, the Alternative for Germany, or AfD, an at least partially far-right extremist party, has

attracted considerable support—and not just in the country's formerly
Communist east but also among West German bourgeois circles. It is
telling that Elon Musk has advocated for voting AfD in the latest German election campaign. Right-wing populism is a global movement with
worrying transnational ties. In short: Concern for democracy has become
a defining feature of a new historical epoch.

The failure of the Weimar Republic led to the Third Reich. Germany's first democracy ended in the transfer of power to Adolf Hitler.
There is no overlooking Weimar when we ponder the question of how
and why democracies die. The fate of the first German republic is both
a warning and an object lesson not only in Germany but also globally.
Prophecies that Germany or other Western democracies could return
to the "conditions like Weimar" aren't new.[1] What is new is the actual
global fragility of democracy, which recalls the period between the two
world wars. That alone is reason enough to remind ourselves of what
really happened in and to the Weimar Republic.

Weimar's democracy is still fascinating, not least because of the astonishing contradictions this merely fourteen-year period encompassed. It
was a time of new beginnings, experimentation, and a willingness to
innovate. A laboratory of modernism full of vibrant culture, particularly—
though not exclusively—in the metropolis of Berlin. A period when traditional gender roles loosened, and people were more sexually free. But it
was also a time of seemingly endless crises and upheavals, including the
hyperinflation of 1923 and the Great Depression starting in 1929. A time
of political instability, of rapidly changing governments, violence, and
militancy, which led to civil-war-like fighting in the system's dying days.

It has rightly been demanded that Weimar history not be treated
solely ex post facto as a prelude to the National Socialist dictatorship but
as an epoch of its own, full of ambivalence and contradiction.[2] Of course,
given the catastrophe of Hitler's ascent to power, there is no avoiding the
question of why German democracy ultimately failed. "No one can think
of the Weimar Republic without thinking about its demise," wrote historian Hagen Schulze.[3] Moreover, the current global crisis of democracy has
given renewed urgency to the question of what caused the German disaster in 1933. But that's precisely why it's important to emphasize the open-
endedness of the situation at the time. Otherwise, we ignore alternatives

and spaces to maneuver—and risk overlooking something that is essential to answering the question of the demise of Weimar democracy.

Historians have advanced various explanations. Some point out the difficult legacy of Wilhelmine German authoritarianism: the continuing influence of pre-democratic elites in heavy industry, the large agricultural estates east of the Elbe River, the military, the government administration, and the justice system. Others emphasize the burden placed on the young democracy from the start by Germany's military defeat in the First World War and the harsh terms of the Treaty of Versailles. Still others stress the structural shortcomings of the Weimar Constitution, which granted sweeping powers to the Reich president as a kind of ersatz kaiser—the constitution's Article 48 gave him an instrument of rule by emergency decree that practically invited misuse in times of crisis. Another school of thought points the finger at Germany's political parties' confinement within ideological front lines and their refusal to compromise for chronically weakening the parliamentary democracy. But as heavy as the initial burdens and failings, resulting mainly from the foundation of the republic, may have been, Germany's first democratic experiment was not destined to fail. There were alternatives—and reasons why they were disregarded or insufficiently pursued. The end of the story was far more open than those fixated on the Weimar Republic's ultimate demise would have us believe.

There was no shortage of opportunities to change course and go in different directions. For instance, during the revolution of 1918–19, the governing Social Democrats could have pushed through greater societal change and retained less of the past. Or the suppression of the Kapp Putsch in March 1920 and the great wave of pro-democratic solidarity following the murder of Foreign Minister Walther Rathenau in June 1922 could have been the occasion for those in power to take the offensive against the anti-democratic camp. That opportunity remained unused.

During the hyperinflation of 1923, when the republic was teetering on the abyss, the forces of democratic self-preservation proved stronger than many people expected. But the election of the dyed-in-the-wool monarchist Paul von Hindenburg as Reich president in April 1925 represented a caesura. His rise could have been prevented, had the Communists been willing to go against their usual grain. Likewise, the collapse of the grand coalition in March 1930, which marked a de facto end to parliamentary democracy, could have been avoided had the political parties involved been more willing to compromise. No one forced the mainstream parties in the state of Thuringia to include the Nazis in the regional government in 1930. They did that of their own free will, granting the fascists the opportunity to rehearse their rise to power on the national level. There was no reason for Hindenburg to yield to his advisers and dismiss Reich Chancellor Heinrich Brüning in late May 1932, thereby terminating the moderate phase of presidentially appointed government. With Brüning in office, his successor Franz von Papen would not have been able to stage his coup d'état in Prussia in July 1932, removing one of the final bulwarks of the Weimar Republic.

Even Hitler's triumph in January 1933 wasn't unavoidable. There were still ways to keep him from power. One of the bitterest ironies of German history is that the leader, or *Führer*, of the Nazi Party assumed the office of chancellor thanks to a sinister game of intrigue—at a juncture when Hitler's movement was in decline and many keen contemporary observers had already, and prematurely, written him off.

History is always open. The only thing a historian can say for certain about the future is that it will turn out differently than people at any given time imagine. The decisive factor is how individual people behave in concrete situations. That was true during the Weimar Republic, and it still is today. It's in our hands to decide whether democracy fails or survives. The true goal of this book is to illustrate that point.

We should constantly recall that the Weimar Republic didn't go out with a bang. It was gradually undermined by the erosion of the constitution and democratic practices. This "quiet death" should serve as a negative example of how Western democracies like the United States, whose stability has long seemed unshakable, could fail despite their long and storied tradition.[4] The failure of the Weimar Republic remains a lesson of how fragile democracy is and how quickly freedom can be squandered, if democratic institutions cease to function and civil society is too weak to keep the anti-democratic wolves from the door.

FATEFUL HOURS

1

A Magical Beginning

THE 1918–19 REVOLUTION

November 9, 1918, in Berlin: Soldiers side with striking workers in front of the Garde-Ulanen barracks. (The sign reads "Brothers! Don't shoot!")

It's November 9, 1918. Berlin is gripped with a feverish tension. Rumors of a German navy officers' uprising in Kiel and the rapid spread of revolution has been keeping the imperial capital on tenterhooks for days. "All circles of society are nervous with anticipation that something extraordinary is about to happen," writes one of the era's keenest observers, the art patron and diplomat Count Harry Kessler.[1] The commander in chief of the Germany March, General Alexander von Linsingen, orders the suspension of rail travel and demands additional troops to protect Berlin. But all measures of this sort soon prove useless.

On the morning of November 9, workers in Berlin's major factories declare a general strike. The Naumburg Riflemen, a German military unit considered particularly reliable, sides with the protesters. Massive demonstrations, led by armed workers and soldiers, move from the city's outer districts to the government quarter, marching up and down before the state buildings on Wilhelmstrasse. Theodor Wolff, the editor in chief of the liberal *Berliner Tageblatt* newspaper, writes in his diary: "From the window of the editorial office I can see huge masses of people with red flags pressing forward down Leipziger Strasse. Colleagues arrive with news that people on the street are ripping the cockades from officers' uniforms, that nothing is being guarded anymore, that the city has been completely transformed in one fell swoop, that the streetcars are no longer running, that revolutionaries have occupied the telegraph office, and that the red flag is flying over the Brandenburg Gate."[2]

Working the telephone ceaselessly, Reich Chancellor Prince Max von Baden tries in vain to convince Kaiser Wilhelm II, who is still at his headquarters in the Belgian town of Spa, to abdicate. In the end, around noon, Prince Max decides to take matters into his own hands and orders the telegraph office to spread the news that Wilhelm has in fact vacated the throne. A short time later, he transfers the chancellorship to the chairman of the majority wing of the Social Democratic Party,

Friedrich Ebert. When asked whether he is prepared to exercise that office "even under the monarchist constitution," Ebert equivocates, "Yesterday I would have definitely answered this question in the affirmative, but today I must first consult with my allies." When Prince Max broaches the option of a royal regency, Ebert retorts, "It's too late for that." Behind him, his party comrades chant, "Too late, too late!"[3]

At two in the afternoon, the deputy chairman of the Majority Social Democrats, Philipp Scheidemann, proclaims a "German republic" from a balcony at the Reichstag. "The German people have emerged victorious across the board," he tells the crowd. "The old and decayed has collapsed. Militarism is over! The Hohenzollerns have stepped down!"[4] The leader of the radical leftist Spartacus Group, Karl Liebknecht, only recently released from Luckau Prison on October 23, leaves no doubt in his speech that the real work of revolutionary upheaval still lies ahead. "We must gather all forces to construct a government of workers and soldiers and create a new state system of the proletariat, a system of peace, happiness, and freedom for our German brothers and our brothers throughout the world."[5]

That afternoon, historian Gustav Mayer goes to downtown Berlin. "What a different sight jumps out at me!" he notes. "Everywhere soldiers without cockades. People standing, strolling around and talking (but not singing) in Potsdamer Platz. Trucks and gray military vehicles come and go constantly, packed (even on top of the roofs) with soldiers, their jackets unbuttoned, between them large numbers of workers and youths with rifles slung over their shoulders. Every car has someone waving a red flag."[6] The red flag becomes the symbol of the revolution. "Red cloth seems to have been handed out from some distribution points to the movement's followers—everyone is carrying this symbol of revolution, which until only recently was considered an outrage," writes a bewildered reporter from the *Deutsche Zeitung* newspaper, a mouthpiece for the radical nationalist Pan-Germanic League.[7]

That evening, Theodor Wolff composes an editorial for the morning edition. "The greatest of all revolutions has brought down the imperial regime and all parts of it, high and low, like a suddenly brewing storm. You can call it the greatest of all revolutions because never before has a surge like this overwhelmed such a mightily constructed bastille festooned by solid walls."[8] Reviewing events the following day, Kessler arrives at a similar conclusion: "The revolution began less than 24 hours ago in Berlin, and already nothing is left of the old order and army. Never has the entire inner framework of a major power been so completely pulverized in such a short time."[9]

The revolution, however, did not erupt nearly as suddenly as many people believed. In fact, it had taken more than one attempt to bring down the Hohenzollern monarchy's seemingly secure order. The upheaval of November 1918 was not only a result of Germany's military defeat and the shock suffered by the German populace. For some time, dissatisfaction had been brewing at the core of Wilhelmine society. The truce declared in 1914 between rival forces in Germany in the interest of winning the Great War may have papered over social tensions, but four years of conflict had exacerbated them extraordinarily. The material welfare of not only blue-collar workers but also white-collar employees had deteriorated dramatically, while industrialists and arms manufacturers had made gigantic profits.

Dramatic food shortages particularly fueled discontent. "Everything is held back for the wealthy and the property owners," complained one working-class woman from Hamburg during the "winter of turnips" in 1916–17. "As soon as sacrifice is called for, the lords of society no longer want to be the brothers and sisters of the working class. The magnificent speeches about the need to 'hold out' only apply to the working class. The ruling class with its sacks of money has already provided for itself."[10]

The unjust allocation of food, more than shortages per se, raised ire and left people embittered, and as of 1916 they began venting their pent-up frustration in strikes and protests. The longer the war persisted, the more Germans' outrage at their economic misery drove them to demand peace. The 1917 Russian Revolution served as an example. Spies from the German political police constantly reported desperate women standing in line to buy groceries saying things like, "We only have to do what they did in Russia, then everything will change immediately."[11]

The Independent Social Democratic Party (USPD)—which was formed as an opposition force in April 1917 as the Majority Social Democratic Party (MSPD) continued to support imperial Germany's war aims—became a rallying point for anti-war protest.

In late January 1918, hundreds of thousands of armaments workers in Berlin and other cities went on strike, demanding "Peace, Freedom, and Bread." Civilian and military authorities once again succeeded in suppressing the movement, but it was clear how decrepit the foundations of Hohenzollern rule had become. "These were the first tongues of flame from the smoldering fire," concluded one Hamburg Social Democrat.[12]

The situation was becoming incendiary on the battlefront as well. "I'm not putting my neck on the line anymore for the Prussians and the capitalist fat cats," wrote one soldier home to Munich in August 1917.[13] His was not the only voice of the kind. "Equal pay and equal food / Would make the war be gone for good" was a popular saying in the trenches.[14] When the final major German offensive in the west came to naught in the spring of 1918, accounts of soldiers breeching discipline and refusing orders multiplied. More and more men reported sick, tried to lie low in back lines, or surrendered. "Three-quarters of the units here want it all to end," one soldier wrote home in August 1918. "They don't care how."[15]

By the end of September 1918, the German Army Supreme Command under Paul von Hindenburg and Erich Ludendorff had no choice but to admit the war was lost and press for an immediate ceasefire and "parliamentization" of the Reich Constitution. In other words, facing defeat, the most influential leaders of the Wilhelmine Empire were prepared to accept what they had always vehemently rejected: the formation of a German government based not on the will of a monarch but on a majority, even including the Social Democrats, who had been the largest party in the Reichstag since 1912. On October 26, the German parliament passed laws mandating a transition to a parliamentary monarchy. The Reich Constitution was amended to read: "The Reich chancellor needs the consent of the Reichstag to exercise his office." Moreover, in his role as commander in chief, the kaiser would be subjected to parliamentary scrutiny. The special status of the military, a central element of the Reich Constitution engineered by Otto von Bismarck, was thus eliminated.[16] Reform from above was intended to head off revolution from below. That was the basic idea behind the government reforms introduced in October 1918.

But this tactical maneuver came too late. The powers that be lost their authority with breathtaking speed. The desire to end a senseless war under any circumstances and as quickly as possible spread beyond the working classes to broad segments of the populace. US President Woodrow Wilson's responses to the ceasefire offers made by the new, parliament-elected government of Prince Max von Baden swiftly made it clear that there would be no peace without the abdication of Kaiser Wilhelm II. But the kaiser would hear nothing of voluntarily renouncing the throne. "A successor to Friedrich the Great does not abdicate," he pompously declared—only to leave the increasingly uncertain situation of the Reich capital, Berlin, for the more comfortable surroundings of Spa on October 29.[17] As a result, the mass rebellion also turned against the monarch. "Here in Berlin, the mood is exceedingly bad," wrote historian Friedrich Thimme. "The masses have completely abandoned themselves to the psychosis of peace and talk about almost nothing but the kaiser and the crown prince stepping down."[18]

It was no accident that the revolution was sparked on large warships of the Imperial Navy, where crewmen and officers lived together in cramped quarters and where social inequality and the whims of commanders took on outrageous dimensions. When the naval command ordered the high-seas fleet to set sail for a final battle against Britain, ordinary seamen refused to obey.[19] At the beginning of November, the mutiny in Kiel spread to land, and from there it stretched out to all of Germany. Emulating the Kiel model, workers and soldiers everywhere formed revolutionary councils. "The physiognomy of revolution is beginning to take shape," Kessler noted on November 7. "Gradual seepage, an oil slick, caused by mutinying sailors off the coast. They're isolating Berlin. Soon it will be nothing more than an island. In the opposite way as in France, the provinces are revolutionizing the capital, and the sea, the land. Viking strategy."[20]

The leaders of the MSPD still believed they could save the monarchy if the kaiser stepped down immediately. If he refused, Ebert was said to have told Max von Baden, the "social revolution" would be "unavoidable." Ebert added that he didn't want any such revolution; indeed, he abhorred it "like sin itself."[21] It is uncertain whether the Social Democrat expressed himself this directly, as the Reich chancellor related in his memoirs, but there's no doubt that Ebert thought he had achieved his goals with Germany's transition to a parliamentary monarchy and that he considered revolution superfluous. In any case, the constitutional reforms undertaken in late October were transparently more of a promise than a political reality. The military's power remained omnipresent. It would take joint action by revolutionary navy men, workers, and soldiers to ensure that systemic change was irreversible.

On November 8, too, all attempts by Prince Max to persuade the kaiser to give up the throne proved futile. Wilhelm II even threatened to deploy the military to the Reich capital: "If you in Berlin don't change your minds, I will come with my troops to Berlin after the ceasefire and blast the city to bits, if I have to."[22] This was the prelude to the events of November 9.

The leaders of the MSPD found themselves in a difficult situation. They hadn't wanted revolution. Indeed, they had tried their best to prevent one. But there was no way they could stand on the sidelines after the upheaval and retain any influence whatsoever on the course of events. Thus, on the afternoon of November 9, Ebert did an abrupt about-face and proposed to the USPD that they form a joint revolutionary government consisting in equal measure of both parties. He didn't make any personnel demands. When asked by USPD parliamentary deputy Oskar Cohn, he even declared his willingness to work with his bitterest rival, Karl Liebknecht, if the Independent Social Democrats put him forward for office.[23] The USPD did make some demands in return for joining the proposed government. For starters, Germany was to become a "social republic," to which the MSPD agreed under the condition that the "people be allowed to decide in a constitutional conference." The USPD also insisted that executive, legislative, and judicial power rest exclusively "in the hands of elected representatives of the entire working populace and soldiers." This went too far for the MSPD, which responded: "If

this demand entails a dictatorship of a part of the social class not supported by the majority of the people, we must reject it as violating our
democratic principles."[24]

By noon the next day, the coalition agreement had been finalized, and
a Council of Popular Representatives, as the cabinet was now known,
convened for its constituent meeting. The council was made up of three
members of the MSPD and the USPD: Ebert, Philipp Scheidemann,
and the lawyer and parliamentary deputy Otto Landsberg for the former; for the latter, party and parliamentary faction chairman Hugo
Haase, party secretary Wilhelm Dittmann, who had been sentenced to
five years in prison for leading the January 1918 general strike, and Emil
Barth, a representative of the Revolutionary Stewards, nonunion representatives elected by workers who possessed great influence in Berlin's
larger factories. Liebknecht refused to join the government because he
was unwilling to work with the leaders of the MSPD, whose support for
the war had, in his eyes, forever compromised them. Nominally, Ebert
and Haase shared the chairmanship. But practically, Ebert—who had
inherited the Reich chancellor's desk on November 9—claimed the role
of leading the new government.[25]

There was no guarantee that the MSPD and USPD would agree
on a coalition. The rupture of the Social Democratic movement in the
spring of 1917 had not only uncovered differences of opinion but exacerbated personal animosities. It was primarily due to pressure from below
that squabbling Social Democrats came together. After the collapse of
Hohenzollern rule, desires for an end to the "war between working-class
brothers" erupted with almost elemental fury. That anger was on ample
display at a meeting of some three thousand delegates of the Berlin workers' and soldiers' councils in Zirkus Busch on the afternoon of November 10. When Liebknecht—the great symbol of opposition to war—took
the podium and warned, gesturing toward the MSPD delegates, against
"those who today walk with the revolution but were its enemies the
day before yesterday," he was drowned out by cries of "Unity! Unity!"[26]
That was a major personal defeat for Liebknecht, who had obviously
overestimated his influence on the masses.

The conference elected an "Executive Council of the Workers' and

The Council of Popular Representatives. Left, from top to bottom: Hugo Haase, Otto Landsberg, Wilhelm Dittmann. Right, from top to bottom: Friedrich Ebert, Philipp Scheidemann, Emil Barth. Center: Scheidemann proclaims the republic on November 9. (The banner reads "The Founding of the German Republic")

Soldiers' Councils in Greater Berlin," which convened the next day, with Richard Müller, the speaker of the Revolutionary Stewards, as its chairman. That body consisted of fourteen soldiers' and fourteen workers' representatives along with seven representatives each from the MSPD and USPD. The executive council was supposed to supervise the work of the Council of Popular Representatives. But its powers were so vaguely defined that in case of conflict the government had reason to hope it would prevail.[27] MSPD leaders could be satisfied with the first two days of the revolution. They had been able to attach themselves to the revolutionary movement and were now preparing to expand their power step-by-step. Their hand was strengthened by the fact that the majority of the soldiers' councils supported their positions and moderate views also predominated among the workers' councils.

On November 12, the Council of Popular Representatives issued a public proclamation that has rightly been described as the Magna Carta of the revolution.[28] It began with the words: "The government that has emerged from the revolution, whose political leadership is purely socialist, has tasked itself with achieving the socialist platform." With the stroke of a pen, all the wartime decrees of the old authoritarian state were abolished: the state of emergency, the restrictions on the right to assemble, and government censorship. Freedom of expression and religion were once more guaranteed, political prisoners were granted amnesty, and the 1916 Auxiliary Services Act, which mobilized German men between the ages of seventeen and sixty for the war effort, was revoked. In addition, the new government promised to introduce the eight-hour working day as of January 1, 1919, and guarantee equal, secret, direct, general voting in future parliamentary elections for all Germans, including women, over the age of twenty. Those promises fulfilled two standing central demands of the Social Democratic movement. The constitutional National Assembly, which would convene in the near future, would be elected according to the new rules. The proclamation did not envision state confiscation of means of production. On the contrary, the new government pledged to "maintain orderly production" and "protect property against attack."[29] The MSPD newspaper *Vorwärts* (Forward) expressed its satisfaction with the document: "The platform is excellent. It will show the world that the new powers in Germany desire an order based on liberty and not coercion, anarchy, or chaos."[30] The Majority Social Democrats remained constantly and painfully aware of the negative example of how the Russian Revolution had ended.

After the formation of the Council of Popular Representatives and the election of the Executive Council of the Workers' and Soldiers' Councils in Greater Berlin, a modicum of calm returned. The revolution had proceeded relatively peacefully, with only a handful of deaths. The leader of Germany's Center Party, Matthias Erzberger, signed the ceasefire agreement on November 11 in the forest near Compiègne. The new German government seemed determined to ensure order and protect private property. Nothing commonly associated with revolution had come to pass, the *Berliner Volks-Zeitung* newspaper declared. On November 10, it wrote: "Anyone who wasn't put off by difficulties of walking through the streets in the driving snow would have taken home the impression that there was no need for the green security police to intervene to prevent any confrontations or riots. There was no sign that the participants of the various rallies, armed with umbrellas and wrapped in thick woolen scarves and freshly washed winter Sunday clothing, had any particular affinity for hand grenades or infantry rifles."[31] During one such Sunday walk through Grunewald forest on November 10, theologian and philosopher Ernst Troeltsch noted that the mood was rather "subdued," but also "calm and comfortable" with everything having "gone so well." He added, "You could see on everyone's faces that their wages were still being paid."[32] Novelist Thomas Mann made a similar observation in Munich, where the revolution had triumphed on November 7 under the leadership of the talismanic USPD politician Kurt Eisner. Mann wrote: "I'm relieved at the relative calm and orderliness with which everything has proceeded, at least thus far. The German revolution is a German revolution, not an intoxicated Russian-Communist bender."[33]

Life in Berlin returned to normal with surprising speed. Before long, the trams were running, telephones worked, and people had natural gas, water, and electricity. Shops were open, and theaters kept staging performances. Everyday life seemed minimally affected by the revolutionary upheaval. "The revolution was never more than a small whirlpool in the normal life of the city, which continued to flow in its accustomed channels," wrote Kessler on November 12. "The massive, earth-shattering upheaval has flashed through everyday Berlin life creating hardly any more of a stir than a detective film."[34] The same was even truer of rural Germany. "Life here is following its usual course despite the mighty volcanic eruption that occurred," wrote Dorothy von Moltke, the matron of a provincial eastern estate in Kreisau, Silesia, to her parents in South Africa on November 19.[35]

Once they had overcome their initial shock, the bourgeoisie proved astonishingly adaptable. In no time, bourgeois groups organized themselves in councils similar to those of their proletarian compatriots. "A competition is underway to form all manner of councils: farmers' councils, citizens' councils, intellectuals' councils, artists' councils, theater councils," scoffed the medieval historian Karl Hampe in mid-November. "The German mania for clubs has fled into the arms of the revolution." For Hampe, as well as for more than a few members of the conservative bourgeoisie who had been loyal to the kaiser, November 9, 1918, had been the "most miserable day" of his life.[36]

How would things continue after the promising start of the first days? The MSPD pursued a clear agenda whose immediate priority was to address the pressing everyday problems of securing the food supply, transitioning from a wartime to a peacetime economy, demobilizing the troops, implementing the ceasefire, and preparing for peace negotiations. "Our next tasks must be to swiftly bring about peace and secure our economic existence," Ebert declared at a national conference of the Council of Popular Representatives with Germany's regional states on November 25.[37] Ebert saw the workers' and soldiers' councils as nuisances suitable at most for providing emergency assistance for a transitional period. After that, they would have to make way for a democratically legitimated national assembly. All fundamental decisions about Germany's social and political future were to be reserved for that freely elected parliament.

The USPD was unsure about what national political system it wanted. The party's right wing had no objection to the convening of a national assembly, although it wanted to postpone the election as long as possible to enact social-structural reforms that would create a solid foundation for parliamentary democracy. "Democracy has to be so firmly anchored that a conservative counterrevolution will be impossible," demanded the party's intellectual leader, Rudolf Hilferding, in mid-November.[38]

But the USPD's left wing rejected the national assembly and called for the introduction of a council system. At a general meeting of the Greater Berlin workers' councils in Zirkus Busch on November 19, Richard Müller cautioned: "The national assembly is the path to establishing the dominance of the bourgeoisie. . . . The path of the national assembly is over my dead body."[39] This statement earned him the nickname "Dead Body Müller." Their uncompromising rejection of a national assembly put the left wing of the USPD on ideological common ground with the Spartacus League, as the Spartacus Group had renamed itself on November 11. It was formally part of the party but pursued a de facto agenda of its own. Adopting the slogan "All power to the councils," the league was busy agitating for a continuation of the revolution. "Scheidemann–Ebert are the appointed government of the German revolution in its current state," Spartacus leader Rosa Luxemburg wrote in mid-November in the newspaper *Die Rote Fahne*, which she had edited since being released from prison in Breslau (today Wrocław) and returning to Berlin on November 10. "But revolutions don't stand still. Their natural law is to stride rapidly forward and outgrow themselves." Supporters of a national assembly, she added, were, "consciously or not, dialing back the [socialist] revolution to the historical stage of bourgeois revolutions." The urgent historical question posed by the upheaval in Germany, however, was "bourgeois democracy or socialist democracy."[40]

But the Spartacus League had no great influence. The group was in its infancy, and membership was still limited. Liebknecht and Luxemburg were "well aware that a truly socialist republic could not be established with the means at their disposal," author and Spartacus member Eduard Fuchs wrote to historian Gustav Mayer in mid-November.[41] The radical Left didn't possess any decisive sway in the workers' and soldiers' councils, where MSPD members and moderate representatives of the USPD had the upper hand. Germany was thus very far removed from a Bolshevik-style dictatorship of councils in the late fall of 1918. Nonetheless, bourgeois circles deliberately exaggerated the danger of such. "Spartacus" became a dog whistle for Bolshevism, encouraging popular fears of chaos, terror, and civil war.[42]

The effectiveness of this bête noire was such that even a keen observer like Theodor Wolff fretted about "Spartacus folks and lots of rabble waiting, armed, for an opportunity to launch a putsch, and there's no sufficient organized force that can offer protection."[43] The fear and hatred were focused on Liebknecht. On November 11, Mayer surmised that, in his "monomaniacal ambition," the Spartacus leader was out to become "the Lenin of the German revolution." Eleven days later, Mayer added in his diary: "You hear only voices of pessimism that say that the triumph of Bolshevism in Berlin can no longer be prevented and that Liebknecht is paying the soldiers who follow him ten marks a day."[44] By early December, posters were appearing on Berlin advertising pillars calling for Liebknecht's murder: "Strike down their leader! Kill Liebknecht! Then you'll have peace, work, and bread."[45]

The MSPD leadership also fell for the stereotype of the Bolshevik enemy and had no qualms about instrumentalizing popular fears in domestic political conflicts. The articles in *Die Rote Fahne* played into their hands by using aggressive language that suggested Liebknecht and Luxemburg were scheming to take power by force. Both Ebert and Scheidemann maintained an overblown fear of "a Russia-like situation," combined with an aversion to all forms of disorder and anarchy. Broad segments of the bourgeoisie and the military leadership in particular shared this "antichaos reflex." As Colonel Ernst van den Bergh, an officer in the Prussian Ministry of War, remarked, the two MSPD leaders embodied "the direction all rational people must support with full conviction."[46]

In a phone call with Ebert on November 10, Ludendorff's successor at German Army High Command, Wilhelm Groener, already offered his cooperation. "The officer corps demanded that the government fight Bolshevism and is ready to be deployed," Groener recalled saying in his memoirs. "Ebert accepted my suggestion of an alliance. From then on, we talked every evening via a secure connection between the Reich Chancellery and army command about the necessary measures. The alliance proved its worth."[47] There was no formal agreement between the two centers of power. But they did work together, which would have great effect on how the revolution proceeded.

On November 11, the Council of Popular Representatives acted on a request by Hindenburg and sent a telegram to army command, beseeching the generals "to order the entire field army to maintain military discipline, calm, and strict order under all circumstances." Until they were decommissioned, soldiers were to "follow orders unconditionally," while retaining their weapons and preserving their ranks. The soldiers' councils were tasked with assisting the officers in the "preservation of discipline and order."[48] The officer corps's authority was thus essentially restored, and the soldiers' councils suddenly found themselves reduced to a subordinate role.

A main reason the MSPD extended a hand to the army command was the realization that the orderly demobilization of eight million soldiers was hardly possible without the military leadership cooperating. The political leadership counted on the generals accepting the reality on the ground and behaving loyally to the revolutionary government. In a November 20 cabinet meeting, after Emil Barth demanded that Hindenburg be dismissed to defuse Entente worries about "the persistence of German militarism," Ebert refused, saying that the former commander had "given his word of honor that he would stand behind the government" so there was no need to "dislodge him from his position."[49]

This trust allowed the military leadership to reestablish itself as a force in domestic policy, and before long, officers were confident about going out in public again. By mid-December, when returning guard troops were ceremoniously welcomed back to Berlin, Kessler observed: "The red flags are conspicuous in their absence. Everything is black-white-and-red, black-and-white, and occasionally black-red-and-gold. Common soldiers and officers once again commonly walk around displaying their cockades and epaulettes. It's a big difference from November."[50] Writer Gerhart Hauptmann was excited by the military's return: "Battle helmets, machine guns, field kitchens, and banners. Everything in its right place militarily. The army's deeply rooted popularity has become evident again. Splendid troops. No red symbols . . . I called out 'Bravo.' "[51]

The people's representatives also shied back from rigorous actions concerning the civil administration because they feared they couldn't run the country without the expertise of the old state apparatus. Some of their earliest statements were appeals to civil servants to do their duty. On November 11, Gustav Mayer called it a "reassuring sign" that "a large part of the civil service doesn't want to retreat and pout and that the new men are prepared and eager to collaborate with experienced

*Festive reception: Friedrich Ebert welcomes returning troops
at the Brandenburg Gate on December 10, 1918.*

'technical' experts."[52] The state secretaries in the Reich government retained their posts, and although they were flanked by two "supervisors" from the MSPD and USPD, the latter had no chance to do any genuine monitoring since they depended on information supplied by the ministerial bureaucracy.[53] Other high-ranking officials such as Prussian district administrators also kept their jobs even though they made no secret of their preference for the toppled authoritarian German Reich and their antipathy to the new order. Not a single high-ranking functionary from the old system was dismissed. At a conference of Germany's regional states on November 25, Ebert justified the decision not to push for a wholesale replacement of administrative personnel: "Having seized political power, we needed to make sure that the machinery of the Reich didn't break down. . . . The six of us couldn't do that alone. We needed the cooperation of experienced specialists."[54]

The MSPD popular representatives also took a soft approach on issues of ownership of the means of production. There was no comprehensive agricultural reform, not least because of worries about Germany's already strained food supplies. On November 11, the Council of Popular Representatives assured the agricultural lobby that "the Reich government will vigorously protect [you] against all attacks on property and production."[55] Such assurances were primarily directed at the aristocratic owners of large agricultural estates east of the Elbe River, who were already up in arms at the abolition of Prussia's three-tiered electoral system and the resulting loss of their political domination in Germany's largest regional state. Big agricultural interests held sway in most of the farmers' councils, whose formation the Council of Popular Representatives had approved on November 21, and they stabilized rather than democratized or revolutionized the status quo in the German countryside. One bit of progress was the "Preliminary Ordinance on Rural Labor" of January 24, 1919, which revoked discriminatory Wilhelmine legislation concerning farmhands and allowed them to unionize. Nonetheless, the economic power of the *Junker*, as large-scale estate owners were called, remained untouched—and with it a fundamental pillar of the agrarian-conservative dominance of Prussia.[56]

Along with the estate owners east of the Elbe, the elites who had most vocally called for a war of territorial conquest prior to 1918 and resisted any democratic reforms afterward were the industrial barons of the Rhineland and Westphalia in western Germany. They, too, feared for their privileged position of power after the November Revolution, especially as the call to nationalize key industries represented a core element of the Social Democratic political platform. Members of the USPD pressed the Council of Popular Representatives to act on this demand. Their MSPD colleagues, however, favored deferring the issue so as not to imperil Germany's postwar reconstruction with any hasty experiments. The decision reached by the governing cabinet on November 18 was a compromise, declaring that "those branches of industry that are sufficiently developed for socialization should be socialized" while making clear that the government was in no hurry to see this carried out. It was decided to form "a commission of renowned national economists," to include "people with practical experience from the ranks of labor and entrepreneurs."[57] The commission met for the first time on December 5 under chairman Karl Kautsky, a leading Social Democratic Party (SPD) intellectual before 1914 who had gone over to the USPD during the war. That body met for weeks without achieving any results.

Prior to that, a groundbreaking decision had been reached. On November 15, business owners and unions had signed a formal accord, the Stinnes–Legien Agreement, named after the two chief negotiators, industrialist Hugo Stinnes and the chairman of the General Commission of Unions, Carl Legien. It recognized trade unions as "appointed representatives of the working class" and voided all restrictions on freedom of association. Employers recognized the rights of workers returning from the war to their old jobs and agreed to an eight-hour workday without wage cuts. Moreover, working conditions were to be set by labor contracts, works councils were made the rule in all businesses with more than fifty employees, and mediators with equal numbers of representatives from both sides were to be employed to resolve labor disputes. Responsibility for seeing that the reforms were enacted was given to the Central Working Community of Industrial and Commercial Employers and Employees Associations in Germany—or ZAG, for short.

Germany's trade unions celebrated the agreement as a great triumph, and it did indeed represent significant sociopolitical progress over the Wilhelmine Empire. But the captains of industry were the bigger winners insofar as labor leaders' pledge to preserve the existing economic order, including private ownership of the means of production, basically prevented the nationalization of key industries. In a letter to members on November 18, the Federation of German Employers' Associations (VDA) justified its concessions to unions by arguing that there was still "the greatest reason to fear" that the government could decide to socialize production. Because of that, it had been imperative to "shore up the position of unions, which at present represent the moderate wing of the government, with all the means at our disposal."[58]

From December 16 to 21, the First General Congress of Workers' and Soldiers' Councils, which came from throughout Germany, convened in

Berlin, following a call to do so by the executive council on November 17. The congress was intended, on the one hand, to decide whether Germany should have a national assembly or adopt a system of councils and, on the other, to elect a central council as a new superior executive organ of state.[59] MSPD representatives were rightly satisfied with the results of the delegate elections. Of the 514 deputies who assembled on December 16 in the Prussian House of Representatives, some 300 were affiliated with the MSPD and only 100 with the USPD. Others were party unaffiliated or members of the leftist bourgeoisie, while the Spartacus League was barely represented at all. One of the congress's first acts was to deny Liebknecht and Luxemburg, "who had been of such service to the revolution," the status of "guests with consulting voices."[60] Given the makeup of the congress, there was no doubt how the most important question would be resolved. A large majority rejected a motion to stick with "the council system as the basis of the socialist republic" and to grant the workers' and soldiers' councils the highest legislative and executive authority. In the end, the congress decided to call an election for a national assembly on January 19, 1919.[61] That was almost a month earlier than February 16, the date the Council of Popular Representatives had previously agreed upon.

For the spokesman of the left wing of the USPD, Ernst Däumig, the "celebratory endorsement of a national assembly" was equivalent to a "death sentence" for the council system, and he accused the delegates of having mutated into a "political suicide club."[62] But from the beginning, the introduction of an "unadulterated" council system, as propagated by USPD left-wingers and followers of the Spartacus League, was a pipe dream. Most local workers' and soldiers' councils saw themselves not as alternatives to a freely elected parliament but as temporary, provisional organs that wanted to help ensure order in the transitional phase until the convention of a national assembly.

USPD delegates refused to follow their party leadership during the election of the Central Council. On December 19, they petitioned that the Central Council should have "the full right to approve or reject laws before they are proclaimed." That went well beyond Haase's proposal that there should be joint consultations on major draft laws. After Ebert vigorously opposed the motion, saying that it would largely impair the government's ability to act, the USPD petition was rejected, whereupon USPD delegates refused to participate in the Central Council election. In essence, the USPD voluntarily renounced a significant part of the power it had achieved in early November.[63]

Ebert and his supporters' satisfaction at the congress was hardly complete, however, as delegates passed two resolutions that didn't suit their plans at all. For starters, the congress called upon the government "to begin immediately with the socialization of all industry ready for it, in particular mining."[64] Moreover, delegates demanded a comprehensive reform of the military along the lines of the "seven points" proclaimed by the Hamburg Soldiers' Council in early December. Those points included the order to transfer supreme command over the armed forces to a people's commissioner under supervision of the executive council, getting rid of all the trappings of rank "as a symbol of the destruction of militarism and the eradication of the idea of obedience to the death," and having soldiers elect officers in the future.[65]

Both resolutions showed that the MSPD delegates remained interested in major social reforms. The demands were unmistakably directed at the Council of Popular Representatives, which had thus far taken no steps worthy of the name in that direction. The formation of a commission had postponed the issue of nationalization indefinitely. And from the beginning, Ebert had pursued a policy of cooperation with the armed forces' high command on military policy.

The military leadership immediately protested the congress's resolutions. At a joint meeting of the cabinet and the newly elected Central Council on December 20, Groener warned about "grave dangers" resulting from them. The connection between troops and the officer corps would be ripped apart, he claimed. The officers would "no longer be willing to cooperate," and the result would be a "complete dissolution of the army." Groener added, ominously, "I predict the most difficult times for our people." Ebert shared those reservations, proclaiming that "action had been somewhat hasty and premature" on the whole issue. He proposed that the congress's resolution be deemed to apply only to military on the home front, not in the field, and that nebulous

"conditions of realization" had to be declared before it could be executed.[66] This was another instance of the MSPD leadership deferring a
decision to avoid a contest of strength with the officer corps. The questions of ultimate authority over the military and the election of officers
would no longer be part of the "conditions of realization" of the "Hamburg points" issued by the Prussian Ministry of War on January 19, 1919.

The situation in Berlin came to a head around Christmas. Conflict had
been simmering for some time between the city commandant, MSPD
politician Otto Wels, and the People's Navy Division, a radical leftist
group of some 1,800 seamen who had quartered themselves in the Berlin City Palace and Royal Stables and were alleged to have engaged in
plunder. Wels demanded that their leader, Heinrich Dorrenbach, vacate
the palace and reduce the size of his force by two-thirds. To exert pressure, Wels withheld their pay, even though it had already been approved
by the Council of Popular Deputies, which angered the navy men, so on
December 23, an armed unit temporarily occupied the Reich Chancellery, cutting its telephone lines. Another group of navy men under Dorrenbach's command marched on the palace and took Wels into custody.
   Late that night, MSPD popular representatives were alarmed to learn
that Wels was being abused and his life threatened, prompting Ebert to
ask the Prussian Ministry of War for military assistance. Before sunrise
the Lequis Commando was ordered to storm the palace and the stables.
The situation was "ripe for a major decision," wrote Kessler. "If the government has sufficient energy, it will use it to remove the entire radicalized navy division from Berlin."[67] But the operation failed. The navy
men received support from the security force of Berlin Police President
Emil Eichhorn as well as from armed workers. The Lequis Commando
was forced to back down, leaving the government with no choice but to
resolve the conflict by negotiating with the People's Navy Division. All
told, eleven navy men and fifty-six members of the commando died in
the fighting at the palace. Radical working-class spokespeople in Berlin blamed the bloodbath on the MSPD popular representatives. At the
funeral for the fallen navy men, protesters carried placards reading, "We

accuse Ebert, Landsberg, and Scheidemann of the sailors' murder."[68] The funeral was a "far bigger affair than expected," wrote Kessler. "A huge crowd stretching as far as the eye could see . . . At the head of the procession, seven identical silver-black coffins, all of them with wreaths of red and white flowers, conveyed on seven royal coaches from the stables . . . Behind that, wreaths and flowers, all either red or a mix of red and white, carried by deputations bigger than I had ever seen before."[69]

The Christmas fighting in Berlin ruptured the government coalition. The USPD popular representatives were particularly angry that their coalition partner hadn't even informed them about the decision to send in troops. In their eyes, this proved that the MSPD leadership had made itself, once and for all, dependent on the military command. Events had shown, Wilhelm Dittmann criticized at a meeting of the cabinet and the Central Council on December 28, "how dangerous it is to try to work together with military power that is based on the old generals and the old army." Emil Barth asked: "Can any socialist government be based on the power of bayonets? Must it not be based on the trust of the people?"[70] On December 29, following Central Council confirmation to the USPD that it had approved the three MSPD representatives' orders to the Prussian war minister, Haase, Dittmann, and Barth resigned from the government.

The MSPD leadership now had a free hand, proclaiming that very day, "The paralyzing divisiveness has been overcome."[71] The three USPD popular representatives who resigned were replaced by two members of the MSPD: union secretary Rudolf Wissell, who was given responsibility for social and economic policy, and military expert Gustav Noske, who took over the department "military and navy." Noske had been sent to Kiel in early November and had made sure to steer the revolution into calmer waters. The new man would "have to have rhinoceros-thick skin," Scheidemann declared at the midnight meeting of the cabinet and Central Council on December 28–29.[72] Noske obviously fulfilled that requirement in the eyes of his MSPD colleagues.

"It's as though the air is electrically charged with an incomparable political tension," wrote a *Berliner Tageblatt* journalist about the mood in the

German capital on New Year's Eve. "The old year comes to an end in feverish excitement." At the same time, however, he noted the outbreaks of unbridled hedonism with consternation. "The confetti of carefree revelers is falling in spirals, and men and girls, hungry for life, are dancing their way into the new year. Music is playing in hundreds of establishments. There is dancing and more dancing: waltzes, foxtrots, one-steps and two-steps. People's legs flit over floors as though they were under a witch's spell. Skirts fly, people gasp for breath, and champagne corks pop. . . . Never has there been so much or such frenetic dancing in Berlin."[73]

The dance mania extended to provincial Germany. "The broad masses have a horrifying lack of sensitivity for what we're going through—people are dancing the nights away, as if nothing has happened," complained historian Karl Hampe in his New Year's Eve diary entry. "Never has the transition from one year to another been celebrated in such a dismal mood."[74] Kessler agreed. "Final day of this terrible year," he noted. "1918 is likely to forever remain the most terrible year in German history."[75] Many educated German bourgeoisie shared these sentiments. They couldn't comprehend how swiftly and weakly the old monarchist authoritarian state had collapsed, and they regarded the new democratic order with skepticism. "My attitude toward this massive upheaval is half numb, half disgusted, and not in the slightest democratic," wrote Romance language expert and diarist Victor Klemperer, summing up the year.[76] Historian Gustav Mayer, who sympathized with the MSPD politically, drew a similar conclusion: "The collapse is not just of the ruling class and a political system. It's simultaneously the moral collapse of an entire people, a destabilization of all its standards, a seismic disturbance of all its values, a questioning of all moral relations and all duties. We're living on the day after an unprecedented earthquake, uncertain whether the last blow was indeed the hardest and whether it makes any sense to start rebuilding the rubble."[77] Hedwig Pringsheim, Thomas Mann's mother-in-law, concluded her New Year's Eve diary entry with the words: "We enter a new year, shaken in all the convictions of our existence, uncertain and helpless. Chaos after the lost war."[78] By that point, little remained of the magic of the early days of the revolution.

Rosa Luxemburg and Karl Liebknecht dared to stage a rival new beginning. On December 30, they helped found the German Communist Party, the KPD, at a convention in the Prussian House of Representatives. One hundred twenty-seven delegates from fifty-six locations in Germany came together for the event. More than a third were Spartacus League members, and nearly a third were part of the International Communists of Germany, a group that had been formed by leftist radicals in Hamburg and Bremen during the First World War.[79] The delegates were a heterogeneous group. Older functionaries from the prewar Social Democratic tradition were flanked by young workers and intellectuals radicalized by their experience of war and revolution. The latter were full of revolutionary élan but incapable of soberly assessing the political realities, as became evident in the debate over whether the Communists should take part in the elections for the national assembly on January 19. A clear majority at the convention thought they should not.

Luxemburg threw her entire authority behind the contrary position. "I'm convinced you want to make your radicalism a bit comfortable and hasty," she shouted at delegates, adding that the masses needed to be educated before there could be any thought of socialism. "That's what we want to do using parliamentarism."[80] Luxemburg was supported by her ally Käte Duncker, who reminded delegates that half of all voters would be women going to the polls for the first time ever. "Do you really think," Duncker asked, "that after telling these women for decades that they should fight for their right to vote, they'll follow us now if we tell them not to exercise it?"[81] But it was no use. In the end, the party convention decided by a margin of 61 to 23 to reject the recommendations of the Spartacus League leadership and boycott the election of the national assembly. Luxemburg tried to console her friend Clara Zetkin, who was horrified by the decision, by saying, "Our 'defeat' was only the triumph of a somewhat childish, immature, one-dimensional radicalism. . . . Don't forget that the 'Spartacists' are mostly from a fresh generation, which is free from the stultified traditions of the 'old, proven' party—we have to see both the light and dark sides of that."[82]

Karl Liebknecht had spoken forebodingly at the party conference that the next few days would "bring surprises" and that the events might "go over the heads of the so-called leaders."[83] That was precisely what happened with the Berlin riots in January 1919, which went down in the history books incorrectly as the "Spartacus Uprising."[84] They were sparked by the dismissal of Berlin Police President Eichhorn on January 4. He was a member of the USPD, and his was one of the last positions not controlled by the MSPD leadership. Moderate Social Democrats particularly resented him for deploying security officers to support the People's Navy Division in the battle for the City Palace around Christmas, while radical members of the working classes in Berlin were incensed when he was fired. The USPD board of directors, the Revolutionary Stewards, and the KPD leadership jointly called for a demonstration on January 5, and more people than expected turned out to protest. *Die Rote Fahne* wrote of the "most massive crowd the Berlin proletariat ever mobilized."[85]

During that demonstration, things got out of hand, as groups of armed revolutionaries occupied the printing presses of the newspapers *Vorwärts* and the *Berliner Tageblatt*, as well as the Mosse, Scherl, and Ullstein publishing houses, in Berlin's newspaper district. This spontaneous action was followed that night by the improvised formation of a "Revolutionary Committee" headed by Georg Ledebour of the USPD's left wing, Liebknecht of the KPD, and Georg Scholze of the Revolutionary Stewards. Carried away by the heated atmosphere, the majority of the committee called upon Berlin workers to go on a general strike and topple the government, although it was completely unclear how that was supposed to happen. Even Luxemburg, who opposed putsches on principle, proved susceptible to the euphoria and urged the working classes to seize the moment.[86]

Even more people took to the streets the following day, January 6,

Before the January 1919 riots in Berlin: Rebels barricade themselves in Berlin's newspaper district behind paper rolls and newspaper bundles.

but the government had mobilized its supporters, who also turned out en masse. By the time the Revolutionary Committee convened that evening, the euphoria had dissipated. Most of those who had called for an uprising were now concerned with saving face and avoiding a violent confrontation.

The government, however, was determined to meet the challenge head-on with maximum severity. The time had come, the political leadership felt, to use all the military means at its disposal to set an example and restore "calm and order" in Berlin.[87] "If there's no alternative, and someone has to get blood on his hands, I won't shirk that responsibility," Noske was said to have declared upon assuming command of government troops in and around Berlin. He headquartered himself in an empty academy for girls in Berlin's Dahlem suburb and assembled formations of a volunteer militia, so-called Freikorps, which had already begun to coalesce on January 3, that is, before the unrest. On January 7, Ebert reported to his cabinet, "We are in the process of creating forces sufficient to create order."[88] Prominent USPD leader Karl Kautsky's attempt to mediate that day failed after MSPD popular representatives demanded that the occupied newspapers and publishers be vacated before negotiations could begin.

On January 11, government troops began storming the *Vorwärts* building. Five occupiers, who wanted to negotiate over vacating the newspaper, were arrested and shot to death along with two other prisoners. It was the first in a series of atrocities that would go unatoned for.[89] Later that day, Noske marched at the head of three thousand soldiers through the center of Berlin to Wilhelmstrasse to demonstrate that the government was still in control of the situation. On January 12, the other occupied buildings were retaken. The dilettantish, half-hearted uprising ended in bloodshed. "This morning, Potsdamer Platz looks like it does on a peaceful Sunday," noted Kessler. "No trace of revolution. Berlin is awakening from heated fever into a sad reality."[90]

After the suppression of the uprising, Liebknecht and Luxemburg had every reason to fear for their lives and constantly moved from one hiding place to another to avoid ambush. On January 15, they found refuge with friends in Berlin's Wilmersdorf district. There, Luxemburg wrote her final article, "Order Rules in Berlin," whose last words played on poet Ferdinand Freiligrath's ode to the failed democratic German revolution of 1848: "You dull-witted henchmen! Your order is built on sand. The revolution will rise up the heights tomorrow, with sabers rattling, and to your horror announce with a fanfare of trombones: I was, I am, and I will be!"[91]

That evening, members of the Wilmersdorf militia discovered the Communist leaders' whereabouts. Luxemburg and Liebknecht were arrested and taken to the Eden Hotel on Kurfürstendamm boulevard, where Waldemar Pabst had quartered himself with his Guards Cavalry Rifle Corps. It is unclear whether, as would be asserted in the 1960s, Pabst called Noske to ask what to do with his prisoners. What is certain is that while Noske didn't issue an order to have them murdered, he also did nothing to restrain the troops' bloodthirstiness.[92] Liebknecht

was abused, then taken to Tiergarten park and shot from behind. Luxemburg was beaten while being removed from the hotel, dragged into a
car, and shot in the head. Her killers threw her body into the Landwehr
Canal. "The old pig floats," they were alleged to have said after committing the murder. The next day's edition of the *BZ am Mittag* newspaper
ran the headline: "Liebknecht Shot While Fleeing, Rosa Luxemburg
Killed by Mob!" Many newspapers passed on this misinformation,
which was based directly on a press release issued by Pabst's men.[93]

The news of Liebknecht and Luxemburg's murders hit Ebert like an
electric shock. In his memoirs, later Reich Chancellor Hermann Müller
would recall "rarely seeing him so upset as on that morning of January
16."[94] In addition to being revolted by the killings, Ebert worried that
the two victims might pose more of a threat to his government as martyrs than they did while alive. The government and the Central Council
promised a "thorough investigation" and "the most severe punishment"
for the perpetrators.[95] But there was nothing of the sort. The only trial in
the case, held in front of a court-martial, ended in May 1919 with several
of the main participants being acquitted and two of the accused, rather
minor figures, being sentenced to laughably short terms in prison. Captain Pabst, the man mainly behind the murders, got off scot-free.[96]

Liebknecht was laid to rest on January 25, 1919, together with several
comrades who had been killed in the January fighting, in the central
cemetery in the Friedrichsfelde district. Working-class Berliners flocked
to the burial ceremony. The painter and sculptor Käthe Kollwitz was
permitted to sketch him lying in state. "Red flowers laid around his
forehead with the bullet wound, his face proud, his mouth open slightly
and twisted in pain," was how she described the sight of the Communist leader's body. "His facial expression somewhat surprised. His hands
folded in his lap. A couple of red flowers on his white shirt."[97] It wouldn't
be until May 31 that Luxemburg's already heavily decomposed body
would wash up in a canal lock. She was buried by Liebknecht's side
on June 13.

Politician and journalist Rudolf Hilferding would dub the events
of January 1919 as "the German Revolution's Battle of the Marne."[98]
Indeed, they did represent a caesura, underscoring the unbridgeable gap

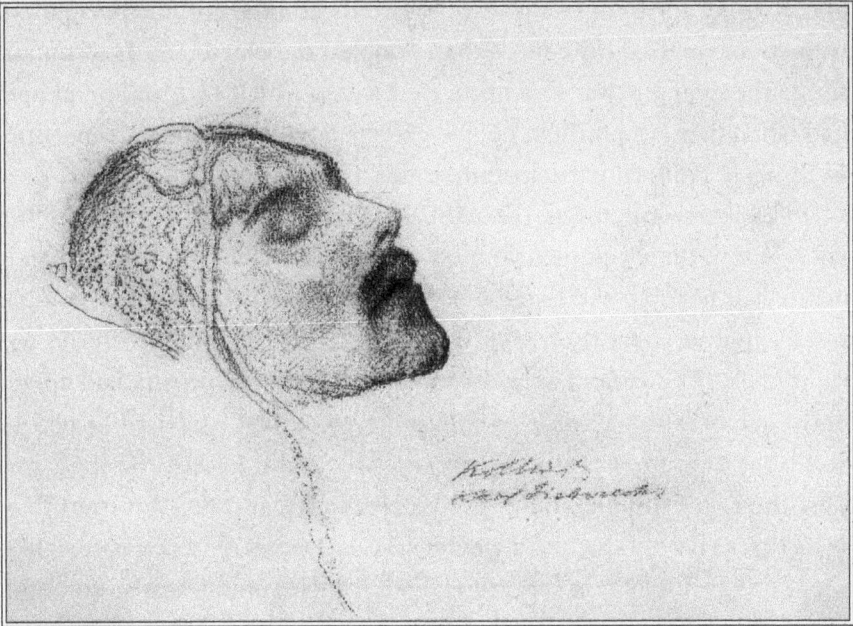

Karl Liebknecht on his deathbed. Drawing by Käthe Kollwitz.

that had opened during the war between the moderate and radical parts of the labor movement. Supporters of the USPD and the KPD were convinced that the MSPD leadership was politically responsible for Luxemburg and Liebknecht's murders, even if it had not been directly involved in them. That would burden the Left for years to come.

On January 19, 1919, National Assembly elections took place as planned. People formed long lines outside polling stations, waiting for hours to cast their ballots. The election proceeded with few disruptions, even in Berlin. "Everything calm and gray on gray—neither commotion nor excitement," wrote Kessler. "Representatives of various parties stand on either side of the conga line and wordlessly hand out ballots. Cooks, nurses, old women, families with fathers, mothers, and servant girls, even children, trudge up and join those waiting. The whole thing as undramatic as an event of nature, like a country rain."[99] The lowering

of the voting age from twenty-five to twenty and the enfranchisement of
women for the first time more than doubled the electorate. In comparison to the final postwar Reichstag election, in which 14.4 million people
had taken part, 37.4 million people cast their ballots on January 19, 1919.
In terms of political participation, it was a veritable revolution.[100]

The clear winner was the MSPD, which took 37.9 percent of the
vote—more than 3 percent more than in 1912, when the Social Democrats had become the biggest party in the Reichstag. MSPD popular
representatives saw the result as confirmation that they were on the
right track. The violent suppression of the January uprising had apparently not hurt the party's popularity. By contrast, the USPD had to
settle for a disappointing 7.6 percent. Of the middle-of-the-road parties, the two Catholic ones—the Center Party and the Bavarian People's Party (BVP)—received a collective 19.7 percent of the vote, while
the German Democratic Party (DDP), which contained the tradition
of left-wing liberalism in the Wilhelmine Empire, got 18.5 percent.
Its right-wing liberal competition, the German People's Party (DVP),
the successor to the National Liberals, achieved only 4.4 percent.
The right-wing nationalist German National People's Party (DNVP)
had to make do with just 10.3 percent. That was significantly less than
the ultraconservative and antisemitic parties had been able to muster
before 1914. All in all, the election clearly reflected voter support for
parliamentary democracy.[101]

On February 6, the National Assembly convened in Weimar's National
Theater. Ebert in particular had pushed for the city in the eastern
regional state of Thuringia as a location for the National Assembly—on
the one hand, because conditions in Berlin were still considered too precarious and, on the other, because Weimar's connection to the cultural
classicism of Goethe and Schiller seemed especially suited to lending
credibility to Germany's new beginning. It would be "favorably looked
upon throughout the world, if the spirit of Weimar can be connected
to the establishment of a new German Reich," Ebert said in a cabinet
meeting on January 14.[102] In his opening speech to the assembly, Ebert
asked delegates to understand the difficulties the popular representatives had been forced to confront. They had been "administrators of the

bankruptcy of the old regime in the most literal sense," with no other option than to do everything they could "to get economic life going again." Ebert added, "If our performance didn't live up to our hopes, at least the circumstances that got in the way need to be recognized for what they are." [103]

Nothing about this "historic day," Theodor Wolff remarked, recalled the "external splendor of the regime that had collapsed." Nonetheless, in its "frugality," the occasion had possessed a certain charm. "It didn't seem very imposing," Wolff wrote. "It was a bit of a return to simple values and modest demands, but it did give the impression of popular upstandingness." [104] Kessler, never one to spare a sarcastic remark, found Ebert's speech "elegant and worthy." [105]

Because the MSPD didn't have an absolute majority, and forming a coalition with the USPD was no longer an option after the events of the past months, the most plausible path to a government was to partner with the DDP and the Center Party. These were the same parties with which the MSPD had worked as of July 1917 in a parliamentary "interfactional committee" and in Prince Max von Baden's cabinet in October 1918. Ebert and colleagues began talks with the DDP on February 1. Less than a week later, on February 7, the Center also agreed to join a new government. The path was thus cleared for what became known as the Weimar Coalition. Together, the three parties commanded a robust three-quarters majority, and on February 11, the assembly elected Ebert the first president of the new German republic. The fact that a former saddle maker, who had enjoyed only a vocational education, now held the highest office in the land was the clearest possible demonstration of a new beginning for Germany. Conversely, it was precisely this fact that stuck in the craw of those Wilhelmine social elites who had previously ruled the country. [106]

Philipp Scheidemann was made Reich premier, an office that was rechristened under its traditional name of Reich chancellor once the Weimar Constitution was passed. Together with him, Landsberg (Ministry of Justice), Noske (Military), and Wissell (Economy) were retained from the government of popular representatives. They were joined by the MSPD leaders Gustav Bauer (Labor), Robert Schmidt (Education), and Eduard David (without portfolio). The Center Party and the DDP each provided three ministers, while the career diplomat and former German ambassador in Copenhagen Count Ulrich von Brockdorff-Rantzau, who had no party affiliation, was put in charge of the Foreign Ministry. Initially the Reich president and the Reich government had to govern within the framework of a provisional constitution, the Preliminary Reich Authority Act of February 10. It remained in force until the new Reich constitution took effect in August 1919. Nonetheless, the course of events seemed to be entering calmer waters. "A massive step forward has been taken," commented Colonel van den Bergh.[107]

In fact, however, the spring of 1919 marked the beginning of a second, more radical phase of the revolution, characterized by local revolts, Soviet-like council experiments, major strikes, especially in the industrial centers on the Rhine, in the Ruhr Valley, and in central Germany, and even street fighting reminiscent of a civil war. This new revolutionary wave was no longer directed against the monarchical authoritarian state, as it had been in November 1918, but against the MSPD-centrist coalition supported by the military. And everywhere the Freikorps, under Noske's direction, set about enforcing order with an iron fist.[108]

In March 1919, following a general strike, armed clashes broke out again in Berlin. "During these two weeks, the long-held fear that political revolution could only come with unprecedented levels of violence reached a crescendo that was unprecedented at any point in the history of the German Empire," writes the English historian Mark Jones.[109] The government troops deployed machine guns, grenade launchers, heavy artillery, and even warplanes. There was a de facto state of civil war in some districts in the center and east of the city.

On March 9, the *BZ am Mittag* reported that Spartacists in Berlin's Lichtenberg district had murdered sixty captured police officers in cold blood. The leading organs of liberal sentiment such as the *Berliner Tageblatt* and the *Vossische Zeitung* picked up the story, and the Social Democratic *Vorwärts* also joined in the outcry of horror, writing, "The pen recoils at having to describe renewed atrocities committed here by Spartacist mobs against defenseless prisoners." [110]

But this news, too, was false—a fiction invented by Captain Pabst, who needed the brazen lie about the "Lichtenberg prisoner murder" to persuade Noske to sign a momentous decree on March 9. "The increasing cruelty and bestiality of the Spartacists fighting against us compels me to give this order," Noske would write. "Any person found fighting against government troops with a weapon in his hand is to be shot immediately." [111] This command effectively amounted to a license to kill, and, freed from any restrictions, Noske's paramilitaries used it to justify full-blown massacres in the German capital.

One of the worst acts of murder took place on March 11 at Französische Strasse 32, the pay office of the now disbanded People's Navy Division, twenty-nine members of which were taken prisoner and summarily executed by Lieutenant Otto Marloh. Marloh was acquitted of any wrongdoing in subsequent military court proceedings. [112] Similarly, constable Ernst Tamschick killed Leo Jogiches, Rosa Luxemburg's longtime companion, on March 10 by shooting him in the back of the head as he was being taken to the Moabit prison, but Tamschick was never even prosecuted. Two months later, he murdered the former commander of the People's Navy Division, Heinrich Dorrenbach, in similar fashion. [113] According to conservative estimates, a total of 1,200 people, most of them civilians, lost their lives during the fighting in Berlin in March 1919. Government troops tallied only 75 dead. "The public should know that the military is testing its strength and extending itself again," Kessler wrote. "Gradually, a core of military might is consolidating, and, backed by that force, the propertied, fearful classes can regroup. Their power is increasingly relegating the government to the background." [114]

In the spring of 1919, Munich also witnessed unprecedented violence. It began on February 21, when the Bavarian state premier and USPD leader, Kurt Eisner, was shot dead in broad daylight by a young lieutenant, Count Anton Arco auf Valley. Ever since overthrowing the

Wittelsbach dynasty on November 7, 1918, and proclaiming the "Free State of Bavaria," Eisner had been the target of fierce antisemitic attacks. In particular, his enemies blamed him for publishing documents from the archives of the Bavarian Foreign Ministry proving decisively that the leadership of the German Reich had triggered the First World War.[115]

Eisner's assassination radicalized the revolutionary movement in Munich. On the night of April 6–7, the state parliament was dissolved and a first Bavarian Soviet republic proclaimed, soon to be replaced by a second one led by Munich Communists. The government under the state premier and MSPD leader, Johannes Hoffmann, fled to Bamberg. It tried to regain power by raising a "Republican Soldiers' Army," but that attempt failed, prompting the German national government in Berlin to order a "Reich executive intervention" against the Soviet republic in mid-April. Prussian Lieutenant General Ernst von Oven took charge of the military operation, which included Freikorps units under the command of Bavarian Colonel Franz Ritter von Epp. The Bavarian Soviet leadership with its hastily assembled, ragtag Red Army units had no chance against the thirty-thousand-strong government troops.

By the end of the month, Munich was surrounded and besieged. Last-minute attempts to head off bloodshed failed. On April 30, supporters of the Soviet republic killed ten hostages, including members of the far-right Thule Society, in the courtyard of the Luitpold Gymnasium in retaliation for the shooting of captured Red Army fighters by government soldiers on the outskirts of the city. The "hostage murder" horrified the Munich bourgeoisie and was used by national government troops as an excuse to commit numerous atrocities.[116]

On May 2, Victor Klemperer reported that the jubilation with which the people of Munich had welcomed national troops had subsided. "Since yesterday afternoon and all through the night . . . the bitterest battle has raged without interruption, and shells and grenades are constantly rocking everything, drowning out the wild rattle of machine guns and the cracks of gunfire. Much blood is flowing in the inner city, where the Spartacists are desperately holding on since they can expect nothing whatever from surrender."[117] In total, over six hundred people, many of them civilians, lost their lives during the days of terrible violence.

After taking the city, the Reich's military henchmen began hunting down the leaders of the two Soviet republics. Freikorps soldiers murdered the party-unaffiliated socialist and writer Gustav Landauer in barbarous fashion after taking him to Stadelheim Prison on May 2. The next day, the commander in chief of the Red Army, navy man Rudolf Egelhofer, was shot to death in the inner courtyard of the former Bavarian dynasty's royal residence. Communist Eugen Leviné was arrested on May 13, sentenced to death after a brief show trial, and executed on June 5. Writer Ernst Toller, who had played a prominent role in the first Munich Soviet republic, was able to hide until June 4, which saved his life. He was sentenced to five years in prison. On May 7, Munich anarchist Erich Mühsam, who had been sentenced to fifteen years' incarceration, wrote from his prison cell: "You take a look around in your mind's eye: all the dead, all the murdered. . . . This is the revolution I once cheered on. After half a year, a giant pool of blood: It horrifies me." [118] In the months and years to come, Munich would become a reactionary, counterrevolutionary hotbed. It was no coincidence that Adolf Hitler, at the time an unknown former private in the First World War, launched his career in the Bavarian capital.

On May 7, 1919, the victorious Entente powers presented the German delegation in Versailles with the terms of peace. As Ernst Troeltsch wrote in retrospect, this marked the end of "the dreamland of the armistice period, in which, in ignorance of the conditions and real consequences of the impending peace, everyone could imagine the future in whatever fantastic, pessimistic, or heroic way they wanted." [119] Broad segments of the German population had been seduced into believing in the illusion of a "Wilsonian peace"—an agreement inspired by the spirit of understanding and reconciliation of American President Woodrow Wilson's "Fourteen Points" of January 1918. When the actual terms of the draft Treaty of Versailles emerged, it was like a slap in the face for Germany's government, political parties, and populace. The agreement would make the German Reich into a "brutally exploited colony," complained historian Gerhard Ritter, who had volunteered to fight in the

First World War in 1914.[120] In the *Berliner Tageblatt* newspaper, Theodor
Wolff criticized the draft treaty as "a document of the most retrograde
policy of subjugation, far removed from any and all ideas of the League
of Nations, untouched by even the slightest new spirit and putting force
above law. . . . If it remains as is or similar to what it looks like today,
there can be only one response: No!"[121]

The draft agreement had Germany losing an eighth of its territory
and a tenth of its population. Alsace-Lorraine, which had been annexed
in 1871, was to be returned to France, while Upper Silesia and large parts
of the Prussian provinces of Posen and West Prussia were to be ceded
to Poland. Danzig would become a "free city" under the mandate of the
newly created League of Nations, and the Memel region farther to the
east was to be subjected to Entente administration. In the southwestern
region of Saarland, a vote would be held after fifteen years to decide
whether it wanted to be part of Germany or France. German territory
west of the Rhine would be divided into three occupation zones, also for
a maximum of fifteen years. Germany would be forced to renounce all
its colonies and was also expressly forbidden to incorporate the German
parts of Austria. The Reich army was limited to one hundred thousand
men. To cap things off, Germany would be required to make reparations
for all war damage and losses. This punitive requirement was justified
by the draft agreement's Article 231, which held Germany and its allies
solely responsible for the war.[122]

This "war-guilt paragraph," in particular, unleashed howls of indignation. The revolutionary government's failure to enlighten the German
populace about imperial Germany's fatefully cavalier actions during the
diplomatic crisis of July 1914, following the assassination of Archduke
Franz Ferdinand of Austria, now came back to haunt it. In November 1918, the Council of Popular Deputies had decided to publish the
most important documents concerning the outbreak of war and charged
Marxist philosopher and author Karl Kautsky with preparing them. But
in April 1919, the Scheidemann cabinet reconsidered and decided not
to publish the material. As Eisner's release of the material made clear,
the documents showed that the Reich leadership had urged Austria-
Hungary to declare war on Serbia and thus bore the main responsibility

for starting the conflict. Scheidemann's cabinet feared that if such machinations were made public, it would weaken their position at the Versailles peace conference.[123]

Immediately after the peace terms became known, a broad front of resistance formed. At a meeting of the National Assembly, which had moved to the main auditorium of Berlin University, on May 1, Scheidemann declared the treaty unacceptable, asking, "What hand would not wither that puts itself and us in these shackles?" All the political parties, from the ultraright DNVP to the MSPD, were united in objecting to the draft treaty. Even USPD spokesman Hugo Haase, while conceding that Germany would have no choice but to sign in the end, reacted harshly.[124] Nor did Ebert mince words. "It would be dishonorable and undignified if we did not muster all our strength to fight the disgrace we are being threatened with," he proclaimed at a protest in Berlin on May 18.[125]

Public outrage was one thing. What would happen if the Allies insisted on the treaty's wording was another. Were Germany to reject the treaty, it would likely mean the end of the armistice and the resumption of fighting. General Groener made no effort to conceal that the German army could no longer put up any serious resistance if attacked—and that there was no popular support for going back to war.[126] The German delegation in Versailles was left trying to embroil the Entente powers in a "war of memoranda" to gain time and perhaps the odd concession. They focused their efforts on Article 231.[127]

Entente statesmen were unimpressed. In fact, the arrogance with which Foreign Minister Brockdorff-Rantzau rejected any responsibility hardened their position. On June 16, the secretary of the peace conference handed the German delegation the final text of the treaty. Apart from a few minor concessions—for example, a referendum in Upper Silesia to decide whether the region wanted to be part of Germany or Poland—it summarily rejected the German proposals. Germany was given an ultimatum of five days, later extended to seven, to sign the treaty. The German delegation returned to Weimar on the evening of July 16. "It all looks like a new war," noted Harry Graf Kessler. "It's like 1914, and just as oppressively humid and sunny as it was at the end of July."[128]

A week of frantic consultations in the cabinet and parliamentary groups ensued. Under pressure from the ultimatum, opposition to the treaty began to crumble. In a cabinet vote on June 18, seven ministers voted in favor of and seven, including Scheidemann, against signing the agreement. On June 19, despite his threat to resign if his parliamentary group refused to back him, seventy-five MSPD MPs voted in favor of the treaty and only thirty-nine against. The DDP had already decided to reject the treaty, while the Center Party opted on June 19 to approve the treaty "under certain conditions and under protest." This forced Scheidemann, committed, as he was, to a no vote, to resign. Brockdorff-Rantzau followed suit. On June 21, Ebert appointed Gustav Bauer, the former minister of labor, as Scheidemann's successor. Hermann Müller, who had been elected MSPD chairman a few days earlier, took over the Foreign Ministry. Matthias Erzberger, who had argued most emphatically in the Center Party in favor of accepting the treaty, became minister of finance.[129]

On June 22, the National Assembly approved the Treaty of Versailles by a vote of 237 to 138 (with five abstentions and one invalid vote)—albeit with the proviso that Germany did not consider itself the "author of the war" and did not consider itself obliged to hand over "war criminals." The Entente immediately rejected those qualifications and insisted on unconditional acceptance by the deadline they had set. Ultimately, on the afternoon of June 23, after further frantic deliberation, the National Assembly authorized the government "by a large majority" to sign the peace treaty. On June 28, the fifth anniversary of the Sarajevo assassination, Foreign Minister Hermann Müller and Transport Minister Johannes Bell from the Center Party signed the treaty in the Hall of Mirrors at Versailles.[130]

There is no doubt that the Treaty of Versailles was a peace dictated by the victors to the vanquished. But at least in comparison to what a victorious imperial Germany would likely have forced upon its adversaries, it was not overly harsh. The Treaty of Brest-Litovsk, which the Reich had imposed on revolutionary Russia in March 1918, was a clear indication of what the Allies could have expected had they lost the war. Nevertheless, most Germans regarded the Treaty of Versailles as a humiliation, a national "disgrace" against which they needed to defend themselves.

Henceforth, nationalist and military circles never stopped longing for revenge. Conservatives rejected "the lie of German war guilt" while promoting the myth that the German army had been "stabbed in the back"—that is, cheated of victory by traitorous left-wingers and Jews. This toxic combination poisoned the political atmosphere in Germany for some time. The irony was that the treaty undoubtedly contained points that could have been exploited by a patient German foreign policy geared toward international understanding. "In order to relieve ourselves of the burden of what today brings," warned Theodor Wolff on June 28, "we must pursue a policy of creating trust and alliances."[131] And on June 30, Hedwig Pringsheim noted: "'Shameful peace' or not, and hard and cruel as it may be, at least it is peace! And a chance for the future, however small! The hope for a better time still dawns in this agreement, despite everything."[132]

When the Weimar National Assembly began deliberating the constitution on February 24, 1919, important preliminary decisions had already been made. The leadership of the MSPD had insisted that the result was to be a representative parliamentary democracy. With the reform of October 1918, the proclamation of the republic on November 9, and the declaration of universal and equal suffrage on November 12, the course had been set. A further step in this direction was the appointment of constitutional law expert Hugo Preuss as state secretary of the interior on November 15, 1918. He was assigned to draw up a draft constitution. The left-wing scholar stood for cooperation between the democratically minded segments of the bourgeoisie and moderate forces in the workers' movement. That quality was why Ebert considered him particularly suitable for this new task.[133]

Preuss quickly got to work. From December 9 to 12, 1918, his office hosted a conference attended by government representatives, ministerial advisers, and a number of academics, including economist and sociologist Max Weber. By January 3, based on those discussions, Preuss could present a first draft of the new constitution with sixty-eight articles. The foundation was the principle of popular sovereignty. Nevertheless, the wide-ranging authority of the parliament, the Reichstag, representing popular will, was given a "counterweight" in the form of a powerful Reich presidency. Moreover, the federal structure of imperial Germany was to be reorganized to promote central, national authority.[134]

The Council of Popular Deputies discussed and approved the draft on January 14, 1919, albeit with two alterations. Firstly, Ebert and his allies demanded that the document include an enumeration of citizens' fundamental rights. Secondly, specific proposals for the reorganization of Germany's regional states were replaced with a more general clause that retained the possibility of subsequent changes to the Reich's federal structure.[135] The draft constitution was submitted to the National Assembly on February 21, and after the first reading from February 24 to March 3, it was referred to a twenty-eight-member committee consisting of representatives from the parliamentary groups. It was chaired by southwestern German DDP deputy Conrad Haussmann, who was also backed by the MSPD.[136]

The committee initially focused on the relationship between the nation and the regional states. Although there had been strong resistance to Preuss's insistence on central national authority, he still hoped the committee would curb the ambitions of the individual states. And indeed, he succeeded in extending the powers of the Reich over financial administration, the military, the postal service, and transportation. The Reich Council, as the body representing the regional states at the national level was now called, was much weaker than the Wilhelmine Empire's old Federal Council. Article 18 of the draft constitution also allowed for the regional states to be reorganized, although no use was made of the provision. But the draft document made no effort to address one core problem: the predominance of Prussia, by far the largest regional state, which accounted for around three-fifths of the German populace.[137]

Even more contentious was the status and authority of the Reich president. The powerful presidency favored by Preuss and Weber attracted considerable support from the middle-of-the-road bourgeois parties as protection against "parliamentary absolutism," in particular, the prospect of a socialist majority in the Reichstag. The MSPD parliamentary group opposed the creation of such a powerful office. On February 28, during the first reading of the draft, MSPD spokesman Richard Fischer warned: "We must reckon with the fact that one day someone from another party, perhaps a reactionary, coup-loving one, will occupy this position. We must take precautions against such eventualities."[138]

Nonetheless, amid the violence of the spring of 1919, which often verged on civil war, and with one of its own, Friedrich Ebert, holding the highest office of the land, the MSPD was increasingly willing to bend on this issue. The Reichstag, to be elected every four years on the basis of proportional representation, remained Germany's most important governmental body, responsible for legislation and deciding on matters of war and peace. Governing cabinets needed parliamentary approval, and the Reich chancellor could be toppled by votes of no confidence. The Reich president, on the other hand, was to be chosen by a direct popular vote for a term of seven years and had the power to appoint and dismiss the national government and dissolve the Reichstag. He was also Germany's supreme military commander. Most fatefully, it would turn out, the draft constitution's Article 48 granted him emergency powers, authorizing him to take the "necessary measures" if "public security and order" were "seriously disturbed or endangered." That meant that the president could suspend certain fundamental rights and order military interventions. The combination of rule by emergency decree, the fact that the president was directly elected, the long term of the office, and the right to dissolve the Reichstag gave the Reich president massive influence, although he was supposed to exercise it only during crises to protect the constitutional order. It was in this spirit that Paul Löbe, the MSPD vice president of the National Assembly, justified his party's support for Article 48 as a "weapon to defend the democratic republic and its protection against violent attacks."[139]

The canon of fundamental rights also came in for lengthy discussion. At the insistence of the popular deputies, in his draft Preuss had included provisions based on the classic democratic liberal rights that German advocates of democracy had demanded going all the way back to the Paulskirche Constitution of 1848. In the Constitutional Committee, the great representative of liberal democracy and DDP deputy

Friedrich Naumann proposed expanding this catalog to include further "basic rights of the populace," which would reflect changing economic and social circumstances. This prompted various groups and political parties to make demands of their own and pursue special interests. The Catholic Center Party, for example, succeeded in introducing articles concerning the church and schools, while representatives of the working classes insisted that the constitution include the possibility of transferring "private economic enterprises to public ownership," when suitable, and guaranteeing the right to works councils (Article 165).[140]

Finally, there was also dispute over the flag to be used by the new German republic. The MSPD preferred black, red, and gold—the color scheme used by Germany's failed democratic revolution of 1848–49. "In Germany, black, red, and gold is the color that democracy has always fought for," argued MSPD deputy Hermann Molkenbuhr in the National Assembly. But both right-wing parties, a majority of the DDP, and a minority of the Center Party wanted to retain black, white, and red—the colors of the Wilhelmine Empire. The result was a dubious compromise. The new German flag was black, red, and gold, but the imperial colors black, white, and red were featured in a canton atop the hoist side.[141]

The National Assembly ratified the constitution by 262 votes to 75 on July 31, 1919. *Vorwärts* called it a day of "the greatest historical significance," writing that "the entire life of the German nation . . . has now been placed on a new and finally secure foundation." The *Frankfurter Zeitung* approvingly quoted the minister of the interior, Eduard David of the MSPD, who said that the constitution made Germany "the most democratic democracy in the world."[142]

On August 11, Ebert signed the constitution in his eastern German vacation home in Schwarzburg. The epochal act took place without any ceremony at all. The businesslike sobriety also applied when Ebert was sworn in according to the constitution on August 21 in Weimar's National Theater. "Everything was very proper but also dispassionate—like a confirmation in a bourgeois home," Kessler reported. "The republic should avoid ceremonies. This form of government is ill-suited to them."[143] The less-than-glamorous beginning of the new German democracy didn't lessen what the authors of the constitution had achieved through hard work and under extremely adverse internal and external conditions. Despite all the compromises and shortcomings, particularly regarding the balance of power between the Reichstag and the Reich president, the constitution represented a framework of rules that, in the right hands, could help consolidate and bolster Weimar democracy. The decisive factor was how its provisions and possibilities would be used. As Hugo Preuss noted a few years later, even "the best constitution" was of no use if it was "applied incorrectly or amateurishly by its enforcers."[144]

In his memoirs, written in exile after 1933, Wilhelm Dittmann, one of the three USPD popular representatives, described November 1918 as an "unprecedentedly favorable historical moment" to "push political, economic, and social development forward with a tremendous jolt."[145] In the first weeks after November 9, before the old imperial functionaries and elites had gathered themselves, it would have been possible to nationalize the mining industry, enact agrarian reforms on the large East Prussian estates, remove top imperial officials, democratize the state bureaucracy, and establish armed forces loyal to the republic. But the MSPD leaders acted more like trustees of the bankrupt imperial past than committed advocates of a new future. They shied away from structural reforms. Their first concern was to democratically legitimize power relations by convening a national assembly and adopting a constitution. They were interested only secondarily, at best, in the idea that social changes would be required to provide a solid foundation for the democracy they envisioned. Even if we concede that the popular representatives' scope for action was limited by the difficult conditions they faced, historian Heinrich August Winkler was right when he concluded: "If their drive to shape things had been stronger, the MSPD could have changed more while retaining less."[146] The reality, however, was that many enemies of democracy still occupied positions of power from which they could attack the new political order.

At the same time, we shouldn't neglect the revolution's achievements and accomplishments. It cemented the change from monarchy to republic and established the first democratically constituted state in German history. "This extraordinary event in the history of democracy gives the November Revolution historical status," writes historian Alexander Gallus.[147] The proclamation of the Council of Popular Representatives on November 12 already sealed the most important achievements: guarantees of freedom of speech and assembly, the abolition of censorship and the massively discriminatory servants' code, universal suffrage for women, and the introduction of the eight-hour workday. The constitution of August 1919 enumerated liberal-democratic civil rights and laid the foundations of a modern welfare state. The achievements of the popular deputies undoubtedly also included the swift reintegration of most ex-soldiers into the processes of economic production, which kickstarted the transition from a wartime economy to a peacetime one.

Despite all its shortcomings and encumbrances, the course of the revolution of 1918–19 did not doom Weimar democracy to inevitable failure. It was an open question whether the foundations on which it had been built would stand the test of time. Much depended on the alliance between the moderate wing of the labor movement and the democratically minded segments of the middle classes, which would be crucial for parliamentary democracy to function. Likewise crucial was whether a majority of Germans could be won over to the new state order in the long term—and whether those who despised democracy could be kept in check.

On the first anniversary of the November Revolution, which he had greeted so effusively, Theodor Wolff was forced to concede that "much of the spirit of the monarchical state" had been preserved. But he added: "Anyone who believed that a people schooled in a long monarchical tradition, force-fed rigid views, and with only vague notions of how to stand on its own feet, could transform itself—as in the fairy tale—from a bear into a bridegroom after one day of revolution has a strange understanding of history and knows nothing of the psychology of nations." The German Republic would endure, Wolff argued, if it succeeded in turning schools and universities into its "heralds," educating future generations in democratic beliefs. "We should ask not today, but in twenty years' time, whether there is still much of the old spirit left," he wrote.[148] Sadly, the Weimar Republic would not get that much time.

Marching on Berlin

THE KAPP–LÜTTWITZ PUTSCH

Swastika on the steel helmet: Soldiers of the Ehrhardt Brigade occupy Berlin on March 13, 1920, and distribute leaflets.

In the late evening on March 12, 1920, Berlin was alarmed by news that the Ehrhardt Naval Brigade was marching on the German capital to overthrow the coalition government under Social Democratic Chancellor Gustav Bauer and to eliminate the Weimar Republic, which was at that point only a few months old. An hour after midnight, Reichswehr Minister Gustav Noske summoned the leading military officers for consultations in his ministry on Bendlerstrasse, telling them that force alone could put down the potentially violent putsch. Only the chief of army command, General Walther Reinhardt, agreed. The other senior officers all rejected the idea, arguing that, given the marine brigade's determination and the Reichswehr and security police's likely unwillingness to fight, any resistance would quickly collapse. "Soldiers don't shoot at fellow soldiers," the head of the troop office, General Hans von Seeckt, is said to have declared, asking, "Mr. Minister, do you really want to see a battle in front of the Brandenburg Gate?" We don't know whether Seeckt actually said these words, but there is no doubt that he wanted to keep the Reichswehr neutral and out of the imminent conflict. In effect he was defying his superior. "Have I been completely abandoned?" the desperate minister asked the group.[1]

At the end of the consultations, Noske asked Chancellor Bauer to convene the cabinet. Their meeting began at around four o'clock in the morning and was attended by the ministers, Reich President Ebert, and members of the Prussian regional government. With Seeckt reaffirming his position that resisting the putsch would only shed blood in vain, the cabinet decided to renounce force and allow the troops already mobilized to secure the government district to withdraw to their barracks. That led Reinhardt, who had once again vehemently decried surrendering without a fight, to demand his dismissal as head of the army command.

*The counterrevolutionary: Lieutenant Commander
Hermann Ehrhardt (left) with officers.*

A heated debate ensued over whether the government should remain in Berlin. It ended in a compromise. Ebert, Bauer, and most of the ministers would go to Dresden, where Noske considered the city commander, General Georg Maercker, to be reliable. Vice-Chancellor and Justice Minister Eugen Schiffer from the centrist German Democratic Party (DDP) would remain in Berlin with two other ministers.[2]

At 6:15 in the morning, Ebert departed his official residence by car, accompanied by Foreign Minister Müller and his senior deputy, State Secretary Otto Meissner. When Meissner expressed his displeasure at having to leave so abruptly, with no time to pack, Müller declared half jokingly, "We'll get through this revolution with only one shirt."[3] He would be proved right. Bauer set off with Noske and his adjutant, Major Erich von Gilsa, just in time. Ten minutes later, the rebellious troops arrived at Wilhelmstrasse. Reich Interior Minister Erich Koch-Weser

(DDP), who boarded a regularly scheduled train to Dresden at 8 a.m. together with Postal Minister Johann Giesberts from the Center Party, overheard two workers at a newspaper kiosk saying: "Let them come, soon it will be our turn!"[4]

The attempted coup came as little surprise. Ever since the signing of the Treaty of Versailles on June 28, 1919, the political Right had stepped up its hostility toward the Weimar Republic. "What's currently marching on the streets is the counterrevolution," noted Count Harry Kessler at the beginning of September 1919, "with the monarchy already clearly reappearing in the background."[5] Ernst Troeltsch, like Kessler an attentive observer of the times, identified a "wave from the right" in December 1919, particularly at German universities: "If you spoke to students a year ago, you had to be prepared for offbeat, pacifist, revolutionary, even idealistic Bolshevik contradictions. Today you have to be ready for antisemitic, nationalist, antirevolutionary backlash. In some legal faculties, people scuffle their feet in displeasure whenever the word 'constitution' is mentioned."[6] In fact, faced with economic hardship and bleak career prospects, most German students turned their backs on the republic. It was one of the most serious flaws of Weimar democracy.

The officer corps was also filled with resentment, worrying in particular that the new German government would follow the Treaty of Versailles to the letter and reduce the army to 100,000 men. Many officers were scared that they would lose the basis of their material existence and social prestige. In July 1919, the general in charge of Reichswehr Group Commando 1 in Berlin, Baron Walther von Lüttwitz, reported massive unrest among the troops to Noske. "The legitimate question, When will I be put out on the street?" was haunting everyone's minds, Lüttwitz complained.[7] In a meeting with Ebert in August, Lüttwitz and General Maercker told the German president it was "urgently desirable" to reach an agreement with the Entente powers that would clarify "in what strength and for how long the Reichswehr could be maintained beyond the contingent of 100,000 men stipulated in the peace treaty."[8] In January 1920, the Reichswehr still numbered around 250,000. In its negotiations with Germany's former enemies, the German government succeeded only in getting them to agree that the deadline for the troop reduction would be pushed back from March 31, 1920, to July 10, 1920, and that it could be carried out in two stages. That at least bought three months' time.[9]

Freikorps militias were especially reluctant to disband. They included the so-called Baltic men—volunteer units that had fought "Bolshevism" in Estonia and Latvia and were spirited back to Germany in October 1919 only under pressure from the Entente. Some joined the naval brigade named after its commander, Corvette Captain Hermann Ehrhardt, that Noske had deployed during the unrest in central Germany in the spring of 1919. It was a powerful force of around five thousand men. In January 1920, the brigade relocated to Döberitz, twenty-five kilometers from Berlin. It made no secret of its hatred of the Weimar Republic, rejecting the democratic black, red, and gold and wearing swastikas on its steel helmets—already a clear symbol of right-wing radical sympathies.[10]

The old conservative strongholds in Prussia vigorously supported the anti-democratic backlash. Although the aristocratic East Prussian large-estate owners, the *Junker*, had successfully prevented a major redistribution of property during the revolution of 1918–19, they still had to forfeit the predominance over state and society they had enjoyed in the Wilhelmine Empire. The *Junker* were united with large swathes of the officer corps in rejecting the purportedly bloodless, technocratic, corrupt "system" of Weimar and longing for a restoration of the monarchy.

It was therefore no coincidence that an East Prussian general regional administrative director, Wolfgang Kapp, became one of the key figures in the attempted coup d'état of March 1920. In September 1917, Kapp had founded the German Fatherland Party together with Grand Admiral Alfred von Tirpitz. It coalesced from a protofascist mass movement that had insisted on "peace through victory" with massive territorial annexations. After 1918, Kapp became chairman of the East Prussian chapter of the newly founded German National People's Party (DNVP) and a member of its main executive committee in Berlin. He was a member of the Deutsche Bank's supervisory board and maintained close relations with ultraconservatives like the Ruhr Valley industrialist Hugo Stinnes.[11]

Since the summer of 1919, Kapp had been plotting to launch a "counterrevolution from the right," for which, as he confided in a letter to Colonel Wilhelm Heye, the chief of the General Staff of the Northern Border Guard High Command, "the East was the only possible starting point." The chances of a coup were promising, Kapp argued, as long as "the military leaders" were prepared to "support this movement with all their strength and also take the lead."[12]

On July 8, 1919, Kapp met with the generals Otto von Below and Friedrich Karl von Lossberg in his Berlin apartment. They were joined by Erich Ludendorff, who had headed Army Supreme Command along with Paul von Hindenburg and functioned as a de facto military dictator during the last two years of the First World War. Ludendorff had returned from exile in Sweden at the end of February 1919. "The greatest stupidity of the revolutionaries was leaving us alive," he wrote to his wife Margarethe at the time. "I'll return to power one day, and when I do, I will know no mercy. With a clear conscience, I will see Ebert, Scheidemann, and comrades hanged from the next lamppost with their feet dangling."[13]

It was Ludendorff who pulled the strings in the preparations for the coup, albeit without attracting too much attention. During the July 8 meeting, Below recommended waiting another two years before taking action, arguing, "The troops are not yet sufficiently back in their commanders' hands, and the people would be against us."[14] But Kapp and Ludendorff insisted on overthrowing the government and establishing a dictatorship. In a memorandum from September 1919, Kapp explained why, in his opinion, the operation needed to commence as soon as possible: "Within a short period of 11 months, enormous progress has been made toward the complete ruin of the state and economic order. Abroad, the complete ruin of Germany's reputation, disgraceful treaty clauses, and continual disgraceful treatment instead of the promised conciliatory peace. It's the nadir of Germany's international currency. At home, the collapse of state authority, the failure of legal protection against all kinds of criminals, shortages of coal, and unemployment. In a nutshell,

Bolshevism awaits just around the corner. . . . If an iron fist has any chance of stopping this trend, the time is now."[15]

The National Association, founded under Ludendorff's patronage in October 1919 and based at Schellingstrasse 1 in Berlin, was the plot's headquarters. The coup was jointly directed by Colonel Max Bauer, Ludendorff's right-hand man during the war, and Captain Waldemar Pabst, the main mastermind behind the murders of Rosa Luxemburg and Karl Liebknecht. Pabst had already attempted a putsch with his Guards Cavalry Rifle Corps on July 21, 1919, but the rebellion had failed to get off the ground, whereupon he was forced to resign from the Reichswehr.[16]

The National Association benefited from generous financial support from big business leaders, including Stinnes, although he was very skeptical about the chances for a successful coup. "[He] considers any violent revolution from the right to be completely hopeless and disastrous and believes workers will put up a fierce front . . . against any reversal of conditions," noted Vice Admiral Albert Hopman after a conversation with the Ruhr industrialist in August 1919.[17]

The aim of the National Association was to unite those right-wing forces ready for action and to directly prepare a coup. In addition to spewing propaganda against the Weimar Republic and its leaders, the group also primarily devoted itself to recruiting reliable armed units. Former Freikorps soldiers were quartered on estates in Pomerania and Uckermark, where, disguised as agricultural laborers, they stood at the ready.[18]

The ball started rolling faster than the conspirators had expected. In February 1920, the Allies demanded the disbandment of the Ehrhardt Naval Brigade and a similar unit under the command of Wilfried von Loewenfeld. The two naval brigades had not been integrated into the postwar Reich navy, taking instructions instead from Reichswehr Group Commando 1 under Lüttwitz. On February 29, Noske ordered that they be disbanded within the next ten days. But Lüttwitz, who saw himself as the protector of the Freikorps and the Ehrhardt Brigade in particular, defied the order. "I will not tolerate such a central force being broken up in this stormy time," he proclaimed on March 1, 1920, at the Döberitz military training area, where the Ehrhardt Brigade was celebrating its first anniversary with a religious service and a grand parade.[19] Lüttwitz's words were tantamount to a declaration of war on the government.

Noske hesitated to dismiss the general, whom the troops held in high esteem, and tried to reach an amicable agreement. Lüttwitz remained adamant, refusing to budge even when his chief of staff, General Martin von Oldershausen, and his son-in-law, Major Kurt von Hammerstein, urged him not to make the conflict any worse. On March 10, following a suggestion by Seeckt and Reinhardt, Noske transferred command of the two naval brigades from Lüttwitz to Vice Admiral Adolf von Trotha, head of the Admiralty.[20]

Early that evening, Ebert received Lüttwitz for talks, to which Noske—at his own request—was also invited. Right from the outset, the atmosphere was frosty. In an immediately provocative gambit, the general demanded not only that Noske rescind the order to disband the brigades but also that the National Assembly be dissolved, new Reichstag elections held, "specialist ministers" appointed for the Foreign Ministry and the Ministry of Economics and Finance, and the government loyalist Reinhardt dismissed. To top it all off, Lüttwitz insisted that he himself be named commander in chief of the Reichswehr.

Ebert rebuffed the general's presumptiveness calmly and firmly. Noske, however, lost his temper, rejecting the general's demands as a de facto ultimatum, which he should under no circumstances be allowed to get away with. The minister informed Lüttwitz that he had stripped him of command over the two naval brigades and warned him against taking any steps he might regret. A military putsch, Noske cautioned, would have unforeseeable consequences, cause a rift in the Reichswehr, and provoke workers into going out on a general strike. That had no impact on Lüttwitz, and they parted in anger.[21]

Instead of having the mutinous general arrested, Ebert and Noske only advised him to resign. It was another instance of the Weimar Republic leadership's reluctance to take decisive action against right-wing opponents of democracy—a tactical mistake that would come back to haunt the government. When Lüttwitz's resignation letter hadn't arrived

by midday on March 11, Noske informed him that he was fired. That
enabled the general to travel unhindered to the Ehrhardt Naval Brigade
in Döberitz to discuss the next steps. Ehrhardt agreed to allow his men
to march on Berlin on the evening of March 12. They arrived at the Brandenburg Gate on the morning of March 13.[22] Lüttwitz's actions forced the
hand of the conspirators around Kapp and Ludendorff, who had expected
to launch their rebellion at the end of March or the beginning of April.
Now they had to take action without having made final preparations.[23]

Warnings were pouring in from all sides to Noske. For example, on
March 8, 1920, the Prussian state commissioner for the supervision of
public order, Herbert Ritter von Berger, pointed out the "strong sentiment fermenting in right-wing extremist circles, especially in the
Reichswehr and among members of the old army." This undercurrent
had to be taken"very seriously." But Berger's report did not contain any
concrete information about an impending coup, and Noske received it
only during the course of March 11.[24] He issued arrest warrants for the
main conspirators, Kapp, Bauer, and Pabst, but they were forewarned by
someone at police headquarters and able to evade arrest.[25]

The following afternoon, Noske told the cabinet that he had reliable
news of "regular discussions having taken place for some time now in
a closed circle . . . with the aim of changing the makeup of the Reich
government." At the center of the plot were Director General Kapp and
Captain Pabst, Noske said, so he had ordered their arrest. A rumor was
circulating, he added, that the Ehrhardt Naval Brigade intended to strike
the following night. Thus, as a precautionary measure, a state of alert
had been declared and tighter security imposed in the government district.[26] Nonetheless, neither Noske nor his fellow cabinet members seem
to have taken the threat very seriously. When Prussian Interior Minister Wolfgang Heine burst in at the end of the meeting with the news
that the Ehrhardt Brigade was preparing to march, Noske reassured
them that this was a "false alarm, as has repeatedly been the case." He
also said he had sent Vice Admiral von Trotha to Döberitz to talk sense
into Ehrhardt.[27]

Threatening backdrop: Rebels set up artillery in front of the Brandenburg Gate.

Trotha, who secretly sympathized with the conspirators, telephoned ahead to announce his arrival, so Erhardt had time to conceal his plans. When Trotha showed up in Döberitz, accompanied by Lieutenant Captain Wilhelm Canaris, he found the camp "completely silent." Noske's emissary also avoided asking any overt questions when he spoke with Ehrhardt one-on-one. After returning to Berlin at around 8:30 p.m. on March 12, Trotha reported that he had not seen anything suspicious. He added, however, that he could not guarantee that Ehrhardt's brigade would *not* march that night, since Ehrhardt's men could be expected to get up to "all sorts of mischief." [28]

Noske could rest easy for the time being. But before long he got a rude awakening. At around 11 p.m., Reichswehr Group Commando 1 received news that the Ehrhardt Brigade was on the march. After being filled in, Noske made one last attempt to dissuade Ehrhardt from the attempted coup, sending Lüttwitz's chief of staff General von Oldershausen and Lieutenant General Burghard von Oven to Döberitz. On their way, the two envoys encountered the navy men marching with full assault packs and waving black, white, and red flags. In the meantime, their commander had fallen asleep and had to be woken up. Oldershausen and Oven forcefully reminded him of the consequences of his actions. The government had Reichswehr troops and security police at their command in Berlin, and bloodshed was inevitable. Ehrhardt protested that he could not disobey orders from Lüttwitz. Nevertheless, he was prepared to put down his conditions for negotiations in writing. They largely mirrored the list of demands that Lüttwitz had presented in his confrontation with Ebert and Noske—although Ehrhardt, on his own initiative, added a demand for amnesty for all those involved in the coup.

At an officers' meeting convened an hour after midnight, the two generals, having returned to Berlin, proposed negotiating with Ehrhardt, but Noske and Reinhardt strictly refused. Conversely, like before, they were unable to push through their demand that the rebellion be put down by force.[29]

Shortly after 5 a.m., Colonel Adalbert von Thaysen, who was tasked with protecting the government district, received the order to withdraw his regiment to their barracks in the nearby district of Moabit. A little later, the Ehrhardt Brigade arrived in western Berlin to the sound of marching music. There, the soldiers were greeted with cheers from predominantly middle-class onlookers. Young women presented flowers, and black, white, and red flags flew from many of the apartment buildings. "The street was once again colorfully decked out with uniforms— Where had all those half-forgotten Iron Crosses around people's necks suddenly come from?" asked one eyewitness.[30] In the working-class district of Prenzlauer Berg, Käthe Kollwitz observed: "The counterrevolution has now begun. . . . People are gathered in packs on the streets, all of them as though under orders. What will happen next?"[31]

Kapp and Lüttwitz inspected the columns of military men at the Brandenburg Gate. Ludendorff was also present, in civilian clothing, although he was by no means taking a harmless morning stroll, as he later claimed. Ehrhardt greeted Kapp with the words: "So you're taking over the government—don't forget to govern."[32] The occupation of the government district proceeded smoothly. At around 7 a.m., Kapp entered the Reich Chancellery together with the former Berlin police president and his designated minister of the interior, Traugott von Jagow, and the former undersecretary of state in the Ministry of Agriculture, Baron Friedrich von Falkenhausen. They were met in the reception hall by the undersecretary of state, Heinrich Albert. When Albert asked what they wanted, Kapp replied, "We are seizing governmental power." In response to the subsequent question as to what legitimated that action, Kapp simply said, "The law of November 9, 1918." Albert asked the intruders to leave immediately, but Kapp only gestured at the troops gathered on Wilhelmstrasse. It was his way of saying that power now resided with him and that any resistance would be futile.

Kapp then wanted to speak to Vice-Chancellor Schiffer. Twenty minutes later, when Schiffer and Albert entered the library on the upper floor, the new lords and masters of the Reich Chancellery had already settled in and were hard at work. Kapp and Schiffer exchanged heated words, with the former ordering the vice-chancellor and undersecretary of state to leave the Reich Chancellery at once or be forcibly removed. Schiffer was later put in protective custody in his apartment, but the guards were withdrawn in just a few hours after he gave his word of honor not to leave the building.[33]

As Kapp and his followers assumed responsibility for governing, Lüttwitz, Colonel Max Bauer, and the staff of the brigade took control of the Reichswehr Ministry on Bendlerstrasse. Ludendorff also turned up there, declaring to anyone who would listen, "We're going to finish the job."[34]

In his first proclamation on March 13, Kapp declared the previous government deposed and appointed himself Reich chancellor and Prussian state premier, and Lüttwitz Reichswehr minister and commander in chief. His second proclamation promised to establish a "strong state power," to eradicate "the government of party interests," to "ruthlessly" suppress strikes and sabotage, and to combat "any rebellion against the new order with merciless determination." Lüttwitz extended the state of emergency he had imposed in Berlin at the beginning of the putsch to the entirety of Germany. The National Assembly was declared dissolved on the grounds that it had violated the spirit of the constitution by postponing new elections. Bans on assemblies and parades as well as a temporary ban on all newspapers followed. Editors who spread "false rumors" about the new government—a kind of "fake news" accusation avant la lettre—were to be taken into protective custody.[35]

In a meeting with representatives of the right-wing German People's Party (DVP) that afternoon, Kapp was at pains to appear moderate. The putschists were "good republicans," he assured the politicians, and nothing could be further from their minds than a restoration of the monarchy. Dictatorship would "of course only be introduced temporarily" and the constitutional state restored "as soon as possible." To this end, new elections would be called soon. Kapp also voiced regret at the introduction of women's suffrage but said abolishing it would be unnecessary because women would soon lose the desire to vote anyway. Finally, he emphasized his government's desire for "good relations with the right-wing parties," that is, the DNVP and DVP.[36]

At a hastily convened press conference during the morning, Kapp had appealed to the representatives of the right-wing media to support the would-be new government in overcoming the "immense difficulties" it faced. He emphatically denied that the putsch was a "coup carried out by sinister reactionaries." He reiterated that he regarded republican government as a fact of life and intended to restore constitutional conditions after a dictatorial transitional phase. He also introduced his good friend Baron von Falkenhausen as the new head of the Reich Chancellery.[37]

But it quickly became apparent how poorly planned the government takeover was. The self-appointed Reich chancellor did not even have a complete list of names for his cabinet and struggled filling the ministries with allies. Two close associates, the medical councillor Georg Wilhelm Schiele and the pastor and German nationalist Reichstag deputy Gottfried Traub, turned Kapp down, citing their own unsuitability, when he asked them to head the Ministry of Economic Affairs and the

Ministry of Culture, respectively. Chief Finance Councillor Paul Bang initially declared himself willing to take over the Ministry of Finance, but soon changed his mind when he realized how shaky the whole enterprise of the coup truly was.[38]

An even more serious problem for the putschists was that they had not been able to arrest members of the old government, as they had envisaged. Kapp was incensed at Ehrhardt for allowing Ebert and most of the ministers to escape, complaining to Falkenhausen that he would prefer to "put the whole matter in people's hands."[39] A few months later, he would go on record saying that the parallel existence of old and new governments had created an "unfortunate dualism that gave the supporters of the old government a rallying point and unreliable elements and opportunists time to wait and see how things turned out."[40] There was indeed a kind of double government, so people didn't immediately have to take one side or the other.

The decisive factor for the success or failure of the coup, however, was the putschists' ability to extend their power beyond Berlin to other parts of Germany while garnering support from major segments of society. Not surprisingly, conservatives from the eastern provinces of Prussia were most enthusiastic. "Perhaps this is Prussia's final battle, but it has been seized by the evil hands of the worst sorts of political Cagliostros, rapacious condottieri and roving thieves from the East," noted Kessler, who followed the developments from the Swiss city of Bern.[41] Many district councillors and even the Social Democratic supreme president of East Prussia, August Winnig, who had long since distanced himself from the party, celebrated the putsch. In a joint declaration on March 13 with the commander of Military District Commando 1, Lieutenant General Ludwig von Estorff, Winnig recognized the Kapp government as the "holder of the actual power." The two men wrote, "Surrounded by hostile neighbors, we East Prussians must welcome every development that promises our province peace and the chance to create prosperity."[42]

Commanders of military districts in not only East Prussia but also

Pomerania, Silesia, Mecklenburg, Schleswig-Holstein, Hamburg, Thuringia, and Saxony backed the new regime and removed officials loyal to the Weimar Constitution from their posts. In Bavaria, the commander of Reichswehr Group Commando 4, General Arnold von Möhl, succeeded in overthrowing the Social Democratic state government under State Premier Johannes Hoffmann and installing the governmental president of Upper Bavaria, Gustav Ritter von Kahr, as government commissioner and a new strongman.[43]

Many Reichswehr officers vacillated or tried to avoid taking a stand until the situation was decided. At the same time, they also had clear reservations about the new masters. In a speech to ranking members of the equipment office in the Reichswehr Ministry at noon on March 13, Colonel Hans von Feldmann left it up to all those present, individually, to decide what to think about the putsch, but made no secret of his conviction that the coup was "the most foolish possible" course of action, since any necessary changes to the political situation could also have been achieved by constitutional means. Feldmann said that he continued to feel bound by his oath and would follow whatever instructions the president issued.[44] For his part, in a conversation with Vice-Chancellor Schiffer on March 14, Seeckt conceded that the would-be usurpers of power had "some positive qualities" but dubbed them "politically muddled fantasts, reckless madcaps, and dilettante blowhards." As a result, Seeckt reasoned, they would prove unable to build on their "initial success" and "ultimately be forced offstage as failures."[45]

Paul von Hindenburg, the former head of the Army Supreme Command, sympathized with the putschists' aims but disapproved of the course they had chosen. "As much as my heart was in favor, my mind could not be," he wrote in a letter in April 1920. But when his old brother in arms General Wilhelm Groener implored him in a telegram to publicly reject the coup—"one word from you is enough to bring the Reichswehr back down to its constitutional foundation"—he declined to come out and say what he thought.[46]

Skepticism also prevailed among industrialists, although they, too, refused to take a public stand against Kapp. Stinnes considered the coup to be a dangerous adventure that could lead to serious economic upheaval, but he initially avoided condemning its main leaders. A March 14 resolution of the coal syndicate merely stated that it remained committed to the aims and principle of the mining industry working with the trade unions, "regardless of the current turmoil and any turmoil to come." A day later, Stinnes agreed to a modified resolution that rejected any attempt at "violent changes to the government and constitution" and announced that the syndicate would not follow any instructions from the Kapp government.[47]

The chemical industry was the most resolute in distancing itself from the coup. "Everything is now being put at risk by a small group who are foreign to industrial life and workers' psychology," wrote Julius Bueb, a member of the board of the Badische Anilin-Soda-Fabrik in Ludwigshafen on March 15. He added that the putsch had "refueled" the workforce's inherent, latent mistrust of employers, and recent events would necessarily have a "downright devastating" effect abroad. Germany's opponents could now say—rightly—that "Prussian militarism" had by no means been overcome. On the contrary, it could still "send the socialist government packing in the twinkle of an eye."[48] At a rally the same day, chemical industry leaders declared their "unlimited solidarity with workers in their defense against the attacks upon the state and economic order."[49]

Most civil servants initially adopted a wait-and-see attitude in the conviction that things had yet to be decided and that making any premature declarations of allegiance risked undermining or losing their privileged positions. On March 14, however, the undersecretaries of state of the Reich ministries formally decided to accept instructions only from the constitutionally elected government. Almost without exception, the ministerial officials of the Reich and Prussia followed suit, refusing to act on any orders by Kapp and his followers.[50]

The positions taken by Germany's political parties varied. District and regional associations of the DNVP and its press organs were very positive toward the putschists. On the other hand, although Kapp himself was a member of the DNVP's main executive committee, he had not informed the party leaders of his plans and had even ignored the warnings of party chairman Oskar Hergt not to use violence. Thus, the party executive's March 13 statement was correspondingly restrained. It said the party presumed that the "new government" would pursue the goal of "immediately restoring constitutional conditions" and called for new elections within the prescribed period of sixty days. Until that point, the DNVP was prepared to "cooperate to ensure peace and order, freedom, and national dignity, by uniting all the forces of the German people."[51]

The party leadership of the DVP was caught completely off guard by the events of March 13. At an emergency meeting that afternoon, leaders tried to find a middle ground between supporting and rejecting the coup. Party chairman Gustav Stresemann declared it necessary to find a stand "that does not cause difficulties for the new government but that leaves the possibility open for us to act as mediators between Dresden and Berlin." On the one hand, he came out against "going through thick and thin with the new government"; on the other, he called for the "new facts" created by the coup to be recognized. The resolution that passed at the end of the meeting reflected this dichotomy. It accused the "previous government" of having provoked the coup by postponing new elections, called for the "swiftest transition of the current provisional government to one based on law," and demanded "immediate new elections to the legislative bodies on the basis of the previous liberal system."[52]

By contrast, the DDP and the Catholic Center Party, the SPD's coalition partner, unambiguously rejected the putsch. Center Party deputies in the National Assembly and the Prussian State Assembly excoriated the attempted coup as "a crime against the German people" that "raised the specter of civil war." The DDP's main executive committee and parliamentary groups denounced the conspirators as "champions of the harshest agenda of Germany's former lords and masters and the most reactionary views from east of the Elbe." The coup's leaders, the DDP added, represented only "a small minority," consisting of those who bore "the heaviest responsibility from the time of the war." The statement ended confidently, stating: "We remain on the foundation of our constitution and of the law. We stand by the legal authorities. . . . We expect swift and energetic action from the government and the National Assembly."[53]

Despite the undecided situation, the Kapp regime might have triumphed, were it not for the determined resistance of the working class. On the morning of March 13, President Ebert, the Social Democratic members of the government, and SPD party chairman Otto Wels issued an appeal in Berlin condemning the "military coup" in the strongest terms and calling for an "across-the-board" strike. "We did not launch the revolution to subjugate ourselves once again today to a regime of bloodthirsty mercenaries," the document read. "For that reason, we need to defend ourselves with the most vigorous means at our disposal. Let no business run as long as the military dictatorship of Ludendorff and his henchmen is in power! Stop work! Go on strike! Cut off the oxygen to this reactionary cabal. Fight with everything you have to save the republic! . . . Proletarians, unite! Down with the reactionary counterrevolution!"[54] This was an obvious about-face for the SPD leadership, which had instructed the military under Noske to put down all labor strikes in late 1918 and early 1919.

We don't entirely know how the appeal came about. It was penned by the Reich Chancellery press officer, ministerial director Ulrich Rauscher, and was not personally signed by the leaders in whose names it was issued. It appears that Noske and Chancellor Bauer read and approved the draft. In the early hours of March 13, with the members of the government having already set off for Dresden, Wels and the Berlin SPD district chairman Franz Krüger dictated the text to the twenty SPD district organizations by telephone. Rauscher himself transmitted it to ministerial councillor Arnold Brecht in the Chancellery, who immediately released it to the press.[55]

Upon arrival in Dresden, at a meeting with the commander of the city's Military District Commando 4, General Georg Maercker, the ministers disavowed the appeal, saying that their signatures had been placed on it without their knowledge. A second appeal on March 14, entitled "To the

German People!," no longer called for a general strike. It dubbed events in Berlin "a presumptuous swindle on a grand scale" and demanded that civil servants follow the instructions of the legally elected Reich government, in accordance with their oath to the constitution. Anyone who served the usurpers would be fired. Ebert and Noske also appealed to the soldiers of the Reichswehr to defend the constitution and to remain "loyal to the old legitimate government." The appeal added: "Let no one now seek to make himself jointly responsible for this criminal insanity." [56]

But the call for a general strike had gone out, and trade unions were adopting the cause. In the course of the morning of March 13, the executive committee of the General German Trade Union Federation (ADGB) met with the party chairmen of the MSPD and USPD. Although efforts to agree on a joint proclamation foundered because USPD representatives held the Bauer government partly responsible for the putsch, the ADGB and the Working Community of Independent Employees' Associations (AfA) did issue a joint call for a strike: "The defensive action of the workforce must be a powerful and overwhelming one. No profession and no group should be allowed to stand on the sidelines. Everyone must do his duty. The reactionary counterrevolution must fail because of the united resistance of the people." [57] The German Civil Servants' League (Deutscher Beamtenbund) also joined the strike directorship formed by the ADGB and AfA.

The USPD formed its own "Central Strike Directorship of Greater Berlin." The German Communist Party, the KPD, at the time still a small group, initially refused to participate in the call to strike, saying that it would "not lift a finger for the government of the murderers of Karl Liebknecht and Rosa Luxemburg, which had been toppled in shame and disgrace." The party changed its position a short time later after realizing that it meant isolating itself from the working masses. [58]

On Sunday, March 14, the biggest strike Germany had ever seen began, although its full force became apparent only on Monday. Work came to a standstill in most factories and many stores were closed. Traffic was almost completely paralyzed. Newspapers were not published because the typesetters refused to work. "We are sitting here without electric light, without gas, without railroad connections, and without any newspapers," wrote the Berlin historian and Friedrich Engels biographer Gustav Mayer to his colleague Hermann Oncken on March 15. "We only learn what's going on via rumors spread by telephone."[59] At the end of the month, theater critic Alfred Kerr recalled those fateful days in Berlin, which he had spent sitting in the dark with the flu, "without light, without heating, and without knowing what was to become of Germany, which has been taken off guard." He added: "There was not even any telephone contact with the world at large. Outside you couldn't see your hand in front of your face. A great week."[60] Water, too, was only sporadically available. "When the water comes back on, we refill the bathtub and all our containers," noted Colonel Ernst van den Bergh, head of the soldiers' welfare department at the Reich Ministry of Defense. "At night, all the streets are dark. You can see odd candles lit in the buildings. Then suddenly the power would return at half strength and the rooms would gleam again in the moonlight."[61] The Technical Emergency Aid tried to restore electricity, gas, and water service but were prevented from doing so by striking workers.[62]

Kapp was still optimistic. He was "determined to take ruthless action," he informed a DVP delegation on March 14, and "did not doubt success for a moment" because it wouldn't be long before the Reichswehr fully backed him.[63] But the putschists were completely unprepared for the resounding effect of the general strike and the work stoppage of the ministerial bureaucracy. Increasingly isolated from the outside world, they sat by candlelight in the Reich Chancellery. Orderly government activity was impossible. Moreover, the Reichsbank refused to make payments, leaving Germany's would-be new rulers high and dry financially. The more insecure they felt about their cause, the more draconian the measures they took to salvage what they could. On March 15, Kapp issued a decree threatening strike leaders and pickets with the death penalty. It took Stinnes intervening by telephone to persuade Kapp to rescind that decree.[64]

While the workers demonstrated their power, paralyzing the entire country with their protest, the Reich government, which had been dispatched to Dresden, initially proved unable to respond. "Bauer almost broken," noted Interior Minister Koch-Weser. "Ebert also numb."[65] In the early afternoon of March 13, Ebert met for the first time with Maercker, who informed him that he had received an order from Lüttwitz to take the Reich president and the ministers into protective custody. For the time being, he added, he was interpreting this command to mean that he had to ensure their protection. But he refused to issue a clear statement that he stood by the constitution and the democratically elected government. Once again, Noske had misjudged the attitudes of one of his military leaders.

In the face of Maercker's ambivalence, the government decided on the evening of Saturday, March 13, to travel on to Stuttgart the following Monday and convene a national assembly there. However, on March 14, when Maercker announced he would travel to Berlin to confer with Lüttwitz, Ebert feared that he might once again side with Kapp and order the government taken into custody. So Ebert and the ministers set off for Stuttgart that afternoon. The Württemberg military district commander, General Walter von Bergmann, had promised protection and assistance.[66]

It was a difficult journey. Workers' councils repeatedly stopped and checked Ebert and the ministers' cars. They ran out of gasoline before reaching Chemnitz, so they had to travel on to Stuttgart by train, where they first arrived on March 15. There they were greeted in the afternoon by Württemberg President Wilhelm Blos, who expressed the hope "that we will soon succeed in defeating the Kappists' criminal attack and restoring the peace and order so necessary to the Reich."[67]

By then, it was already becoming apparent that the coup had failed. "People understand the situation better here than in Berlin," noted Koch-Weser on the evening of March 15. "The Kapp government is collapsing."[68] For that reason, the government, which had regained confidence, rejected all attempts at mediation. "Negotiating with Kapp is pointless," Koch-Weser wrote to Schiffer in Berlin. "It strengthens him, discredits us, and only prolongs the crisis. Kapp must resign, or his movement must burn itself out."[69]

Thus, when Maercker showed up in Stuttgart on March 16 to negotiate a compromise on behalf of Kapp, Ebert, the ministers, and the president of the National Assembly, Constantin Fehrenbach, rebuffed him. They were also motivated by fears that an arrangement of any kind with the putschists might further radicalize the working classes and encourage separatist tendencies. "If we negotiate, we face the threat of Bolshevism and the secession of southern and western Germany," declared Ebert at a cabinet meeting on March 16, with Maercker in attendance. The government would insist that the putschists completely capitulate. Maercker relayed this and other conditions, formulated by Noske, to Berlin by telephone that evening. Among other things, the government demanded that Kapp and Lüttwitz resign immediately, that their troops be placed under the command of General Seeckt or some other general who had not been involved in the revolt, and that a new commander be named to remove the Ehrhardt Brigade from Berlin and disband it. Pabst, whom Lüttwitz had promoted to the rank of major, summarily rejected those conditions.[70]

In the meantime, efforts had begun in Berlin to broker a deal, with the DVP leading the way. True to his policy of remaining open on both sides to negotiation, Stresemann put forward a compromise, under which both governments would resign and Ebert would appoint an interim cabinet. This proposal went down badly with the representatives of the SPD, and the two other governing parties, the Center and the DDP, refused to negotiate without their coalition partner. Stresemann therefore decided to change course and try to engineer Kapp and Lüttwitz's resignation, offering them an "honorable way out" in the form of a generous amnesty arrangement.

Having been informed by Stresemann that Kapp and Lüttwitz were prepared to resign if the terms were reasonable, and despite having been warned from Stuttgart against doing so, Schiffer began talks with Major Pabst on the evening of March 16. Prussian SPD Minister President Paul Hirsch and his party colleague, Prussian Finance Minister Albert Südekum, also took part. After hours of deliberations, the following points were agreed upon: "Kapp resigns, Lüttwitz resigns supreme command;

the Reich government appoints another commander in chief. The deputy to the Reich chancellor will make the following proposals to those concerned. The National Assembly will dissolve itself no later than four weeks after it convenes; popular election of the Reich president; cabinet reshuffle as quickly as possible. The Reich minister of justice will lobby the National Assembly for a general amnesty."[71]

The putschists had not yet conceded defeat. But when reports arrived increasingly of striking workers and soldiers clashing violently, troops being stripped of their arms, and subordinates refusing to follow orders, Kapp and Lüttwitz faced growing pressure to draw the logical conclusion that the coup had failed. In his response to Schiffer's proposals, which Pabst had forwarded to him, on the morning of March 17, Kapp declared himself willing to resign from the office of Reich chancellor, although he sought to portray that step as voluntary, motivated solely by his desire not to block joint action against the "danger from the left." Kapp declared that he was "placing executive power in the hands of the military commander in chief in order to ensure the coming together of all existing forces to save our culture in the forthcoming, decisive battle against Bolshevism."[72]

Lüttwitz took somewhat longer to throw in the towel. After Kapp's resignation, he continued to see himself in the role of a "military dictator," initially refusing to relinquish his post as military commander in chief. This gave Schiffer the opportunity to renege on the promises he had made to Pabst and to end his relationship with the putsch government, which his colleagues in Stuttgart felt compromised their authority.

On the afternoon of March 17, a delegation of officers sought out Lüttwitz in the Reich Chancellery, with their spokesman, Colonel Wilhelm Heye, getting straight to the point. Although they had "full understanding" for the putsch, Heye said, everyone concerned had to face the fact that the coup had failed and Lüttwitz would have to resign. "Lüttwitz became very upset, rapped me with his sword and threatened to have me arrested," Heye recalled years later.[73] But after a further meeting with Berlin commanders, which Ludendorff also attended, Lüttwitz was forced to admit he had lost the confidence of the troops and resigned.

That evening, after consulting with Ebert by telephone, Schiffer named General von Seeckt Lüttwitz's successor and reappointed him to his former position as commander of Reichswehr Group Commando 1. There was a stir during the announcement when an SPD member of parliament, unaware that Seeckt was in the room, exclaimed loudly: "I don't trust that piece of carrion!" Everyone present, including the general himself, burst into "raucous laughter."[74] But the Social Democratic deputy was only saying out loud what many of his fellow party members were thinking. After all, Seeckt had behaved ambiguously when the putsch began, avoiding any clear commitment to the legitimate democratically elected government.

The following day, the Ehrhardt Brigade quit Berlin to the strains of the German national anthem. They were met with catcalls and jeers from an angry crowd at the Brandenburg Gate. The soldiers opened fire. Twelve people were killed, and thirty wounded.[75]

"Never before has a gang of usurpers been swept away as quickly as Kapp and his comrades," journalist Carl von Ossietzky rejoiced in the *Berliner Volks-Zeitung*. "Never before has a popular rallying cry had such a rapid and powerful effect as the call to strike."[76] In the *Berliner Tageblatt*, Ossietzky's colleague Theodor Wolff wrote of a "victory of the people," adding that no one could claim that "German democracy was a pathetic illusion" any longer. "At the moment when Germany was about to be brought down to its lowest depths, it rose up before the eyes of the world. . . . People have complained that the history of the birth of the German Republic lacked great symbolic moments. This was our storming of the Bastille."[77]

But the end of the coup did not mean the end of the general strike. The trade unions, who could take most of the credit for defending the republic, now wanted to be rewarded, calling not only for the resignation of Noske, whom they rightly held responsible for reactionary tendencies in the Reichswehr, but also for "a decisive voice in the reorganization of social conditions." They laid out their ideas in a nine-point agenda. The most important demands were for all those involved in the putsch to be punished, the state administration to be thoroughly purged and democratized, the mining industry to be immediately socialized, all counterrevolutionary military units to be disbanded, and the working classes to take over Germany's security forces.[78]

After everything that had happened, it was clear to many that Noske could hardly remain in office. On the way to Dresden on March 13, Interior Minister Koch-Weser already noted in his diary: "Who will replace Noske, who cannot be kept on after this display of naivete?"[79] Colonel van den Bergh was also convinced that Noske had completely "failed," criticizing the Reichswehr minister for having "too much confidence in the senior officers" and failing to "break the swelling wave of militarism."[80] On March 18, in the National Assembly in Stuttgart, Philipp Scheidemann, the former SPD Reich minister president, sharply attacked Noske's policy toward the military: "Anyone who didn't deliberately close their eyes and ears should have been able to foresee what we have been forced to our disgust and indignation to experience over the last few days." Noske began composing his letter of resignation during the session itself, and when Koch-Weser implored him not to do anything hasty, he replied, "Not a single hour more."[81] But Ebert, seeing Noske as a guarantee for fruitful cooperation with the Reichswehr, didn't want to let him go under any circumstances. And Noske initially secured the backing of the majority of the SPD parliamentary group, who were reluctant to rebuff their own Reich president.

Chancellor Bauer and some of the ministers returned to the capital on March 19, while Ebert and Koch-Weser remained in Stuttgart until the following evening. At the first cabinet meeting in Berlin on the afternoon of March 20, SPD chairman Otto Wels immediately called for Noske's dismissal. Confidence in the Reichswehr minister was gone, Wels said, and he was "no longer politically tenable." Although General Seeckt, who had been called in for the meeting, tried to argue Noske's case—he had "proved himself with the troops, both personally and militarily"— the cabinet members' minds were made up. The SPD undersecretary of state in the Ministry of the Interior, Heinrich Schulz, countered that while he respected "the gentlemanly manner" in which Seeckt had stuck up for Noske, "politically, Noske has no future since his name entails an agenda."[82]

Ebert remained unconvinced, even threatening to step down himself if his party and the trade unions insisted on Noske's resignation.
On March 22, Wels and ADGB chairman Carl Legien again stressed to
the Reich president that a change in the Reichswehr Ministry would be
necessary to end the general strike. Faced with such massive pressure,
Ebert finally gave in and accepted Noske's resignation.[83]

Starting on March 18, the trade unions held negotiations with representatives of the majority parties and the Reich and Prussian governments, but they never received the decisive political say they desired.
Not only the SPD's middle-of-the-road coalition partners but Ebert
himself raised serious objections to greater union influence within the
government. Indeed, if organized labor's demands had been met, the
Weimar Republic would have become the sort of "trade-union state"
conservative critics of the compromise of 1918 had held up as a bête
noire. Legien's proposal to replace the Bauer cabinet with a "workers'
government" of the MSPD and USPD was dead on arrival. Neither party
had any desire or will to reestablish the coalition that briefly existed in
the Council of Popular Representatives in 1918. And the Center Party
and DDP were not at all inclined to tolerate such a coalition, which had
no majority in the Reichstag. Nonetheless, the government was at least
prepared to make the odd concession to the trade unions, and the general strike was declared over on March 22.[84]

One of the political consequences of the putsch was a reshuffling of
the Reich and Prussian governments. On March 27, Ebert appointed
former Foreign Minister Hermann Müller, co-leader of the SPD alongside Wels, to succeed Bauer, who was accused even by his own party of
lacking leadership qualities. Schiffer, discredited due to his negotiations
with the putschists, was forced to vacate his posts as justice minister and
vice-chancellor. Wels was initially considered as a potential successor to
Noske, but he declined, and no leading Social Democrat was willing to
take on the unpopular post, so Ebert finally appointed the former mayor
of Nuremberg, Otto Gessler, from the conservative wing of the DDP.
The SPD thereby gave up a key position it didn't need to. Otherwise,
the orientation of the cabinet remained basically unchanged.[85]

The situation was different with the Prussian government. There, the bland State Premier Paul Hirsch was replaced by the extremely assertive former Minister of Agriculture Otto Braun from East Prussia. Another political heavyweight, Carl Severing, became Prussian minister of the interior. Braun and Severing aggressively tried to democratize the Prussian governmental administration. Prussia subsequently developed into a "bulwark" of the Weimar Republic, in stark contrast to Bavaria, which became a reactionary, anti-democratic stronghold under the rule of lawyer Gustav von Kahr and his successors.[86] "Here we're wading deep into a reactionary backlash, antisemitism, fatigue with the nation, and similar faults," wrote Thomas Mann's mother-in-law and Munich resident Hedwig Pringsheim to her friend and publicist Maximilian Harden in early May 1920.[87]

"If the German Republic, awakened by the military coup, makes up for what it failed to do in November 1918, then all will not have been in vain," wrote satirist Kurt Tucholsky in the weekly newspaper *Die Weltbühne*.[88] But that opportunity was left untaken. There was nothing even approaching a radical reform of the Reichswehr, especially after General von Seeckt, of all people, who had proved so unreliable when the putsch came to a head, succeeded Reinhardt as head of the army command. Under his leadership, the rift between civil society and the military deepened, and the Reichswehr of the Weimar Republic developed into a "state within a state."[89]

Chancellor Bauer's promise to the trade unions that state authorities would not attack armed workers, especially in the Ruhr region, was quickly broken. In the Ruhr, a "Red Ruhr Army" had formed out of the mass movement to repel the putsch. It numbered around fifty thousand armed fighters, mostly USPD and KPD supporters. After efforts to find a peaceful solution to the conflict had failed, the new government under Hermann Müller sent troops to the Ruhr in early April 1920. Freikorps units, such as the Loewenfeld Marine Brigade, which had supported the military coup, were among those deployed. The pitched battles were extremely vicious. Over a thousand Red Army soldiers were killed, most of them after being captured. Carl von Ossietzky hit the mark when he criticized: "The military, which has switched from Lüttwitz to Seeckt, continues to operate unchecked. Attacks of the worst kind are the order of the day. Workers who have taken up arms to defend the republic are being dragged before courts-martial by Seeckt's 'republican' troops."[90]

Nor did the leadership keep its promise to bring those responsible for the coup to justice. Most of the conspirators were able to avoid arrest. Kapp fled to Åsa in Sweden, where he was cordially welcomed at Hugo Stinnes's vacation home. After returning to Germany in March 1922, he was arrested, but he died in custody in June 1922 before proceedings against him could begin. Lüttwitz absconded to Hungary, and Pabst to Austria after a stopover in Munich. Ludendorff, Bauer, and Ehrhardt went to Bavaria, whose right-wing government shielded them from prosecution. Only one man was ever convicted of high treason, Kapp's interior minister, Traugott von Jagow, and even he had to serve only three years of a five-year prison sentence, after the Reichstag passed a general amnesty law in August 1925.[91]

Ludendorff, the coup d'état's real mastermind, was never charged with any crimes, which allowed him to attempt a second rebellion from Munich in November 1923 against the democratic government in Berlin, this time in alliance with the up-and-coming local hero of the radical Right named Adolf Hitler. In March 1920, he had traveled to the Reich capital to offer himself to the would-be new political masters as a propaganda figure. But he didn't get there until the collapse of the putsch was imminent. "The way you look and speak, people will laugh at you," Pabst claims to have sneered to the beer-hall demagogue.[92] Underestimating Hitler was a constant feature of his disastrous political career.

Instead of strengthening the Weimar Republic, the successful defense against the Kapp–Lüttwitz Putsch made the middle classes more right wing while pushing the working class further to the left. The next time Germans went to the polls, they dramatically punished the Social Democrats and left-wing liberal democrats. The MSPD's share of the vote fell from 37.9 to 21.7 percent in national elections on June 6, 1920, while the USPD's rose from 7.6 to 17.9 percent, making the party almost as strong as the mainstream SPD. The shift reflected the disappointment among large sections of the working class with the results of the revolution as well as outrage at the excessive force used by the Freikorps under Noske's leadership. The KPD received only 2.1 percent of the vote—it would become a mass party only after the USPD split in October 1920 and the numerically stronger left wing of that party joined the Communists. DDP support was cut in half from 18.6 to 8.3 percent of the vote, while the Center more or less held its own. The DVP was not punished for its wavering stance on the putsch. On the contrary, it was able to increase its support from 4.4 to 13.9 percent, and the DNVP was also able to improve its share of the vote from 10.3 to 15.1 percent. The governing "Weimar Coalition" lost its majority and would fail to regain it throughout the remaining years of the republic. In late June 1920, Ebert appointed the president of the National Assembly, the Center Party politician Constantin Fehrenbach, chancellor of a centrist minority cabinet consisting of the Center Party, the DDP, and the DVP. It was the first government since the November Revolution in which the SPD was no longer represented.[93]

"By the summer of 1920, insofar as the November Revolution wished to establish a democracy under the leadership of the socialist working class, it had failed once and for all," was the verdict rendered by left-wing socialist historian Arthur Rosenberg.[94]

"The Enemy Is on the Right"

THE MURDER OF WALTHER RATHENAU

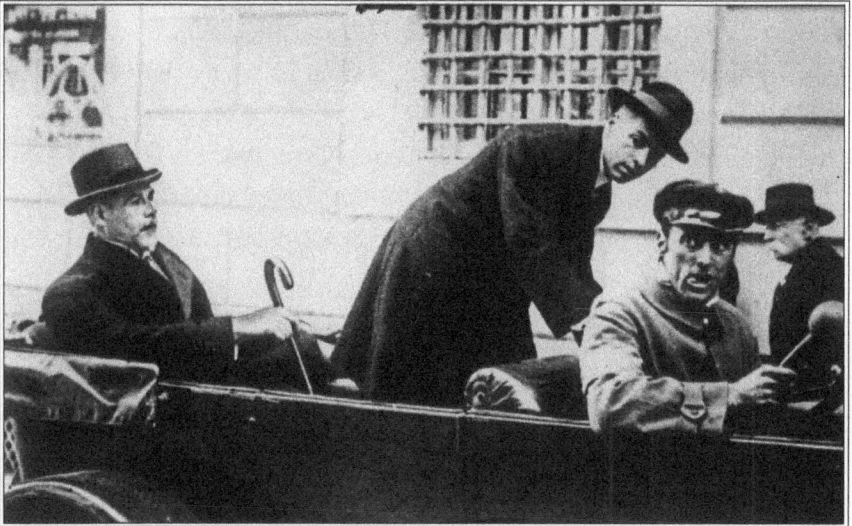

Reich Foreign Minister Walther Rathenau, sitting in the car in which he would be shot on June 24, 1922.

On the morning of June 24, 1922, shortly before eleven o'clock, German Foreign Minister Walther Rathenau left his villa in Berlin's upper-class Grunewald district to be driven to his ministry on Wilhelmstrasse. Although the weather was rainy and cool, the top of his convertible remained down. On Königsallee boulevard, his driver slowed down to take a steep curve. At that moment, his car was overtaken by a large, powerful Mercedes, also an open convertible, with two men in leather coats sitting in the back. An eyewitness, construction worker Walther Krischbin, who was employed on a building site at the location, described what happened next to the *Vossische Zeitung* newspaper: "When the large vehicle was about half a car length ahead . . . , one of the men in the fine leather coats bent forward, grabbed a long-barreled pistol, the butt of which he pulled into his armpit, and pointed it at the man in the other car. He was so close he didn't even need to aim. . . . Then the shots rang out, rapid fire like a machine gun."[1]

Rathenau was hit by five bullets and collapsed. At that point, the second man in the Mercedes jumped out and threw a hand grenade into the other car. The power of the blast lifted the foreign minister up from his seat. As the assassins' car raced off, passersby hastened to the scene of the attack. One of them was a nurse named Helene Kaiser, who had been waiting at a streetcar stop. "I was startled by the bang, jumped up, and saw the passenger in the stationary car leaning over to the side," she would testify two days later. "I assumed that he had been injured by the explosion, and as a nurse, I rushed over to help him. As I approached, I saw that the man was bleeding profusely from his face and lower limbs and that there was a large pool of blood in the car. The floor of the car was also on fire. I stamped out the fire and got in, introducing myself to the driver as a nurse and telling him I was there to help."[2]

The chauffeur turned the car around and drove back to Rathenau's villa with the dying man. But when they got there, the doctor on hand

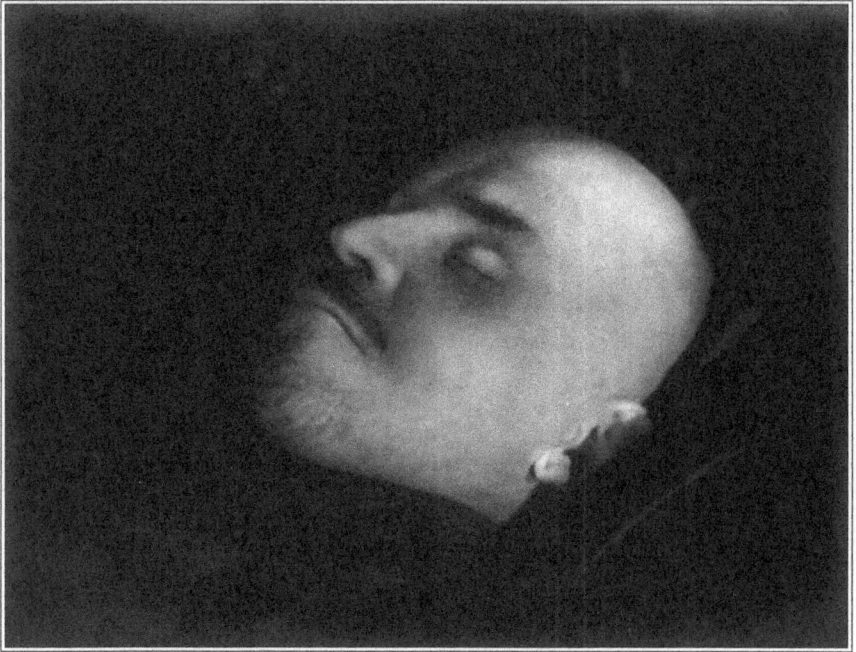

*"His expression was so unspeakably peaceful": Rathenau's
body lying in state in his villa in Berlin-Grunewald.*

could only pronounce him dead. Rathenau was laid out in his bedroom on
the second floor. His sister Edith Andreae, who rushed from Cologne to
Berlin, saw him there. "Walther's expression was so unspeakably peaceful, so saintly and serious—I felt so solemn," she wrote to a friend. "It
was the kind face of someone who says, you poor people, I forgive you."[3]
    It was no accident Walther Rathenau was targeted for assassination.
Since joining the cabinet of Reich Chancellor Joseph Wirth of the Center Party as minister of reconstruction at the end of May 1921, and even
more so since taking over the Foreign Ministry in January 1922, he had
been subjected to German nationalist smear campaigns. Rathenau represented everything the political Right hated. He was Jewish and a
staunch supporter of the Weimar Republic. He was an heir to AEG, the
large electrical company. Yet he was not only a businessman but also

a talented writer—with an intellect far superior to that of most of his cabinet colleagues.

From the spring of 1922, following the reparations conference in Genoa and the signing of the Treaty of Rapallo in April, hostility built to the point of open death threats. Rathenau's attempt to reach an agreement on the issue of reparations with the victors of the First World War was tar-brushed as a "policy of fulfillment"—that is, a traitorous submission to the demands of Germany's enemies. Moreover, his efforts to reach a settlement with the Soviet Union were maligned as a sign of his secret complicity with the Bolsheviks. The main Nazi Party newspaper, the *Völkischer Beobachter*, slandered Rathenau as the prototypical "stock market and Soviet Jew."[4] In the June issue of the journal *Konservative Monatshefte*, in an article entitled "The True Face of the Rapallo Treaty," nationalist Reichstag deputy Wilhelm Henning wrote: "No sooner has the cosmopolitan Jew Rathenau gotten his hands on responsibility for maintaining Germany's honor than that honor is a thing of the past. . . . German honor is not some cheap commodity for international Jewry to buy and sell! . . . German honor will be avenged. But the German people will hold you, Mr. Rathenau, and all those behind you, accountable."[5] A song became popular among racists and antisemites gathered in their local bars to carp about politics; it exhorted: "Gun down Walther Rathenau / that goddamn Jewish sow."[6]

Rathenau was not the first political victim of right-wing terror. Aside from Rosa Luxemburg, Karl Liebknecht, and Leo Jogiches, and Kurt Eisner and Gustav Landauer, there was also Hans Paasche, a former imperial naval and colonial officer who had become a committed pacifist and democrat. On May 21, 1920, soldiers from a Reichswehr rifle regiment had murdered Paasche on his Waldfrieden estate in the Neumark region in eastern Germany. An investigation into the killing concluded, as was becoming the rule in such cases, that he had been "shot while fleeing." Count Harry Kessler commented, "Politically unpopular individuals currently enjoy less security in Germany than in the most disreputable South American banana republics or in Borgia's Rome."[7] And in *Die Weltbühne*, Kurt Tucholsky channeled his outrage into satiric verse:

It's becoming a habit in the Reich
Another one down, the same for all alike
Every day the same old story
The social question in this country
Is solved by a lieutenant and his men. Is that dog a pacifist?
Don't bother shooting it in the ribs!
Put a bullet straight in his heart! And the authorities will just
Repeat the lie that he was evading arrest
There'll be editorials, denials, and a lot of wailing.
And in fourteen days once again smooth sailing.[8]

Political murder was the order of the day in the early Weimar Republic, and time and again the trail of the perpetrators led to the same circles: radical right-wing nationalist groups and paramilitary Freikorps associations, whose members hadn't reintegrated into postwar civilian life. One secret society made a particular name for itself. The Organization Consul (OC) was a direct successor to the Ehrhardt Naval Brigade, which had been disbanded due to its involvement in the Kapp–Lüttwitz Putsch of March 1920. Members were obliged to demonstrate "unconditional obedience" to the group's leadership and to maintain "absolute silence" toward strangers. "Traitors will be dealt with by Vehmic court," stated paragraph 11 of the organization's statutes, referring to the draconian, secret "hanging courts" of medieval Westphalia.[9]

Not coincidentally, this clandestine organization had its headquarters in Munich. After the suppression of the Bavarian Soviet Republic in May 1919, the southern German metropolis had become a center of reactionary counterrevolution and an Eldorado for right-wing opponents of democracy. Although wanted for arrest, the navy captain Ehrhardt was able to move around the city freely, using false passports generously provided by Munich Police President Ernst Pöhner. But the OC's network spanned the whole of Germany, it maintained close relations with the Reichswehr, through which it gained access to weapons depots, and it kept blacklists of individuals to be assassinated.

The aim of the group's terrorist actions was to provoke the Left into an uprising. The hope was that as the state put down such a rebellion, opportunities would arise to eliminate the Weimar democracy and bring a right-wing government to power. The OC was involved not only in Rathenau's assassination but also in previous attacks on the former Reich Finance Minister Matthias Erzberger and on the republic's first head of government, Philipp Scheidemann.

As the initiator of the peace resolution of July 1917, the head of the German armistice delegation of November 1918, and creator of a financial reform in 1919–20 that burdened the wealthy, Erzberger was particularly hated by the Right. On August 26, 1921, he and his companion, the Center Party MP Carl Diez, were attacked by two men during a walk near Bad Griesbach in the Black Forest. Erzberger was shot seven times and died, while Diez survived, albeit seriously wounded. Investigators in Baden quickly identified the perpetrators: First Lieutenant at Sea Heinrich Tillessen and former Lieutenant Heinrich Schulz. Both were registered in the spa town under the address "Maximilianstrasse, Munich" and had connections to a fake timber company—the "Bayerische Holzverwertungsgesellschaft mbH."—an OC cover firm. But before the police could arrest them, the assassins managed to flee to Hungary, and on June 13, 1922, the retired Lieutenant Captain Manfred Killinger, who had trained them before they committed their crime, was acquitted of the charge of accessory to murder.[10]

Just nine days earlier, on Whitsunday 1922, an attack was made on Philipp Scheidemann, the man who had proclaimed the German republic on November 9, 1918, and who had become mayor of Kassel after his time in government. During a walk in the woods of Wilhelmshöhe Park with his daughter and granddaughter, two men ambushed him. One of them, disguised as a hiker, overtook Scheidemann, pulled a rubber syringe out of his pocket, and sprayed the politician three times in the face with hydrogen cyanide. Scheidemann was able to fire two shots at the fugitive before collapsing unconscious. He was lucky to survive— strong winds that day had lessened the effect of the poison. The two attackers, former Lieutenant Karl Oehlschläger and his henchman

Hans Hustert, were among the OC operatives entrusted with "special tasks." In August 1922, they were arrested in Upper Silesia, where they had gone underground as forest workers on an estate.[11]

Rathenau knew his life was in danger. In a conversation with Kessler on March 20, 1922, he complained that although the long-term burden of his office was already becoming physically unbearable, "the worst thing was the vicious enmity in Germany itself." Kessler reported, "Every day he received not only threatening letters, but also police warnings that had to be taken seriously." Nevertheless, he refused to allow special protective measures, as the police advised.[12] It was almost as if he had resigned himself to his fate. "What do you want from me?" he asked the left-leaning liberal-democratic reporter Hellmut von Gerlach. "There's no way to protect oneself without becoming a prisoner, locking oneself up or being constantly guarded by the police. When I took office, I knew the risk I was taking. All I can do now is wait and see how things go."[13] And he wrote to a pen pal, *Vorwärts* editor Lore Karrenbrock: "You shouldn't worry about my survival. If a life not wasted is to end, it will not be arbitrary, but because it has come to a conclusion. I am grateful for every hour I have been granted to affect the world, and it's not worth asking which sentence, which brushstroke of my work will be the last."[14]

The news of the foreign minister's assassination spread like wildfire on the morning of June 24. Berlin artist Max Liebermann recalled: "I cannot forget that terrible day when my neighbor . . . came weeping into my backyard in Wannsee. It was at eleven o'clock in the morning. I was standing over there in the yard where my easel is. 'Walther has been murdered,' he shouted."[15] The theater critic Alfred Kerr, whose apartment was only a few hundred meters away from Rathenau's villa, had just returned from the United States and was about to travel on to England, when a member of his wife's family rushed in and, "trembling with agitation," reported: "They've shot Rathenau—he's lying over there."[16] At 11:30 a.m., Kessler's private secretary told him that Carl von Ossietzky had just phoned to say Rathenau had been murdered. "It was as though I'd been punched," Kessler wrote in his diary.[17] Historian Erich Marcks was in the Foreign Office that morning, preparing to interview prospective diplomats. "A horrified whisper went through the room, and we were sent home," he recalled. "Rathenau had been murdered while on his way to us."[18] Franz Kafka received the terrible news from his friend Max Brod. His reaction was cynical and bitter: "It's a wonder he was allowed to survive so long. Rumors of his impending assassination were already circulating Prague two months ago." The writer added that the murder of the foreign minister was "so very much part of Jewish and German destiny" that it should have been expected.[19]

Reich President Ebert was at his vacation home in Freudenstadt in the Black Forest when the news reached him. He immediately sent a telegraph to Berlin, saying that the "cowardly murder" had deprived the government of a highly capable member, "whose experienced advice will be particularly hard to do without these days." The murder shook Ebert to such an extent that he developed a painful bilious colic. Nonetheless, against his doctor's advice, he set off for the German capital that very night.[20]

Theodor Wolff expressed his shock and horror in an editorial in the *Berliner Tageblatt* newspaper. "What a shock that this brilliantly talented man, so extraordinary and warm in his love for his country, has now been murdered, like so many others before him, by an emissary of the conspiracy dwelling in darkness. [I feel] the deepest horror at the unspeakable conditions in which we live and under which our government exists today." Wolff made no bones about who was responsible for the murder. "Rathenau was slandered and defamed in the most boundlessly base and unfathomably vile of fashions at German nationalist and German racist events as well as in most of the newspapers aligned with those circles, and this intellectual groundwork made the deed possible, indeed inevitable."[21] In a letter to his friend the Frenchman Romain Rolland, writer Stefan Zweig, still reeling from the shock of the murder, also interpreted Rathenau's killing as part of a massive conspiracy aimed at "murdering all the courageous, all the true leaders of the pacifist or revolutionary parties . . . in order to grab power."[22] In an article whose headline asked "Who Will Protect the Republic?," Georg Bernhard, the editor in chief of the *Vossische Zeitung*, cautioned: "The shots that fatally hit Walther Rathenau this morning outside in Grunewald are shots of alarm. An alarm that should awaken all healthy instincts in the German people and rally the masses of those who still believe that decency and reason must keep political passions in check. The republic must now finally pull itself together and protect the men laboring to rebuild Germany on its behalf. Because the republic itself is in danger."[23]

On the afternoon of June 24, at 3 p.m., the Reichstag convened for a special session. Scenes unfolded the likes of which the parliament had never seen before. A deafening din greeted the chairman of the DNVP, Karl Helfferich, when he entered the chamber and took his seat. He was one of Rathenau's harshest critics and had castigated the latter's "policy of fulfillment." Erich Dombrowski, head of the politics section of the *Vossische Zeitung*, reported: "The Social Democrats, Independents, and Communists pressed toward his seat, gesticulating animatedly, almost in a closed phalanx. 'There's the murderer,' they shouted at him a hundred times. . . . The situation grew tenser with every passing second, threatening to turn violent. . . . The parliamentary deputies had all risen from their seats to better follow this electrifying clash between Right and Left. The Social Democrats clenched their fists and kept making threats against Helfferich."[24] Reichstag President Paul Löbe rang his bell for order in vain. Only when he threatened to suspend the session did tempers settle. Chancellor Wirth announced that harsh measures would be taken against the gang of murderers and their accomplices. His speech was, as Kessler observed, "repeatedly interrupted by thunderous applause on the left from the Social Democrats and the Center." He added: "Observers in the gallery also clapped their hands. At one point, half of the Reichstag stood up and thunderously shouted 'Long live the republic' three times."[25] In a second session of the Reichstag that evening, Wirth read out a decree issued by Ebert on the basis of the powers granted to him under Article 48 of the Weimar Constitution. In it, the Reich president threatened to ban associations and assemblages hostile to the republican form of government and made it a criminal offense to insult the republic or its representatives. A state court to protect German

*June 25, 1922: Reich Chancellor Joseph Wirth delivers the
official eulogy for Rathenau in the Reichstag.*

democracy was to be established in Leipzig. Five days later, Ebert would
issue a second decree allowing the death penalty to be given to participants in associations that aimed to assassinate members of the Reich and
state governments.[26]

On Sunday, June 25, the trade unions called a rally in central Berlin's Lustgarten park. Hundreds of thousands marched silently under
the black, red, and gold flag through the streets of the German capital
from early morning until late evening. It seemed that the divided Left
was coming back together. A wave of sympathy for the Weimar Republic swept through the country. "The hatred of Rathenau's murderers is
profound and genuine, as is the determination to preserve the republic, which runs far deeper than the prewar monarchical 'patriotism,'"
Kessler noted.[27]

At twelve noon that day, the Reichstag reconvened to discuss the
emergency ordinances. Wirth took the opportunity to commemorate the
dead with moving words and to excoriate the enemies of the republic.

His extemporaneous speech ended with the words: "There stands the enemy, dripping his poison into the wounds of a people. There stands the enemy—and there is no doubt: The enemy is on the right." The parliamentary minutes recorded at this point: "Prolonged thunderous applause and hand clapping in the center and on the left and in all the gallery. Lots of prolonged movement."[28] Journalist Georg Bernhard wrote that the Reichstag session "left a deep impression" on all those in attendance: "The Reich chancellor's speech was the best he ever delivered and perhaps the best piece of oratory ever heard in this building."[29]

Rathenau's state funeral took place on June 27 in the Reichstag chamber. "The coffin lay raised behind the lectern under a massive black baldachin suspended from the ceiling," observed Kessler from the gallery. "The hall was lined in black and decorated with a veritable sea of flowers and leafy plants. . . . At twelve o'clock, the chancellor led Rathenau's aged mother into the imperial box. . . . The old woman's waxen skin was pale, and her face stony, as if chiseled under her veils. Complete self-control for all to see. Her veiled, white face, bleached by pain, was what moved me most."[30] In his eulogy, an obviously suffering Ebert declared: "The despicable act did not strike Rathenau alone. It struck Germany as a whole. This bloodthirsty crime was directed against the German republic and against the idea of democracy. . . . It is an attack upon the nation."[31] When the funeral march from Wagner's *Götterdämmerung* was played, many people could no longer maintain their composure. "Many of those around me wept—the epochal import of this fateful death floated through their souls in the music," said Kessler.[32] Despite the rain, a huge crowd lined the streets as Rathenau's coffin was taken to his family's burial plot in the Berlin-Oberschöneweide Cemetery.

From noon onward, work ceased everywhere in Germany. Huge demonstrations took place in almost all major cities, with bourgeois liberals marching side by side with Social Democrats and Communists. "The head of one of the largest capitalist companies in the world had been killed, and Communist workers wept at his grave and cursed the murderer," recalled Friedrich Stampfer, editor in chief of *Vorwärts*.[33] It almost seemed as if the republic were gaining the broad majority support it had previously lacked. The uproar over this act of violence extended far into the conservative middle classes. "The disgustingly vile murder has pushed me far to the left," noted linguistics professor Victor Klemperer.[34] That summer, still reeling with shock, Thomas Mann wrote his speech "On the German Republic," in which he distanced himself more clearly than ever before from the positions he had taken in his book *Reflections of a Nonpolitical Man*, declaring his support for the new democratic government. The speech, which he would deliver in Beethoven Hall in Berlin on October 13, 1922, ended with the appeal: "Long live the republic!"[35]

Nevertheless, the mourning wasn't as universal as the many such statements might have made it appear. Mann's mother-in-law Hedwig Pringsheim complained that outrage at the murder was "making huge waves everywhere . . . except in Munich."[36] Many German nationalist circles secretly rejoiced at Rathenau's death. Although the head of the army command, General von Seeckt, issued a decree to the troops disputing accusations that the military sympathized with Rathenau's murderers, there were celebrations and carousing in numerous barracks after the murder became known. Some Reichswehr officers refused to take part in mourning ceremonies or to fly the black, red, and gold flag.[37] The situation was similar at universities, where antisemitic professors and students set the tone. In Heidelberg, for example, Nobel Prize laureate in physics Philipp Lenard refused to close the Institute of Physics, which he headed, for the afternoon of Rathenau's funeral or to fly the German flag at half-mast. Pro-democracy students who protested this provocation, including Carlo Mierendorff, who later became a prominent SPD politician and resistance fighter against Hitler, were officially reprimanded. Meanwhile, disciplinary proceedings against Lenard were dropped.[38]

The Berlin police department's political division was responsible for tracking down Rathenau's killers. It was headed by Bernhard Weiss, who, as a Jew, also faced antisemitic attacks, and he pursued the investigation of the crime with great vigor.[39] Following a tip-off from right-wing extremists, the police were able to locate the assassins' car after just a few days and arrest the driver, twenty-one-year-old student Ernst Werner Techow. After a week-long manhunt, the two main assassins, twenty-three-year-old law student Erwin Kern from Kiel and twenty-six-year-old mechanical engineer Hermann Fischer from Chemnitz, were surrounded at Saaleck Castle near Kösen in the eastern German regional state of Thuringia. Kern died in the shootout with police, while Fischer shot himself.[40] After 1933, the Nazis reinterpreted the two men's deaths as a tale of heroism, erecting a memorial stone to the pair of "martyrs of the movement," as they were now known. Saaleck Castle would become a place of pilgrimage for the radical Right for years.[41]

In October 1922, the newly formed State Court for the Protection of the Republic opened legal proceedings against the assassins' accomplices and those who knew about their plot. The defendants included former Freikorps militiamen: Ernst von Salomon (later a writer), who had been tasked with finding a driver for the murderers' car, and Karl Tillessen, the brother of one of the Erzberger murderers. The majority of the seventeen men in the dock were young, mostly university and high school students. They all came from so-called good homes and had deviated from the straight and narrow amid the turmoil of war and the immediate postwar period. Disoriented and insecure, they had sought refuge in nationalist and right-wing extremist organizations. Some had been members of the Ehrhardt Brigade, had actively participated in the Kapp Putsch, and had subsequently joined the OC. "These people profess their love for everything 'national,' but what they mean is the rifle. They work for the 'national cause' but what they mean is preparations for murder," wrote the novelist Joseph Roth, who reported on the trial for the *Neue Berliner Zeitung*.[42]

The court handed down stiff sentences. Techow was sentenced to fifteen years in prison as an accessory to murder, while Salomon received five years' incarceration. Those shown to have failed to report the planned crime got sentences of up to three years. The Weimar judicial system is frequently—and rightly—accused of being overly lenient toward right-wing perpetrators of violence, but that was not the case here, or with the two Scheidemann assassins, who were sentenced to ten years in prison in December 1922.

Still, the trial had no satisfactory outcome. The court failed to investigate the question of who was truly behind the killing. In his closing remarks, senior Reich prosecutor Ludwig Ebermayer declared: "The threads leading back from the Rathenau murder and its perpetrators in a wide variety of directions are too knotty to be untangled today."[43] In truth, even in 1922, sufficient evidence pointed to the OC as the mastermind of Rathenau's killing as well as the attacks on Erzberger and Scheidemann. It was not until October 1924, more than two years after the Rathenau murder, that the State Court opened proceedings against the organization, and when it did, the trial devolved into farce. The judges in the case didn't bother to conceal their sympathies with the right-wing terrorists, whom even the senior prosecutor Ludwig Ebermayer described as "honorable, fatherland-loving, and fearless men." Sixteen of the twenty-six defendants were sentenced to ridiculously short prison terms of three to eight months for being members of a "secret association." And the trial did nothing to clarify the Ehrhardt organization's role in the assassinations of Weimar politicians.[44]

In *Die Weltbühne* in late June 1922, Tucholsky exhorted an imaginary reader in rhyme to finally take energetic action against the enemies of democracy:

> Fight back for once! Punch them in the face.
> Don't fall asleep again after fourteen days!
> Out with the monarchist judges,
> the officers—and the thugs
> who exploit and sabotage you,
> smearing swastikas on your homes as they do.
> . . . .
> Strike out! Hit them! Hit them hard![45]

But the chance passed to mobilize the strong pro-republican sentiment after the murder to stabilize democracy in the long term. Although the majority of the parties were able to agree on a law to protect the republic in July 1922, the Bavarian government refused to adopt it. Thus, while radical right-wing organizations were banned in Prussia, they were permitted to operate largely unhindered in Bavaria. Only a year later, Hitler and Ludendorff were to stage a coup in Munich.

The final words in the tragedy belonged to Rathenau's mother. During the hearings before the State Court in the fall of 1922, Techow's defense lawyer read out a letter that she had written to the assassin's mother: "In unspeakable pain, I extend my hand to you, you poorest of all women. Tell your son that I forgive him in the name and in the spirit of the man he murdered, as God may forgive him if he makes a full and open confession before the organs of earthly justice and repents before the divine one. Had he known my son, the noblest man born of this earth, he would have turned the murder weapon on himself. May these words give peace to your soul."[46] But this example of human generosity left little impression on the woman to whom it was addressed. Techow's mother's only response was to have her lawyer acknowledge receipt of the letter.

Madhouse

THE OCCUPATION OF THE RUHR VALLEY AND HYPERINFLATION

The start of the Ruhr Valley occupation: On January 11, 1923, French troops take over Essen.

The *Berliner Tageblatt*'s correspondent in the western German city of Essen could hardly believe his eyes on the early afternoon of January 11, 1923. "The French marched into the city at around 2 o'clock," he reported. "A few cyclists led the way, followed by infantry and then several thousand cavalry at a trot. Slowly, three heavy armored cars rattled through the streets, followed by infantry and artillery, and machine guns could also be seen. At the end were several trucks with crews. All public buildings and the railroad station, as well as all road junctions, were occupied by troops with fixed bayonets."[1]

The commander of these French occupying forces, General Jean-Marie Degoutte, immediately declared a state of siege. Within a few days, the French military had also occupied Gelsenkirchen, Bochum, Recklinghausen, Hattingen, Dortmund, and other cities and towns in the Ruhr region. By March 1923, between seventy thousand and one hundred thousand soldiers were stationed there. A relatively small Belgian contingent of eight thousand men was also placed under Degoutte's command.

Spectacular as it was, the occupation didn't come as a complete surprise. The victorious Entente powers had threatened for years to impose sanctions if the German government failed to meet its reparations obligations. After a conference on the subject in Paris ended without result on January 4, the situation quickly escalated. "French invasion imminent after failed reparations conference," linguistics professor Victor Klemperer had noted in his diary on January 5.[2]

Ever since the end of the war, disputes over reparations had further strained the already toxic relations between the defeated Reich and the victors. The latter's claim to compensation was derived from Article 231 of the Treaty of Versailles, which held Germany and its allies solely responsible for the outbreak of war and liable for all losses and damage.

At a conference of the Supreme Council of the Entente in Paris in January 1921, the British and French presented their former enemies with a bill. Germany was to pay a total of 226 billion gold marks over the span of forty-two years, with annual installments starting at 2 billion and gradually rising to 6 billion gold marks. This demand was a rude awakening to the German populace. Only "fools" could have believed that "the worst was already behind us," Reich President Friedrich Ebert confided in a letter.[3]

The German government rejected the payment plan from Paris, arguing that it far exceeded Germany's economic capacity. In late April 1921, the Allied Reparations Commission submitted a new proposal, reducing its demands from 226 billion to 132 billion gold marks. That, too, was rejected. It would take a further Entente ultimatum for the German government under the centrist Joseph Wirth to accept the revised proposal—and even then, Germany was only demonstrating goodwill while ultimately hoping that it could demonstrate that the demands could not be met and negotiate a reduction to a level Berlin deemed reasonable.

But the prospects for a compromise dwindled. In early 1922, new French Prime Minister Raymond Poincaré took a hard line on reparations. Convinced that Berlin was unwilling, not unable, to pay, he set his sights on "productive collateral," specifically the rich coal deposits of the Ruhr Valley. If they could be brought under French control, Poincaré believed, Germany would be permanently weakened and would never again be able to pose a threat.

In late November 1922, the Council of Ministers in Paris decided to occupy the Ruhr region. Poincaré needed only a pretext. The Reparations Commission provided it. On December 26, it deemed that Germany had fallen behind on deliveries of lumber and telegraph poles, and on January 9, 1923, Germany was also found to be in arrears with its coal deliveries. Two days later, French and Belgian troops marched across the border.

The invasion unleashed howls of outrage and a powerful wave of nationalism within the German populace. Some observers felt reminded of the mood in August 1914, when fiercely feuding parties and interest groups had concluded a "strategic truce" on behalf of the nation. "For the moment, all class hostility of the workmen against the owners has been submerged by the patriotic wave. The whole country appears to be united," wrote the British ambassador in Berlin, Lord Edgar Vincent D'Abernon, in his diary.[4] In the Ruhr area, "the situation is tense to the breaking point," reported the correspondent of the *Vossische Zeitung* in Essen. There was a threat of "a catastrophe of unimaginable proportions . . . barring a miracle."[5] Anti-French sentiment came to a boil throughout the Weimar Republic. Playwright Gerhart Hauptmann noted on February 1: "Germany is quaking with inner agitation. . . . The hatred and anger over the peacetime invasion by France could not be stronger. Germany is almost completely unified in this hatred and rage, which, if weapons were available to express them, would be devastating for the French."[6]

But the force of one hundred thousand men to which the Reichswehr had been reduced was incapable of launching any sort of military response. Instead, Wilhelm Cuno, the former general director of Hapag shipping company, who had succeeded Wirth as Reich chancellor in November 1922, announced a policy of passive resistance. The very day of the invasion, coal-mine owners in the Ruhr region were instructed to cease all deliveries to France and Belgium. On January 13, the government prohibited civil servants from following any orders issued by the occupiers. This applied to the staff of the national rail service, the Reichsbahn, as well as to the employees of the Reichspost and telegraph administration.[7]

Initially, the strategy worked. In the first weeks of the Ruhr campaign, it seemed as if Poincaré's attempt to take possession of the coal mines as "productive collateral" would fail. In early 1923, France "didn't profit at all from its Ruhr adventure," wrote the editor in chief of the Social Democratic newspaper *Vorwärts*, Friedrich Stampfer. "It's been left to pay for the military operations on an as yet unknown scale."[8]

The French government had underestimated the determination of German resistance, but it refused to back down in any respect. To break their former enemy's passive resistance, the occupiers came up with sometimes drastic sanctions. As early as January 29, General Degoutte declared an "enhanced state of siege," under which armed force would be used against any attempt at sabotage, and any demonstrations would be put down with equal rigor. Mining companies that defied the French orders were threatened with harsh punishments. Civil servants who refused to cooperate with the occupiers were arrested and often expelled, along with their families, from the occupied territory to other parts of Germany.

One particularly drastic measure was the establishment of a customs border between the occupied and unoccupied parts of Germany. By the end of January, occupied Germany was prohibited from exporting anything to the rest of the Reich. When the railroad workers went on strike, the occupiers took over the railroads to continue the transport of coal to France. This was a major step in breaking Germany's initially effective passive resistance. The occupying forces also increasingly took control of coal companies, locking out the German workforce and recruiting foreign workers, including Polish miners, as replacements.

The situation in occupied Germany was coming to a head, and the occupiers reacted to violations of their orders with increasing severity. The most serious unrest occurred on March 31, the day before Easter Sunday, when the French military killed thirteen workers at the Krupp company in Essen, injuring numerous others. A week and a half later, on April 10, hundreds of thousands in Germany took to the streets for the funeral procession to protest the bloodbath. "Never before has German soil seen such a funeral," reported the *Kölnische Zeitung* newspaper. "Employers and employees, civil servants and white-collar workers, all the entire spectrum of political parties from right to left marched together behind the dead with wreaths with imperial black-white-and-red ribbons and Communist colors."[9]

The more French soldiers acted against German civilians, the more they empowered those forces that wanted to transition from passive to active resistance. In March and April, squads of saboteurs waged a minor war, blowing up railroad tracks and bridges to prevent coal from being taken to France and attacking the occupying forces' facilities and individual members of the foreign troops. One of the insurgents, former Freikorps fighter Albert Leo Schlageter, was arrested in Essen in early April and sentenced to death. He was executed in May.

Schlageter was styled into an icon of resistance—and not only by the jingoistic DNVP or the Nazi Party. In a sensational speech, Karl Radek, the Communist International's expert on Germany, lionized Schlageter as a "martyr of German nationalism" who deserved "to be honored, in the best tradition of manly honesty, by us, the soldiers of the revolution." It was a ham-fisted attempt to appeal to supporters of the extreme Right.[10]

Over the course of the spring, it became clear that something would have to give. Chancellor Cuno faced increasing pressure to negotiate with France and Belgium. The trade unions in particular urged him to use the time while the workers' resistance was still unbroken. However, the German government hesitated, fearing that any concessions could be interpreted as a sign of weakness. Meanwhile, Poincaré categorically ruled out any negotiations until Germany formally changed its policy.

Time was on France's side. For Germany, passive resistance ultimately proved to be a bottomless pit of costs. The government had to support the civil servants expelled from the occupied regions and pay the wages of striking workers. Companies, particularly in heavy industry, received generous loans to compensate for production disruptions and lost income. At the same time, tax revenues from the occupied territory collapsed, and the lack of coal from the Ruhr region forced the German government to purchase expensive imports from England. The only way to cover exploding state expenditures was to print reams of money, but the Reich's debt still skyrocketed, while the German currency, the Reichsmark, began to plummet in value.

Inflation had already set in during the First World War. The Reich had financed its military campaign not by raising taxes but predominantly by issuing domestic bonds—in the mistaken belief that the enemy, once defeated, could be forced to pay them off. Moreover, the postwar democratic German governments made no effort to rebalance the budget. Germany's loose monetary policy had several advantages. For starters, a devalued mark was good for exports. Between 1920 and 1922, unlike the major industrialized countries of the West, Germany experienced an economic boom with low unemployment. In turn, this made it possible

to finance war debts and additional social benefits. Democratic politicians prioritized social harmony over price stability. Finally, rampant
inflation was also an effective means of demonstrating to the Allies that
their reparation demands could not be met. There was no dismissing
the suspicion, particularly maintained by the French government, that
the Germans were deliberately allowing the value of their currency to
decline in order to shirk their obligations.[11]

The initially gradual devaluation of the mark soon accelerated. Following Foreign Minister Walther Rathenau's murder on June 24, 1922,
foreign confidence in the German currency dwindled. "Like the fever
curve of a seriously ill patient, the exchange rate against the dollar level
illustrates our decline on a daily basis," remarked Count Harry Kessler at
the beginning of November 1922.[12] At that point, one dollar was already
worth 9,000 marks. Between February and April the following year,
Germany's national bank, the Reichsbank, succeeded in stabilizing the
value of the German mark on the foreign market at around 21,000 to one
against the dollar. But afterward, Germany's currency plunged into an
abyss. By the end of July, the dollar was already trading at over 1 million marks.[13] "The mark completely ceased to deserve the appellation
'currency'—it became simply an illusion," recalled Hamburg banker
Max Warburg. "Worthless scraps of paper, each nominally representing
1 million marks and stuffed into huge sacks, dominated the market."[14]

Meanwhile, prices were rising not on a daily but on an hourly basis.
In early August 1923, Victor Klemperer recorded an episode on the way
back from vacation on the Baltic Sea, in which his wife ordered a cof-
fee in a train station: "The price on the board was 6,000 M[arks]. It
was taken down while she was drinking up. When she went to pay, the
waiter asked for 12,000. She said the price had just been 6,000. 'Oh, you
were here during the old price? Then give me 6,000!'"[15]

Hyperinflation hit the various social groups differently. The main losers were people who had saved large sums of money or subscribed to
war bonds. They now could do nothing but watch their assets dissolve.
Pensioners and public benefits recipients also suffered because payments were constantly delayed and never fully adjusted to the rampant
monetary devaluation. The same was true of civil servants, white-collar

employees, and workers on fixed monthly salaries. Conversely, hyper-inflation benefited property owners, as their land and building assets remained untouched, and those in debt, who could now pay off liabilities with basically worthless money.[16]

But the biggest beneficiaries of inflation were large industrial enterprises. Their fixed assets remained stable, and they could get cheap credit, which enabled them to acquire factories, real estate, and entire companies at ridiculously low prices. The Ruhr industrialist Hugo Stinnes was particularly unscrupulous in this regard, buying up everything that could be purchased: businesses, estates, ships, hotels, newspapers. The result was a huge economic empire, the likes of which had never been seen in Germany. In March 1922, *Die Weltbühne* wrote that no one else in the country had "concentrated as much power in his hands as Hugo Stinnes."[17] In March 1923, Stinnes made it onto the cover of *Time* magazine and was dubbed the "New Emperor of Germany."[18]

Foreigners who had foreign currency also profited from hyperinflation. For them, Germany was a land of milk and honey where they could live in luxury. The capital, Berlin, was a particular favorite among Americans, who populated houses of entertainment, resided as pampered guests in fancy hotels, and acquired treasures at bargain prices in antique stores and at art auctions. The contrast to the growing impoverishment of the locals was glaring and elicited considerable xenophobia. One anonymous commentator in *Die Weltbühne* raged at the luxurious lifestyle of foreign diplomats in Berlin, writing that while they existed "in an earthly paradise," many Germans were going hungry, and the middle classes were being plunged into "physical and moral" ruination.[19]

Germany's currency wasn't the only thing in precipitous decline. Social norms and morals also lost their validity. Mainstream values such as reputability, decency, and civic responsibility no longer counted for much. Many Germans turned unscrupulous, cynical, and selfish. After the trauma of war and revolution, people now had to witness "the daily spectacle of the failure of all the rules of life and the bankruptcy of age and experience," recalled journalist Sebastian Haffner about being a sixteen-year-old schoolboy in Berlin in 1923.[20] Germany lost faith in the status quo. What could still be relied on, given all that had happened? Like many members of his generation, seventeen-year-old Klaus Mann, Thomas Mann's eldest son, asked himself: "With everything around us crumbling and shaking, what were we supposed to cling to, what laws were we supposed to follow? . . . We were introduced early on to apocalyptic moods and became quite experienced in dissipation and excess."[21]

One side effect of the doom and gloom fueled by the economic catastrophe was the appearance of so-called inflation saints—itinerant preachers who traveled the country as self-styled saviors promising salvation from all evil. "Everything, especially the weak of character who are unable to exist without external support, is playing into the hands of these modern-day saviors with their long hair and presumptuous fantasies," the *Kölnische Volkszeitung* newspaper warned in September 1922.[22]

The mark's rapid plummet was all anyone could talk about. "Living conditions and money inevitably intrude on every conversation," wrote the philosopher and cultural critic Walter Benjamin in an essay entitled "Journey Through German Inflation."[23] The faster the currency declined, the more people accepted the absurdities of hyperinflation. Just a few months earlier, it had been "a scary idea" to exchange 100,000 marks for one dollar, remarked Georg Bernhard, the editor in chief of the *Vossische Zeitung*, at the end of July 1923. But people had "become accustomed to all the zeros," and most were no longer frightened at "whether the number in front of those zeros was a little more or a little less."[24]

In search of a supposedly safe place to put their money, more and more people were lured into playing the stock market. Stock exchanges and bank counters were bustling, and it wasn't just professional investors driving the action. "From the half-starving pensioner to the hackney driver, everyone is at it," observed *Die Weltbühne*. "Gambling mania is rampant."[25] Klemperer also caught stock-market fever. In May 1923, he bought shares for the first time and quickly became obsessed. "Dreams of making a killing fill every brain and every hour," he wrote in his diary. "The age has gone astray to the point of excess."[26]

No one embodied a world that had become derailed quite like the racketeers, or *Raffkes* (greedheads), as they were popularly known in

Berlin. Most were young men who had made quick fortunes with high-risk stock investments and had no scruples about flouting conventions and rules. They drove fast cars, smoked expensive cigars, dined in luxury restaurants, and surrounded themselves with attractive women. "The young and quick-witted did well," recalled Haffner. "Overnight they became free, rich, and independent. It was a situation in which mental inertia and reliance on past experience were punished by starvation and death, but rapid appraisal of new situations and speed of reaction were rewarded with sudden, vast riches. The twenty-one-year-old bank director appeared on the scene, and also the high school senior who earned his living from the stock-market tips of his slightly older friends. He wore Oscar Wilde ties, organized champagne parties, and supported his embarrassed father."[27]

The bottomless pit that was hyperinflation defied rational explanation, leaving Germany veritably stunned. In his autobiography *A Small Yes and a Big No*, artist George Grosz wrote that everything he saw and experienced at the time often seemed to him "like a fantastic dream." He added: "But funnily enough, the higher the prices rose, the more it increased our lust for life. Hooray, was life ever good!"[28] The paradoxical flip side of inflation misery was this sort of euphoria. Germans were hopelessly consumed with desires for amusement and all sorts of debauchery. The entertainment industry experienced an unprecedented boom. Bars and nightclubs sprang up everywhere, and a dance craze comparable to the revolutionary months of 1918–19 set in. Klaus Mann, who visited Berlin for the first time in the summer of 1923 with his sister Erika, was both fascinated and bewildered by the licentious party scene: "Millions of helpless, impoverished, bewildered people capered and swung in a delirium of hunger and hysteria. Dance was a mania, a religion, a racket. The stock market danced. The members of the Reichstag hopped about as if mad. The poets were convulsed with rhythmic spasms. The cripples, the prostitutes, the beggars, the reformers, the retired monarchs and astute industrialists—all of them swayed and skipped. They danced the shimmy, tango, fox trot, and St. Vitus' dance. They danced despair and schizophrenia and cosmic divinations. . . . Jazz was the great balm and narcotic of a disconcerted, frustrated nation."[29]

Nudity was tolerated like never before. In Berlin, the erotic dancer Anita Berber became a sensation. With her garish makeup and fondness for alcohol and drugs, the boyishly slim young woman personified a life between glamour and vice.[30] Alongside an unbridled passion for nightlife, sports distracted and entertained Germans during the years of hyperinflation. In addition to the Six Days cycling race in Berlin's Sportpalast arena, boxing grew increasingly popular. Mavens of high society, dressed to the nines, among them numerous film and theater celebrities, could be seen in the box seats and at ringside.

With its cinemas, theaters, cabarets, and newspapers, Berlin developed into a magnet for artists, writers, and journalists. "Berlin was worth going the extra mile for," recalled the playwright Carl Zuckmayer. "The city had an unparalleled appetite for talent and energy, digesting, grinding it up, and spitting it out again just as quickly as it had been devoured. With the force of a tornado, it sucked in everyone who aspired to get to the top in Germany, the genuine articles and the pretenders, the zeros and the heroes. But first, it showed all of them the cold shoulder."[31]

The luxurious and hedonistic lives of those who profited from inflation stood in stark contrast to the misery into which broad sections of the population had been plunged when their savings suddenly became worthless. Spending what little money one had as quickly as possible before it completely lost its value became a prerequisite to survival. In phases of particular hyperinflation, people panic-bought. In August 1923, the *Berliner Illustrierte Zeitung* newspaper ran an article with the headline "Overstimulated Nerves" that read: "There's nothing much left to say. It hammers on the nerves every day. The insane numbers, the uncertain future, the sudden questions about people's immediate prospects. An epidemic of fear and the barest sort of need. Long lines of consumers who had long been weaned from window shopping are once again standing in front of stores."[32]

Inhabitants of many cities had no choice but to pilfer from greengrocers and bakeries to survive. Others traveled to the countryside with rucksacks to hoard food. In lieu of increasingly worthless paper marks, farmers demanded to be paid in material items—jewelry, paintings, carpets, and porcelain. Those who had no commodities of the sort to offer tried to steal what they needed from fields. Traditional bourgeois notions of property dissolved along with traditional moral standards. Crime increased in inverse proportion to devaluation of the mark. In the hurricane of hyperinflation, it was everyone for themselves. The result was what author Jens Bisky has called "everyday anarchism." Dog-eat-dog became the law of the land.[33]

Social tensions openly intensified in the summer of 1923. The sociopolitical "truce" that had prevailed at the beginning of the Ruhr conflict had long since broken down. Wages and salaries lagged far behind price increases, especially for food. At the same time, unemployment was soaring. By mid-June, Reich Chancellery State Secretary Eduard Hamm registered "great agitation and deep bitterness" in broad segments of the populace.[34] A series of strikes shook the country. On July 27, in an editorial entitled "In Dire Straits," the centrist Berlin newspaper *Germania* excoriated the Cuno government as an "utter disappointment" and cast doubt on whether the German leadership had the guts to take comprehensive action.[35] The article created a massive stir. The opinion-making liberal press in the German capital joined in the criticism. Cuno's position became untenable, and on August 12, he submitted his resignation.

The following day, Ebert appointed Gustav Stresemann, the chairman of the conservative democratic German People's Party (DVP), Cuno's successor. The rhetorically brilliant and tactically adroit parliamentarian, who had backed German aggression during the First World War, had transformed himself from a "monarchist at heart" to a "republican of reason" after 1918 and seen to it that his party constructively participated in parliamentary democracy. Stresemann negotiated a big-tent "grand coalition" among the DVP, the left-wing democratic German Democratic Party (DDP), the Catholic Center, and the SPD.

"Never before has a government taken office at a more difficult moment than the present one," reported the Austrian ambassador in Berlin, Richard Riedl. The problems Stresemann and his cabinet faced were indeed overwhelming. Prices were spiraling out of control, and Reich finances were a disaster. At the same time, extremists on the right

A difficult office in difficult times: Gustav Stresemann
shortly after his appointment as chancellor and foreign
minister of the grand coalition, August 1923.

and left were readying themselves to overthrow the Weimar Republic, and separatists were making waves on the left bank of the Rhine.
Without currency reform, economic recovery was out of the question.
That, however, required the government to stop subsidizing resistance
in the Ruhr.[36]

Stresemann demonstrated courage. On September 26, he announced
the end of passive resistance. It was an unpopular decision, prompting
the nationalist Right to unleash a vicious campaign that accused him of
"betraying" the national cause and "capitulating" to the French. Essen's

Rheinisch-Westfälische Zeitung, a newspaper with close ties to heavy industry, went so far as to demand that the new chancellor be brought before the State Court.[37]

That same day, the Bavarian government declared a state of emergency and appointed the president of Alpine Bavaria, Gustav Ritter von Kahr, as "state commissioner general," equipping him with far-reaching powers. That was tantamount to an act of rebellion against the imperial government. In response, the government imposed a state of emergency on September 27, entrusting Minister of the Armed Forces Otto Gessler with executive power. But Stresemann drew a line at an open test of strength with renegade Bavaria because he was unsure of the loyalty of the Reichswehr.[38]

The smoldering conflict with Bavaria wasn't the only strain on the grand coalition. In the autumn of 1923, the Soviet government in Moscow thought the time was ripe in Germany for a Communist October uprising that would extend the international proletarian revolution and remove the Soviet Union from its isolation. The springboard was supposed to be German Communists' entry into the SPD-led regional state governments of Saxony and Thuringia. On October 10, the SPD and KPD agreed to a joint government in Saxony, and six days later a united front was also formed in Thuringia. However, at a conference of works councils in Chemnitz on October 21, it became clear that the Executive Committee of the Communist International and KPD leadership had overestimated German workers' willingness to fight. A large majority rejected a motion to go on a general strike, which was to trigger a national uprising.[39]

The works council conference's decision to call off the "German October" was followed everywhere—with one exception: Hamburg. It has never been fully clarified why that was. One version of events blames a mishap—due to a series of unfortunate circumstances, the directive from the KPD headquarters may not have reached Hamburg in time. Another theory proposed that the Communist Party leadership in Hamburg under Ernst Thälmann deliberately disregarded the Chemnitz resolution in hopes of sparking a revolutionary uprising throughout the Reich. Whatever the reason, on the morning of October 23, insurgents stormed several police stations. The fiercest fighting broke out in

Barmbek, a traditionally "red" working-class district. "The barricades sprouted up everywhere, multiplying with incredible speed," wrote Russian revolutionary Larissa Reissner in her report on the events.[40] But the far more powerful police forces made the insurgents surrender the very next day. Twenty-four Communists and seventeen police officers paid for the failed insurrection with their lives.

Whereas the Reich government showed astonishing leniency toward the right-wing provocations from Munich, it was all the more severe in reacting to the left-wing united-front governments in Saxony and Thuringia. On October 22, trains full of Reichswehr troops from all over Germany rolled across the Saxon border. "Saxony is being flooded with Reichswehr troops," observed Thea Sternheim, wife of the playwright Carl Sternheim, in Dresden. "In countless squads of 6–8 men, heavily armed military troops from Württemberg and Mecklenburg patrol our streets."[41]

On October 29, after Saxony State Premier and left-wing Social Democrat Erich Zeigner and his cabinet refused to step down, the Reich began seizing power in the regional state, appointing a Reich commissioner who immediately dismissed the Zeigner government. Outraged at the unequal treatment of Saxony and Bavaria, the SPD ministers resigned from the grand coalition national government on November 2. From then on, Stresemann led a centrist minority coalition. Four days after the breakup of the grand coalition, Reichswehr troops moved into Thuringia and ended the SPD-KPD government in that regional state as well.[42]

It was not only the extreme Left plotting a coup in the fall of 1923. The radical Right also sensed that its time could be at hand and stepped up its calls for an iron-fisted "strongman" to bring order to all the chaos and free Germany from the shackles of the Treaty of Versailles. The focus of such hopes was above all the head of the army command, Hans von Seeckt. Starting in mid-September, the general received one visit after another from key representatives of the Reichslandbund (Reich Rural League), the powerful lobbying organization of the archconservative East Prussian aristocratic estate owners; the ultranationalist DNVP;

and the extreme right-wing Pan-Germanic League. They urged him to declare his willingness to become "military chancellor" in an authoritarian solution to the crisis. Seeckt was hardly averse to the idea. In the event that Stresemann's government lost its parliamentary backing, he could imagine a three-man directorate in which he himself would play a leading role.[43] In September, in conversation with the US ambassador in Berlin, Alanson Houghton, Hugo Stinnes also came out in favor of appointing a dictator who would, among other things, abolish the eight-hour working day, the greatest social achievement of the November Revolution.[44]

Plans to establish a "national dictatorship" were most advanced in Bavaria, where it was above all the National Socialist German Workers' Party (NSDAP)—the Nazi Party—that profited from the catastrophic economic situation. From January 1923 onward, the previously obscure Nazis recorded an exponential influx of members, registering more than fifty-five thousand by November.[45] The party's biggest attraction was its chairman, Adolf Hitler, who had won a power struggle against his internal rivals in July 1921. With his incendiary speeches against the "November criminals," the "shameful peace of Versailles," and "Jewish high finance," he drew crowds to the largest assembly halls in Munich week after week. Stefan Grossmann, one of the two editors of the left-wing democratic weekly *Das Tage-Buch*, warned early on, after experiencing Hitler live, against underestimating the danger he posed: "In Zirkus (Krone), which he has recently favored as a speaking venue, he commands the huge space. He possesses a national pathos that comes from within and sweeps listeners off their feet. He knows exactly how much gravity people in Munich will put up with and when he has to switch to Bavarian-Alpine Austrian dialect or, as a last resort, parodic Jew-speak."[46] The frenzied enthusiasm Hitler regularly inspired in his audiences boosted his self-confidence and convinced him that he was a chosen man on a special historical mission. Increasingly he enjoyed styling himself in the role of the maximum leader, a Führer, who would free Germany from humiliation and misery and restore its former greatness.

Rumors of an imminent Nazi coup began swirling that summer. In early September, Hitler and Ludendorff, who had moved to Munich after the failed Kapp Putsch and continued his counterrevolutionary efforts there, linked up at a so-called German Day rally in Nuremberg. With the ex-general as his ally, the would-be Führer hoped he could win over the Reichswehr for his plans to overthrow the government. At the end of the month, Hitler assumed political leadership of the German Combat League, an amalgamation of several paramilitary units, including the Sturmabteilung (SA), commanded by Hermann Göring.

Potential Hitler allies and rivals in Bavaria were the "triumvirate" of Kahr, Colonel Hans von Seisser, the head of the Bavarian state police, and Lieutenant General Otto Lossow, the head of the Reichswehr in Bavaria, who had been fired by Gessler the previous October for defying orders but whose command Kahr had restored immediately afterward. The three men were aiming to set up a "national dictatorship" backed by the Reichswehr leadership in Berlin. They were aware of Seeckt's plans for a directorate and wanted to join him. Hitler, however, wanted to emulate Benito Mussolini's "March on Rome" in October 1922 by proclaiming a dictatorship in Munich and starting a march on Berlin from there. In his speech at the Zirkus Krone on October 30, 1923, he left no doubt about his intentions: "Bavaria is on a great mission today. . . . We must take the battle elsewhere and stab the blade into the heart. . . . For me, the German question will only be resolved when the black, white, and red swastika flag flies from the Berlin Palace."[47]

While the triumvirate bided their time, after making such grandiose proclamations, Hitler could no longer wait, and on November 6, he decided to strike. The insurgency was originally planned to take place on November 11, the fifth anniversary of the armistice in the First World War. But the date was brought forward to November 8 after it emerged that Kahr was to deliver an evening speech in the Bürgerbräukeller beer hall that evening, with the whole of political Munich in attendance. This offered a unique opportunity to take Bavaria's leadership hostage. Kahr, Lossow, and Seisser would be presented with a fait accompli and forced to join forces with Hitler and Ludendorff, providing the initial spark for a national coup.

At first, Hitler's plan looked as though it might work. After storming the Bürgerbräukeller together with Ludendorff, he forced the three men to agree to join his putsch—drawing enthusiastic celebrations from the crowd. But no sooner had the triumvirate managed to leave the beer hall than they reversed course, sending a telegram to German radio stations that very night. It read: "State Commissioner General von Kahr, Colonel von Seisser, and General von Lossow reject Hitler's putsch. Statement extorted by force at Bürgerbräu meeting invalid."[48] The Reichswehr and the Bavarian state police opposed the putschists, so their cause had effectively failed. Hitler and Ludendorff's attempt to turn the tide by marching through downtown Munich ended in a hail of bullets in front of the Feldherrnhalle monument. Fourteen putschists and four policemen were killed. Hitler fled to the vacation home of his friend and ally Ernst Hanfstaengl in Uffing am Staffelsee. He was arrested there two days later and taken to a fortress prison in the town of Landsberg am Lech.[49]

As amateurish as the putsch and as ridiculous as the staged act of solidarity in the Bürgerbräukeller had been, the events in Munich on the night of November 8–9 were a sign of things to come, which deserved to be taken seriously. During the few hours Hitler's storm troopers believed they had in fact seized power, they immediately began to terrorize and arrest members of the political Left and German Jews. The quick collapse of the putsch prevented worse from happening. But the acts of terror previewed those that would be carried out across Germany ten years later, once Hitler had been appointed Reich chancellor.[50]

Another omen of bad things to come was an event that took place on November 5, three days before Hitler's coup, in Berlin's Scheunenviertel, a neighborhood populated by many poorer Jewish immigrants from Eastern Europe. A crowd incited by antisemitic agitators looted Jewish-owned stores and homes and abused Jews in the streets. "Berlin has had its Jewish pogrom," wrote *Vorwärts*. "Berlin has been desecrated. What a disgrace for a people that counts itself among the civilized."[51]

The failed coup in the Bürgerbräukeller discredited the radical Right's coup plans for the time being. "The hollowness of national dictatorship as a call to arms has been exposed," commented journalist Ernst Feder in the *Berliner Tageblatt*.[52] Unintentionally, Hitler and Ludendorff had helped to shore up the Weimar Republic they so hated. After four years of seemingly unstoppable ascent, the right-wing populist and Munich beer-hall demagogue Hitler was now confronted with the prospect of losing all political significance. *The New York Times* predicted that the failed coup would mean the certain end for Hitler and his followers.[53] But when he was put on trial before the Munich People's Court I in the spring of 1924, the Nazi leader was given only the minimum sentence of five years in prison, with eligibility for parole after just a few months. As a result, he was able to leave Landsberg in December 1924 and restart his political career. A unique opportunity had been wasted to remove the future Führer from circulation and in all probability squash any chance of a comeback.[54]

On the night of November 9, having received news of the putsch, Ebert transferred executive power, which had been held by Reichswehr Minister Gessler since September 26, to General Seeckt. In view of the ambivalent role the head of the army command had played in the previous weeks, some observers considered this a risky move. In fact, though, it was a clever step that undercut the hopes the enemies of the Weimar Republic had invested in the general. By placing Seeckt directly under his authority, Ebert simultaneously constrained him and committed him to defending the existing constitutional order. With that, any plans for a directorate had also come to an end.[55]

At the beginning of November 1923, hyperinflation reached its surreal peak. "One billion is now our smallest currency unit—as of Monday [it will be] the price of a domestic postage stamp," Dorothy von Moltke—the mother of the famous German resistance fighter against Hitler, Helmuth James von Moltke, wrote to her parents. "Oh, it's really terrible. And all those people who can't even afford day-old bread."[56] On November 14, the value of one dollar passed the trillion mark for the first time; the following day it stood at 2.52 trillion.[57] At that point, a new currency, the Rentenmark, was issued. In mid-October, the grand coalition had agreed to form the Rentenbank, or "Pension Bank," to create a new

At the peak of hyperinflation:
Children play with worthless banknotes.

mark whose value would be guaranteed by charges on land and bonds on
industry and agriculture. Within a week, the exchange rate against the
US dollar was stabilized at 4.2 trillion, and the Reichsbank determined
that 1 trillion paper marks would be worth one Rentenmark. Effectively,
that meant a return to the prewar dollar-exchange rate of 4.20 marks.[58]
At the end of November, Klemperer received his first salary in Renten-
marks, immediately lifting his mood: "The fear of the sudden devaluation of money and the pressure of having to spend it as soon as possible
have come to an end for the time being."[59] Optimism also prevailed on
the von Moltke family estate in Kreisau. "It's a great relief for all of us to

be able to deal with small amounts and stable prices again," wrote Dorothy von Moltke. "At least we know where we stand."[60]

Although contemporaries spoke of the "miracle of the Rentenmark," it did not happen overnight. The populace needed time to gain confidence in the new means of payment. But by early December, signs of improvement were already visible. "You can see happy shoppers in the grocery stores again," observed Kessler in Berlin. "A first ray of hope is penetrating the darkness."[61]

In the middle of this stabilization phase, Stresemann was toppled from power. Anticipating a motion of no confidence by the SPD, on November 23, he asked the Reichstag to confirm him in office and lost that vote. "What prompted you to overthrow the chancellor will be forgotten in six weeks, but you will feel the consequences of your stupidity for ten years to come," Ebert told his former allies.[62] In fact, the SPD would remain outside the national government for almost five years. Stresemann's chancellorship had lasted only around one hundred days, but it achieved remarkable results. By discontinuing passive resistance in the Ruhr, he laid the groundwork for an understanding with France, a cause he was to pursue single-mindedly as Germany's foreign minister in the years to come. Inflation had been brought under control, and the conditions for economic recovery created. Last but not least, he effectively combated military, economic, and political adversaries who wanted to impose dictatorial solutions to the crisis, thus successfully defending the Weimar Republic's constitutional order.

Stresemann was succeeded by Wilhelm Marx, the party and parliamentary group leader of the Center Party. On November 30, he formed a minority centrist government consisting of the Center, DVP, DDP, and Bavarian People's Party (BVP). Using an enabling act from the Reichstag on December 6, the cabinet resolutely continued the policy of economic stabilization. It rigorously curtailed expenditures by reducing staff in the public sector and cutting civil servants' salaries, while significantly boosting revenues with a series of emergency tax decrees. For the first time in a long while, the government was able to present a balanced budget again.[63]

"Thus ends a year of crisis," noted the British Ambassador D'Abernon on December 31, 1923, adding that only when one looked back did one realize "how near to the precipice this country has been." D'Abernon credited Germany's democratic politicians with heading off complete catastrophe. "Political leaders in Germany are not accustomed to receive much public laudation; those who have seen the country through these perils deserve more credit than is likely to be their portion."[64]

Looking back on 1923, author Stefan Zweig wrote in his autobiography, *The World of Yesterday*, "I have a pretty thorough knowledge of history, but never, to my recollection, has it produced such madness in such gigantic proportions." Nothing had ever made the German people "so furious with hate and so ripe for Hitler as the inflation," he added.[65] Sebastian Haffner came to a similar conclusion in his memoir, *Defying Hitler*, written in exile in England in 1939: "[No nation] has experienced the gigantic, carnival dance of death, the unending, bloody Saturnalia, in which not only money but all standards lost their value. The year 1923 prepared Germany, not specifically for Nazism, but for any fantastic adventure."[66] In his essay "Memories of German Inflation," written in exile in California in 1942, Thomas Mann also saw the events of 1923 as a prelude to what was to come: "There is a straight path from the madness of German inflation to the madness of the Third Reich."[67]

The extremes of the inflationary period did indeed deeply engrave themselves into the collective memory of Germans. 1923 left people feeling that everything was fundamentally shaky, there was no security anymore, and nothing could be relied on. For many Germans, the sudden loss of their assets and savings—"one of the greatest robberies in world history," as left-wing socialist historian Arthur Rosenberg called it[68]—was a trauma from which they would never fully recover. A deep bitterness lurked below the surface of people, especially from the middle classes. In nostalgic retrospect, the decades before 1914 seemed like "the good old days," an era of stability and bourgeois solidity.

Nevertheless, there was no straight line from 1923 to 1933. The Weimar Republic may have been on the brink of the abyss, but it met every challenge, demonstrating an astonishing ability to survive, and emerging not weakened but strengthened. The government continued to consolidate its domestic and foreign policies during 1924. Once the fever of inflation broke, the economy recovered remarkably quickly. The state of emergency was lifted in February 1924. At the London Conference in July and August, France promised to leave the Ruhr within a year. By the end of August 1924, the Dawes Plan had presented a temporary solution to the reparations problem acceptable to all sides, and the Reichstag approved it. The day the London Agreement was signed, August 30, the Rentenmark was replaced by the Reichsmark, backed by 40 percent gold or foreign currency exchangeable into gold. Foreign, mainly American, capital began to pour in. The postwar period was over once and for all, paving the way for Germany's return to the international community as an equal member. If the international economy remained favorable, the prospects for steady economic growth were not at all bad.

Of course, it remained to be seen whether the survival of the Weimar Republic would stabilize the parliamentary, democratic order in Germany in the long run. Weimar democracy's ability to get through the crises of 1923 was due in part to the fact that the state was led by a man like Ebert. He had doggedly utilized all the constitutional leeway of the office of the German presidency, including the emergency powers of Article 48, in order to prop up and defend the republic from the onslaught of its opponents. But the question remained: What might a successor to Ebert do?

The Turn to the Right

EBERT'S DEATH AND HINDENBURG'S ELECTION

Last respects for a great patriot: Friedrich Ebert's coffin is transferred from the Potsdamer Bahnhof in Berlin to his birthplace in Heidelberg on March 4, 1925.

In the final days of 1924, Reich President Friedrich Ebert began feeling ill, complaining of fatigue and a variety of ailments. His personal physician, Arnold Freudenthal, advised him to take it easy. But the pressures of his daily business didn't allow for any significant rest. In February 1925, his health seemed to rebound. On February 21, for instance, Ebert received Gustav Stresemann, now Germany's foreign minister, for a lengthy meeting. But the very next day, he was bedridden and in severe pain. Freudenthal initially diagnosed biliary colic, an affliction Ebert had suffered for several years, and prescribed warm compresses. When the pain didn't subside, he called in the surgeon August Bier, who arranged for the Reich president to be taken to the West Hospital in Berlin's Charlottenburg district, where he immediately underwent an operation. But it was too late. He never regained consciousness. At 10:12 a.m. on February 28, Friedrich Ebert, only fifty-four years old, died.[1] The autopsy determined the cause of death to be acute appendicitis and peritonitis. Ebert's family and his closest companions, however, were convinced that the attacks to which the Reich president had been subjected over the previous years had weakened him, contributing to his untimely demise.

After being named as Reich president by the Weimar National Assembly in February 1919, Ebert had been subjected to a vicious smear campaign unlike any other in the young republic. The elites in power before 1918 could not stand the fact that a man of humble origins—a trained saddler and Social Democrat—now held the highest office in the state. Jokes about "Fritze Ebert," playing on his working-class background, did the rounds, and he was targeted by spiteful caricatures in the anti-democratic press. One oft-used visual motif was an unflattering photo from August 1919 of Ebert and Reichswehr Minister Gustav Noske in swimming trunks at the Baltic seaside resort of Haffkrug. It served as a template for many insults intended to denigrate the reputation not only of the head of state himself but also of the new democratic order that he embodied. Although Ebert continued to lead a modest private life as Reich president, he was not spared accusations of corruption and personal enrichment. In his first year in office, he reacted cautiously to the numerous insults and slander. This changed after the assassination attempts on Erzberger in 1921 and Rathenau in 1922, and by the end of 1924 Ebert had filed a total of around two hundred lawsuits. The aim was to defend not only his own person but the dignity and reputation of the Weimar Republic.[2]

The most vicious of these attacks was the accusation of "treason" in conjunction with the role Ebert had played in a major strike by workers in arms factories in Berlin in late January 1918. In his function as SPD chairman, he had joined the strike leadership—not, however, to support but rather to end the work stoppage, so that imperial Germany's war effort wouldn't be impeded. During a visit to Munich in June 1922, the chemist Emil Gansser, an early Hitler supporter, publicly defamed the postwar Reich president as a "traitor to his country." Ebert filed a lawsuit but withdrew it on the advice of his defense attorney and party colleague Wolfgang Heine, who convinced him that a trial before a Munich court would be inopportune. Gansser felt emboldened and called in an open letter for the president to resign, claiming it would be "too perilous a test" for the Weimar Republic "if a man remains at its head who does nothing about accusations of treason."[3]

A provincial nationalist newspaper, the *Mitteldeutsche Presse* in Stassfurt, near the city of Magdeburg, echoed Gansser's slander in late February 1924, demanding, "Mr. Ebert, prove that you are not a traitor!" That prompted Ebert to file another criminal complaint against the editor responsible, twenty-five-year-old Erwin Rothardt, who had already been convicted of multiple instances of character defamation. What began as a libel suit quickly turned into a political trial in which the political Right sensed an opportunity to pillory everything the Social Democrats had done during the First World War, causing irreparable damage to the reputation of Ebert as the former SPD party chairman. During discovery, the presiding judge at Magdeburg District Court, Gustav Bewersdorff,

Reich President Friedrich Ebert and Reich Minister of Defense Gustav Noske at the Baltic Sea resort of Haffkrug, August 1919: The opponents of the republic used the "swimming trunks photo" to vilify the head of state. On this postcard, it is framed by Wilhelm II and Hindenburg in full-dress uniforms, to emphasize the difference between the splendor of the empire and the alleged lack of style of the republic. (The heading reads "Then and Now!")

allowed the defense to present a series of low-credibility witnesses. The trial proper began on December 9, 1924, and ended on December 23 with a scandalous verdict. Rothardt was sentenced to three months in prison for insulting the Reich president, but the court also found that Ebert had "objectively and subjectively fulfilled the conditions of treason through his participation in the strike leadership and through individual actions in this position."[4]

The ruling sparked outrage among supporters of democracy. Renowned lawyers, politicians, and artists issued sworn statements on behalf of the president. But Ebert was deeply wounded. Of all people, he—a man who had lost two sons in the First World War and whose patriotism was beyond question—now had to live with the stigma of being branded a traitor. In October 1922, the Reichstag had decided by a two-thirds majority to extend his term in office until June 30, 1925. Ebert no longer wanted to run in the first popular presidential election, telling confidants that he was tired and needed rest. He appealed the Magdeburg verdict in February 1925. Preparing for the new trial ate away at his time and contributed to his constant illness. He would not live to see the start of his appeal in March.[5]

The obituaries for Ebert reflected the sharp polarization between the opponents and defenders of Weimar democracy. Those who had vilified the German president during his lifetime had nothing good to say about him in death. Supporters of the Weimar Republic, however, felt great grief and concern at Ebert's passing. It was a particularly bitter blow for Foreign Minister Stresemann, who had come to appreciate the Reich president, especially during his chancellorship in the dramatic crisis of the fall of 1923. In his obituary in *Die Zeit* newspaper, which took up the entire, black-edged front page, he emphasized that Ebert "had . . . in his work as a statesman . . . outgrown dogma and dependence on any party beliefs." Although he came from a humble background, the former president led with an "innate dignity" and "impeccable tact."[6] The editor in chief of the *Vossische Zeitung*, Georg Bernhard, recalled Ebert as "a tower of strength in stormy times" during the revolutionary turmoil, someone who "stood unwaveringly at the helm and, despite all the attacks and accusations raining down on him, fought to steer the ship of the Reich into the harbor of democracy."[7] The senior political editor of the *Berliner Tageblatt*, Erich Dombrowski, paid tribute to a "great patriot" who "always remained a man of the people . . . simple, sincere, and straightforward."[8]

The SPD did its best to forget the conflicts it had experienced with

Ebert as Reich president. The party had frequently criticized the head of state, especially following the Reich's intervention in Saxony in October 1923. Ebert had "remained a Social Democrat in heart and mind," wrote the SPD newspaper *Vorwärts*, despite the nonpartisanship with which he had conducted his office. "After all the great theorists and the great agitators, Ebert was the first great statesman of the German workers' movement. . . . The movement honors itself when it honors Friedrich Ebert."[9]

On the night of March 1, Ebert's coffin was taken to the presidential palace. The state funeral service took place there on the afternoon of March 4. The eulogy was delivered by Reich Chancellor Hans Luther, who since January 1925 had led a "People's Bloc" government, the first coalition to include the ultranationalist DNVP. Luther, too, praised Ebert as a statesman who had preserved the unity of the nation "beyond all party barriers and political divisions." The funeral procession moved from Wilhelmstrasse along Unter den Linden boulevard through the Brandenburg Gate to the Reichstag building, where the coffin was placed in front of the steps leading to the main entrance. A huge crowd lined the streets, and thousands accompanied the procession when it moved on to Potsdam Train Station. "It was very touching how in the evening, when everything was over, people stood like walls on the high arched canal bridges to see Ebert pass by one last time, namely in a special train over the rail bridge," wrote Katia Mann to her husband Thomas.[10] That night, the train with the coffin traveled to Heidelberg, Ebert's birthplace. Members of the socialist militia Reich Banner Black-Red-Gold paid their last respects to the deceased at all major stations the train passed through. Ebert was laid to rest in Heidelberg's Bergfriedhof cemetery, again in front of huge crowds.[11]

Who would succeed Ebert? This question was all the more crucial because the Weimar Constitution gave the presidency huge potential power far beyond symbolically representing the state. The president was a counterweight to parliament. After initially opposing this arrangement, Social Democrats had come to terms with it because one of their own,

Friedrich Ebert, held the office. Abuse seemed impossible. But what if the far-reaching presidential powers fell into the hands of an outspoken opponent of Weimar democracy? Would he use his authority to pry apart the constitution?

The rules governing the popular presidential election required an absolute majority in the first round of voting. If no candidate achieved one, a second ballot would be held in which a relative majority was sufficient. At the suggestion of the governing coalition, the Reichstag set March 29 as the date for the first ballot and April 26 for a possible second one.[12]

From the very beginning, the political Right's stated aim was to wrest the presidency from the Social Democrats. The sine qua non was a candidate who would unite the parties of the mainstream and the middle classes. The driving force behind the selection of such a man was the president of the Reich Citizens' Council, former Prussian Minister of the Interior Friedrich Wilhelm von Loebell. In December 1924, before Ebert's death, he set up a committee made up of representatives of all centrist parties except the DDP. Nonetheless, the search for a suitable candidate proved difficult, especially as the Center Party and the Bavarian People's Party (BVP) soon withdrew from the committee. For a time, General Hans von Seeckt, head of the army command, was discussed, but he withdrew himself from consideration, doubting that he would have much chance of being elected. On March 7, the Loebell committee finally agreed on Karl Jarres, mayor of Duisburg and former Reich minister of the interior, a member of Stresemann's DVP, who enjoyed the German foreign minister's strong support.[13]

The SPD was determined to put forward a candidate from its own ranks in the first round of voting, but here too, however, the party executive faced unexpected difficulties. Reichstag President Paul Löbe, who was initially suggested, adamantly refused to be nominated. Otto Braun, an East Prussian and perhaps the SPD's most popular politician, also initially rejected his party's call but eventually allowed himself to be persuaded. Braun had resigned as Prussian state premier on January 23, 1925, after the two DVP ministers in his cabinet left the coalition—a condition the DNVP had set for joining Luther's national government. The result was a lasting governmental crisis in Prussia. Former Reich

Chancellor Wilhelm Marx made two attempts in February and March 1925 to form a new Prussian government but failed on both occasions.[14]

On March 7, the SPD executive announced Braun's nomination. The *Vossische Zeitung* heavily criticized the decision, declaring that it made "a united front of pro-democracy parties impossible for the first ballot."[15] Having been presented by Social Democrats with a fait accompli, the Center Party had no choice but to nominate a candidate of its own. Adam Stegerwald, the former Prussian minister for public welfare and chairman of the Christian Trade Unions, was initially put forward. However, at a meeting of the Center factions of the Reichstag and the Prussian House of Representatives on March 8, Stegerwald failed to garner sufficient support. As a result, on the evening of March 10, the party's executive committee recommended the nomination of Wilhelm Marx.[16]

But the next day, before the Reich party committee could decide on Marx, a new proposal for a joint centrist candidacy was announced for the first ballot. Otto Gessler, who had served as Reichswehr minister since March 1920, indicated a willingness to throw his hat into the ring. As a member of the DDP, he was sure to have its support, and as an experienced politician, he was also viewed favorably by the other centrist parties. The Loebell committee initially seemed inclined to accept Gessler's candidacy, providing the Center Party also consented.[17]

In the end, though, Stresemann himself put his foot down and rejected the idea. His reasons primarily had to do with foreign policy. In early February 1925, Stresemann had taken the initiative to propose a security pact to the French government, which was to include the final recognition of Germany's western border and a mutual renunciation of force—a bold step that was to lead to the Locarno Treaties of October 1925. On March 11, he informed Gessler of his concerns that a candidacy by the Reich minister of the armed forces would greatly strain Franco-German relations. Many people in France, he added, believed that the head of the army command, Seeckt, was "the real dictator in Germany" and that the Reichswehr minister "followed him in lockstep." If Gessler were to become Reich president, it would reinforce the French public's impression "that political leadership was to a certain extent being transferred to the Reichswehr."[18]

On the evening of March 12, the Loebell committee officially named Karl Jarres as the candidate of the right-wing unity "Reich Bloc." Meanwhile, the Reich Party Committee of the Center Party voted unanimously for Wilhelm Marx. The centrists' failure to agree on a unity candidacy meant that, in addition to Jarres, Braun, and Marx, four other candidates ran in the first round of voting. The DDP nominated the president of Baden, Willy Hellpach, who had been that regional state's minister of education from 1922 to 1925. The leading pro-democracy newspapers in Berlin had particularly lobbied for him, with *Berliner Tageblatt* editor in chief Theodor Wolff praising his combination of "both a clear democratic stance and the finest manner." [19]

The BVP also named a candidate: party chairman and Bavarian Minister President Heinrich Held. He was the same man who had given Hitler a second chance in late February 1925 by permitting him to reestablish the Nazi Party, which had been banned, in Munich. For their part, the National Socialists presented Erich Ludendorff, one of the putschists of November 1923. Hitler supported his candidacy, speculating that the ex-general would lose face if, as expected, he performed poorly. It was a chance for Hitler to get rid of an annoying competitor in the extreme right-wing racist-nationalist camp. [20] The KPD also took the opportunity to put forward its chairman, Ernst Thälmann, although his candidacy was transparently pro forma. [21]

As anticipated, Karl Jarres received the most votes in the first round of voting on March 29, with 10.4 million (38.8 percent), but fell well short of an absolute majority. Social Democratic candidate Otto Braun came in second with 7.8 million votes (29 percent)—better than the SPD's performance in the last Reichstag elections on December 7, 1924. In third place was the Center Party candidate, Wilhelm Marx, who received 3.9 million votes (14.5 percent). All other candidates polled in single digits: Thälmann, 1.9 million (7 percent); the DDP's Willy Hellpach, 1.6 million (5.8 percent); Held, 1 million (3.7 percent); and Ludendorff, 186,000 votes (1.1 percent). Turnout, at 68.9 percent, was lower than in all previous Reichstag elections.

The extremist parties' poor performance was particularly striking. Thälmann received 800,000 fewer votes than the KPD in the previous Reichstag election; and Ludendorff, 600,000 fewer than the National Socialists and other racists had gotten in December 1924. There was an obvious "trend toward de-radicalization," to use a phrase of historian Heinrich August Winkler, due mainly to Germany's economic recovery in 1924.[22] Hitler was very satisfied with Ludendorff's defeat. "That's good—now we've finally finished him off," he told confidants. Indeed, Ludendorff descended into political insignificance with breathtaking speed.[23]

All told, the parties of the Weimar Coalition—SPD, Center, and DDP—had achieved 49.3 percent of the vote. They could therefore expect, if they could agree on a mutual candidate, to emerge victorious from the second round of voting, in which a simple majority was sufficient. This time, it was the Center that took the initiative, with the party executive proposing the rather bland Marx on March 31. Although the popular Otto Braun had been far more successful in the first round of voting, on April 2, the Social Democrats agreed to support Marx based on their prewar experience that middle-class voters tended not to support SPD candidates in run-off elections. In return, the SPD party executive insisted that the Center pledge to support Braun's reelection as head of government in Prussia. That was exactly what happened. On April 3, the Prussian parliament elected Braun as Prussian state premier with 216 out of 430 votes. The governmental crisis in Germany's largest regional state was finally over.[24]

On April 4, the three parties, now united in the "People's Bloc," agreed to present Marx as a joint pro-democracy candidate. DDP chairman Erich Koch-Weser had been able to dispel initial resistance in his party by pointing out that no alternative to Marx could command a majority. If Marx became Reich president, it would be a "significant step" toward making Germany "a republic not only in name but in heart."[25]

The Reich Bloc realized that Jarres was unlikely to win the race against the common candidate of the Weimar Coalition. It was thus made to look for an alternative who would be able to tap into new groups of vot-ers beyond the usual conservative circles. The rules allowed for the nomination of someone who had not run in the first round of voting, and the DNVP saw Paul von Hindenburg as a strong candidate. The seventy-seven-year-old field marshal, who had been living in retire-ment in Hanover since stepping down as the head of the Supreme Army Command in July 1919, enjoyed the nimbus of the "victor of Tannen-berg," the battle that had liberated East Prussia from Russian invasion in August 1914. Despite his less-than-glorious role at the end of the war, his name had an appeal that reached far into republican circles as well.[26]

The DNVP and DVP had already put the highly regarded army com-mander forward as a candidate for the first popular election in the sum-mer of 1919. Hindenburg was initially reluctant to accept the nomination before giving in, albeit not without first securing permission from former Kaiser Wilhelm II, who was living in exile in Doorn in the Netherlands. But the Kapp Putsch of March 1920, which discredited the two right-wing parties, thwarted those plans and prompted Hindenburg to draw back from politics.[27]

Before the first ballot on March 29, 1925, Hindenburg had asked his former companion Ludendorff to withdraw his candidacy, as it was "hopeless" and he could only "disgrace" himself. "Instead of uniting, as we so desperately need, you are once again splintering the national forces that have been united with so much effort at a crucial time," Hin-denburg said.[28] He indicated that he could certainly imagine himself running for Germany's highest office in the decisive second ballot.

There was resistance to this, especially among those in DVP circles, who were determined to stick with Jarres. The foreign policy concerns with which Stresemann had blocked Gessler applied even more to Hin-denburg, whose name had been at the top of the Allied list of German war criminals in 1919 and who was regarded abroad as an embodiment of hated Prussian militarism.[29] There were thus numerous obstacles to Hindenburg's nomination, and the candidate initially kept a low profile. Nevertheless, when the first delegation from the DNVP knocked on his door in Hanover on April 1, he indicated his willingness in principle to run for election. When two DNVP delegates followed up three days later, they were already able to elicit a firm commitment, albeit on the condition that the Reich Bloc unanimously support his candidacy.

By April 6, Hindenburg was already wavering. At Stresemann's behest, two DVP politicians and personal acquaintances of the field marshal, Wilhelm Spiekernagel, a member of the regional state parliament, and Heinrich Tramm, the mayor of Hanover, seem to have advised him not to run, pointing out that the campaign could turn bitter and potentially damage his reputation. These concerns made an impression on Hindenburg. The next day, he sent a telegram to the DVP's national office declaring that he was unable to accept the role he had been offered, due to his advanced age. "I remain steadfastly committed to Jarres's candidacy and urge all those who place their fatherland above their party to join me and prevent a disastrous fragmentation," Hindenburg wrote.[30]

However, the nationalists refused to admit defeat. Determined to make Hindenburg their candidate at all costs, they played their final card: Grand Admiral Alfred von Tirpitz, the father of the Wilhelmine Empire's naval fleet, the co-founder of the German Fatherland Party in 1917, and a member of the ultranationalist parliamentary group in the Reichstag. On the evening of April 7, he and his parliamentary colleague Walter von Keudell succeeded in persuading the fickle field marshal to reverse his decision. If the Reich Bloc unanimously backed him, Hindenburg said, he would agree to be its candidate. On April 8, after Jarres had finally withdrawn himself from consideration, the Loebell committee officially proclaimed Hindenburg the Reich Bloc candidate. DVP representatives, caught off guard, had no choice but to put on a brave face, and the party leadership instructed constituency organizations to work "with all their strength" to ensure Hindenburg emerged victorious.[31]

The Center Party's sister party in Bavaria, the BVP, also endorsed the elderly field marshal. Their antipathy toward Marx, a Rhenish Catholic supported by the SPD, was greater than any reservations against Hindenburg, a Protestant from northern Germany, who could now also hope to outperform Jarres with southern German Catholics.[32] Conversely, Marx could not count on much support from the radical Left. On April 11, the KPD leadership went against the recommendation of the Executive Committee of the Communist International (ECCI) and stuck with Thälmann's candidacy. "It is not the task of the proletariat to choose the most skillful representative of the interests of the bour-geoisie, to choose the lesser evil between the civilian dictator Marx and the military dictator Hindenburg," the appeal from KPD headquarters argued. "Every class-conscious worker needs to vote against Hinden-burg and Marx and for Thälmann!"[33] The party leadership consciously accepted the fact that this could lead to the election of a convinced mon-archist and opponent of parliamentary democracy.

Observers abroad saw Hindenburg's nomination for exactly what it was, an act of provocation, and the reaction in the American, British, and French press was scathing.[34] There was no lack of concerned voices in Germany either. "Republicans, the republic is in peril!" warned the SPD party executive on April 11. "Hindenburg's candidacy endangers peace! His election would bring immense misfortune upon the entire German people."[35] In an editorial with the headline "Save Democ-racy!" in several newspapers, including the *Berliner Tageblatt*, Thomas Mann warned of the "disastrous consequences" of Hindenburg's can-didacy, arguing that his election "would plunge the country back into a state of unrest, insecurity, and internal strife that seemed happily over-come." The German people, Mann advised, would do well to "refrain from electing a warmonger from the past as their supreme leader."[36] The *Vossische Zeitung* wrote of a "tragedy," calling Hindenburg's nomination "a slap in the face of the foreign minister" and asking: "Will Dr. Strese-mann be able to remain silent if German foreign policy, at a moment when the scales are to be tipped, perhaps for decades, is burdened with a field marshal whose mere name is enough to provide months of material to anti-German propaganda around the world?"[37]

Stresemann was trapped. On the one hand, he saw Hindenburg's can-didacy as a millstone around his foreign policy; on the other, he couldn't publicly criticize the decision of the Loebell committee without disavow-ing his party colleagues on it. In a conversation with Kessler on April 19, he revealed the full extent of his dilemma. He had fought "to the last" against Hindenburg's nomination, he said, but had been outmaneuvered by DNVP intrigue. "Two years of work has been destroyed," Kessler recorded Stresemann saying. When the former suggested "informing the public about the dangers of this candidate," Stresemann replied that such a campaign "could easily have the opposite effect" and "lead people who rejected foreign interference in our internal affairs to vote for Hindenburg." Kessler added that "the longer we talked, the gloomier he became." In the end, the foreign minister could only console himself with the hope that Hindenburg might lose the election.[38]

In his diary, Stresemann spoke of himself and his party being in an "almost impossible situation."[39] Instead of publicly calling upon voters to reject Hindenburg, he sought to allay concerns at home and abroad. In an article in *Die Zeit* on April 19, Stresemann argued that the election was not about choosing between a monarchy and a republic and expressed confidence that Hindenburg "as president of the German Reich, free from all outside influences, will exclusively focus on the welfare of the fatherland and respect for its constitutional institutions."[40]

The election campaign was conducted with a vehemence the Weimar Republic had never experienced. The supporters of the People's Bloc and the Reich Bloc faced off as bitter enemies. "The election campaign is raging—In one corner Hindenburg!—In the other Marx! No end is in sight," noted Max von Stockhausen, state secretary in the Reich Chancellery, on April 15. "Germany is split down the middle, and the worst thing is that whoever is elected will have to govern with one half against the other."[41] German nationalist election propaganda launched an anti-Catholic culture war. A leaflet published by the Fatherland Association and the right-wing parties demonized Marx as a "representative of the grimmest reactionary sentiment" and a "friend of those ultramontanes" who "since 1918 have been waging the fiercest campaign of annihilation against the Protestant Church with the help of the Jesuits." By contrast, in Catholic Bavaria, Marx was accused of having allied himself with "Christianity's worst enemy, the Social Democratic movement." A leaflet by BVP politician Georg Heim concluded with the appeal, "If you don't want to destroy Christian culture, if you don't want to hand over the Christian school of thought to these neo-pagans, then don't vote for Marx!"[42]

Meanwhile, the right wing presented Hindenburg as a national beacon, a savior destined to lead Germany from decline and chaos to new greatness. A campaign poster featuring Hindenburg's very familiar face and blood-red letters reading "The Rescuer!" was pasted on advertising pillars all over. But what was the field marshal supposed to be saving the country from? asked the *Vossische Zeitung*: "The fact that Germany is gradually recovering, that conditions are once again orderly in the Reich, and that bright prospects are opening up for the future is thanks to all those men who, since November 1918, have been vilified, slandered, and persecuted in a constant struggle with the so-called nationalist opposition of the DNVP. These men have pursued cool, sober, realistic policies and refused to embroil the Reich in any wild adventures."[43]

Hindenburg deliberately kept himself out of the daily fracas of campaigning, remaining in his hometown of Hanover and playing the role of the nonpartisan patriarch his campaign strategists had concocted for him. In a public declaration of policy on April 12, he intoned: "I extend my hand to every German who thinks patriotically, upholds the dignity of the German name both at home and abroad, and wants religious and social peace." It was the leitmotif of his campaign. Hindenburg made only one personal appearance, on April 19 in the Hanover city hall, in front of a large crowd of domestic and foreign reporters. On this occasion, too, he emphasized "the importance of the will to unity, which has nothing to do with party politics, but rather corresponds to the healthy national emotions of the German people."[44]

In contrast, Wilhelm Marx went on an exhausting campaign tour, beginning on April 14 in East Prussia and ending on April 23 in Stuttgart. In his speeches, he avoided attacking Hindenburg personally and expressed his admiration for the field marshal. At the same time, he styled himself as a guarantor of national unity who wanted to overcome divisions and pave the way for a "true national community."[45] The high point and conclusion of the election campaign was on April 24, when first Hindenburg, then Marx addressed Germans directly on the radio for the first time. "Friday evening . . . we were able to listen on the radio to Grandpa Hindenburg's speech in Hanover and Marx's in Nuremberg," reported Betty Scholem in her letter to her son Gershom. "This technical fact in itself was far more interesting than the candidates' canned phrases."[46]

On the eve of the run-off election, cultural philosopher Theodor Lessing, who taught at the Technical University of Hanover, published a psychological profile of Hindenburg in the *Prager Tagblatt* newspaper. It ended with the words: "According to Plato, philosophers should be leaders of the people. If Hindenburg ascends the throne, it won't be as a philosopher, just as a representative symbol, a question mark, a zero. You could say: 'Better a zero than a Nero.' Unfortunately, history shows that behind every zero there's always a Nero."[47] Lessing's assessment would prove prophetic. Nationalist students in Hanover embarked on a vicious smear campaign against the Jewish scholar. His teaching license was revoked, and in February 1933 he would he assassinated by the Nazis.

The weather was poor in Berlin on Election Sunday, April 26—an omen in the eyes of some pro-democracy observers. Kessler went to the polling station on Linkstrasse in the morning: "A fine rain is pouring down and emptying the streets. On Potsdamer Platz square only a few swastika youths carrying big truncheons, blond and stupid, like young calves. Few flags in this area and those few are fairly evenly distributed between black-white-red and black-red-gold. Spent the whole day in an anxious mood." Kessler reckoned that it would be a neck-and-neck race, with Marx getting a majority of half a million to one million votes at best.[48]

Even that forecast proved too optimistic. When the result was announced at midnight, Hindenburg had won the election by a clear margin, garnering 900,000 more votes than Marx. Some 14.6 million votes (48.3 percent) had been cast for him, 13.7 million (45.3 percent) for Marx, and 1.9 million (6.4 percent) for Thälmann. Although the candidate of the People's Bloc had received almost half a million votes more than Braun, Marx, and Hellpach together in the first round, the Reich Bloc candidate had exceeded the results of the three right-wing candidates Jarres, Held, and Ludendorff by almost 3 million votes.[49]

"Hindenburg by the Grace of Thälmann!" read the headline in *Vorwärts* on April 27, while the Catholic newspaper *Germania* wrote of the "crutches" that "Comrade Thälmann" had "helpfully slipped under the field marshal's tired armpits."[50] The votes that had gone to Thälmann would in fact have been enough to help Marx to victory, but no one had seriously expected Communist voters to change their minds. The BVP, which had endorsed Hindenburg, leading the vast majority of its core supporters to vote for him, bore at least as much responsibility for the field marshal's victory. Hindenburg did particularly well in the Protestant areas of northern and eastern Germany, but quite a few Catholic voters outside Bavaria had also refused to follow Marx—whether because they disapproved of his alliance with the Social Democrats or because they admired Hindenburg. Moreover, the Reich Bloc succeeded in mobilizing nonvoters. Turnout rose from 68.9 to 77.6 percent compared to the first ballot. The increase had obviously benefited Hindenburg.[51]

Hindenburg's victory sparked jubilation on the right. "Who would have thought it possible two years ago that Hindenburg could become Reich president," exulted Forestry Councillor Georg Escherich, the founder of the Bavarian Residents' Defense Forces, in his diary. "We now have an absolutely impeccable, sensible man back at the helm."[52] The conservative *Berliner Börsen-Zeitung* newspaper expressed satisfaction that "the national idea with the name Hindenburg on its banner" had triumphed: "Our confidence in the German people turning away from pacifism, internationalism, and Marxism has not betrayed us." However, Hindenburg's victory was "only a battle, not yet a campaign," the paper pointed out. "And this campaign, the struggle for the soul of our people, continues uninterrupted, without a second's rest."[53]

Despite his considerable forebodings, Stresemann, who had been confined to his bed with a severe sore throat on Election Day, was still surprised by the result. "Everything will now depend on how Hindenburg conducts himself in his new office," the foreign minister wrote, "and whether the consequences that foreign countries partly fear and partly hope for actually materialize."[54]

Hindenburg's triumph shocked the pro-democracy segment of the German public. Theodor Wolff expressed a "feeling of shame" felt by many: "We are ashamed of the political immaturity of so many millions, which now once again displays itself before the eyes of the shrugging world." The editor in chief of the *Berliner Tageblatt* saw the real peril not in Hindenburg himself but in the "deviousness" of the clique of advisers around him, who, Wolff feared, would exploit "the political inexperience of the military-educated and military-minded Reich president" to seize control of state affairs.[55] Concerns about the influence of Hindenburg's camarilla were justified, as the final years of the republic would show.

Kessler's first reaction was sheer horror at what "will probably be one of the darkest chapters in German history."[56] When she heard the news in Switzerland, Thea Sternheim, the wife of playwright Carl Sternheim, felt "the same sensation of horror and helplessness" as she had at the start of the First World War on August 1, 1914. "You can already hear the thunderous avalanche of national madness again, and the only consolation right now is not being outside having to look at the twisted faces of the victors."[57] From Paris, Victor Klemperer was also reminded of the beginning of the First World War: "I have the impression of something similar to what happened on June 28, 1914, when the Austrian heir to the throne was murdered. What will become of Germany now?"[58] In *Die Weltbühne*, Kurt Tucholsky answered the question "What now?" with a healthy dose of black humor: "Now a bitter, terrible, blood-spilling lesson. One deserved a thousand times over." In Tucholsky's eyes, one of the deeper causes of the republicans' defeat was their skittishness about attacking Hindenburg during the election campaign. "In all their speeches and essays they repeatedly emphasized the great admiration and love they felt for this idol of Prussian manhood; they celebrated the old man, looked up to him with respect, adored him—and then they recommended voting for Marx."[59]

Hindenburg's election was greeted with particular dismay in France. The editorialist of the Parisian daily *Le Temps* wrote, "Germany has removed the mask with which it tries to make people believe in the sincerity of its democratic sentiment and is now revealing its former face, across which its bellicose instincts and lust for power are clearly written."[60]

Two days after the election, Chancellor Luther visited Hindenburg in Gross-Schwülper, the estate of his son Oskar's mother-in-law near Braunschweig. "The field marshal received us on the steps of the manor . . . physically quite spry despite his 77 years and fundamentally fresh and clear-minded," recorded Stockhausen in his diary.[61] The chancellor spent two hours briefing the newly elected Reich president on the political situation. On his return, he reported to Stresemann his definite impression that Hindenburg "wanted solely to govern within the constitution" and would not try to change the cabinet.[62] That was to be expected, since Luther led a right-wing-centrist government, including ministers from DNVP, the party to which Hindenburg was politically close.

On May 11, Hindenburg left Hanover by train for Berlin. It was a triumphal journey. At every stop, supporters showered the new head of state with applause. That afternoon, Hindenburg arrived at Heerstrasse station, where he was received by the chancellor and the entire cabinet. To the cheers of many thousands of Berliners lining the streets, he made his way in an open carriage through the Tiergarten park to the Reich Chancellery on Wilhelmstrasse. There, Hindenburg temporarily occupied Bismarck's old apartment before moving permanently into the presidential palace.[63]

He was sworn in the following day in the plenary chamber of the Reichstag. "The gallery in the Reichstag was already overflowing at 11 a.m., an hour before the swearing-in ceremony," noted Kessler. "Fortunately, I had a numbered seat from which I could see well. . . . The hall was rather sparsely decorated. Behind the president's chair, the black-red-and-gold standard of the president of the Reich was mounted on a wall covering and a black, red, and gold bunting flanked by blue hydrangeas on the president's table: That was all. . . . At 12 o'clock Hindenburg and Löbe, both attired in black frock coats, entered without ceremony

*Arrival in Berlin: Newly elected Reich President Paul von Hindenburg
is greeted by an enthusiastic crowd in Berlin on May 11, 1925.*

through one of the small doors behind the presidential chair. Hardly anyone noticed they were there. But suddenly cheers came from the far left.
The Communists hailed the Soviet republic and then marched in single
file."[64] The KPD deputies don't seem to have been bothered that Thälmann's candidacy had helped put Hindenburg in the saddle.

Hindenburg read the prescribed oath in a somewhat uncertain, falter-
ing voice: "I swear by God Almighty and Omniscient that I will devote
my strength to the welfare of the German people, increase their benefit, avert harm from them, uphold the constitution and the laws of the
Reich, conscientiously fulfill my duties, and do justice to all. So help me
God." After a short speech by Löbe, Hindenburg took the floor once
again and reiterated his core message that as Reich president he wanted
to "serve the cause of nonpartisan unification of all the capable and con-
structive forces of our people."[65]

The inauguration ceremony made a big impression on everyone present. An acquaintance of Kessler called out to him as he left the Reichstag: "We have just witnessed the birth of the German Republic." Even

Kessler, who had predicted catastrophe on the day of Hindenburg's election, was now able to see something positive in the event. With the new Reich president, the Weimar Republic, including its colors, would become "acceptable in high society since the black-red-gold will now appear everywhere together with Hindenburg as his personal standard colors." Kessler added, "If the republicans do not renounce their vigilance and their unity, Hindenburg's election may even become quite useful for the republic and the cause of peace."[66]

Stresemann was also impressed. "For the time being I do not think that Hindenburg will be under the influence of any political camarilla, at least not consciously," he wrote in his diary on May 12. If this impression proved correct, then the election "could be a plus, because then one can say that the whole German people, on both the right and the left, are behind the government policy."[67]

In fact, pro-democratic fears in Germany and other Western countries concerning Hindenburg's nomination and election weren't initially borne out. The Reich president disappointed all those who had expected him to shift the government decisively to the right, including in terms of personnel. State Secretary Otto Meissner, who had served under Ebert, and his staff remained in charge of the Reich president's office. "If I take over a company as a captain, I don't throw out the sergeant!" Hindenburg is said to have replied to his DNVP allies who insisted that Meissner be dismissed.[68]

On foreign policy, too, the signs pointed to continuity. On May 19, Stresemann had his first lengthy meeting with Hindenburg and discovered that the Reich president was more positively oriented than he had assumed and indeed was open to the security-pact project with France. No rallying cries demanding that France renounce Alsace-Lorraine escaped his lips, and overall, Stresemann came away from this meeting feeling that he was dealing with a man "who grew up in conservative traditions and makes no secret of them . . . but who thinks constitutionally and intends at any rate to work alongside the government honestly and without ulterior motives." Everything now depended on "not allowing *hasardeurs* to gain influence over him." But after a follow-up meeting on June 9, the foreign minister's verdict was already less favorable. It was, Stresemann noted, "extremely difficult to discuss the intricacies of foreign policy with the Reich president, as he is trapped in certain natural one-sided biases."[69] As it turned out, Hindenburg was to hinder Stresemann's foreign policy in various ways.

Hindenburg's election to the Reich presidency was undoubtedly a turning point in the history of the Weimar Republic. The predemocratic elites from the large East Prussian agricultural estates and the Reichswehr attached great importance to again having one of their own as a head of the state, through whom they had direct access to power. The power Hindenburg possessed thanks to Article 48 of the Weimar Constitution was also crucial. Of course, as the example of the United States had shown, a strong president independent of political parties was not per se a threat.[70] Moreover, Article 48, which Ebert had also made use of, did not necessarily mean automatic transformation of Weimar party democracy into an authoritarian presidential regime. Hindenburg swore an oath to the constitution and obviously felt bound by his word. Nonetheless, unlike Ebert, parliamentary democracy was not close to his heart, as he made clear in conversations with the Bavarian State Premier Held and Bavarian Crown Prince Rupprecht during a summer vacation in 1925. The Weimar Constitution was "simply a fact" and "he had to respect it," Hindenburg declared, only to add "that he by no means regarded it as gospel and could envisage it being gradually dismantled."[71] Thus, from the outset, Hindenburg was keen on using the constitutional possibilities of his office to shift the balance of power from the legislative to the executive. What took place in the spring of 1925 was therefore, as historian Heinrich August Winkler pointedly put it, "nothing less than a tacit constitutional change, a conservative refounding of the republic."[72]

Hindenburg's election was by no means inevitable. If Stresemann had not torpedoed Gessler as a consensus candidate, the Reichswehr minister might have won an absolute majority in the first round of voting. And if the KPD leadership had been willing to compromise its principles in the run-off and urged its supporters to vote for Marx, he might have won the vote, and German history would have taken a different course. The fact was, however, that the victory of the imperial field marshal represented a major defeat for the Weimar Republic.

6

A Dark Day

THE COLLAPSE OF THE FINAL GRAND COALITION

The grand coalition cabinet, June 1928. Sitting, from left: Erich Koch-Weser (Justice), Hermann Müller (Chancellor), Wilhelm Groener (Defense), Rudolf Wissell (Labor). Standing, from left: Hermann Dietrich (Food), Rudolf Hilferding (Finance), Julius Curtius (Economics), Carl Severing (Interior), Theodor von Guérard (Transport and Occupied Territories), Georg Schätzel (Post). Missing is Foreign Minister Gustav Stresemann, who was convalescing in Baden-Baden.

On the evening of December 26, 1929, a conspiratorial meeting—one that would play a central role in determining the fate of the Weimar Republic—convened in the apartment of former General Staff Officer Baron Friedrich Wilhelm von Willisen in Berlin's Charlottenburg district. Present were General Wilhelm Groener, who had replaced Otto Gessler as Reichswehr minister in January 1928; his closest colleague, Colonel Kurt von Schleicher, who had been appointed to head the newly created ministerial office in the Reichswehr Ministry in March 1929; State Secretary Otto Meissner, the head of the Office of the Reich President; and Heinrich Brüning, who had been elected chairman of the Center Party's Reichstag faction a few weeks earlier. After a meal, Schleicher and Meissner came straight to the point, telling Brüning they wanted him to form a presidentially appointed government based on Article 48. President Hindenburg, they declared, wanted to end the governing big-tent or "grand" coalition under Social Democratic Chancellor Hermann Müller and was "under no circumstances" willing to leave the Müller cabinet in office. He expected Brüning to heed his call.

Brüning didn't reject the idea outright but warned against hasty decisions. The grand coalition, he argued, should be allowed to govern until the fall of 1930. Germany didn't have that much time, his interlocutors countered. No concrete agreements had been reached yet, but connections were being made. Groener arranged to take a discreet walk with Brüning through the forest in nearby Potsdam to discuss how things would unfold.[1]

During that conversation, the Reichswehr minister once again made it clear that he saw no future for the Müller cabinet and that everything pointed toward a presidentially appointed government under Brüning. Hindenburg would not be dissuaded from his decision to make him chancellor, and Groener solemnly promised: "I will stand behind you, through thick and thin." Although Brüning remained skeptical that the grand coalition could be terminated that quickly, he assured Groener that he would "never shirk responsibility in a difficult situation for the fatherland." With that, the Reichswehr leadership knew it could count on the centrist in the event of a breakup of the government.[2]

Hindenburg now felt that he was close to achieving the goal he had been pursuing, since taking office, of curtailing the influence of Germany's political parties and parliament and making full use of the constitutional powers of his office. On March 1, 1930, he received Brüning for a confidential discussion, and asked him "whether the Center Party was prepared to support a different government." Brüning replied that his party had an interest in "maintaining the current coalition for a while longer" to get some reforms through the Reichstag. At the same time, he reiterated his willingness not to ignore "any call made out of patriotic conviction."[3] In the spring of 1930, the course seemed to be set for a presidential regime. Another turning point in Weimar history was in the offing.

Surprisingly for many, the Social Democrats had emerged as the clear winners of the Reichstag elections of May 20, 1928, increasing their share of the vote to 29.8 percent—a rise of 3.8 percent over the elections of December 1924. The Social Democrats thus entered the new Reichstag as the strongest parliamentary group by far, with 152 seats. In contrast, the DNVP suffered dramatic losses. Although it remained the second-strongest party with 73 seats, its share of the vote fell from 20.5 to 14.3 percent. The traditional centrist parties also suffered slight declines: The Center Party took 12.1 percent of the vote (down from 13.6); the DVP, 8.7 percent (down from 10.1); the DDP, 4.9 percent (down from 6.3); and the BVP, 3.1 percent (down from 3.7). There was also electoral movement on the extremes. While the KPD earned 10.6 percent of the vote, up from 9 percent, the National Socialists dropped from 3 to 2.8 percent of the vote and sent only twelve deputies to the Reichstag.

The loss of support for the parties of the bourgeois mainstream primarily benefited special-interest splinter groups like the Reich Party of the German Middle Class (Economic Party), the Christian Farmers and Rural Party, and several others. All told, these groups commanded

14.7 percent of the votes. Together with the relatively low voter turnout of 76.6 percent, the drift to special-interest parties was an alarm signal. There was broad unease among the middle classes that the Weimar Republic was turning into a "state for the parties" rather than for the people.[4] But on balance, the democratic camp, and especially the SPD, were rightly satisfied. The years of relative normalcy since 1924 were paying dividends. The *Berliner Tageblatt* newspaper interpreted the election as a sign of the "German people fundamentally turning against nationalist demagoguery and strife and committing strongly to the German republic, whose foes have been utterly defeated."[5] There was every reason to expect further stabilization as long as the Weimar Republic continued its positive economic development and was able to marginalize its extremist foes to the right and left.

In his diary, Victor Klemperer lamented the poor performance of the DDP, for which he and his wife had voted. The election "did so little to change actual conditions," he complained.[6] In fact, the result handed a clear leadership mandate to the SPD, and the party was determined to return to the government, from which it had withdrawn in the fall of 1923. But who should it nominate as its candidate for chancellor? The popular Prussian Minister President Otto Braun, who had won the Prussian state parliamentary elections, also held on May 20, even more convincingly than his colleagues at the national level, was occasionally suggested. A union of these two top offices in one person might have resolved the "dualism" between the Reich and Germany's largest regional state, which had been a smoldering issue throughout the Weimar Republic. Braun knew, however, that Hindenburg would hardly agree to such power being concentrated in his hands. Braun was also in poor health and reluctant to take on an additional burden.[7]

The choice fell to SPD party leader Hermann Müller, who had already served as Reich chancellor for a few months after the Kapp Putsch in March 1920. Müller was not a charismatic politician, nor a rousing speaker, but he was held in high regard in the party and parliamentary group due to his expertise and calm temperament. He was a reluctant candidate. In a letter to Austrian Chancellor Karl Renner, he remarked that he would have preferred it if Otto Braun had been willing.

He would "then have been able to be of the most service to the government as the head of the parliamentary group."[8]

On June 12, Hindenburg charged Müller with forming a government "on the broadest possible basis." Since the parties of the Weimar Coalition—the SPD, the Center Party, and the DDP—had no majority, the only alternative was a grand coalition, as had already existed under Stresemann from August to November 1923. However, negotiations proved unexpectedly difficult. The DVP would take part only if it were also made part of the government in Prussia. Otto Braun, however, had no intention of jeopardizing the stability of his cabinet, with whom he had implemented successful democratic reforms, by including the notoriously unreliable DVP. He sought to get around the DVP's demand for a conjunction of the Reich and Prussian governments with delaying tactics and a vague promise to decide on expanding his coalition in due time.[9]

The parties were also unable to agree on substantive issues such as the additional wealth tax demanded by the SPD. As a result, talks seemed to have reached a dead end before they had even really begun. On the evening of June 22, 1928, Müller informed Hindenburg that his efforts to engineer a grand coalition had failed. Hindenburg immediately authorized him to resume negotiations to form a "smaller" partnership, that is, a reprise of the Weimar Coalition. But since such an alliance would not have commanded a majority, the renewed mandate was probably just a tactical maneuver by Hindenburg to pressure the parties to reach agreement after all.[10]

In this muddled situation, the DVP party chairman and foreign minister, Gustav Stresemann, who was taking a cure at the Bühlerhöhe sanatorium near Baden-Baden, personally intervened. In a telephone call with Müller on June 23, the content of which emerged from a telegram published immediately afterward, he declared that he still considered a grand coalition to be "the best practical option for creating reasonably stable conditions of government." However, instead of attempting to "form it on the basis of an agenda approved in advance by the parliamentary groups," leading "personalities from the parliamentary groups" should reach deals they would take to the Reichstag, where they would stand or fall. "Such a cabinet also reflects the spirit of the constitution of the German Reich, which recognizes only the personal responsibility of Reich ministers, but not the responsibility of parliamentary groups."[11]

Stresemann's intervention caused quite a stir. The press wrote of a "shot fired from Bühlerhöhe." But the fact that the party chairman had effectively presented his parliamentary group with a fait accompli also caused great resentment. The leader of the DVP parliamentary group, Ernst Scholz, already on tense terms with Stresemann, felt duped and initially wanted to prevent Julius Curtius from joining Stresemann as a minister in the Müller cabinet. In the end, he withdrew his objection to joining the government with the proviso that the parliamentary group was "in no way" bound by the cabinet membership of its two ministers to support the government in votes of confidence and no confidence. In a further resolution, the parliamentary group also stated that proper leadership of the party "presupposes constant contact between all those involved in political decisions and with the parliamentary group leader." This was a barely veiled rebuke to party chairman Stresemann.[12]

The Center Party distanced itself from the new government. After failing to get former Chancellor Joseph Wirth named vice-chancellor and to secure an important portfolio such as the Ministry of the Interior, it dispatched its parliamentary group leader Theodor von Guérard to the government as an "observer" only.[13] On June 29, Müller was finally able to present his cabinet. In addition to Stresemann and Curtius as foreign minister and economics minister and Guérard as minister for transport and the occupied territories, it included three Social Democrats: Interior Minister Carl Severing, who had previously headed the corresponding ministry in Prussia, Finance Minister Rudolf Hilferding, who had held that post in the first grand coalition under Stresemann in 1923, and Labor Minister Rudolf Wissell. The DDP provided two ministers: Erich Koch-Weser, who had been minister of the interior from 1919 to 1921, took over the Ministry of Justice; and Hermann Dietrich, the Ministry of Food. The BVP was represented by Reich Postal Minister Georg Schätzel, and the party-unaffiliated Groener remained on as Reichswehr minister.[14]

What became known as the "cabinet of personalities" thus started on shaky ground. With no formal coalition agreement, and the parliamentary groups of the DVP, Center, and BVP declaring that they were not obliged to support the cabinet, the government existed "under the constant Damocles sword of no confidence."[15] For this reason, Müller refrained from calling for an explicit vote of confidence after his government statement on July 3, contenting himself with a motion jointly proposed by the parliamentary groups represented in the cabinet. It read: "The Reichstag approves the declaration of the Reich government and moves on to the agenda." This motion was approved on July 5 by 261 votes to 134 (with 28 abstentions), and the government was able to take up its work.[16] But there was no trace of optimism or spirit of renewal.

It took only a few weeks for the cabinet to be confronted with its first serious domestic political conflict: a dispute over armored cruiser A. Shortly before its demise, the preceding People's Bloc government under Wilhelm Marx had decided to build the warship, which Germany's naval leadership considered indispensable for defending the Baltic coast. However, at the end of March 1928, the second chamber of the German parliament, the Reichsrat, insisted that construction should not begin until the budget situation had been reviewed. In its election campaign, the SPD had fiercely attacked the navy's plans, calling for "food for children instead of armored cruisers."[17]

At the cabinet meeting on August 10, 1928, Groener announced that the finance minister had expressed no objections to beginning construction on the armored ship as planned on September 1, which Hilferding confirmed to the chancellor. The Social Democratic ministers were aware that canceling the project would likely lead to Groener's resignation and trigger a cabinet crisis. They therefore voted to proceed with the warship's construction.[18]

The cabinet decision outraged SPD supporters. Driven by the party rank and file, the Social Democratic parliamentary group introduced a motion in the Reichstag on October 31 to stop the project after all and use the money saved for feeding children. This put the chancellor in a major bind. On November 14, Müller informed his cabinet that the Reich president had told him that "for reasons of state, he was absolutely in favor of the continued construction of the armored ship and was seriously considering resignation if the Reichstag rejected that continued construction."[19]

SPD parliamentarians, however, were of no mind to take the government's difficult situation into consideration. That same day, the parliamentary group refused Müller's request to abstain from voting in the Reichstag and imposed a party-line vote on all deputies, including the chancellor and the SPD ministers.[20] Thus, it came to pass on November 16 that although a majority in the Reichstag rejected the SPD's motion, Müller and the three SPD ministers voted in favor of it—"in a sense expressing no confidence in themselves."[21] This public humiliation dealt a serious blow to the credibility of both the largest governing party and the reputation of parliament. The ridiculous spectacle provided welcome ammunition for those Reichswehr leaders, large-estate owners, and right-wing parties who were already thinking about ways to undermine parliamentary democracy. Stresemann did not have just his own party in mind in February 1929 when he complained during a major speech to his party's central executive committee: "How grotesque is it that, as a result of the parliamentary regime, we have de facto government of parties but at the same time believe we can continually oppose the government that has emerged from those parties?"[22] A pattern of behavior from the German Empire was also at play here. Germany's political parties failed to recognize that in a parliamentary democracy the main dividing line was not, as in a constitutional monarchy, between the government cabinet and the parliament, but between the government as a whole and the opposition.[23]

The dispute over armored cruiser A was not yet settled when the grand coalition had to deal with another far-reaching conflict: a dispute over retirement rules. As part of a drive for better pay, German trade unions terminated the wage agreement with the Northwestern Group of the Iron Industry on November 1, 1928, demanding an hourly raise of fifteen pfennigs. Employers refused to increase wages at all and, after all attempts to reach an agreement had failed, announced on October 13 that there would be mass lockouts effective November 1. On October 26, the arbitrator, Superior Regional Court Councillor Eugen Joetten, the chairman of the Düsseldorf Arbitration Chamber, rendered judgment. It provided for a wage increase of six pfennigs per hour for workers on contract and a supplement of two pfennigs per hour for piecemeal laborers. Metalworkers accepted the result of the arbitration, while employers rejected it. On October 31, Labor Minister Wissell declared the arbitration binding. But employers stuck to their guns and locked out 230,000 workers on November 1. It was the start of the most serious labor conflict of the Weimar Republic.[24]

Employers were obviously trying to set an example and destroy the instrument of compulsory state arbitration, which had been enshrined in law in October 1923. The Federation of German Employers' Associations and the Reich Association of German Industry backed the barons of heavy industry, promising support. But the public was very critical of the employers' attempt to play hardball. The *Frankfurter Zeitung* newspaper wrote: "It must be said with all clarity that sabotaging a binding arbitration judgment by shutting down ironworks is an attack not only on the workers but against a state institution, that is, against the state itself, and therefore represents a revolutionary act of a sort."[25] The plight of the locked-out workers, who were not entitled to unemployment benefits, prompted compassion and a willingness to help, and on November 17, the Reichstag decided by a large majority to provide funds to assist them.

Under pressure from public opinion, industrialists were finally forced to give in. At the cabinet meeting on November 28, Stresemann suggested that employers and employees should "agree on a final mediation action" by a "person of the greatest possible authority." At the suggestion of Curtius, Severing was entrusted with this task.[26] Employers agreed to accept Severing's decision in advance, although trade unions assented only after prolonged hesitation. The lockout ended on December 3, 1928. On December 21, Severing rendered his judgment, which took the form of a classic compromise. The trade unions were to make significant concessions on their wage demands, but in return they received improvements in employees' working hours.

On January 21, 1929, the Reich Labor Court ruled that the provision of the 1923 Arbitration Ordinance that authorized the chairman of the arbitration committees to make arbitration awards on his own was inadmissible. Joetten's judgment from October was thus subsequently declared null and void. Industrialists had won a partial victory, while the Reich minister of labor had suffered a defeat. But the significance of the retirement dispute went beyond these specifics. Rhenish-Westphalian industry had sought open confrontation in the battle of state arbitration, thereby calling into question the Weimar welfare-state compromise. This marked a new era in social and political disputes that did not bode well for the future. The success of the SPD in the Reichstag elections of 1928 had also raised fears among businesses of an expansion of and further burdens from the "trade-union state." Leaders of heavy industry also began to ponder how to force the Social Democrats from power and install a government that would be independent of parliament.[27]

The German business sector wasn't the only segment of society moving rightward. The bourgeois centrist parties were growing more conservative as well. Along with the general spirit of the day, government quarreling and the poor public impression it made may have played a role in the shift. The right wing of the DNVP, which had only grudgingly participated in the preceding People's Bloc governments, was also gaining influence. Electoral defeat in May 1928 had shown that more moderate policies weren't paying off. In October 1928, media mogul Alfred Hugenberg, an extreme nationalist, was elected party chairman to succeed Count Kuno Westarp. He charted a new party course of uncompromising opposition to the Weimar "system." Hugenberg's empire encompassed not only the Scherl publishing house in Berlin and its daily newspapers Der Tag and the Berliner Lokal-Anzeiger but many other companies, ranging from the news agency Telegraphen-Union (TU) to the advertising firm Allgemeine Anzeigen GmbH (AlA) and the cinema studio Universum-Film AG (Ufa). Via his wire services, Hugenberg supplied local newspapers with finished articles, thus greatly influencing many periodicals that weren't officially part of his group. In his maiden speech as party chairman, he declared war on the Weimar Republic: "The day will come when the German people will rise up and shake off all this garbage. But before that, we as a party must also shake off all the garbage today's system has thrown over us."[28]

The Center Party, *the* political association of middle-class centrism and one that was indispensable to the stability of parliamentary democracy, also moved right. The signs of the shift began when the party leadership removed Heinrich Brauns, an experienced expert on social issues, whom Hermann Müller would have liked to retain as minister of labor, from the government. At the party conference in Cologne on December 8, 1928, prelate and church lawyer Ludwig Kaas from Trier was elected to take over from Marx as party chairman. His election reflected the growing influence of conservative clergy. In a speech at the Freiburg Catholic Congress in August 1929, Kaas revealed his true political leanings when he called for "leadership on a grand scale" and demanded that the government seek independence from the "unpredictable contingencies of changes in the parliamentary weather."[29]

The DNVP and the Center Party's shift to the right was outmatched by the KPD's even sharper lurch to the left. The new "general line" was defined at the Sixth World Congress of the Communist International in Moscow in September 1928. It held that the world was in a period of the "final crisis" of capitalism, which opened new perspectives for the proletarian revolution. The "main enemy" was the Social Democratic movement, which, according to the Communist line, was serving as the "last reserve of the bourgeoisie" and had "many points of intersection with the ideology of fascism."[30] The "ultraleft turn" was due not least to the internal power struggles in the Soviet Union between Joseph Stalin and the "right-wing" opposition around Nikolai Bukharin. The general secretary of the Soviet Communist Party relied on the support of the other parties of the Communist International, and Ernst Thälmann was one of his unconditional supporters in Germany. In September 1928, Thälmann was dismissed as chairman of the KPD following a corruption scandal, but he was reinstated after Stalin intervened. Under Thälmann's leadership, the KPD now fully fell into line with Stalin and his ideology.[31]

The KPD's electoral success in the May 1928 election and the party's accompanying martial rhetoric were enough to stir up fears of a revolution among the middle classes. Since the fall of 1928, clashes between the Communist Red Front Fighters' League and the Social Democratic Reich Banner Black-Red-Gold were becoming more common. In their wake, the SPD police chief of Berlin, Karl Friedrich Zörgiebel, banned all Communist meetings and demonstrations that December.

Despite the prohibition, following a call from the party leadership, KPD supporters gathered in Berlin on May 1, 1929, to celebrate the traditional day of working-class struggle. Three days of clashes ensued, during which police brutally attacked demonstrators. Thirty-three people were left dead, 198 were injured—some seriously—and 1,228 arrests were made. Berlin's "Bloody May" of 1929, which was one of the key events of the Weimar Republic, deepened the rift between Communist and Social Democratic members of the working class. Whereas the KPD rank and file had previously attached little credence to the "social fascism" slogan, which defamed the SPD as a peacemaker for fascism in Germany, the events in May suggested that it might have been valid after all. The split in the labor movement would prove disastrous for the further history of the Weimar Republic, because it undermined workers' ability to mount a common defense against the fascists and the German extreme Right in alliance with National Socialism.[32]

Since the end of 1928, Chancellor Müller had been attempting to convert his "cabinet of personalities" into a formal grand coalition. "If we do not achieve secure conditions of government in the Reich, it will mean the bankruptcy of parliamentarianism in the Reich, which was founded on the Weimar Constitution," he warned in a letter to SPD chairman Otto Wels.[33] But it took several more governmental crises—for example, the Center Party withdrew Transport Minister Guérard from the cabinet at the beginning of February 1929 to lend weight to its demand for a redistribution of portfolios—before the path to a coalition agreement became clear. On April 11, 1929, after the parliamentary groups had agreed on a budget for 1929 following laborious negotiations, Koch-Weser handed over the Ministry of Justice to Guérard. The latter was joined in the cabinet by his party colleagues Adam Stegerwald, the chairman of

Berlin's "Bloody May," 1929: After a ban on demonstrations,
there are serious attacks by the police on Communist workers.
Here, officials clear a street in the Neukölln district.

the Christian Trade Unions, as minister of transport and former Chancellor Joseph Wirth as minister for the occupied territories. The cabinet expected that the parliamentary groups would now support its work and that "proposals of fundamental importance would be made and pursued only by mutual agreement," as stated in a declaration drafted by the state secretary in the Reich Chancellery, Hermann Pünder, and approved by all the governing parties.[34] Only then was the grand coalition sealed. Yet it soon became clear just how fragile the new government alliance was.

The dominant topic in German foreign policy in 1929 was a new accord on reparations. The Dawes Plan of 1924 had left open a definitive solution to the issue. In his report of January 1928, American reparations commissioner Parker Gilbert recommended that the total amount of reparations now be set and that Germans be given full responsibility for the collection and transfer of payments without foreign supervision.[35] His ideas were welcomed with open arms by the German government. According to the Dawes Plan, Germany's full annual installment of 2.5 billion Reichsmarks would come due for the first time in 1928–29. But with the economy slowing and the budget tight, Berlin wanted to reduce that burden. Moreover, a resolution to the reparations problem offered the prospect of French troops evacuating the Rhineland early— one of Stresemann's primary goals.

A meeting of the League of Nations in Geneva in September 1928, with Müller standing in for Stresemann, who was ill, decided to set up an expert commission to draw up proposals for a final settlement. In early January 1929, Reichsbank president Hjalmar Schacht was appointed the head of the German delegation. Back in the autumn of 1923, together with then–Finance Minister Hans Luther, Schacht had succeeded in stabilizing the mark, and ever since, he enjoyed a stellar reputation in both domestic and international financial circles. Schacht cofounded the DDP but left the party in 1926, moving closer and closer to German nationalist positions.[36] He was assisted by his second delegate, Albert Vögler, general director of the Vereinigte Stahlwerke steelworks and an influential member of the right wing of the DVP. The deputy delegates were the Hamburg private banker Carl Melchior from Bankhaus Warburg and the managing director of the Reich Association of German Industry, Ludwig Kastl. The composition of the German delegation highlighted the government's interest in involving industrial and banking represen- tatives in the negotiation process. It was a way of shielding the outcome of the commission's work from possible criticism from the right.

The experts began negotiating in Paris on February 9, 1929, under the direction of American Owen D. Young, chairman of the supervi- sory board of the General Electric Company, who had already repre- sented the United States at the 1924 Paris reparations conference. Unlike then, the German delegation now sat at the conference table as an equal partner. The Müller cabinet had refrained from giving it any specific instructions, and Schacht used his negotiating leeway to link proposals for reparations payments with political demands for a revision of Germany's eastern border and the return of German colonies. By mid-April 1929, the negotiations were on the verge of collapse after Schacht responded to an offer made by creditor states with a counteroffer that fell far short of the sums proposed. As a result, foreign investors with-drew large amounts of capital from Germany. The ensuing credit crunch made it clear to the German government that it could not afford for the reparations negotiations to fail. Schacht was forced to back down. Vögler resigned on May 23, explaining that he considered the Allied demands economically impossible.[37]

In the end, on June 7, 1929, the experts signed off on the Young Plan. It foresaw Germany paying reparations until 1988, with annuities rising from 1.7 to 2.4 billion Reichsmarks by 1966 before falling again. Foreign control of German finances was lifted. The Reich government, rather than the reparations agent, was responsible for the transfer of money. A new institution, the Bank for International Settlements, in Basel, was created to handle payments. In the event that it had difficulty meeting its obligations, Germany could turn to an international expert commit-tee responsible for proposing revisions to the payment schedule.

With the Young Plan, Germany regained its full economic policy sovereignty, and the first annuities were significantly lower than under the Dawes Plan, thus providing financial relief. The prospect of having to pay reparations for another fifty-eight years may have been depress-ing, but hardly anyone in the Müller cabinet expected that this would actually happen.[38] At a reception for the German delegation experts on June 14, the chancellor explained that no one could predict what the situation would be in ten to fifteen years, and there was reason to hope that "global economic reason" would prevail from now on. In the mean-time, "the utmost" should be done "to loyally fulfill the terms of the new plan."[39]

At a conference in The Hague in August 1929, Germany's creditors agreed to the experts' plan, but requested revision of details before the reparations issue could be finally settled. Nonetheless, the German del-egation under Stresemann's leadership reaped a huge reward for agree-ing to the Young Plan. On August 30, an agreement was signed on the early evacuation of Rhineland. Entente troops had already withdrawn from the first zone in the winter of 1925–26. Now a second zone was to be evacuated by November 30, 1929, and a third and final zone by June 30, 1930, five years before the deadline set in the Treaty of Versailles. Stresemann was able to claim the agreement as a personal success. In a missive to Reichstag President Paul Löbe, he wrote that the conference in The Hague had concluded a "stage of foreign policy" and enabled Germany to "pursue a generous policy of understanding in the future, free and independent of the eternal battles over the reparations issue and the occupied territory."[40]

As the government had feared, the nationalist Right mobilized opposition to the Young Plan. The duration of the reparation schedule and the still-high annual payments offered them welcome points of attack. On July 9, 1929, at the instigation of, above all, Hugenberg, a "Reich Committee for the German Referendum" was formed. It brought together all right-wing opponents of the Weimar Republic: the Stahlhelm paramilitary militia, the racist Pan-Germanic League, the DNVP, the Reich Rural League, and the Nazi Party. Hitler joined the initiative after it was agreed that the campaign should be directed not only against the Young Plan but also against the so-called lie that Germany was solely to blame for the First World War. For the first time since the failed putsch of 1923 and the Nazis' miserable performance in the May 1928 election, Hitler was able to play a significant role on the political stage, presenting himself as an equal to the national leader of the Stahlhelm, Franz Seldte, DNVP chairman Hugenberg, and Heinrich Class from the Pan-Germanic League.[41]

In mid-September, the Reich Committee published the wording of a public referendum on the "Law to Prevent the Enslavement of the German People," which its initiators called the Freedom Law for short. Its first two points excoriated Germany's "forced admission of guilt" and called on the German government to void the corresponding article in the Treaty of Versailles and demand the immediate and unconditional evacuation of all occupied German territory. Paragraph 3 prohibited the German government from taking on any "new burdens and duties" based on the "war-guilt lie." This also included the proposals made by

Bis in die dritte Generation

müßt ihr fronen!

Wehrt Euch! Geht zum Volksbegehren!

Demagogic campaign: The nationalist Right mobilizes against the Young Plan of June 1929. The campaign ended with the failed referendum of December 22, 1929. (Poster from October 1929.)

the Paris conference of experts, which would, in turn, have negated the Young Plan. The demagogic high point came in the law's fourth paragraph, which branded "Reich chancellors, Reich ministers, and agents of the Reich" traitors who should receive prison sentences of no less than two years. The category "agents of the Reich" included Hindenburg, an honorary member of the Stahlhelm, which put Seldte in a tricky situation. To exempt the Reich president from this stricture, the wording was changed to "Reich chancellors, Reich ministers, and *their* agents."[42] For his part, Hindenburg declared in a letter to Müller that he regarded paragraph 4 to be "an unprofessionally emotional and personal attack" that he regretted and condemned."[43]

On September 21, the Reich Committee submitted the referendum to Severing for approval, which he gave. According to the constitution, national referenda required the signatures of at least one-tenth of eligible voters to be admissible. Yet despite unrestrained agitation by the Hugenberg press, initiators barely managed to achieve the necessary quorum, with 10.2 percent.

The Reichstag debated the Freedom Law in the final week of November. As generally expected, it was rejected. The DNVP parliamentary group was divided, which caused a stir. Of its seventy-three members, only fifty-three voted in favor of the law—an unmistakable warning to Hugenberg not to overdo his hard-line approach. In early December, twelve deputies left the party, including well-known parliamentarians such as the former Reich Minister Walter von Keudell; large landowner Hans Schlange-Schöningen; the managing director of the Association of Commercial Employees, Walter Lambach; retired Lieutenant Captain Gottfried Treviranus; and historian Otto Hoetzsch. They founded a "German National Working Group," from which the People's Conservative Association emerged in January 1930 after merging with the Rural Popular (Landvolk) Party. Count Westarp also resigned his position as parliamentary group leader.[44]

Following the Reichstag's rejection of the legislation, the referendum went ahead. For it to pass, turnout had to be more than 50 percent (21 million votes), with a majority voting yes. However, on December 22, 1929, only 5.8 million, or 13.8 percent of eligible voters, voted in favor of the bill. This was a clear failure and "a terrible blunder by Hugenberg," Pünder noted.[45] The political Right had not succeeded in turning the Young Plan into an issue that could mobilize masses of dissatisfied voters. But Hitler benefited from the initiative. It had made the Nazi chairman socially acceptable to conservative circles and, with the help of the Hugenberg press, he had been able to attract national attention. "The Munich coup apostle has notched his first real success," wrote *Vorwärts*. "He has hitched [the DNVP] to his wagon and is driving the black-white-red chariot, cracking his whip, in the direction of his wider aims."[46] During the referendum campaign, the Nazi Party had been able to portray itself as a right-wing protest party with far better organization and a greater willingness to take action than its conservative allies.

It had already become evident from the state elections in the fall of 1929 that the National Socialists were gaining ground. In Baden, on October 27, they took 7 percent of the vote, and in Thuringia on December 8, a still higher 11.3 percent. In January 1930, the Nazis entered into a coalition with the DVP and DNVP and occupied a key position in the regional government of Thuringia, with Wilhelm Frick, one of the ringleaders of the Hitler Putsch of November 1923, named Thuringian minister of the interior and national education.[47]

Amid the campaign against the Young Plan, the man who stood more than anyone for reconciliation with Germany's former enemies died. Gustav Stresemann had worn out his already fragile health fighting internal party rivals and the intra- and extraparliamentary opponents of his policy of international understanding. He suffered a stroke on the night of October 3, then another, fatal one early the next morning. "It's an irreplaceable loss, the consequences of which cannot be foreseen," noted Kessler, who was in Paris at the time. He described the reaction of the French: "Everyone is talking about it, the hairdressers, the restaurant waiters, the chauffeurs, the newspaper women. . . . The whole of Paris perceives his death as the next thing to a national calamity. . . . It is almost as though the greatest French statesman had died. The mourning is universal and genuine."[48] Who in 1923 would have thought such a reaction possible?

The democratic camp in Germany felt much the same way. Wolff praised Stresemann in the *Berliner Tageblatt* as a "German statesman" and a "courageous and intelligent realist," who had "restored Germany from its foreign policy isolation to its rightful place among the nations."[49] In *Die Weltbühne*, Carl von Ossietzky praised him as a "unique talent in Germany" who "towered so high above the swollen-headed heroes of the factions" and could hold his own with "the best diplomatic minds of the present day" at the international negotiating table.[50] At Stresemann's funeral on October 6, hundreds of thousands of Berliners paid their last respects. "Sunday was dominated by Stresemann's funeral," wrote Betty Scholem to her son Gershom, who had emigrated to Palestine. "Germany has a lot of misfortune with its statesmen. There was one who did his job well and died at the age of 50."[51] It is difficult to say how things would have turned out if Stresemann had lived longer. In any case, his death dealt a huge blow to the Müller government.

As a staunch advocate of the grand coalition, Stresemann had succeeded in keeping together the divergent forces in the government alliance. The SPD chancellor had thus lost his most important supporter, a virtuoso in handling parliamentary business. The death of its chairman was also an irreplaceable loss for the DVP. He had led the party from opposing Weimar democracy to being part of the government. In the last years of his life, however, he had found it increasingly difficult to get the DVP's parliamentary group to follow his centrist policies. He occasionally toyed with the idea of founding a new middle-class party together with Erich Koch-Weser from the DDP. After his death, the right wing of the DVP, which had made life so difficult for Stresemann and was dominated by industrialists, finally gained the upper hand, as was reflected by the election of Ernst Scholz to party chairmanship as Stresemann's successor. Curtius became foreign minister and was in turn replaced as economics minister by Paul Moldenhauer, a Cologne professor of insurance policy and board member at IG Farben. He had been a member of the Reichstag since 1920 but had previously attracted little attention.[52]

Three weeks after Stresemann's death, on October 24, 1929, came "Black Friday" (actually a Thursday). The collapse of the New York Stock Exchange and the prelude to the Great Depression hit Germany particularly hard, since the economic upswing of the "golden years" of the Weimar Republic had largely been financed with foreign, primarily American, loans. After the stock market crash, US banks were forced to reclaim their short-term investments, accelerating the downturn of the German economy.

A shadow had already befallen the economy in the second half of 1928. Company profits dropped, investment dried up, and bankruptcies increased significantly. After a harsh winter, the number of unemployed climbed for the first time to over 3 million in February 1929. And it remained relatively high, at 1.25 million, in July.[53]

With the rise in joblessness, the Reich Institute of Job Mediation and Unemployment Protection, which had been created in July 1927 as a major extension to the German social insurance system, encountered grave difficulties. Those with compulsory insurance had a legal entitlement to unemployment benefits. But contributions were not allowed to exceed a maximum of 3 percent of people's basic wages and were to be paid equally by employers and employees. The revenue thus generated was sufficient to support approximately eight hundred thousand unemployed and, in months of crisis, an "emergency fund" that could temporarily cover a further six hundred thousand. But when funds were insufficient to cover need, the Reich had to step in with loans, with no cap on the sums involved.[54]

The spike in unemployment in the winter of 1928–29 thus quickly developed into a politically explosive problem. With tax revenues falling because of the incipient economic downturn, Reich finances became increasingly precarious. In March 1929, Finance Minister Hilferding struggled to raise the necessary subsidies for the Reich Institute, ultimately having to enlist the help of a banking consortium.

Without unemployment insurance reform, there was no way to restructure the Reich's finances. No one doubted that. But opinions differed on the proper remedy. Whereas employers advocated tax relief and a reduction in social spending, trade unions opposed any reduction in benefits and favored increasing unemployment insurance contributions. The conflict, which soon escalated into a matter of principle, inevitably made itself felt within the grand coalition government. The DVP supported employers' demands, while the SPD, together with trade unions, vehemently rejected them.[55] The contradictions within the coalition could hardly be resolved; that much was clear early on. The impasse prompted anti-democracy forces in industrial circles, right-wing parties, and the Reichswehr to intensify their search for ways to govern without parliamentary majorities.

When the governing cabinet discussed the problem of unemployment insurance for the first time on May 6, 1929, the two sides clashed severely. Labor Minister Wissell demanded that contributions be immediately increased from 3 to 4 percent, arguing that a "systematic reform of unemployment insurance" could be undertaken only once a government inquiry had collected sufficient information. In contrast, Economics Minister Curtius opposed increasing contributions for the time being. He proposed that an immediate program for the reform should be drawn up, and only thereafter should the question be clarified of "what resources are required to finance the insurance in its revised form."[56]

In June 1929, at Wissell's request, the cabinet decided to appoint a commission of experts to try to mediate, but the attempt to bridge the gap failed. Instead, the fronts hardened. The Müller cabinet found itself under increased pressure from the business community. At the end of August 1929, the Federation of German Employers' Associations declared an increase in contributions "incompatible with the current situation of the economy and the Reich." Rather, costs had to be cut so that the Reich Institute could be restructured. One month later, the Reich Association of German Industry followed suit, demanding that reform of unemployment insurance be carried out in a form "that excludes a burden on the Reich budget." The association insisted, "If a loan cannot be avoided in special cases, the Reich government must ensure that the loan is covered by reducing benefits."[57]

At the beginning of October 1929, after hard-bitten negotiations with the parliamentary groups, the government finally proposed an amendment to the Unemployment Insurance Act, intended to eliminate benefits abuse. But it skirted the controversial issue of increasing contributions. Just one day before his death, Stresemann was able to persuade his parliamentary group to abstain from voting so that the amendment would pass in the Reichstag. The legislation was ratified on October 3 by 237 votes to 155 (with 40 abstentions). Once again, a serious government crisis had been averted, but the issue had only been postponed. The conflict continued to simmer and necessarily came to a boil again as the economic situation deteriorated following the crash of the New York Stock Exchange.[58]

Throughout the fall and winter of 1929, the financial situation of the Reich became increasingly precarious. Shortfalls in tax revenue and rising unemployment insurance subsidies tore gaping holes in the budget.

By the end of October, the Reich had 1.2 billion Reichsmarks in outstanding debts. Within this drama, the financial relief promised by the Young Plan was just a drop in the ocean. But Germany had no chance of consolidating its finances, anyway, until the agreement was sealed. Against this backdrop, Hilferding had increasing trouble securing loans to close the budget deficit. Since August, he and State Secretary Johannes Popitz had been working hard to obtain a long-term foreign loan from the American bank Dillon, Read & Co., which had already helped the Reich out of a financial crisis in June 1929.[59] They conducted their negotiations behind the back of Reichsbank president Schacht, who did not miss the chance to bring about a test of strength. That was hardly a surprise. Since the Hague Conference in August 1929, Schacht had distanced himself from the government, which he accused not only of having an unsound financial policy but also of being too accommodating toward Germany's creditors. At the end of November, Pünder wrote about Schacht in his diary: "Now he's running around everywhere saying that the Reich government is ruining his beautiful Young Plan by continuing to make new concessions."[60]

On December 4, the cabinet convened for a debate. Schacht began by declaring that he had "absolutely no intention of interfering in [the] cabinet's political decisions," but immediately attacked the state's conduct of its finances. Expenditures had to be cut, and if they weren't, the Reichsbank would refuse to help in raising new loans, and he would put his criticism before the public "in an appropriate form."[61]

The very next day, he made good on that thinly veiled threat. In a memorandum leaked to the press, he complained that the Young Plan had been "adulterated" following the Paris conference of experts. At the time, Schacht said, he had made his signature conditional on the Reich government getting its finances in order and taking measures to strengthen the economy before the treaty was accepted. But "nothing at all has happened," he complained. The budget deficit had not been eliminated. On the contrary, shortfalls were increasing and could be covered only by new taxes, thus further burdening businesses in particular. For this reason, Schacht said, he must "emphatically reject being held responsible for the implementation of the Young Plan."[62]

The memorandum had a massive impact. Never had a Reichsbank president attacked government policy like this. "In Spanish-speaking countries, what the president of the Reichsbank has done is called a *pronunciamento*," wrote Carl von Ossietzky in *Die Weltbühne*. "A general issues an ultimatum, and the government has to accept it or fall on its sword."[63] Pünder noted, "The indignation in the cabinet is huge, especially since Schacht is stabbing the government in the back like this in the middle of negotiations."[64]

In a statement on December 6, the government condemned Schacht for taking to the public sphere, calling it "an incomprehensible violation of the duty to show consideration for the authority of the state." At the same time, it announced that it would be submitting a "comprehensive financial plan" to the Reichstag the following week.[65]

On December 9, Hilferding presented the details of that plan to the cabinet. By significantly reducing direct taxes, it went a long way toward meeting the wishes of the business community. In return, Moldenhauer agreed to increase unemployment insurance contributions from 3 to 3.5 percent as of January 1. But the cabinet deal did not mean that the parties were on the same page. The SPD was anything but enthusiastic about the business-friendly plans, and the DVP parliamentary group opposed increasing unemployment contributions. One critic declared that "the only option might be to leave the government." However, in the meeting with the parliamentary group leaders on December 11, Müller insisted that the plans be "accepted unchanged." If the parliamentary groups could not reach an agreement, the government would go before the Reichstag "to bring about the decision in open battle."[66]

Another serious government crisis seemed imminent. There was a frantic back-and-forth of cabinet and parliamentary group meetings. When Müller issued his government statement on December 12, he couldn't be sure of the coalition partners' approval. Finally, on the morning of December 14, a compromise, again drafted by Pünder, was agreed upon: "The Reichstag approves the statement presented by the Reich government and trusts that the government's financial plans will be implemented in accordance with the basic principles announced by the government, subject to the final formulation of the individual laws."[67]

In the decisive session on December 14, the Reichstag passed a vote of confidence by 222 votes to 156 (with 22 abstentions). Of the DVP MPs, 22 voted in favor, 14 against. Twenty-eight SPD MPs remained absent from the vote. Once more, the fissures in the coalition had been plastered over. But the only actual interest the DVP had in the coalition was preventing its collapse before the Young Plan could be accepted.

Anyone who had hoped that Schacht would give in now was mistaken. On December 16, he increased the pressure on the government, declaring to the Reich president and the Reich chancellor that he did not consider the emergency financial measures to be sufficient, and demanding, in what approached an ultimatum, that a sum of 500 million Reichsmarks be included for debt repayment in the 1930 budget.[68] This put the cabinet in a tight spot. If Schacht refused to provide a bridging loan, the Reich could become insolvent. Ultimately, the government had no choice but to accede to Schacht's request. On December 19, the coalition pledged to immediately introduce the bill to the Reichstag on a repayment fund to cover the Reich's outstanding debt of 450 million Reichsmarks. Parliamentarians passed the legislation on December 22. That day, the government received the loan it needed from a domestic banking consortium led by the Reichsbank.[69]

In the previous days, Müller had come close to giving up and resigning as chancellor. After the crisis, Pünder noted: "The scariest thing was that only a few people suspected what was imminent. Thank God the great danger is now finally over."[70] But the government had only bought itself some breathing space, and it had lost another important cabinet member. Finance Minister Hilferding was tired of Schacht constantly impinging upon his authority and had tendered his resignation to Müller on December 20. His work had been disrupted by "external interference," Hilferding complained, so he could no longer continue.[71] The remark was directed against not only Schacht but the DVP as well. Hilferding's deputy Popitz also left. Hilferding was succeeded by Moldenhauer, while the Ministry of Economics was taken over by the Social Democrat Robert Schmidt, who had already held that office in several cabinets.[72]

Toward the end of 1929, the industrialists stepped up their attacks on the grand coalition. On December 12, the Reich Association of German Industry (RDI) presented a memorandum with the telling title "Rise or Decline." RDI managing director Ludwig Kastl and lignite industrialist and member of the RDI executive committee Paul Silverberg were the men behind the memo. "The German economy is at a crossroads," it read. "If we do not finally succeed in changing course and turning around our economic, financial, and social policies, then the decline of the German economy is sealed." Among other things, the RDI called for a far-reaching withdrawal of the state from the economy; limits on social spending, above all by reforming unemployment insurance; a reduction in corporate taxes; and a veto for the government against spending increases ratified by the Reichstag. All these measures would serve, the RDI claimed, to "put an end to the progressive decomposition of the German economic corpus."[73]

For the chemical magnate Carl Duisberg, the chairman of the RDI, it was clear that time had run out on the grand coalition. "We cannot avoid the fact that we must have fundamental change, an overturning of the whole system," he declared to the association's managing directors' conference at the beginning of December 1929. "And that would be the most important thing we can achieve—a completely different capitalist, and not socialist, direction."[74] The obvious goals were to relieve Germany of the burdens of the welfare state, force the SPD from the government, and further transform the country's parliamentary democracy into an authoritarian system.

Advocates of a radical change from the grand coalition were also gaining momentum in the DVP. One of its Reichstag deputies, Erich von Gilsa—a former aide to Gustav Noske—maintained close contact with industrialist Paul Reusch, chairman of the Gutehoffnungshütte mining and machine-building conglomerate, regularly reporting to him about internal party and parliamentary group developments—for example, a meeting of the right-wing DVP critics of the coalition on January 24, 1930, at which it was decided to "accelerate a change in party policy." To this end, they had agreed on a platform that included the main demands of the RDI memorandum for lowering taxes and reforming unemployment insurance. "If the Social Democrats don't agree to the stipulation, they must either leave the coalition or the DVP must topple Chancellor Müller's government."[75]

Stresemann's successor, Ernst Scholz, also took this line, working toward the end of the grand coalition from the turn of the year 1929–30. In early February, Gilsa told Reusch of the party chairman's informing him, in confidence, that once the Young Plan had been adopted, "domestic matters should be put in order with the greatest acceleration." Scholz intended to "issue the cabinet an ultimatum to make legally binding commitments to financial and tax reform." In doing so, he was "consciously working toward a break with Social Democratic ideas." To this end, he had already contacted the chairman of the Center Party, Heinrich Brüning, and a moderate group of German nationalists around Gottfried Treviranus, who had split from the intransigent Hugenberg-led DNVP at the beginning of December 1929.[76]

The Reichswehr leadership and the Reich president's entourage had long been pursuing precisely these plans. Kurt von Schleicher—who maintained friendly relations with Hindenburg's son Oskar, his former regimental comrade—played a key role. At the turn of 1926–27, Schleicher had already suggested to the Reich president that if a right-wing coalition with the DNVP could not be arranged, he should appoint a "government of his confidence without consulting the parties and regardless of their wishes" and "arm it with the dissolution order" that would give it "all the constitutional possibilities to obtain a majority in parliament."[77] By the spring of 1929, Schleicher—now the appointed head of the ministerial office of the Reichswehr Ministry—was discussing with Brüning the concept of an autocratic presidential government: "The Reich president sees the danger of all domestic and foreign policy getting stuck in the mire," Schleicher said. "He's determined, together with the Reichswehr and the new forces in parliament, to put things in order before his death." When Brüning asked whether the parliament would be involved, Schleicher replied: "The Reich president will not violate the constitution, but he would send parliament home for a while when the moment is right and put things in order during this time with the help of Article 48." [78]

In the winter of 1929, as the economic situation deteriorated and the conflicts within the grand coalition intensified, the Reichswehr leadership's plans for a deparliamentarization and authoritarian transformation of the Weimar Constitution took concrete shape. The meeting between Groener, Schleicher, Brüning, and Meissner on December 26, recounted at the beginning of this chapter, got the ball rolling. Schleicher described what made Brüning the military's preferred candidate to lead a presidentially appointed cabinet. He was a man "of conservative attitude," an "experienced politician and nationally minded former front-line soldier." The right-wing parties "would not be fundamentally opposed to him," and he "also enjoyed the trust of the Reichswehr." [79]

In early January 1930, Groener expressed his satisfaction with the progress of the exploratory talks. His "cardinal in politics" Schleicher had done "excellent work behind the scenes and laid the groundwork for future progress." [80] On January 15, Hindenburg received Westarp, who had resigned as leader of the DNVP parliamentary group in December in a dispute with Hugenberg, for a strictly confidential meeting, asking whether there was any prospect of "the DNVP directly or indirectly supporting" a government he might potentially form. He had put the same question to Hugenberg on January 6 but had received a curt no. Hindenburg was concerned that "the DNVP would act to scuttle the formation of an antiparliamentary and anti-Marxist government formation" and that "there would be no break with governing with the Social Democrats." Westarp expressed his private opinion that the DNVP should support a "Hindenburg cabinet" governing on the basis of Article 48. However, he was very doubtful whether Hugenberg and a party majority could be won over to such a course: "Hugenberg is currently very firm in his policy in the field and especially among the leading institutions, the party executive, etc."

In a subsequent discussion with Westarp, Meissner once again defined the structure of the planned presidential cabinet: "(a) antiparliamentary, that is, without coalition negotiations and agreements; (b) anti-Marxist—in his view it was also absolutely necessary for the sake of the economy and finances to eliminate Social Democratic influence, at least in the near future." Even though there was no chance of the DNVP participating, Meissner emphasized, it was important for the party to "internally approve of the cabinet and expressed as much publicly and in the press."[81] Hindenburg's state secretary was aware of the journalistic power of the Hugenberg group and wanted to enlist it for his cause.

On January 3, 1930, the second Hague Conference convened to finally approve the Young Plan, which had been negotiated in August 1929. The atmosphere was tense, as the German right-wing campaign and Schacht's potshots had increased creditor nations' fears that Germany could evade its obligations under a new conservative government. As a result, there was considerable debate about whether to insert a sanctions clause to prevent this. Schacht once again stirred up trouble, declaring on January 13 that the Reichsbank could participate in the Bank for International Settlements (BIS) only if the alleged "falsifications" of the original submission by the commission of experts were reversed. Moldenhauer had to pledge to enact specific legislation to ensure that the Reichsbank took part in the BIS to avoid a scandal. Laws to enact the Young Plan were signed on January 20 and approved by Müller's cabinet on January 30. Now it was time for the reparations agreement to clear the parliamentary hurdle.[82]

But once again, unexpected difficulties arose. Two days earlier, on January 28, the parliamentary leadership of the Center Party had decided, at Brüning's suggestion, to inform Müller that it would not vote for the legislation "unless the government proposes and obtains approval for measures in good time to ensure reform to Germany's finances before the Young Plan is adopted."[83] The idea was not yet to break up the grand coalition, but rather to give it one last chance. "The renovation was the test case; without it, this government alliance could not survive," historian Heinrich August Winkler has written.[84]

For Müller, the drive to link the Young Plan and the financial and tax reform could not have come at a more inopportune time. At the cabinet meeting on January 30, he raised "serious concerns" that taking the Center's demand into account would lead to a "considerable delay" in the ratification of the Hague Agreement. This was "a great danger, because the longer the negotiations dragged on, the greater and more threatening the pressure would grow from those quarters that wanted to reject of the laws."[85] In the meeting with the party leaders on February 7, however, Brüning refused to yield: "Budgetary restructuring must not be delayed until the Young Plan has been adopted. After the Young laws are passed, it will probably no longer be possible to reach the agreement absolutely necessary between the parties. The resulting situation would be extremely dangerous."[86] Brüning failed to say a word about the plans to end the coalition and install a "Hindenburg cabinet" with himself at its head.

Despite the financial relief provided by the Young Plan, the budget presented by Moldenhauer at the beginning of February foresaw a record deficit of around 700 million Reichsmarks, 250 million of which was caused by the unemployment insurance subsidy. The parliamentary groups debated how to cover the shortfall throughout February but failed to reach agreement. The DVP vigorously rejected the SPD's proposal of increasing the contribution from 3.5 to 4 percent and raising direct taxes. The idea of an "emergency sacrifice" for people on fixed salaries was bandied about for a while, but although even Hindenburg warmed to it, the DVP wouldn't budge. On March 2, the party's parliamentary group issued a resolution calling for significant relief for the economy and "a restructuring of unemployment insurance while avoiding any further increase in direct taxes." It was clear that Scholz and the party's right wing were prepared to risk a break with the grand coalition.[87]

"The general expectation is that the government will resign," noted Pünder on March 3.[88] But two days later, the unexpected took place, as the ministers agreed on proposals to balance the 1930 budget. Moldenhauer made the most important concession on unemployment insurance and authorized the board of the Reich Institute to increase contributions from 3.5 to 4 percent, pending approval by the majority of employer and employee representatives on the board. In return, the Social Democratic ministers agreed to an austerity program, to be drawn up by the Ministry of Finance, "which will create the basis for a tax reduction and keep running expenditures in the 1931 regular budget below 1930 levels."[89]

The response to the compromise was mixed. The business-friendly *Deutsche Allgemeine Zeitung* lamented: "The real winner is again the SPD. It has once more prevented finance reform, especially of unemployment insurance, and imposed the costs of the Marxist spending economy on the business community." The liberal *Frankfurter Zeitung*, on the other hand, expressed the suspicion that "all those forces working to break up the current coalition, less for objective than for personal reasons, are concentrating their efforts on the DVP, sending the party a storm of telegrams from the countryside and applying external pressure to force the parliamentary group to reject the government."[90]

And in fact, on March 6, despite Moldenhauer's threat to resign, the DVP parliamentary group did reject the key points of the compromise. Moreover, the large industrial organizations protested the next day that the plans presented "didn't align with the necessity of a financial and economic policy aimed at reviving the economy and reducing unemployment."[91] Carl Duisberg told Moldenhauer that should he resign due to the DVP's rejection of the proposals, he would "by no means lose the business community's confidence—on the contrary, you'll be even more assured of it."[92] The message could not have been clearer. Big business wanted an end to the grand coalition.

And that wasn't all. On March 7, Schacht stepped down as Reichsbank president—a move designed to increase the pressure on the Müller government. But this time he had overplayed his hand. He had lost a lot of goodwill due to his obstructionism over the preceding few months. "Schacht has been a dead man for quite some time," noted Pünder. "He's left behind scorched earth everywhere." The cabinet immediately accepted Schacht's resignation, and the general council of the Reichsbank elected former Chancellor Hans Luther as his successor on March 11.[93]

All that prevented the forces pushing for a presidentially appointed government from making the break immediately was the need to pass

the Young Plan legislation through the Reichstag. After that, they calculated, the SPD would no longer be required. Nonetheless, the Center
Party still made its support conditional on the link it had proposed with
the budget in late January 1930. To break the deadlock, Hindenburg
summoned Brüning on March 11 and assured him that if the parties
didn't reach a budget agreement, he would make use of all "constitutional possibilities," including, if necessary, Article 48, to enact fiscal
reform at the beginning of the new financial year on April 1. Brüning saw
this assurance from the Reich president, as he explained in a parliamentary group, as a "huge success for the Center Party," which fulfilled the
end of the proposed linkage,[94] and the parliamentary group decided by a
wide majority to vote for the Young Plan laws. On March 12, in the third
reading, the Reichstag adopted the legislation 265 votes to 192 (with 3
abstentions). Hindenburg signed the treaty the following day.

The Reichswehr leadership was surprised and annoyed when it
learned from the president's office that Hindenburg had dangled the
prospect of using emergency presidential decrees to preserve the Müller
government. No effort was now spared to persuade the Reich president to change his mind. Groener visited Hindenburg on March 11
and apparently succeeded in bringing him back into line. In any case,
senior government councillor Erwin Planck, Schleicher's liaison with the
Reich Chancellery, wrote in a confidential letter to his wife on March
14: "Schleicher is now very close to the old man again."[95] On March
18, Reusch's informant Gilsa was able to report that Hindenburg had
refused, "at the instigation of Groener and Schleicher," to provide the
government with the powers under Article 48 or to pressure the two
DVP ministers Moldenhauer and Curtius to remain in the cabinet.[96] The
die was finally cast.

As if to confirm that fact, Hindenburg sent Müller a letter on March
18 in which he brusquely demanded that Müller immediately under-
take "an effective financial aid campaign" for the struggling agricultural estates in Germany's east.[97] For his eightieth birthday, on October
2, 1927, German businesspeople had given Hindenburg the Neudeck
estate in East Prussia, and ever since, he had always been receptive to
the interests of agriculture. Given the extremely tight financial situation

in the spring of 1930, advocating so vigorously for such state aid injected even more conflict into the grand coalition. With reference to Hindenburg's letter, a satisfied Meissner informed Schleicher on March 19: "This is the first stage on the path to your desired outcome! It's also the foundation for our best option, a Hindenburg leadership."[98]

The following day, Hans Redlhammer, legation councillor in the Foreign Ministry, told Curtius of learning "from an absolutely reliable source" that the Reich president intended to appoint Brüning chancellor after the expected failure of the negotiations on financial reform. Preparation for a "Hindenburg cabinet," Redlhammer said, had "already progressed far enough . . . that a rapid formation of the new government could be expected."[99] On March 21, Brüning commissioned senior government councillor Erwin Planck to draw up a proposal for the composition of the new cabinet. On March 22, Planck wrote to his wife: "My cabinet list for Brüning has turned out excellently and should be acceptable. May God grant that it becomes a reality."[100]

Basically, all that those pulling the strings now needed to do was to engineer a way to blame the Social Democrats for the breakup of the grand coalition. At the DVP's party conference in Mannheim on March 21 and 22, Scholz struck an unusually moderate tone. While accusing the SPD of pursuing "fundamentally anticapitalist policies," he also stated that "governing against the will of or even just without the Social Democrats is hardly possible in the long term." Scholz must have learned from Curtius that the formation of a presidential cabinet under Brüning's chancellorship was imminent, so his conciliatory speech was, in the words of one historian, "nothing more than a tactical maneuver with the aim of transferring culpability for the intended rupture of the grand coalition to the Social Democrats."[101] A party conference reaffirmed the substance of what the Reichstag parliamentary group had decided on March 2, ruling out any compromise on the issue of unemployment insurance.

At a party leaders' meeting on March 25, the two parties on the right and left wings of the coalition clashed again. Scholz insisted that he could agree to increase unemployment insurance contributions above

3.5 percent only after an "internal reform" of the Reich Institute, that is, a reduction in benefits for the unemployed. For the SPD, benefit cuts were out of the question, and it also resisted the DVP's demand for tax cuts in the 1931 budget. At the end of the meeting, Müller declared that he wanted to give the parliamentary groups more time for consultations, while cautioning that, if there was no agreement the next day, "the Reich cabinet will convene immediately and make the decisions required by the parliamentary situation."[102] The chancellor seems already to have known at this point what Brüning had told the parliamentary group leadership of the Center Party on March 26: "The Reich president will not give this cabinet the powers contained in Article 48."[103]

The irreconcilable positions remained entrenched on March 26, so Müller issued the party leaders a new deadline, postponing the debate until the following day. But by then, he stressed, "the final decision has to be made."[104] The designated chancellor of the "Hindenburg cabinet," Brüning, was at pains to avoid the appearance that he had not done his all to save the grand coalition. On March 27, together with DDP parliamentarian Oscar Meyer, he submitted a compromise proposal that essentially would have postponed the particularly contentious issue of increasing unemployment insurance contributions. Brüning put his idea up for discussion at the party leaders' meeting on the morning of March 27, and they decided to give the parliamentary groups the opportunity to comment on it. At the cabinet meeting, which began at twelve noon, all ministers except for Labor Minister Wissell agreed to the compromise.[105] In the afternoon, the majority of the DVP parliamentary group also came out in favor of Brüning's proposal. The buck was passed when the SPD parliamentary group, which behaved just as Brüning and his allies hoped they would, rejected the compromise almost unanimously.[106]

At 5 p.m., the grand coalition cabinet convened for its final meeting. Moldenhauer stated that the government no longer had "sufficient backing in the Reichstag" and that the only option was therefore for it to step down. Interior Minister Severing pleaded for the government to face the Reichstag "in open battle." When Meissner, who was also present, was asked whether the Reich president would give the cabinet the powers under Article 48 if the government lost a vote of confidence in the

Reichstag, Hindenburg's confidant made a statement that, while con-
voluted, made it perfectly clear the government could no longer count
on support of this kind. The meeting adjourned, and when the meeting resumed at 7 p.m., Moldenhauer declared that his position had not
changed. Müller had no alternative other than to admit that the cabinet's
resignation was unavoidable and that he would "immediately submit"
the decision to dissolve the coalition to the Reich president.[107]

"The Müller cabinet has been toppled—the second attempt in the German Republic to govern with a grand coalition has failed," commented
editor in chief Fritz Klein in the *Deutsche Allgemeine Zeitung* newspaper.
"We are facing a political phase that can bring a turning point and, we
believe, will do so far beyond parliament and the coalition politics of the
Reich, if the men of the hour are found."[108]

The *Frankfurter Zeitung*, on the other hand, spoke of a "black day"
for the Weimar Republic and expressed incomprehension at the Social
Democrats' failure to compromise: "Have they considered what this
could mean for our entire domestic political development, for the future
of democracy in Germany? Because now everything is gloomy and
uncertain."[109] The *Berliner Tageblatt* seconded that opinion, blaming
the SPD for the resignation of the government: "More precisely, it is
the Social Democratic minister of labor, Wissell, who brought down the
cabinet."[110] The *Vossische Zeitung* also singled out Wissell for criticism:
"As understandable as it is that the Social Democratic minister for social
policy would defend the achievements of unemployment insurance, it's
difficult to understand why a member of the Reich cabinet seemingly
closed his mind to the higher general political interests."[111]

There was even criticism from the ranks of the SPD itself. In the
eyes of Prussian State Premier Otto Braun, the SPD had made a serious
mistake in foregoing power: "You can't influence the direction of the carriage if you're running alongside it," he told his personal adviser Herbert
Weichmann. "You have to stay in the driver's seat."[112] Former Finance
Minister Hilferding had very harsh words for the SPD parliamentary
group in the magazine *Die Gesellschaft*, which he edited. The fear that

there would be a split in the autumn anyway did not justify taking "such a serious step," he argued, quipping, "It's no good committing suicide for fear of death." On a more fundamental level, Hilferding predicted that if parliament and the parties failed in their basic task of forming and supporting a functioning government, then the balance of power would shift in favor of the Reich president. The real danger for the future of German parliamentarianism came not from outside, he realized, but from within: "Avoiding this danger was always a compelling reason for the Social Democrats to take responsibility in difficult situations." [113]

The breakup of the grand coalition on March 27, 1930, was undoubtedly a major turning point in the history of the Weimar Republic. It marked the last time a government would be based on a parliamentary majority. The dissolution of the Weimar Republic had begun.[114] Certainly, the tactical ineptitude of the SPD had contributed to the coalition's failure, but the true responsibility lay with others, first and foremost the DVP and its industrialist backers. Since Stresemann's death, the moderate supporters of a coalition with the Social Democrats in the party had lost more and more ground. As the economic crisis worsened, the right wing, heavily influenced by big business, gained the upper hand and sought to end cooperation with the SPD and to join the extraparliamentary Right. The bitter dispute over unemployment insurance, which was essentially about who should bear the burden of economic and financial restructuring, was a welcome vehicle to bring about the coalition's collapse. The final impetus came with the certainty that Hindenburg intended to deny the Müller government the emergency powers of Article 48 and was single-mindedly pursuing a presidentially appointed cabinet under Brüning.[115]

Naturally, the Reichswehr leadership, above all Reichswehr Minister Groener and his closest adviser, Schleicher, also bore great responsibility for the end of the last parliamentary elected-majority government. Since 1929, they had been convinced that the Weimar "state of political parties" was in a serious crisis. In the event that the grand coalition proved unable to deal with Germany's economic and financial problems, they were only too willing to look for an authoritarian alternative in the form of a government presidentially appointed on the basis of the emergency-decree article, which largely excluded the German parliament. These plans coincided with Hindenburg and his entourage's conviction that the grand coalition would eventually fail. The meeting on December 26, 1929, and the pact Groener made with the designated chancellor, Brüning, while out on their walk through the woods were important stations on the way to the installation of a "Hindenburg cabinet." Groener's intervention with the Reich president on March 11, 1930, succeeded in persuading Hindenburg to back away from his promise to grant the Müller government presidential emergency-decree powers. That authority might have given the chancellor another chance to extend his cabinet into the fall of 1930. However, neither the Reichswehr leadership nor the Reich president nor the DVP nor large sections of the business community had any real interest in continuing the grand coalition. On the contrary, they single-mindedly pursued a change of power.[116]

The day after Müller's resignation, Hindenburg charged Brüning with forming a government that, "in view of the parliamentary difficulties," was not to be "based on coalition commitments." The new chancellor would be able to rely on the powers of Article 48, which the Reich president had denied to his predecessor. By March 30, Brüning was able to present that cabinet. Most of its members, including Curtius, Moldenhauer, Wirth, and Groener, had already been part of the Müller cabinet. Hermann Dietrich took over the Ministry of Economics; Adam Stegerwald, the Ministry of Labor. The only new additions were Justice Minister Victor Bredt from the Economic Party; Food Minister Martin Schiele, the president of the Reich Rural League; and Gottfried Treviranus from the Popular Conservative Association as Minister for the Occupied Territories.[117] The speed with which the change of power took place clearly indicated how well it had been prepared in advance. "Behind the scenes," the principals in the new government had been working toward it "for weeks," noted Pünder.[118]

In his government declaration of April 1, 1930, Brüning made it clear that his cabinet would be the "last attempt to implement a solution with this Reichstag." This was a barely veiled threat to dissolve parliament if it refused to cooperate with the new government.[119] A few months later, that was precisely the case. On July 16, the Reichstag rejected a government bill to close the budget deficit. Brüning declared his disinterest in any further negotiations with parliament and enacted the bill by means of presidential emergency decree. When the Reichstag voted to repeal that decree, Brüning announced he was dissolving parliament.

That decision was as shortsighted as it was momentous. Ever since the regional elections of 1929, the Nazi Party had been on the rise. The Reichstag elections of September 14, 1930, would turn out to be a spectacular success for the Nazis, who were able to increase their share of the vote from 2.6 to 18.3 percent and their number of seats from 12 to 107. That made them the second-strongest party after the Social Democrats. Many of those who cast their ballots for the Nazi Party were first-time voters and previous nonvoters. At 82 percent, turnout in the election was quite high, and it's doubtful that such voters had fully formed National Socialist views. On the contrary, voting for Hitler and his henchmen was a way of protesting against the status quo. Although the SPD remained Germany's strongest party with 24.5 percent, it lost 5.3 percent compared to 1928, while the KPD increased its share of the vote from 10.6 to 13.1 percent. The Catholic parties—the Center and BVP—remained relatively stable with 11.8 and 3.0 percent respectively (compared to 12.1 and 3.1 percent in 1928). The big losers were the mainstream parties of the center and the right. The DNVP achieved only 7 percent (down from 14.2 percent); the DVP, 4.5 percent (down from 8.7 percent); and the DDP (or the German State Party, as it was known since July 1930), 3.8 percent (down from 4.9 percent).[120]

The headline in the *Vossische Zeitung* the day after the election read "Victory for Radicalism." Despite the Nazis' preceding successes in the state elections, the outcome of the vote took the paper completely off guard. The center had been "shattered," the liberal newspaper wrote, by a defeat that affected "all of bourgeois Germany, which today has good reason to worry about the short-term future." Nevertheless, the paper also warned against excessive pessimism: "The German Republic will not sink in the National Socialist tide, which has risen so quickly and will ebb again one day. But the parties wanting to preserve and maintain this state must finally understand that—beyond any mandates, factions, and platforms—they have something much more important: a common mission." [121]

"107 National Socialists—what a disgrace and how close we are now to civil war!" noted Klemperer. "But we are politically numb. There has been war, revolution, inflation, and we're still alive." [122] Kessler commented that "we are facing a national crisis that can only be overcome by tightly knitting together all the forces that support or at least tolerate the republic." He also saw the "possibility of a civil war and, further down the line, a new Great War." [123]

The left-wing socialist historian Arthur Rosenberg ended his 1935 *History of the Weimar Republic* five years earlier: "In 1930, the bourgeois republic in Germany perished because its fate was entrusted to the bourgeoisie and because the working class was no longer strong enough to save it." [124] Rosenberg wrote these lines in exile, completely in the shadow of 1933, after power had been transferred to Hitler, officially sealing the fate of the Weimar Republic. But despite the breakup of the grand coalition and the September elections in 1930, the demise of the first German democracy was by no means as clear to contemporaries as Rosenberg's account suggested. There was no direct path from 1930 to January 30, 1933. The situation was fluid, and the crisis of state could have been overcome in various ways. Parliamentary paralysis had created a power vacuum in which the actions of individuals accrued additional significance. [125] This was particularly true for Hindenburg and his camarilla, who were determined to marginalize the Reichstag and move toward an authoritarian presidential system. Much depended on how Hindenburg's chancellor, Brüning, interpreted his role. Did he regard governing by emergency decree as an interim stage enabling a return to parliamentarianism once the economic crisis had been overcome and the National Socialist movement had been pushed back? Or did he, too, see it as a transitional stage paving the way for a definitive authoritarian outcome, perhaps for a restoration of the monarchy?

The Thuringia Model

WILHELM FRICK'S FASCIST CULTURAL REVOLUTION

Hitler with his followers in front of the German National Theater in Weimar with the Goethe–Schiller monument, 1931: It was here that Ebert opened the National Assembly on February 6, 1919.

On January 23, 1930, there was a heated debate in the parliament of the regional state of Thuringia about the formation of a new right-wing government including one of Hitler's most ardent followers and a co-putschist of 1923, Wilhelm Frick, as minister of the interior and public education. The debate began with the former state premier and SPD parliamentary group leader, August Frölich, criticizing the fact that the president of the parliament had taken down the democratic black, red, and gold flag from the building. Was this intended to demonstrate, he asked, "that the colors of the Third Reich under Hitler and Frick should take the place of the national colors?" In Frick, the speaker continued, "a high traitor"—who had already broken his oath to the constitution as a Bavarian civil servant and who had never made a secret of his opposition to the parliamentary-democratic system—"has been appointed a minister in charge of the [regional] constitution."

Frölich recalled that Frick had pleaded in the Reichstag for amnesty to be given to Ernst Werner Techow, who had been involved in Rathenau's murder, and had demanded impunity for the Erzberger assassins, Schulz and Tillessen. He reminded the DVP, which wanted to join the right-wing government, that not long ago, in December 1929, Frick had vilified the late Foreign Minister Gustav Stresemann as a paid foreign agent for accepting the Nobel Peace Prize. Repeatedly interrupted by the National Socialists, Frölich concluded his speech with the words: "The election of Mr. Frick makes today a day of political and cultural shame for Thuringia."[1]

That afternoon DVP parliamentary group leader Georg Witzmann tried to justify his party's stance. Despite considerable reservations, he said, his party had decided to join the government in the spirit of cooperating with all parties "who have the goodwill to serve our country with their work." Frick had promised to swear an oath to the constitution and also declared that he would drop his accusations of corruption against Stresemann. A firewall on the political right was out of the question for the Thuringian DVP. On the contrary, Witzmann said, the National Socialists were "ideologically and politically closer" to the DVP than the Social Democrats were.[2] In the end, the government was confirmed by 28 votes to 22 from the SPD, KPD, and DDP. Frick became the first National Socialist minister of a regional German government.

The fact that Weimar of all places—the Thuringian capital, in which Germany had adopted its democratic constitution—served as a springboard to elevate the National Socialists to an important position of power was not a coincidence. After the interlude of the Thuringian united-front leftist government of the SPD and KPD in the fall of 1923, which ended with the Reich intervening there and in Saxony, the Right had begun to gain strength. The "Thuringian Order League"—a conglomeration of the DNVP, DVP, and Thuringian Rural League—emerged as the strongest force in the state elections on February 10, 1924. However, with thirty-five of seventy-two state parliamentary seats, it fell short of a majority and therefore had to rely on being tolerant of the Popular-Ethnic Social Bloc, a successor organization to the then-banned Nazi Party, which surprised everyone by winning 9.3 percent of the vote and seven parliamentary seats. In the city of Weimar itself, it had even received almost twice as many votes, with 18.6 percent.[3]

One of the new government's first measures was to cut funding for Walter Gropius's unpopular Bauhaus in Weimar. In response, the director and the "masters," as the instructors were known, declared their contracts with the state of Thuringia null and void. The world-famous architecture and art school found a new home in Dessau, the capital of the regional state of Anhalt.[4]

It was the minister of the interior in this conservative–extreme right government who in February 1925, after the reestablishment of the Nazi Party, lifted a nationwide ban on Hitler speaking publicly. Gradually, Thuringia replaced Bavaria as the primary stomping ground for the Far Right. "Nowhere in Germany did Hitler, the Nazis, the racist antisemites,

The Nazi Party's second rally in Weimar, early July 1926:
Hitler reviews the SA men marching in the city center.

the military associations, and extreme nationalists find a better place for their activities," historian Karsten Rudolph has concluded.[5]

In March 1925, Hitler gave his first speeches in Weimar at several packed events. Further appearances followed in October 1925.[6] When in the city, the party leader preferred to stay at the Hotel Elephant, the traditional hotel on the market square, which rolled out the red carpet early on. The hospitality he received was one reason that, after the ban on him speaking was rescinded, Hitler decided to convene the NSDAP's first Reich Party Conference in early July 1926 in Weimar. In contrast to previous quarrels within the far-right ethnic nationalist movement, the Nazi Party presented a new unity, tightly focused on the "Führer" as the undisputed integrating leader. On the afternoon of July 4, Hitler was allowed to speak at the Deutsches Nationaltheater—the same venue where Friedrich Ebert had opened the National Assembly on February 6, 1919, and where the National Constituent Assembly had met. "Where

Ebert once sat, today Adolf Hitler sits and stands," boasted the gauleiter, or Nazi regional leader, Arthur Dinter, at a "general roll call" of the SA (Sturmabteilung) and SS. "This is the beginning of a new era."[7]

In September 1927, Hitler dismissed Dinter, who was also the author of the antisemitic bestseller *Die Sünde wider das Blut* (The sin against blood), from his post because his sectarian idea of restoring the "pure doctrine of salvation" was upsetting people in the party leader's circles. As his replacement, Hitler appointed the former managing director Fritz Sauckel, an unconditional true believer who would enjoy a long career.[8] It was also in the Weimar Nazi Party administration that an inconspicuous functionary began a career as a cashier and accountant, which would see him become one of the most powerful men in the Third Reich. His name was Martin Bormann.[9]

Likewise, the young Baldur von Schirach, a son of the last grand-ducal theater director, also found his way to Hitler in Weimar. He wrote verses of homage to the Führer, who would later, in October 1931, appoint him Reich Youth Leader of the Nazi Party. Along with the racist literary historian and avowed antisemite Adolf Bartels and his pupil Hans Severus Ziegler, deputy gauleiter since 1925, it was Schirach who gave Hitler access to conservative, upper-middle-class circles in the city. "I love Weimar," Hitler proclaimed in 1928. "I need Weimar like I need Bayreuth. And the day will come when I'll give this city and its theater a lot more support. I still have big plans for Weimar and Bayreuth."[10]

The Nazis took 11.3 percent of the vote in the Thuringian state elections on December 8, 1929. This was more than three times as much as in the regional elections in February 1927 (3.5 percent). In Weimar, they got no less than 23.8 percent. Their success wasn't accidental. Under Sauckel's leadership, the party had built up a powerful machine and had aggressively campaigned and stirred up unrest in small rural Thuringian communities.[11] Its success came primarily at the expense of the mainstream parties—a sign of how voter behavior was shifting and a harbinger of the coming landslide in the Reichstag elections of September 14, 1930. The *Berliner Tageblatt* was thus very wrong when it dismissed the result as "a fad surrounded by carnival hype that has to be tolerated."[12]

Although the Nazis won only six seats in the regional parliament,

they were still in a key position. As in 1924, the mainstream parties of
the center and right lacked a majority. Their twenty-three seats (Rural
Association: nine; Business Party: six; DVP: five; DNVP: two; DDP:
one) were outweighed by the twenty-four seats for the SPD (eighteen)
and the KPD (six). Since they had ruled out a coalition with the Social
Democrats, they needed the support of the six National Socialist MPs
to form a government. This time around, Hitler did not want merely to
tolerate a coalition. On the contrary, from the very outset, he wanted to
be part of the government.

Hitler was unusually frank about his motives in a letter, dated February 2, 1930, to a supporter of the Nazi movement living overseas, in
which he noted a "great turnaround" in the public perception of Nazism.
It was "astonishing how the knee-jerk, arrogant, snobbish, or stupid
rejection of the party of just a few years ago has given way to expectations and hope." However, he added, such hope would be disappointed
if they were to remain in the opposition out of principle. But in return
for the party's participating in coalition negotiations, Hitler demanded
two key posts, the Ministry of the Interior and the Ministry of National
Education. "The Ministry of the Interior is responsible for the entire
administration, the personnel department, that is, the appointment and
dismissal of all civil servants and the police. The Ministry of Public
Education is responsible for the entire school system, from elementary
schools to the University of Jena, as well as the theater system. Whoever
is in possession of these two ministries and uses his power ruthlessly and
persistently can achieve extraordinary things." [13]

Hitler was thus interested not only in participating in government
but in taking over the executive from within. "We will pass the first
test of our mettle," predicted Berlin gauleiter and later Nazi Propaganda
Minister Joseph Goebbels on January 8, 1930.[14] Hitler added that "only
a National Socialist through and through with both great expertise and
unconditional National Socialist convictions" could be considered as a
candidate to take over the dual ministry. Hitler believed he had found
the right person in Frick, an early party supporter, the former head of
the political division in the Munich police headquarters, and the acting
chairman of the Nazi parliamentary group in the Reichstag, calling him

"an energetic, bold, and responsible civil servant of extraordinary ability and a fanatical National Socialist!"[15]

Initially, the DVP rejected the ministerial appointment of someone who had taken part in the 1923 putsch and been convicted of high treason. "So I went to Weimar myself," Hitler reported in the letter on February 2, "and succinctly assured the gentlemen in no uncertain terms that either Dr. Frick would become our minister, or fresh elections would be held."[16] Fresh elections were the last thing the mainstream parties wanted, since they were sure to further strengthen the Nazi Party. Hitler gave his prospective mainstream parties a deadline of three days, from January 10 to 13. Otherwise, he would have a motion introduced to dissolve the regional parliament. But the DVP still had its scruples.

Hitler was in a strong bargaining position, however, and he furthered his cause with a speech to leading representatives of Thuringia's business and industry associations on January 10, which made a huge impression. "In the evening, Hitler spoke to a closed circle," a very satisfied Goebbels noted. "In front of 150 bigwigs, reeking of respectability. Hitler spoke fabulously. I've rarely heard him that good."[17] Business circles were also ramping up pressure on the DVP, and when the ultimatum expired, the party caved in. On January 23, 1930, the coalition government was confirmed in office. "Frick is now a minister in Weimar," Goebbels recorded in his diary. "It was a difficult birth."[18] Frick's party comrade Wilhelm Marschler was appointed state councillor, a position that gave him a vote in the cabinet.

There was no lack of warning voices in the DVP. "It hurts my soul to see you in such company," shouted DVP Reichstag deputy Siegfried von Kardorff to the delegates from Thuringia at the party's conference in Mannheim in March 1930.[19] But the fact that the DVP was doing deals with the Nazis at all showed how far the party had drifted to the right under Stresemann's successor, Ernst Scholz. Making common cause with the National Socialists at regional level while being part of a grand coalition with the Social Democrats at Reich level was a complete contradiction. In that respect, the Thuringian experiment already foreshadowed the imminent demise of Hermann Müller's government.[20]

Minister Frick did not disappoint expectations. At the third reading of the laws to enact the Young Plan in the Reichstag on March 12, 1930, he took a seat on the benches of the state representatives and made a statement of vigorous protest immediately before the final vote, railing against the "Enslavement Act," the adoption of which would bring "the greatest national misfortune and end the independence of Germany's regional states." The Thuringian Ministry of State had not authorized him to make this statement. Although the DVP parliamentary group leader, Witzmann, disapproved of his unilateral action a few days later, Frick faced no consequences.[21]

Hitler had set his party colleague two tasks. As Thuringian minister of the interior, Frick was to "carry out a slow purge of the administrative and civil service from all red revolutionary elements." There was "a great deal to do," Hitler said, especially in policing. And as minister of national education, he was to push ahead with the "nationalization of the school system." Hitler demanded, "In the same vein, we will purge the teaching staff of Marxist-democratic elements just as we will adapt the curriculum to our National Socialist beliefs and ideas."[22]

Frick set to work with great energy to remake Thuringia in this sense. In his inaugural speech to the civil servants in his two ministries, he made it clear that a "new spirit" now applied in Weimar, and that it would be fundamentally different from the "treacherous November spirit" of the German republic.[23] On March 18, 1930, he introduced to the state parliament the draft of an enabling act intended to largely free the state government from parliamentary control for six months. The law was passed by a simple majority (28 votes to 25) on March 29. Under the guise of reforming and streamlining the administration, civil servants loyal to the republic were dismissed and replaced by followers of the NSDAP.[24]

The Reich government, however, did not stand idly by as Frick went about doing what he did. On March 18, 1930, the Social Democratic Minister of the Interior Carl Severing informed the Thuringian government that he had received news "giving rise to justified doubts as to whether the conditions for the granting of a Reich subsidy for police purposes" were still fulfilled.[25] Thuringian State Premier Erwin Baum from the Rural League "solemnly appealed" to the Reich not to block the funds. Although the new minister of the interior, Joseph Wirth of the Center Party, who had been in office since March 30, 1930, reached an agreement with the Thuringian state government in April to lift the ban on the Reich subsidy, no agreement was reached on the fundamental question of whether National Socialists should be allowed to join the police force. Frick created a fait accompli by filling the offices of the police directorates of Weimar and Gera with his allies. When Wirth then had police funds blocked again in June 1930, Baum filed a complaint with the State Court in Leipzig. The conflict between Thuringia and the Reich was settled in December 1930, when the former guaranteed the "nonpolitical conduct of individual civil servants without fail while on duty", and the latter agreed to lift the freeze on police subsidies.[26]

Frick was unperturbed by all the objections from Berlin and continued his policy of "cleansing" the civil service. Goebbels, who visited him in Weimar at the beginning of June 1930, was impressed: "He is in good spirits, has the courage of his convictions, provokes people, and behaves insolently toward the bigwigs in Berlin. A true German minister indeed."[27] Civil servants who were members of or close to the SPD were hit particularly hard by the staff cuts the state of Thuringia also had to make due to the precarious financial situation. Frick appointed three of his party comrades to the Ministry of Education, including the deputy gauleiter Hans Severus Ziegler, as "expert advisers." They acted as a kind of shadow government, with access to personnel files, which they used to tar-brush undesirables among the teaching ranks. Suspicion and denunciation became pervasive in the Thuringian administration.[28]

Parallel to his administrative and personnel purges, Frick set about to radically change the country's cultural policy. On April 16, 1930, school prayers were reintroduced by a decree in the official gazette of the Ministry of National Education. The reason given was that "forces alien to the species and people" had long been trying to "destroy the spiritual, moral, and religious foundations of our German thinking and feeling in order to uproot the German people and thus make it easier to control us," the decree stated. The German people could resist these pernicious influences only "if they kept the religious and moral driving forces of their nature pure and passed them on to the next generations of youth." Three of the suggested prayers were clearly directed against the democratic constitutional order of the Weimar Republic, which was viewed as anathema to the spirit of ethnic jingoism. The second of these rhyming prayers went:

> Father, in your almighty hand
> Stand our people and fatherland
> You were our ancestors' honor and strength
> You are our constant weapon and defense
> Therefore free us from betrayal and deceit
> Make us strong for the liberating deed
> Give us the Savior's heroic bravery
> Let honor and freedom be our highest commodity!
> Let our vow and watchword be:
> Germany, awaken! Lord, make us free!
> May God make it so![29]

The Nazi battle cry "Germany awaken" was intended to instill nationalism in schoolchildren. Frick left no doubt as to who was meant by the "forces alien to the species and people" in the state parliament in May 1930. The "prayers for freedom," he explained, were intended to serve as a "defense against the fraud" that had been "committed against the German people by Marxism and the Jews."[30] The Nazis' coalition partners offered little opposition to the mandatory bastardized school prayers, and protests from the Thuringian Teachers' Association and the Protestant regional church were also limited. Conversely, the coalition parties shot down a motion by the SPD parliamentary group to rescind the decree. Frick did, however, lose a lawsuit filed with the Leipzig State Court. In its ruling of July 11, 1930, three particularly offensive prayers were rejected because they impinged on the "sensibilities of dissenters" and thus violated Article 148, paragraph 2, of the Reich Constitution.[31]

Before that, in February 1930, Frick had issued an injunction against Erich Maria Remarque's famous anti-war novel *All Quiet on the Western*

Front, which had been published in spring 1929 and quickly become a bestseller. School boards in Thuringia were instructed to report which schools had purchased the title and which teachers had used the book in class. Further inclusion of the book in reading lists was prohibited. These regulations were in line with the views of the German Fighting League for German Culture, which had been founded in August 1927 under the leadership of the Nazi Party's chief ideologue, Alfred Rosenberg. At its Whitsunday conference in Weimar in 1930, held under Frick's patronage, the league demanded that the "German will to self-defense must be hardened."[32] Nazi cultural watchdogs considered Remarque's bestseller capable of impairing that "will." The same strictures also applied to the film version of the novel. The Nazi Party, led by Goebbels as the gauleiter of the German capital, railed against the film, which premiered in Berlin in December 1930, and on December 11, the Supreme Film Board gave in to SA intimidation and banned it. "The Nazi street fighter is dictating the government's actions," crowed Hitler's propaganda expert.[33]

Frick's next serious intervention in cultural life came at the beginning of April 1930 with the decree "Against Negro Culture and for German Ethnic Identity." In its preamble, it claimed that for years, "foreign racial influences," capable of "undermining the moral fortitude of the German people," had been "increasingly asserting themselves in almost all cultural areas." It was therefore "in the interest of the preservation and strengthening of the German ethnic identity" that everything "glorifying Negroism" should be seen as "signs of decay" to be "prevented as much as possible." The authorities were to apply the "strictest standards" and punish all theater companies that could not be regarded as "morally or artistically reliable."[34] This decree provided the basis for numerous bans. For example, the performance of Friedrich Wolf's abortion drama, *Cyanide*, which Erwin Piscator's Berliner Ensemble wanted to stage in Gera and Jena, was prohibited. Plays by the expressionists Ernst Toller and Walter Hasenclever also disappeared from the repertoire of state theaters.[35]

On May 22, 1930, SPD member of parliament Max Greil, a former minister of popular education, excoriated Frick in front of the Thuringian state parliament, castigating him for trying to politicize all areas of cultural life "along the lines of National Socialist Party beliefs." Frick's "proclamation against Negro culture," Greil argued, was actually directed against Jews, and he demanded that Frick publicly acknowledge this fact. Contrasting Nazi cultural policy with the "classical spirit of cosmopolitanism in the sense of Goethe," Greil said, "It is the spirit of nationalist narrow-mindedness; it is the spirit of chauvinist warmongering."[36]

In his infamous decree, Frick had announced that he had appointed the architect Paul Schultze-Naumburg as the new director of the Vereinigte Kunstlehranstalten (College of Architecture, Fine Arts, and Crafts) in Weimar and that it was to be developed into a "center of German culture." Schultze-Naumburg, whom Frick had also hired as an "art consultant," had made a name for himself as a vehement opponent of the Bauhaus and advocate of a "racially sound" German culture. His house in Saaleck near Bad Kösen, located below the castle ruins, was a popular meeting place for extreme right-wing nationalist circles. In June 1930, Goebbels was a guest there. He was accompanied by Frick and Walther Darré, later the Nazi food minister. "The Schultze house is beautifully situated above the Saale River, wonderfully blended into the landscape, a true gem," noted Goebbels in his diary. "I have never seen such a stylish house." While in the town, the Berlin gauleiter did not neglect to visit the graves of Fischer and Kern, the men who had murdered Walther Rathenau.[37]

In his speech inaugurating the newly designed Vereinigte Kunstlehranstalten on November 10, 1930, Schultze-Naumburg raged against modern art, which, he claimed, consisted "only of obscure, tortured, and distorted images and the visualization of mental and physical inferiority." He was united with Germany's youth, he added, in the goal of "chasing all those corrupters of and traitors to the people out of the German house, in which they have no place."[38]

Deeds followed these words. That October, Schultze-Naumburg had wall frescoes by Bauhaus master Oskar Schlemmer painted over in the Van de Velde building. In early November, at Frick's behest, seventy

Wilhelm Frick (left) with Hitler's closest circle visiting the Saxon spa town of Bad Elster, 1932: Next to Frick are Joseph Goebbels and Adolf Hitler. In front: Ernst Hanfstaengl (foreign press officer of the Nazi Party) and Hermann Göring.

works by modern artists, including paintings and drawings by Otto Dix, Lyonel Feininger, Wassily Kandinsky, and Paul Klee, were removed from the exhibition rooms of the Weimar Palace Museum. Frick justified this preview of the Nazis' infamous 1937 campaign against "degenerate art" by claiming that the ostracized works had "nothing in common with Nordic-German nature" and only "depicted eastern and other inferior subhumanity."[39] There was hardly any resistance in Weimar to this "storming of paintings," as it became known. But the liberal Berlin press, including the *Berliner Tageblatt*, branded it for what it was: "a scandal in a cultured nation."[40]

But even this scandal was surpassed by Frick's most audacious coup: the appointment of the racial theorist Hans F. K. Günther as a professor at the University of Jena. In doing so, Frick was acting on Hitler's expectations in a letter of February 2, 1930, in which the Nazi leader had envisaged the "establishment of a chair for racial issues and racial studies" in Jena as the "first step" in the desired "intellectual upheaval." Hitler himself had suggested Günther, the author of a "racial primer of the German people," for the position.[41] When the university rector, church historian Karl Heussi, opposed Frick's request, the students' association, already dominated by National Socialist sympathizers, rebelled. Frick praised the Jena student body for having shown "more understanding for the need to create the conditions necessary for Germany's renewal" than the professors. The only concession made to the university's teaching staff was that the original title—Chair of Human Civilization—was changed to Chair of Social Anthropology. Hitler personally attended Günther's inaugural lecture, on November 15, 1930, which was entitled "The Causes of the Racial Decline of the German People Since the Migration of Peoples."[42]

On April 1, 1931, Frick's time in government in Thuringia came to an abrupt end, after the DVP joined a motion of no confidence proposed by the Social Democrats and Communists. Yet it was not Frick's actions as a minister that caused the coalition to break up, but rather the insulting remarks made by Gauleiter Sauckel in an editorial in the party newspaper *Der Nationalsozialist* (The National Socialist). In it, Sauckel had belittled representatives of the DVP as "foolish old men, traitors, and swindlers," who "in their bottomless impudence were playing a sacrilegious game with the fate of our people."[43] This proved too much even for a party that had endured months of Frick's provocations. Amid considerable press attention, Hitler had traveled to Weimar the day before the vote to try to change the DVP's mind, but his trip was in vain.[44]

In the parliamentary debate preceding the no-confidence motion on April 1, Philipp Kallenbach of the DDP described the results of Frick's fourteen months in government as "downright disastrous." Kallenbach said: "Peace in our state has been destroyed. The driving force behind these administrative measures is the desire to stir up people and create a spectacle, even to encourage hatred and take one-sided actions against broad segments of the population. To a great extent in the short time in question, all areas of public life have been politicized in the interests of

the Nazi Party. To advance those ends, personnel policy has been ruthless, with allies being permitted to feed at the trough more openly and
self-evidently than ever before."[45]

After Frick resigned in the run-up to the Reich presidential election
in spring of 1932, it became known that he had secretly attempted to
obtain German citizenship for Hitler. The affair caused a sensation. A
parliamentary inquiry, chaired by SPD politician Hermann Brill, was
formed in Weimar to investigate, and Hitler and Frick were summoned
as witnesses. The picture that emerged started in the summer of 1930.
With State Premier Baum away on vacation, Frick had sought to lay the
groundwork for Hitler's naturalization by appointing him gendarmerie
commissioner in the town of Hildburghausen, while at the same time
releasing him from all duties as a civil servant. Two ministry officials
were ordered to initiate the necessary formalities under "strictest official secrecy." At a regional Nazi meeting in Gera on July 12, 1930, Frick
presented Hitler with the certificate of appointment, and he confirmed
receipt with his signature. Afterward, however, the Nazi leader apparently had second thoughts, worrying that the title of gendarmerie commissioner might make him look ridiculous. In any case, he tore up the
document a few days later in Munich. Before the committee of inquiry,
he testified that he had not wanted to accept the appointment in the
first place.[46]

The grotesque story of Frick's attempted naturalization of Hitler
quickly became the talk of the town. "Lots of hounding in the press," an
annoyed Goebbels noted. "Crazy caricatures."[47] The affair was mocked
as a "presumptuous masquerade" and a "prank." But an editorial in the
liberal *Vossische Zeitung* drew attention to the deadly serious underly-
ing meaning. With his "unsuccessful push" to make Hitler a German,
Frick had once again proved that the National Socialists were unwilling to abide by the law. "It would be good if the true character of this
party were finally recognized outside Bavaria, where people have experienced it up close," the paper wrote.[48] In Thuringia, no one heeded the
warning. In the state elections in late July 1932, the NSDAP emerged as
the strongest party, with 42.5 percent of the vote, and Sauckel became
state premier.[49]

Looking back, the Social Democratic politician, journalist, and later member of the anti-Nazi resistance Hermann Brill described the "Frick era" in Thuringia as "one of the most important vanguard skirmishes in the great battle between democracy and dictatorship."[50] Indeed, during his time in office, Frick delivered a foretaste of what could be expected if the National Socialists came to power nationally. For fourteen months, Thuringia served as a laboratory in which they could try out measures they were to implement on a larger scale at Reich level three years later.

In a personal letter dated April 2, 1931, Hitler thanked Frick for "placing Thuringia at the center of Germany's national, political, and economic redevelopment." The Nazi leader added, "We all firmly believe in the hour that will once again, this time forever, call you to serve our people in a responsible position."[51] And Frick was in fact rewarded with the post of Reich minister of the interior—one of the most powerful positions in the land—in the "cabinet of national concentration" formed on January 30, 1933, under Germany's new chancellor, Hitler.

The Beginning of the End

BRÜNING'S FALL

The world economic crisis hits Germany with full force in 1929–30: Unemployed people study the scant Help Wanted advertisements in the newspapers.

C hancellor Heinrich Brüning knew he was in for a rough ride when he arrived for an audience with Hindenburg at eleven o'clock on the morning of May 29, 1932. The Reich president had returned the day before from his estate in Neudeck, where his highly conservative entourage had been pressuring him to finally part company with his chancellor. Brüning had gotten wind of the machinations and, as State Secretary Pünder remarked, entered the meeting "reluctant to take the offensive and not very confident."[1]

Hindenburg received the chancellor in a decidedly cool manner and displayed clear disinterest when Brüning once again explained the details of his main policies. He perked up only when Brüning demanded an end to the "obstructionism" against his government. He could no longer tolerate constant scheming behind his back and his authority being called into question, Brüning complained. Hindenburg must ensure "that this shadow government . . . comes to an end." Otherwise, he, Brüning, would not be able to achieve the "turn to the right" that everyone wanted.

"One hears quite different views about your desire to move to the right," Hindenburg replied brusquely. The aged president then put on his glasses, picked up a document lying on the desk, and, without any further ado, read out in an imperious voice: "(1) Because it is unpopular, the government will no longer receive permission from me to issue new emergency decrees. (2) The government is no longer authorized by me to make personnel changes." This obliterated the basis on which the Brüning government had been appointed in late March 1930.

In his memoirs, Brüning described the ensuing exchange of words: "I replied: 'If I understand what you have just said to me correctly, Mr. Reich President, you want the entire cabinet dismissed.' The president's reply: 'Yes, indeed. This government must go because it is unpopular.' I told him: 'I will summon the cabinet tomorrow and dismiss it.' The president of the Reich: 'I ask that it be done as quickly as possible.' Getting ahold of myself, I replied calmly that I, too, saw it as a state necessity that a new cabinet be formed as quickly as possible. 'I can deliver the resignation as soon as tomorrow morning.' The Reich president: 'Do that.'" When Brüning left the presidential palace at around 11:45 a.m., the fate of his government was sealed.[2]

Brüning's fall was a long time coming. His good relationship with the Reich president soon deteriorated, even though Hindenburg had assured him in May 1931: "You are my last chancellor. I will not part with you."[3] Those were empty words. As fond as the president was of talking about the virtue of loyalty, he rarely felt bound to it himself. More important, Brüning's government had fallen short of the expectations that Hindenburg and his clique of advisers had placed in his chancellorship.

From his first day in office, Brüning had pursued a course of rigorous austerity. In a series of emergency decrees, state spending was cut dramatically. The cabinet reduced civil servants' and government employees' salaries and pensions and curtailed the duration and amount of unemployment insurance benefits as well as pensions for the disabled and for war invalids. At the same time, it raised taxes and levies and imposed a "crisis tax" on hourly wages and salary earners.[4] The Reich defense budget was exempt from the cuts. And in accordance with the interests of the agricultural lobby, many millions in farm subsidies also remained untouched.

Restructuring state finances wasn't Brüning's only priority. He also pursued the foreign policy objective of using the Great Depression to settle the reparations issue once and for all. A commitment to austerity, combined with total fiscal transparency, Brüning believed, would demonstrate to the creditor states that Germany could not meet its payment obligations and would thus force them to forgive German debts long before the deadline stipulated in the Young Plan.

As Brüning explained in a speech to the Reich Committee of the Center Party in November 1931, success in foreign policy was "all the more likely to be achieved if we present the balance sheet of German finances and the German economy clearly and honestly for everyone in

The ascetic head of government: With his strict austerity policy, Reich Chancellor Heinrich Brüning exacerbated the economic crisis.

the world to see." This was "the strongest and most effective weapon," one that his government had forged from the outset and had led to "the question of reparations being judged completely differently by the public throughout the world without exception than in previous years."[5]

Brüning was prepared to accept mass unemployment and misery to achieve the goal of canceling reparations debt. The number of registered unemployed, 3.5 million in October 1930, rose to 4.6 million by October 1931. One year later, it passed the 5 million mark, reaching a peak of 6.1 million in February 1932. In reality, many more people were jobless, as the statistics didn't include the "invisible" unemployed, those who for whatever reason had not registered with the employment office.[6]

The psychological consequences of these measures were devastating. Six years after the traumatic experiences of hyperinflation, the onset of a new crisis overwhelmed many Germans. Despair and anger spread, accompanied by a loss of trust in democratic institutions and parties. That boosted the already widespread resentment against the "system" and all those who were part of it.

Due to benefits cuts, only a minority of the unemployed still received unemployment support. Most got only "crisis care" financed jointly by the Reich and local authorities or, when that money ran out too, an even smaller amount of welfare support. The institution of unemployment insurance, one of the Weimar Republic's great social achievements, was largely dismantled, removing a major foundation of the democratic state's legitimacy. Many families could no longer pay their rent and sought refuge in temporary colonies on the outskirts of the cities. Hunger and deprivation were rife, and simply surviving from one day to the next became increasingly difficult. Children, in particular, suffered severe health problems. Desperate people with signs saying "Looking for work at any pay" were not uncommon. Young unemployed formed gangs, and crime skyrocketed. In addition to poverty and loss of social status, many unemployed felt degraded and useless. Mass unemployment brought insecurity even to those who were still employed, since they too could lose their jobs at any time and fall down the social ladder.[7]

"The cityscape of Berlin has gradually changed, and the crisis is now noticeable in every nook and cranny," wrote Siegfried Kracauer, correspondent for the *Frankfurter Zeitung*, at the height of the misery in 1932. "The streets are littered with beggars, a whole barely penetrable forest of them, which has invaded the city and covered the asphalt. Students and better-dressed older men ring doorbells, selling shoelaces and matches or even asking for alms. In the evenings, a strange, enervating silence reigns in streets that used to be busy well into the night. People quickly get lost. They stay at home or get stuck somewhere else. It's as if they hunker down like animals to be alone with their misery."[8]

For a long time, it was assumed that there was no alternative to Brüning's austerity policies. Germany had yet to adopt the idea proposed by John Maynard Keynes in his 1930 book, *A Treatise on Money*, of stimulating the economy through deficit spending, that is, through credit-financed public contracts, and accepting budget shortfalls. That was a grave mistake. From spring 1931 onward, Brüning was virtually besieged by various national economists, economic journalists, and trade-union experts who tried to convince him to combat the Depression with a large-scale job-creation program. But the chancellor remained unconvinced. This was not only due to his fear that he wouldn't be able to convince the Western powers of the need to cancel reparations if the provision of funds for public job creation gave the impression that Germany had more financial leeway than it pretended. Brüning was also concerned that extensive lines of credit would jeopardize the stability of the new currency. The trauma of the 1923 hyperinflation, ingrained in the nation's collective memory, still made itself felt.[9] The "hunger chancellor," as Brüning became known, stuck rigidly to his deflationary policy. In doing so, he failed to turn the tide and instead exacerbated the economic crisis and contributed to the radicalization of large segments of the population.

After the disastrous election on September 14, 1930, the SPD found itself in a difficult situation. Should it remain in opposition to Brüning's presidentially appointed cabinet, or should it reach out to him in some form? At the end of September, party chairmen Otto Wels and Hermann Müller met with the Reich chancellor for initial exploratory talks. Pünder noted in his diary: "After today's discussion, it does not seem out of the question to me that the Social Democrats will support the Brüning cabinet in order to avoid a right-wing dictatorship."[10]

On October 5, 1930, the SPD parliamentary group in the Reichstag decided to tolerate the Brüning cabinet and not to support motions put forth by the KPD, DNVP, and Nazis to repeal the emergency decree of July and to vote no confidence in the government. The decision was not an easy one for the Social Democrats, as it gave their competition on the left, the strengthened KPD, plenty of scope for attack. However, there was no alternative if the SPD did not want to jeopardize its only remaining position of power, the government in Prussia with the Center Party and the DDP (since July 1930 the German State Party, or DStP). If it brought down the Center Party's Chancellor Brüning, the Center Party might depart the government alliance in Prussia. It was therefore State Premier Otto Braun and Carl Severing—who had again been made Prussian minister of the interior in October 1930—who most emphatically advocated the policy of tolerance. The Social Democrats were being "very sensible at the moment," praised Pünder at the end of November 1930. "They know, of course, that if the Brüning cabinet fails in the Reich, the guillotine will immediately fall on the Prussian coalition."[11] Brüning also announced at his cabinet meeting on November 30 that the Social Democrats would have to provide him with a majority for the new emergency decree he had planned. The minutes of that meeting read: "Should the Social Democrats fail to do so, the Center would question the Prussian coalition. He, the chancellor, assumed that the Social Democrats and especially the Prussian minister president were fully aware of this."[12]

If Brüning failed, not only would the Center Party likely torpedo the Prussian coalition. The Reichstag would be dissolved, and the Nazi Party would make further gains. By tolerating the Brüning government, the SPD became a silent partner in it. This had hardly been Hindenburg's original intent when installing a presidential cabinet, and it put the Reich president at odds with the chancellor. Hindenburg would have preferred it if Brüning had extended his government further to the right by including the DNVP. But as DNVP party chairman Hugenberg refused to cooperate, Hindenburg had to accept the situation for the time being. "Since the Right does not want to help, we must accept the help of the socialists in order to achieve something, albeit without forming a coalition," he wrote to a confidant at the end of October 1930.[13] Even for the chancellor himself, support from the SPD was only a stopgap solution. He confessed in his memoirs that "in cultural terms, an abyss" separated him from the Social Democrats. But like Stresemann and others, Brüning was convinced "that when it came to saving the fatherland in times of greatest need without claiming brutal forms of power, the SPD was more reliable than pan-Germanic Hugenberg right-wingers."[14]

Thanks to the SPD's willingness to tolerate Brüning's presidentially appointed cabinet as a "lesser evil," the chancellor was able to govern relatively smoothly. The SPD voted down opposition motions to repeal the presidential emergency decrees, and it also supported government motions to adjourn parliament or prevent it from convening prematurely. In March 1931, for example, the Reichstag took a six-month break until mid-October. But the declining number of sessions reflected the progressive erosion of the parliamentary system. In the first months of Brüning's government, from April to December 1930, it met sixty-seven times, in 1931 it met forty-two times, and in 1932, between the start of the year and Brüning's fall in May, only eight times.[15]

During Brüning's first term of office, instead of laws being passed by the Reichstag, emergency decrees were increasingly issued based on Article 48. Hindenburg signed them without hesitation. With the gradual sidelining of parliament, the balance of power shifted even more in favor of the office of the president. Meanwhile, Brüning was growing commensurately more dependent on Hindenburg and the forces behind him.[16]

The SPD's tolerance of Brüning's deflationary policies, which caused such social hardship, was not uncontroversial in the party. In the magazine *Freies Wort*, Ernst Heilmann, the chairman of the Prussian Social Democrats' parliamentary group, who staunchly supported the policy, described the SPD's dilemma at the beginning of November 1930. The party base, he wrote, understood that the Reichstag faction had to do everything possible to keep the National Socialists out of power. "But many party members cannot overcome the objection that our tactics are not popular and not generally comprehensible enough for the man in the street."[17]

A test of strength came in March 1931, when the NSDAP and DNVP made a great show of quitting the Reichstag. That left the SPD and KPD with a majority—and the Communists used the opportunity to pressure the SPD to vote with them against the defense budget, which included initial funding for the construction of armored cruiser B. After the disputes over the armored cruiser A in 1928, the SPD would have had to go against some of its most cherished principles to approve the budget. Rejecting it, however, could have prompted Brüning to resign. The parliamentary group therefore decided to abstain from the roll call on March 20. However, nine MPs from the left wing of the party disregarded the parliamentary group's decision and voted against the budget.

At the SPD's party conference in Leipzig at the end of May and beginning of June 1931, a large majority of delegates condemned the breach of discipline and backed the party leadership's policy of tolerance. On

September 29, 1931, the party expelled the spokesmen of the dissidents, Max Seydewitz and Kurt Rosenfeld. They went on to found the Social Democratic Workers' Party of Germany (SAP), which never succeeded in attracting much of the SPD's clientele. The party is chiefly remembered for attracting a young Social Democrat from Lübeck who would later become the first SPD chancellor in the postwar Federal Republic of Germany: Herbert Frahm, or, as he renamed himself in exile from the Nazis, Willy Brandt.[18]

Leftists who ran out of patience with the SPD tended to turn to the KPD. The party developed into a catch-all particularly for the young unemployed. In the Reichstag elections on September 14, 1930, the Communists were able to increase their share of the vote from 10.6 to 13.1 percent and became the third-strongest party after the SPD and Nazi Party, with seventy-seven Reichstag seats. Even as the economic crisis worsened, the KPD stuck to the general line it had laid down prior to 1930. It regarded its struggle as primarily against the Social Democrats as the "social-welfare bulwark of the bourgeoisie" and the vanguard of rising fascism in Germany. The KPD leadership had no truck whatsoever with the policy of tolerating a "lesser evil." On the contrary, it never tired of excoriating the SPD tolerance of Brüning as a betrayal of working-class interests.

Nevertheless, a united left-wing front against German fascism would hardly have been conceivable, even if the Communists had become more moderate. The two working-class parties were basically irreconcilable. Whereas the KPD saw itself as a revolutionary force striving to overthrow the existing system, the SPD was, in the words of historian Heinrich August Winkler, "a paradigm party of the republic that supported the state, and it became so more than ever as of 1930, even as the state in question was less and less their own."[19]

Communist hatred of the "social fascists" was so great that the KPD occasionally considered limited cooperation with the National Socialists. In August 1931, the KPD took part in a referendum launched from the right to prematurely dissolve the Prussian parliament. "With their

THE BEGINNING OF THE END

policies, Braun and Severing became the trailblazers of fascism," read an appeal from the KPD headquarters, in which it attempted to justify supporting the referendum. "The Brüning Front could not have wished for a more devoted sentinel and better defender than the Prussian government."[20] The referendum failed. Many Communists refused to heed the call of the party leadership and stayed home rather than voting. In their blindness, the KPD leadership failed to recognize that the real threat was the National Socialist movement, which was gaining support every month.

The main beneficiaries of Brüning's deflationary policies were Hitler and the Nazi Party. After their triumph in the September 1930 election, they found themselves being courted from all sides. "You have no idea how the situation of the movement and especially of H[itler] himself has genuinely changed overnight—the night of the election," wrote Hitler's private secretary, Rudolf Hess, to his father, who was living in Egypt. "We've suddenly become 'respectable.' People who used to give H[itler] a wide berth suddenly 'have to' talk to him. The domestic and foreign press are knocking down our doors. . . . And new members are joining!" Despite volunteers working night shifts, the party couldn't keep up with filling out the membership index cards, Hess added.[21] By the end of 1930, the number of memberships had risen to 389,000; and by the end of 1931, to 806,294. The actual number of members was lower, as the statistics didn't include resignations, partly to buttress the impression of explosive growth.[22]

The party had long since outgrown its offices on Munich's Schellingstrasse, so in March 1931, a new headquarters, a prestigious villa in Brienner Strasse, nicknamed the Brown House, was inaugurated. The party had purchased the property with money from a generous loan by steel magnate Fritz Thyssen, one of the first prominent business leaders to go over to the National Socialists.[23] Nonetheless, most Rhineland and Ruhr industrialists were still cautious, not least because of the uncertainty surrounding the party's economic platform. The party did not owe its breakthrough into a mass movement primarily to the support of big industry, no matter what the KPD or postwar Communist East German historiography may have claimed. The NSDAP self-financed most of its election campaigns. However, with its often-unrestrained polemics against trade unions and the welfare state, the business community had indirectly helped delegitimize the Weimar Republic, thus contributing to the rise of the radical Right. It was no coincidence that industrial circles applauded and supported the disempowerment of parliament and the installation of the Brüning government.[24]

The party's main attraction was and remained its chairman, Hitler. He embodied the longing for a strong leader who, standing above the base everyday fray of political conflict, would overcome Germany's crisis and lead the country to new greatness. Hitler knew better than any other politician how to present himself as a political messiah and exploit the public's hopes of salvation. "So many people look up to him as their helper, their savior, their redeemer from overwhelming misery," wrote the Hamburg teacher Luise Solmitz after attending a mass rally. "Their faith is moving."[25] In his speeches, Hitler denounced the Weimar Republic as a singular period of decay and contrasted its gloom with the bright future of a united, economically prosperous, and politically strong "German ethnic community" under his leadership. The Nazis' rise continued into the state elections of 1930–31. In Braunschweig, the party achieved 22.2 percent in September 1930; in Bremen, 24.4 percent in November 1930; in Schaumburg-Lippe, 27 percent in May 1931; in Oldenburg, 37.2 percent in the same month; and in Hamburg, 25.9 percent in September 1931.[26] Its image as a young, fresh, dynamic force gave the Hitler movement its growing appeal.

This string of successes opened the possibility that Hitler could be elected within the framework of German law. A trial before the Reich Court in Leipzig in September 1930 of three young Reichswehr officers who sympathized with the Nazis provided him an opportunity to publicly declare his commitment to the legal route to power. In his testimony, the party chairman assured that he did not want to achieve his goals "under any circumstances unlawfully," but would instead "seek to obtain decisive majorities in the legislative bodies in accordance with the constitution." But Hitler made no bones about what he intended to

Staging the cult of the Führer: Hitler in front of a rapt audience
of members of the SA and Nazi Party in the canteen of the
Brown House, the Nazi Party headquarters in Munich.

do after seizing power: "If our movement is victorious in its legal struggle, a German state court will come, November 1918 will be atoned for,
and heads will roll." In other words, Hitler intended to forego unlawful
means only as long as he did not yet possess political power. The sole
tactical purpose of his hollow words of commitment to the constitutional
order was to gain ground for the National Socialists in their fight, under
the cover of legality, to further destabilize and ultimately unhinge the
Weimar Republic.[27]

The transparent hypocrisy of Hitler's "vow of legality" was apparent as early as the inaugural session of the newly constituted Reichstag
on October 13, 1930. Despite a Prussian ban on military-style uniforms,
the 107 Nazi deputies marched into parliament wearing brown shirts
and swastika armbands. And although, as the second-largest parliamentary group, the Nazi Party was represented in the Reichstag presidium

and on all parliamentary committees, it immediately pursued a course of obstructionism, trying to paralyze the body by constantly disrupting proceedings and introducing nonsensical motions and interpolations. In February 1931, when the majority of the Reichstag reacted by tightening parliamentary procedure, the Nazi group marched out of the building chanting "Heil!" and "Germany awaken!"[28]

"Hitler, unequal to the great game of politics, beat a retreat with his followers into hysteria," commented Carl von Ossietzky in *Die Weltbühne*. Like many contemporary left-wing intellectuals, Ossietzky underestimated the danger posed by the demagogue, writing in early February 1931 that the "German *duce*" was a "cowardly, effeminate pajama creature, a trumped-up petty bourgeois rebel interested only in his own comfort."[29] But attempts to ridicule the Nazi leader could not combat the phenomenon of Hitler and his undeniable charisma. They did nothing whatsoever to dispel his followers' willingness to worship him as a national savior.

As the Nazi Party was making its big breakthrough, the SA (Sturmabteilung) was also growing into a mass organization. Its membership tripled over the course of 1931—from 88,000 in January to 260,000 in December. New recruits were mainly young middle-class men fearful of falling into the proletariat. The SA offered these people, who were insecure about their prospects, both a social support network and an arena where they could act out their aggression. The specific subculture of regularly frequented pubs and SA clubhouses engendered a cult of violence that defined the "brown battalions" in the public eye.[30]

From early 1931 on, clashes between the SA and its adversaries, mainly Communists, escalated into pitched battles approaching something like civil war. In most cases, the SA initiated the violence, and its troops sought to spread fear and intimidation by marching through working-class districts, breaking up meetings, and assaulting people in the streets. Their acts of provocation, often culminating in brawls, were symbolic attempts to conquer enemy territory. The KPD responded to the SA's increasing aggression with more violence. Battles in auditoriums and on streets claimed numerous victims—on both sides.[31]

For the Nazi leadership, SA violence was a double-edged sword since it contradicted Hitler's hypocritical pledges to remain within legal boundaries. In February 1931, the party leader cautioned SA men not to be "tempted into unlawful acts," telling them, "Our unshakable legality will rebound against and shatter all measures taken by today's political leaders."[32] Not everyone was happy about Hitler's appeal-cum-order to his men. In the summer of 1930, the Berlin chapter of the SA under Walter Stennes had already rebelled against the party leadership in Munich. In April 1931, after Hitler had dismissed Stennes from his post, tensions flared up again, and Stennes and his followers occupied the offices of the Berlin regional directorship. Hitler rushed to the scene, together with the Berlin gauleiter, Joseph Goebbels, and managed to quell the rebellion quickly, getting the SA organizations to swear loyalty to his own person. But conflict continued to smolder. The cause was a fundamental unresolved issue that ran throughout the group's history. It was unclear whether the SA should be a mere auxiliary force of the Nazi Party in its struggle for power or should play an equal role alongside the party as a "military association" that would be assigned a major military function in the future "Third Reich" after the Nazis had attained power.[33]

The crisis came to a head in the summer of 1931. On June 6, the Brüning cabinet presented another emergency decree to safeguard the economy and finance. Once again it included severe social benefits cuts. To soothe public anger the Reich government also issued, together with the emergency decree, an appeal denouncing the "tribute," that is, reparations payments, in unusually harsh terms. Germany had so far done everything it could to meet its obligations from the lost war, the appeal stated, but that was now "no longer possible." The statement continued: "The mobilization of the last forces and reserves of all sections of the population gives the German government the right and duty to proclaim to the world. We have reached the limit of the privations we can impose on our people."[34] The "tribute appeal" shook the confidence of international creditors in the German government's willingness to continue meeting its obligations. As a result, foreign investors rushed to cash in their short-term loans. Within a short time, the Reichsbank lost a large part of its gold and foreign-currency reserves. Germany was on the verge of insolvency.

On June 20, 1931, with German financial collapse seemingly imminent, help unexpectedly beckoned from across the Atlantic. US President Herbert Hoover proposed a moratorium on German reparations and Entente war debts. In a radio address broadcast by all German stations on the evening of June 23, Brüning welcomed Hoover's initiative while reaffirming his own fiscal conservativism. "The vote of confidence contained within President Hoover's step, unique in world history, can bear fruit only if the German people are determined to continue their own path of the greatest austerity in all areas," Brüning said.[35] While Hoover's proposal met with broad approval in Germany, France felt bypassed. Lengthy negotiations were necessary to overcome French government resistance. It was not until July 6 that the approval of all the stakeholders involved was secured.

The weeks of delay meant that the psychological boost from Hoover's announcement, especially in Germany, fizzled out. On July 13, one week after the moratorium came into force, the Darmstadt and National Bank, Danatbank for short, collapsed. A general run on banks and savings institutions set in, forcing the government to suspend banking activity for forty-eight hours. "Ominous days hovering over Germany," noted Thea Sternheim. "Panic everywhere."[36] The Danatbank bankruptcy brought disaster to many companies. Among them was the Scholems' printing business in Berlin. "And it looks as if we'll lose everything," Betty Scholem reported to her son Gershom. "It's little consolation that the whole commercial sector is in the same state and that many more businesses are collapsing than will survive. Since there is nothing but scorched earth all around us, there's no possibility of starting over. The situation is desperate."[37] Goebbels, on the other hand, was triumphant: "The Reich is on the verge of bankruptcy. Our hour is approaching with uncanny speed. And we'll be ready to use it."[38]

The German banking crisis caused considerable concern on the international financial markets. People not only in the United States but also in England and France increasingly realized that German financial

collapse would also have serious consequences for their domestic econo-
mies. An American-prompted international conference held in London
at the end of July 1931 promised the German government considerable
financial relief and recommended that the Bank for International Settlements have a commission of experts examine Germany's financial situation. In its final report, that commission concluded that the German
economy could not be expected to recover without a resolution to the
reparations issues. Banks in the most important creditor countries agreed
to try to defer Germany's foreign debts for six months. Ultimately, as
far as reparations were concerned, Brüning's rigid austerity policy was
beginning to pay off. But the cost was tremendous. "Fear everywhere of
a winter with seven million unemployed," noted Victor Klemperer at the
beginning of September 1931.[39]

The dramatic events of the summer of 1931 turned powerful economic
forces against Brüning's government. In a petition to Hindenburg on July
22, the Reich Rural League, the influential interest group of large East
Prussian agrarian estate owners, demanded a "complete break with the
forces of international Marxism." The petition read: "The frequently
heard objection that it's impossible to govern without the Social Democrats is wrong. The Social Democratic movement and the working class
are being conflated here. No political course has betrayed the German
worker more than the Social Democratic one. Five million unemployed
and people with reduced working hours are the proof."[40]

The leading industrial associations, which had initially placed great
hopes in Brüning's policies, now also distanced themselves from the
chancellor. For them, Brüning's dismantlement of the welfare state did
not go far enough, and they accused the chancellor of failing to liberate
himself from the influence of the Social Democrats. On September 6, a
leading representative of Ruhr Valley industry, the general director of
Gutehoffnungshütte mining company, Paul Reusch, wrote an incendiary letter to Ludwig Kastl, managing member of the Reich Association
of German Industry. Reusch opined that "since Mr. Brüning has disappointed the expectations we placed in him and since he doesn't have the

courage to separate himself from the Social Democratic camp, industry and the Reich Association must fight him as vigorously as possible, and industry should openly express its distrust." Kastl replied that he "fundamentally" agreed with Reusch's statements about Brüning and that he acknowledged that Brüning's policies had been "greatly disappointing."[41]

In a meeting between top representatives of the Reich Association and Brüning on September 18, Carl Duisberg continued the criticism. They had expressed their confidence in the Reich chancellor on several occasions, Duisberg said, but they now concluded that he was "no longer in a position to master the continuing deterioration of our situation." Brüning's alleged habit of making too many concessions to the SPD was one obvious factor in this. Brüning said he understood "the nervousness in the country" and "the impatience of industry," but at the same time he expressed his determination to continue along the unpopular path he had taken, by presenting a new emergency decree.[42] On September 29, ten leading business associations went public with their criticism in a joint statement. German politicians, they said, had to realize that there could be "no compromise between socialist and capitalist economic models," and should thus "openly and wholeheartedly commit to one path." Only if the government finally acted in the interests of German business could it "be certain of the support of all responsible German citizens who believe in the future of the German fatherland."[43] These sorts of public demands could be read as a declaration of war.

Pressured by its industrialist wing, the DVP now also went over to the opposition. On October 5, Eduard Dingeldey, who had replaced Ernst Scholz as party and parliamentary group leader the previous November, informed Brüning that he no longer had the DVP's backing. A few days later, DVP parliamentarian Erich von Gilsa gleefully informed Reusch that Dingeldey had now decided to "openly distance himself from Brüning . . . and make himself available for cooperation with the nationalist opposition."[44]

Hindenburg didn't fail to notice the Reich Rural League and industrialist circles' intensified criticism of Brüning's policies. At a meeting with the

Reich president on September 13, Brüning noted a change in the atmosphere. Hindenburg, Brüning said, had lacked "his usual equanimity and friendly attitude this time" and insisted that the chancellor "must now move further to the right." At the end of the month, during another meeting with Hindenburg, the president told of how "painful" it was for him to realize that Brüning was "progressively losing ground." He had received "a large number of letters from the best men in the German Reich" opposing Brüning's policies and demanding his removal from office.[45]

The Reichswehr leadership also demanded that the government move to the right, accompanied by a change of attitude toward Hitler and his movement. Since the fall of 1930, after Hitler's appearance before the Reich Court in Leipzig, the Reichswehr Ministry had concluded that the Nazi Party should no longer be seen as a hostile, subversive movement, but rather as a political force that had to be included in its considerations. One motivation for the shift was the ministry's interest in increasing Germany's military strength. As Reichswehr Minister Groener informed Brüning in November 1930, the SA was seen as having "defensive potential" that could be used for the future expansion of the Reichswehr. In March 1931, Schleicher agreed with SA leader Ernst Röhm that National Socialists would be allowed to take part in border-guard training courses.[46]

Despite the obvious hypocrisy of Hitler's declared commitment to legality, the Reichswehr leadership intensified its efforts in the fall of 1931 to involve the NSDAP in political responsibility. The intent was to steer the National Socialists into moderate waters, to "tame" them, as it was often termed, through government participation. Rudolf Hess reported on September 9 that attempts were being made from various sides "to persuade Brüning to at least allow H[itler] to join the government." Hitler's condition was the calling of new elections, which were likely to "bring another huge success for the movement."[47]

On October 3, Schleicher met with the Nazi Party chairman. When asked whether he was prepared to tolerate the Brüning government, Hitler replied in the negative but did declare a willingness to join the cabinet, if new elections were called immediately. "Things are starting to move," Goebbels reported, based on Hitler's account of the meeting.

"If we get a decisive position of power in the Reich, we can put off Prussia. . . . Marxism can then be brought to its knees by [a government-appointed regional] state commissioner."[48] Schleicher was impressed by Hitler, calling him "an interesting man with an outstanding gift of oratory," although he added: "His plans take him to higher spheres. You have to pull him down to earth by the scruff of his neck."[49] The assumption was that he, Schleicher, would be able to contain Hitler's ambitions and limit the destructive dynamism of his movement. That would prove to be a serious miscalculation.

Brüning refused to consider new elections as a condition for the Nazis to join his government. "In all my experience, the only winners would be the radical parties on both wings, and what remained of the mainstream (apart from the Center Party) would be more or less pulverized," he told Hindenburg.[50] But he could not simply ignore the Reich president's request that he expand his cabinet to the right. The resignation of Foreign Minister Curtius, who had failed with his project of a German-Austrian customs union, provided an occasion for a cabinet reshuffle. At a ministerial meeting on October 7, the government decided to resign, with Brüning admitting "that a certain amount of ill-feeling against the current Reich cabinet . . . had been transmitted to the populace and has partly fallen on fertile soil."[51] Ministers whom Hindenburg considered a thorn in his side were replaced. The most prominent victim was Minister of the Interior Joseph Wirth, a member of the left wing of the Center Party. Groener temporarily assumed his portfolio in addition to the Reichswehr Ministry. That made him the most important man in the cabinet alongside Brüning, who took over the Foreign Ministry from Curtius in addition to the Chancellery. Transport Minister Theodor von Guérard made way for Gottfried Treviranus, who had become Reich commissioner for eastern aid following the dissolution of the Ministry for the Occupied Territories in September 1930. That post now fell to the Pomeranian estate owner Hans Schlange-Schöningen, a member of the Christian National Rural Popular Party. After being turned down by the industrialists Albert Vögler and Paul Silverberg, Brüning was also able to win over Hermann Warmbold, a board member of IG Farben, for the long-vacant position at the head of the Ministry of Economics. The extremely conservative

State Secretary Curt Joel, who had already effectively headed the Justice Ministry after Victor Bredt's departure, was now officially named to that post.[52]

With the DVP no longer represented, Brüning's second cabinet had even less allegiance to political parties than the first. Overall, the government was much more conservative, but the shift did not go far enough to the right for the chancellor's critics. Hans Schäffer, state secretary in the Reich Ministry of Finance, criticized him for failing to bring "authoritative personalities of the Right or from groups trusted by the Right" into his cabinet. Schäffer also insisted the dual functions now borne by Brüning and Groener were a purely temporary "emergency solution."[53]

Brüning still depended on the Social Democrats tolerating his government. On October 16, 1931, his cabinet survived the opposition's motions of censure with a narrow majority of 295 votes to 270 (with 3 abstentions)—thanks to the support of the SPD parliamentary group and the Business Party, which the chancellor had once again managed to win over. Parliament adjourned until February 23, 1932. "Brüning has achieved a Pyrrhic victory," Goebbels noted.[54]

On October 10, Hindenburg granted Hitler a first audience. The Reich president was annoyed at shouts of "Germany awaken!" from young National Socialists among the usual cheers of the population during his appearances in East Prussia. But Hitler succeeded in defusing the situation by slipping into the role of the former front-line soldier and flattering the field marshal with gestures of apparent deference. Nonetheless, Hindenburg made it clear to the Nazi Party leader that he would resolutely prevent any attempt to bypass him and seize power. In Brüning's recollection, Hindenburg said afterward: "He spoke quite nicely, but you can't make him a minister."[55] In fact, the impression made by the NSDAP chairman was not as unfavorable as Brüning and some later historians claimed. "I liked Hitler very much," Hindenburg told an old confidant, Colonel General von Einem.[56] For his part, in conversation with Goebbels, Hitler expressed his satisfaction with the course of the audience. Hindenburg had "listened attentively," while he, Hitler, had

"made everything clear to him from a military point of view." State Secretary Meissner had "greatly seconded" him. The upshot, in Goebbels's
telling—"Result: The old man has now been acquainted with us face-
to-face. The boss calls him worthy of respect."[57]

On October 11, 1931, a few days after the formation of the second
Brüning cabinet, the "national opposition" marched in Bad Harzburg, a
small town on the edge of the Harz Mountains. The location was carefully chosen. The Free State of Braunschweig, of which it was part, had
been governed by a coalition of German DNVP and National Socialists since October 1930. Hugenberg initiated the meeting. As the central
publication of the DNVP, *Unsere Partei* (Our party), openly proclaimed,
the purpose of the event was to give the "signal to attack" against the
hated Weimar Republic, "a system gone rotten."[58] All the prominent
figures of the anti-republican Right attended. In addition to the leaders from the National Socialists, the DNVP, the Stahlhelm, the Reich
Rural League, and the Pan-Germanic League, there were also members
of the high nobility, including the second-oldest son of former Kaiser
Wilhelm II, Prince Eitel Friedrich, and ranking military officers such as
the former head of the army command, Hans von Seeckt, who had been
a DVP member of parliament since 1930. Representatives of industry
and banks were also present, including steel magnate Fritz Thyssen and
former Reichsbank president Hjalmar Schacht, whose appearance sig-
naled a change in his political orientation. But only second-tier figures
from Rhenish-Westphalian heavy industry showed up. "It was generally
noticed that not a single one of the real industrial leaders was present,"
wrote Erich von Gilsa to Paul Reusch.[59]

Hitler had only reluctantly decided to take part. Being received
by Hindenburg had given his self-confidence a further boost, and he
came to Bad Harzburg not to demonstrate unity but to underscore his
claim to leadership of the German Right. Throughout the event, he
behaved like a prima donna, repeatedly snubbing his conservative partners. On the morning of October 11, for example, he inspected only the
parade of the SA and SS units and demonstratively moved off when

the Stahlhelm formations arrived. He appeared at the final rally in the Kursaal stadium in the afternoon only after Hugenberg had spent an hour convincing him to do so. When it was his turn to speak, he once more dispelled the impression of a common front by pretending that he was talking exclusively to his own followers, addressing those present as "party comrades." He concluded with the words: "Long live our glorious National Socialist movement!" In the manifesto he read out, he left no doubt as to who would be in charge in the future. The National Socialists, he said, were ready "to assume any and all responsibility for the formation of nationalist governments in the Reich and in the regional states."[60]

Kaiser Wilhelm II's representative, Wilhelm von Dommen, reported back to the former emperor in exile in Doorn that Germany had finally succeeded in "establishing a united national front" and that the hour was approaching in which "the November people have run their race and we can push through a nationalist government."[61] In truth, though, the so-called Harzburg Front was united only in its unconditional rejection of the Weimar "system." There had been no agreement on a platform for a joint government. Behind the scenes, the battle for leadership continued, with everyone suspecting everyone else of pursuing selfish goals. This was especially the case with Hitler and the Nazi Party. If the Brüning government fell, Goebbels wrote in his diary the day after the Bad Harzburg conference, "then it will be our turn." He added: "But then we must boot out the backlash as quickly as possible. We alone want to be the masters of Germany."[62] It became apparent just how fragile the Harzburg Front was on October 18, when Hitler sent some one hundred thousand members of the SA and SS to march through Braunschweig. His intent was not only to demonstrate his independence but to make clear that only the National Socialists could mobilize such masses of supporters.

The Nazis won a triumphant 37.1 percent of the vote in the election in Hessen on November 15, 1931, becoming the strongest party by far in that western German regional state. But just ten days later, an incident occurred that threatened to severely disrupt Hitler's prospects. A former member of the Hessian Nazi parliamentary group leaked explosive material to the Frankfurt police chief, minutes of a meeting that members of the Hessian regional Nazi directorate had held in April at the Boxheimer Hof estate near the town of Laupertsheim. The "Boxheim documents," as they became known, revealed that in the event of a seizure of power, the Hessian NSDAP leadership planned everything from a "ruthless crackdown by the armed forces" to the imposition of death sentences for resistance and sabotage. The author of the documents was the court assessor Werner Best, head of the legal department of the regional directorate and designated chairman of the state parliamentary group.[63]

The revelations of these plans caused a considerable stir, as they seemed to confirm general fears about the National Socialists' true intentions. On Hitler's behalf, Göring hastened to assure Hindenburg that the Nazis would "only act legally and only pursue their goals by legal means."[64] While German supporters of democracy demanded consequences, Chief Reich Prosecutor Karl August Werner tried to play down the incident. He was acting on direct instructions from Brüning, who wanted to prevent any damage to ongoing exploratory talks on the formation of the first conservative-fascist government at the regional level. In fact, the negotiations broke down in December because the Nazis made impossible demands. The investigation against Best was deliberately delayed. In October 1932, the fourth senate of the Reich Court declared him "beyond prosecution" due to a lack of evidence.[65] Instead of using the Boxheim affair to take the offensive against the Nazis' antigovernment and anti-democratic activities, the state and the judiciary worked together to sweep the matter under the carpet, thereby recklessly squandering a golden opportunity.

"If there is anything surprising about the year 1931, it is that it passed without any political explosions," Leopold Schwarzschild wrote in the newspaper *Das Tage-Buch*, which he co-published.[66] "A sad New Year's Eve," noted Kessler on December 31, 1931. "The end of a catastrophic year and the beginning of an even more catastrophic one."[67] The *Vossische Zeitung* wrote of a "year of disaster" that "began with sorrow and ended with hardship and was therefore even harder to bear than the terrible years of 1918 and 1923, the former of which at least brought an end to the horror of bloodshed and the latter the mastering of the hobgoblin of inflation."[68] Klemperer also saw no signs of improvement in 1931: "Now nothing but despair, no future, no faith of any kind. You just want to go on living somehow without really grasping why and how. You're completely numbed."[69] By contrast, the mood in Nazi circles was completely different. "The new year will and must bring the decision," an expectant Goebbels wrote in his diary on New Year's Day 1932. "Now then, let's enter it. With courage, strength, and trust in God."[70]

The dominant domestic political issue in the first months of 1932 was the question of whether Hindenburg, whose term of office expired on April 25, would be reelected. To spare the eighty-four-year-old Reich president the hardships of a second popular election, Brüning came up with the idea of having his term of office extended by a decision of the Reichstag—a path already taken back in 1922 when Ebert's term of office had been lengthened. In a meeting with the Reich chancellor on January 5, 1932, Hindenburg "agreed in principle" while making it known how difficult it was for him to decide "to make himself available to the fatherland again."[71] A two-thirds majority in parliament was required to extend his term of office, and Brüning could obtain one only with the support of the National Socialists.[72] On January 6, Interior Minister Groener met with Hitler on behalf of the Reich chancellor to sound out whether he could be won over. Groener summarized his assessment of the Nazi Party leader a few days later in a military commanders' meeting: "Made a likable impression, modest, orderly man who wants the best. . . . Hitler's intentions and goals are good, but he is a swarm animal, fervently many-sided."[73]

A series of meetings followed, in which Hitler initially seemed to signal a willingness to cooperate, but in the end he made his support conditional on the dissolution of the Reichstag and new elections. Brüning could not agree to this because if the Nazis won those elections, there would no longer be a Reichstag majority willing to tolerate his government. On January 12, Hitler informed Brüning that, "despite all his personal admiration for the Reich president," he could not agree to a parliamentary extension of his term of office. A few days later, in a detailed memorandum, he justified that refusal by citing constitutional concerns that, though not unfounded, sounded strange coming from the mouth of a man who had made no secret of his intent, once in power, to abolish the constitution as quickly as possible.[74] Hugenberg also rejected Brüning's plan.[75]

Now it was up to the chancellor to convince the president to run in the popular election after all. Hindenburg was visibly upset at the failure of Brüning's plan and took his time making up his mind. At the end of January, he made it known that he would run for another term in office only if it "did not meet with the united opposition of the entire Right" and if his reelection on the first ballot "could be regarded as assured."[76] On February 1, a cross-party "Hindenburg Committee" headed by the mayor of Berlin, Heinrich Sahm, launched a public campaign, quickly collecting over three million signatures supporting Hindenburg's renewed candidacy. But even this didn't assuage the Reich president's concerns. He was particularly pained that the Stahlhelm, of which he was an honorary member, declined to endorse him. It was only when the Kyffhäuser League, the umbrella organization of soldiers' associations, declared its support on February 15 that Hindenburg relented and made himself available. "A day of fateful significance for Germany," remarked Pünder.[77] Two days later, Hindenburg wrote to his estate neighbor Oldenburg-Januschau, with whom he was on cordial terms, to say how much he was hurt by the German nationalist press claiming he had been "handed" his candidacy "of the Left or a conservative–Social Democratic coalition."[78]

Hindenburg's decision created a dilemma for Hitler, who had no choice but to throw his hat into the ring. The Nazi leader hesitated for a long time before deciding to run because it entailed considerable risk of losing a direct contest against Hindenburg, and defeat could damage his aura as the seemingly unstoppable Führer of an irresistible movement, storming from victory to victory. "When will Hitler make up his mind?" Goebbels complained on January 30. "Does he lack the nerve? We'll have to give him some."[79] Two days later, in a meeting in the Brown

House, Hitler announced he would, in fact, challenge Hindenburg. However, Hitler's candidacy was not to be announced publicly until the Reich president had declared his renewed candidacy and the Social Democrats had come out in his favor. If the democratic camp supported Hindenburg, Hitler reckoned, he could more easily portray himself as the candidate of the entire Right. Both conditions were met by mid-February 1932. Nevertheless, Hitler waited a further week, until February 22, before allowing Goebbels to announce his candidacy at a rally in the Berlin Sportpalast. The same day, the Stahlhelm, supported by the DNVP, declared its intention to nominate its own candidate, deputy federal chairman Theodor Duesterberg. The fault lines in the Harzburg Front were now on full display. As it had done in 1925, the KPD put forward party chairman Ernst Thälmann.[80]

Hitler still had one obstacle. To run for the office of president, he needed German citizenship—something Thuringian Minister of the Interior and National Education Wilhelm Frick had tried and failed to procure for him in the summer of 1930. The right-wing government of the Braunschweig intervened on Hitler's behalf, appointing the Nazi leader a government councillor at its legation in Berlin on February 26. He took his oath of office, applying immediately for a leave of absence until the end of the Reich presidential election campaign. He would never take up the "service" associated with that office. "So Hitler is a citizen," a cynical Goebbels wrote. "Our congratulations."[81]

Three days earlier, Hitler's propaganda expert had scandalized the Reichstag by accusing Hindenburg of "abandoning the cause of his former voters" and "clearly siding with the Social Democrats," adding, "Tell me who praises you and I'll tell you where you stand!" Hindenburg, Goebbels claimed, was being "praised by the Berlin street press, praised by the party of deserters." That was a gibe against the Social Democrats. SPD member of parliament Kurt Schumacher, a severely wounded 1914 war volunteer, memorably responded to this slander with the riposte: "If we know anything about National Socialism, it's that for the first time in German politics human stupidity has been successfully and completely mobilized."[82]

Instead of siding with the Social Democrats, Brüning could come up with nothing better in the Reichstag debate of February 24 than to turn to the right in parliament and affirm that he didn't want to be associated in any way with the November Revolution of 1918: "On November 9, I was in the troop forming the head of the Winterfeld group to suppress the revolution."[83] In his memoirs, Brüning reported that this passage of his speech had met with "thunderous applause" from the center of the floor to the DNVP, while the reaction on the left was "gloomy silence."[84] The chancellor could not have expressed more clearly his contempt for the parliamentary democracy that had emerged from the revolution.

Nevertheless, in an appeal on February 27, the SPD executive committee was not deterred from urging party members and supporters to vote for Hindenburg: "Use all your strength to strike the decisive blow in the first ballot! Liberate the German people from the fascist threat with this one blow! Defeat Hitler! Vote for Hindenburg!"[85] Otto Braun, the Prussian state premier who had run against Hindenburg in the first round of the 1925 election, now praised the Reich president in *Vorwärts* as "the embodiment of calm and steadfastness, of loyalty to one's self and devotion to duty for the people as a whole."[86] Braun declared that he was voting for Hindenburg and appealed to his supporters to do the same. The political landscape had shifted to such an extraordinary extent that the Social Democrats now felt compelled to endorse a dyed-in-the-wool monarchist as the only alternative to Hitler.

As in 1925, Hindenburg did not campaign. Only once, in a March 10 radio speech, did he address the public. In it, he dismissed the accusation that he had been "handed" his candidacy by the Left or a conservative-SPD alliance. "On the contrary, I considered it a patriotic duty to be the nonpartisan candidate of the German people," Hindenburg proclaimed.[87] Brüning, although his relationship with the Reich president had deteriorated considerably in the preceding months, campaigned with all his energy for Hindenburg's reelection, knowing

Hindenburg campaigns for reelection on the radio on March 10, 1932,
three days before the first ballot of the Reich presidential election.

full well that he alone could defeat Hitler. In his numerous campaign
appearances, the chancellor invoked the myth of the "victor of Tannen-
berg," the battle Hindenburg was credited with winning. Indeed, in a
final rally in the Sportpalast in Berlin on March 11, two days before the
first round of voting, he went so far as to name Hindenburg in the same
breath as the "men sent by God," who in "all the decisive hours during
and after the war" had possessed "the courage" to "persevere and make
correct but difficult decisions."[88]

Meanwhile, the National Socialists ran their campaign using the
most modern technology. Goebbels recorded a speech onto a gramophone record and distributed it in an edition of fifty thousand. A ten-
minute sound film, shown in the streets and on the squares of major
cities, praised Hitler as the coming savior of the German people. Garish

posters proclaimed: "Down with the system! All power to National Socialism!"[89] Hitler avoided attacking Hindenburg directly in his public appearances. He knew that he could not afford to irreparably damage his relationship with the president because, should Hitler lose the election, he could not come to power without Hindenburg's consent. So he constantly expressed his admiration for the former field marshal while suggesting that Hindenburg was a man of the past, even as the future belonged to himself and his movement. "Old man," he exclaimed in Nuremberg on March 7. "You should no longer take on responsibility for us. We, the generation of the war, will take it ourselves. You, venerable old man, can no longer cover for those today whom we want to destroy. So please step aside and clear the way."[90]

After some initial skepticism, the rest of the Nazi Party leadership was impressed by the huge crowds drawn to Hitler's rallies and became confident of victory. "Talked to Hitler this evening," Goebbels noted on March 9. "Going from triumph to triumph. Everything looks good. This will be a success!"[91]

The polling stations closed at 6 p.m. on March 13. "The vote-counting machines have started working full speed—the streets remain quiet," reported the *Vossische Zeitung*. "The restaurants are as empty as on a memorial Sunday. All of Berlin is waiting near the loudspeakers—this cosmopolitan city is holding its breath."[92] By late evening, the result was clear. With well over 18 million votes (49.6 percent), Hindenburg had clearly defeated Hitler, who had received just over 11 million (30.1 percent). But the incumbent had fallen slightly short of an absolute majority, requiring a second round of voting. Thälmann had gotten just under 5 million votes (13.2 percent); and Duesterberg, 2.5 million (6.8 percent). After their high hopes, the outcome of the election shocked the Nazi Party. "We have gone down to defeat," Goebbels confided in his diary. "Terrible prospects . . . We have gained 86 percent since September 1930. But what use is all this? Our party comrades are depressed and despondent. . . . Telephoned with Hitler. He is extremely surprised at the result. We set our goals too high."[93]

In the *Vossische Zeitung*, historian Veit Valentin spoke of a "turning point in contemporary history." With March 13, 1932, "the spell of National Socialism was broken"; the "parties loyal to the state" had "heroically defended themselves." It was now time to "organize the counterattack": "Hindenburg's Germany has been forged into a political unit, a historical power, in the defense against the danger of civil war. May it seize its moment."[94] But Hindenburg and his camarilla had no intention whatsoever of joining the parties loyal to the Weimar Republic against the Far Right.

Hindenburg owed his victory primarily to the discipline of SPD supporters in following the call of their party leadership in voting almost unanimously for him. But the president was humiliated by needing both their support and a second round of voting. Although if Hugenberg and the Stahlhelm had not put forward Duesterberg, Hindenburg would probably have been elected in the first ballot, meeting the condition he had set for his candidacy, he directed his resentment at the chancellor, who had persuaded him to run again. When Brüning called on him the day after the election, he didn't get a word of thanks. On the contrary, Hindenburg only hissed, "The contest ended in a draw,"[95] even though there was no doubt he would triumph in the second round of voting on April 10.

Between the two votes, the idea suddenly emerged that Crown Prince Wilhelm could also run for the presidency. As part of a deal for the German government allowing him to return from Dutch exile to his Oels estate in the eastern German province of Silesia in November 1923, Kaiser Wilhelm II's eldest son had promised to refrain from any political activity. For a few years, he kept his word, but now he abandoned his restraint. In a letter to Hitler dated March 29, Wilhelm asked the Nazi leader to support him as a unified right-wing candidate. Hitler initially seemed prepared to withdraw his own candidacy, but only on the condition that Hindenburg also support Wilhelm. If he helped the crown prince to the presidency, Hitler reasoned, Wilhelm could appoint him chancellor in return. But the nascent plan failed after the former

Kaiser Wilhelm II vetoed it from Doorn. In the end, on April 1, the
crown prince publicly endorsed Hitler in the run-off election.[96]

The government decreed an "Easter truce" from March 20 to April 3 in
which all public gatherings were banned. The election campaign was thus
reduced to a single week. As Goebbels noted in his diary, the tight deadline necessitated "completely new methods" of propaganda.[97] An airplane
was chartered so that Hitler could hold multiple large mass rallies in various cities. "Hitler over Germany"—the slogan intended not only to sug-
gest the party leader's omnipresence but also to demonstrate the National
Socialist movement's claim to embody the coming "ethnic national community" that would transcend social classes and political parties.[98]

Hitler's efforts bore fruit. Although Hindenburg was elected with
53 percent of the ballots, Hitler took over two million more votes and
increased his electoral share to 36.8 percent. A large proportion of those
who had voted for Duesterberg, who withdrew his candidacy, voted for
the Nazi leader. Thälmann received only 10.2 percent, with many of his
supporters staying away from polling stations.[99]

Hindenburg couldn't stand the fact that he owed his election not
to like-minded allies on the right but to the tactical discipline of the
Social Democrats and the Catholic Center. "What an ass I am for having allowed myself to be elected a second time," he told confidants a
few weeks after the election.[100] Brüning immediately felt the president's
disgruntlement when he conveyed the government's congratulations to
him on April 11 and offered to step down with his cabinet, as custom
demanded. Hindenburg did not reject the offer outright, as was also cus-
tomary, declaring only that he was unwilling to accept the resignation
"for the time being" and insisting that his words be noted in the official
communiqué. "The chancellor is understandably very concerned about
this," noted Pünder.[101]

Disputes over a ban on the SA and SS exacerbated the estrangement
between Hindenburg and Brüning. On March 17, a few days after the

first round of elections, Prussian Interior Minister Carl Severing had the offices of the NSDAP and SA in Prussia searched. The confiscated material revealed that the Nazi Party headquarters in Munich had ordered the SA to stand at the ready on March 13. As they had after the release of the "Boxheim documents," the party leadership hastened to give public reassurances about their commitment to respecting legal boundaries. Interior Minister Groener, still enraptured by the "military potential" of the SA, remained reluctant to impose any consequences. But a conference of regional states' interior ministers on April 5 applied massive pressure on him to finally take action against Nazi paramilitary organizations. Only then did Groener decide to act, ordering a draft ban of the SA and SS to be drawn up.

But the draft elicited resistance within his own ministry. Schleicher, who had initially encouraged Groener, now backed off in the belief that he could "tame" the Nazi Party by integrating it into the government. He proposed a different approach. Hitler should be issued an ultimatum in the form of an open letter threatening him with the dissolution of the SA and SS if he was not prepared to demilitarize them. But Groener stuck to his plans. On April 10, he sent Brüning a memorandum arguing that after Hindenburg's victory the moment was right, psychologically, for a crackdown. Delaying the decision any longer would "shake the authority of the Reich government and the Reich president to the core."[102] In a meeting that evening, the chancellor agreed to the ban and rejected Schleicher's proposal—a defeat that very much embittered the ambitious head of the ministerial office in the Reichswehr Ministry. From that point on, he boycotted meetings and began to campaign against the ban behind his superior's back within the ministry and the presidential palace. "A tremendous breach of trust toward his boss, Excellency Groener!" noted an outraged Pünder.[103]

Under the influence of those around him, especially his son Oskar, whom Schleicher had been working on, Hindenburg expressed reservations, and it was only with great difficulty that Brüning and Groener convinced him of the ban's necessity. On April 13, the president signed the emergency decree to "safeguard the authority of the state," dissolving "all paramilitary organizations" of the Nazi Party.

The National Socialists had been warned of the impending ban and had enough time to get rid of weapons and incriminating documents. Although brown shirts disappeared from the streets, the organizational cohesion of the SA and SS was maintained as their members hid under the party's umbrella. In an appeal on April 13, Hitler promised that the ban would be only a temporary measure and called on his followers to exercise restraint. "If you do your duty, our propaganda will ensure this blow from General Groener will rebound a thousandfold on himself and his allies," Hitler said.[104]

The response of the press to the ban was mixed. Supporters of democracy hailed it as long overdue. "The National Socialist Party will lack an essential source of attraction in the weeks to come," rejoiced Benno Reifenberg, head of the domestic politics section of the *Frankfurter Zeitung*. "It has been drummed out."[105] The Hugenberg press, on the other hand, reacted with a storm of indignation, and the presidential palace was besieged by right-wing protests. All of this did not fail to have an effect on Hindenburg. In a decidedly unfriendly letter of April 15, he called on Groener to take measures against "similar organizations."[106] Enclosed was alleged incriminating material against the Reich Banner Black-Red-Gold, which Hindenburg said he had been given by the head of the army command, General Kurt von Hammerstein.[107] It spoke volumes that the Reich president made no distinction between the paramilitary units of the National Socialists, who wanted to destroy the Weimar Republic, and the Reich Banner, a Social Democratic militia founded in 1924 to actively defend the republic. "This is the thanks of the newly confirmed head of the Reich to those who made his triumph on April 10 possible, for the most part maintaining party discipline rather than voting from inner conviction," commented Ossietzky in *Die Weltbühne* when Hindenburg's move became publicly known.[108]

The Hammerstein material, essentially a collection of newspaper clippings, in no way justified a ban on the Reich Banner. Moreover, its national leader, Karl Höltermann, promised the minister of the interior that his organization would keep a low profile and that its defensive units, known as "Schufos," would voluntarily disband. On April 23, Groener and Brüning agreed not to take any action against the Reich

Banner, a decision that elicited Hindenburg's great ire. Groener knew that his position, as well as Brüning's, was becoming increasingly tenuous. "It is clear that everything possible is being done to topple me," he wrote to a friend on April 25. "Brüning has also been the victim of a smear campaign with the Reich president. The situation is quite critical. Hindenburg has discovered his conservative heart and wants a government that is further to the right than Brüning's."[109]

In a nod toward Hindenburg, the cabinet decided on May 3 to issue an emergency decree placing all quasi-military organizations under the supervision of the Reich Interior Ministry. At the same time, Groener reiterated that the SA ban had been necessary and that there was "not the slightest reason to ban the Reich Banner."[110]

But on May 10, Groener experienced his personal Waterloo. The day before, the speaker of the Nazi parliamentary group in the Reichstag, Hermann Göring, had attacked him, demanding that he rescind the ban on the SA and SS. Groener's self-defense was long on substance, but, weakened by illness and thrown off by constant heckling from National Socialist deputies, his rhetorical performance was weak. "Groener unfortunately made a disastrous impression arguing his case before parliament," wrote German State Party deputy Theodor Heuss to his party colleague Reinhold Maier a few days later. "We knew that he wasn't a good speaker. . . . But on this occasion he was very agitated, had his head covered with bandages because of furunculosis, looked bad, spoke without notes, and couldn't finish his sentences following interruptions."[111] After this pathetic appearance, Groener had to go. "Politically, he was dead after that speech," Brüning recalled. "Without a trace of sympathy, the faces of the right-wingers beamed with glee. I looked at every single one of them during his speech. The most disgusting was that of General von Seeckt, who made no attempt to conceal his delight at his old rival's collapse."[112]

On May 11, Schleicher informed the Reich Chancellery that "if Groener doesn't step down now, he and the other top generals of the Reichswehr Ministry would resign immediately."[113] Brüning and Pünder suggested that Groener take a leave of absence until things calmed down, but he refused and, after some hesitation, agreed to resign as Reichswehr

minister, though saying he wanted to stay on as minister of the interior.
As Hindenburg left for Neudeck on May 12, the decision was postponed
once again. But Groener's political career was effectively over, and with
him Brüning had lost his most important cabinet ally.[114] Brüning offered
to name Schleicher as Groener's successor as Reichswehr minister, but
the latter reacted evasively, saying that the decision should "not be
overly rushed."[115] The scheming major general was well aware that the
days of the Brüning cabinet itself were numbered.

On the third day of the Reichstag session, May 12, the chancellor
took the floor in the debate, completely ignoring the issue of Groener
and confining himself almost entirely to foreign policy. With a view to
a forthcoming conference in Lausanne and the prospect of a complete
abolition of reparations, he urged parliamentarians not to lose their nerve
during the "last hundred meters before the finish line." The appeal was
also directed at Hindenburg, on whose support he could no longer rely.
Once again, Brüning's government survived motions of censure by the
Nazi Party, the DNVP, and the KPD. However, the majority willing to
tolerate the government had dwindled to a handful of votes, and the
process of dissolution within the cabinet itself could no longer be overlooked. Economics Minister Warmbold had already resigned on April 28
after the failure of his efforts to persuade the government to adopt an
activist economic policy. And on May 2, Hans Schäffer, state secretary in
the Ministry of Finance, also asked to be relieved of his duties.[116]

Meanwhile, the intrigue against the Brüning cabinet continued, and once
again it was the éminence grise Schleicher pulling the strings. On April 28,
he had conferred with Hitler in an initial secret meeting to sound out the
conditions under which the Nazi Party chairman would enter or tolerate a
right-wing cabinet. According to Goebbels's notes, the meeting, in which
Hammerstein also took part, "went well," with the principals "coming to
an agreement." In early May, Goebbels received word that "the generals
were continuing to agitate." At a further meeting on May 7, this time also
attended by Meissner and Oskar von Hindenburg, a script for the demise
of the Brüning government was laid out. Goebbels noted: "Brüning is to

fall this week. The old man will withhold his confidence. Schleicher is strongly in favor. Meissner was good, only the young Hindenburg was a bit stupid. A presidentially appointed cabinet will come. Reichstag dissolved. The coercive laws will fall. We'll have freedom of action and deliver our masterstroke." In other words, Hitler had refused to participate in the government but had promised to tolerate a presidentially appointed cabinet further to the right. In return, he had obtained a promise that a new election to the Reichstag would be called and the ban on the SA and SS would be lifted. Hitler could be more than satisfied with this agreement, as he had kept all his trump cards without committing himself to a new government. "The boss is in a fine mood," Goebbels wrote. "We were discussing the next Reichstag election campaign. That will be a big hit. The SA marching in brown shirts. Woe betide our enemies."[117]

The conspiracy, however, did not go entirely according to plan. Brüning was able to gain some breathing room by underscoring the detrimental foreign policy consequences of a change of government so shortly before the conference in Lausanne. He also threatened to make a stink about the ingratitude of the Reich president, who ultimately had him to thank for reelection, before the Reichstag.[118] After Groener's resignation and the adjournment of parliament, Brüning's enemies resumed their secret talks. Goebbels's diary entries show how systematically they proceeded to undermine the Reich chancellor's position once and for all. "The crisis continues according to plan. That's good! A series of telephone calls with Hitler. He is very satisfied" (May 14). "Everything here is still in a Whitsun mood. Only Brüning is wavering. So push on" (May 18). "The Schleicher plan is going well. Brüning completely isolated. Desperately looking for new ministers. Schleicher has rejected the R[eichs]W[ehr] M[inisterium]. He wants the whole package" (May 19). "Schleicher continues to agitate. The list of ministers has been discussed. . . . Poor Brüning! He is on the verge of extinction" (May 20). On May 25, Werner von Alvensleben, a Schleicher confidant with contacts with the National Socialists, reported that Brüning would be "hung out to dry" in three days. He also presented the completed cabinet list with the names of the designated chancellor and the future foreign minister: Franz von Papen and Baron Konstantin von Neurath.[119]

On his estate in Neudeck, where he had retreated for two weeks on May 12, Hindenburg was more exposed than ever to the influence of his son Oskar and reactionary aristocrats who encouraged him to jettison Brüning as soon as possible. The final impetus for the fall of the chancellor came with the settlement plans of Reich Commissioner for Aid to the East Hans Schlange-Schöningen. On May 20, the cabinet passed a draft emergency decree he had submitted, authorizing him to acquire estates that were no longer eligible for debt relief by way of forced sale in order to make them available for settlement. Large agriculturalists were up in arms. In a May 24 petition to Hindenburg, the director of the East Prussian Land Society, Baron Wilhelm von Gayl, expressed his organization's "grave concerns." After the numerous encroachments on private property by earlier emergency decrees, Gayl wrote, "the authorities' new compulsory auction law amounted to further encroachment and a new slide into state socialism." The Reich president, he demanded, should subject the ordinance to "special examination."[120]

That day, Count Eberhard von Kalckreuth, a member of the Reich Rural League board, also lodged a protest with Hindenburg. The planned emergency decree, he proclaimed, would go down paths "that must cause tremendous bitterness in the already hard-pressed agricultural community of the East and cause extraordinary damage to the landowner and associated economic circles." The letter was accompanied by an article in the *Deutsche Zeitung*, the main organ of the Pan-Germanic League, bearing the headline: "Disenfranchisement of the East!"[121]

The campaign had the desired effect. When Meissner presented the draft of the emergency decree to Hindenburg on May 25, the latter refused to sign it. At the same time, the Reich president announced that he wouldn't allow Groener to remain in office as Reich interior minister "after his blunder in the matter of the SA and SS units." The state secretary was instructed to convey to Brüning Hindenburg's "urgent wish" that he "reorganize the cabinet, namely to the right" after the conference in Lausanne scheduled for mid-June. Hindenburg also brought up Schleicher as someone "very agreeable" to him.[122]

After Meissner had reported to him on May 26, Brüning knew his time as chancellor was running out, and he was determined to no longer stand idly by and watch his authority be gradually undermined. Instead, he presented Hindenburg with the alternative of either reaffirming confidence in or dismissing him after his return from Lausanne. This was the start of the debate described at the beginning of this chapter, which took place on the morning of May 29. Hindenburg brusquely rejected the request for a "new gesture of confidence." The bridges between the two men were burned. Brüning rejected Hindenburg's counterrequest to continue to make himself available to the government as foreign minister, saying he no longer saw any possibility for fruitful cooperation after the events of the past few months. During their meeting, the Reich chancellor maintained decorum, but he later revealed how much he had been hurt by "the callous manner" with which the Reich president had dismissed him.[123]

The cabinet met for the last time on the morning of May 30. The chancellor reported on his conversation with Hindenburg, and his ministers agreed that after everything that had happened, the government would have to resign. When Groener announced that he was going public about the machinations of the camarilla surrounding the president, Brüning asked him not to, arguing, "Despite everything, Hindenburg is the only one the people can still rally around."[124]

That day, at 11:55 a.m., Brüning presented the Reich president with his letter of resignation. Hindenburg had deliberately scheduled the appointment for that hour, as the naval guard was due to march in front of the presidential palace at twelve noon to mark the upcoming anniversary of the Battle of the Skagerrak. That left a mere five minutes for their farewell audience. Hindenburg once again asked his former chancellor of choice to remain in the office of foreign minister. Brüning once more refused, warning the president not to let advisers "push him down a path that would lead to a breach of the constitution." Their entire conversation lasted only three and a half minutes. "I bowed silently and walked back through the garden while the Reich president entered the portal and the honorary naval company gave him a resounding salute," Brüning wrote at the end of his report. "My final departure was thus celebrated by humiliating me."[125]

"The bombshell has arrived," Goebbels rejoiced in his diary. "At 12 noon, Brüning handed the old man the entire cabinet's resignation. That means the system has fallen. . . . I'm calling Hitler right away. He must come to Berlin."[126] In her diary, Thea Sternheim wrote of "Hindenburg kicking Brüning in the teeth." Apparently, she added, the "merchant of emergency decrees" was "not yet reactionary enough" for the clique around the Reich president.[127] Kessler was also appalled by Brüning's dismissal: "Behind-the-scenes influences have imposed their will just as in the days of Eulenburg and Holstein" under Wilhelm II, he noted on May 30. "Today marks the preliminary end of the parliamentary republic."[128] A commentator in *Die Weltbühne* took a similar view: "For years it has said that Germany was a republic without republicans. Now we are republicans without a republic."[129]

The fall of the Brüning cabinet was indeed a turning point. As Heinrich August Winkler has noted, it marked the end of "the moderate phase of the presidential system," whose most prominent feature since October 1930 had been the Social Democrats' tolerance of the government.[130] But Schleicher, the chief political strategist of the Reichswehr, and the camarilla around Hindenburg were unwilling to allow even this limited form of parliamentarism and sought to completely eliminate the SPD and to establish an authoritarian regime in which the conservative elites from big business, heavy industry, and the military could once again rule, while the National Socialists were to be integrated and "tamed."

Nonetheless, we should not overlook that the erosion of parliamentary democracy—the increase in power of the Reich president and the Reichswehr leadership at the expense of parliament, which was dramatically disempowered—had already begun when Brüning took office. In a certain sense, the chancellor was the victim of a development he himself had helped kick-start and drive with his permanent recourse to Article 48. Whether Brüning envisioned a restoration of the Hohenzollern monarchy as a long-term goal, as he claimed in his posthumously published memoirs from 1970, is debatable. What is certain is that he didn't prioritize a return to a functioning parliamentary system. In fact, he didn't

*The "Cabinet of the Barons," June 2, 1932. Sitting, from left: Magnus von
Braun (Food), Wilhelm von Gayl (Interior), Franz von Papen (Chancellor),
Konstantin von Neurath (Foreign Affairs). Standing, from left: Franz
Gürtner (Justice), Hermann Warmbold (Economics), Kurt von Schleicher
(Reichswehr). Missing: Lutz Graf Schwerin von Krosigk (Finance),
Paul von Eltz-Rübenach (Transport), and Hugo Schäffer (Labor).*

even consider it desirable. The long-standing dispute among historians
as to whether the Brüning era represented a "conservative alternative"
to the failed party democracy, that is, whether it should be seen as an
attempt to salvage what could still be saved from the Weimar Republic,
is thus pointless. Ultimately, the decisive factor was not what Brüning
wanted or not, but what the Reich president and his advisers, on whom
the parliamentary leader of the Center Party had made himself dependent from the very start of his chancellorship, thought was right. The
advocates of authoritarianism had no interest in preserving any remnants
at all of parliamentary democracy. They wanted to dismantle it as gradually, subtly, and completely as possible.[131]

On the afternoon of May 30, Hindenburg received Hitler and Göring as part of his exploratory talks with party leaders. The NSDAP chairman declared his willingness to tolerate a right-wing government under Franz von Papen under the two conditions he had previously negotiated with Schleicher: that the Reichstag be dissolved as quickly as possible and that the ban on the SA and SS be lifted. He was promised both. Goebbels noted with satisfaction: "Conversation with the old man went well. . . . SA ban dropped. Uniforms allowed and Reichstag dissolved. That is the most important thing. Everything else will fall into place." [132]

The new chancellor, a scion of the old Westphalian landed gentry, had not yet made much of a political name for himself. He was a Center Party backbencher in the Prussian regional parliament and the majority shareholder of the party newspaper, *Germania*. During the First World War, as a military attaché at the German embassy in Washington, he had attempted to sabotage the supply of weapons and ammunition from the United States to the Entente. He was discovered and summarily expelled as an "undesirable." When he left the United States, trusting in the immunity of diplomatic baggage, Papen carried important secret documents with him—a serious mistake that led to numerous arrests in his American network. After returning to Germany, he served as a battalion commander between summer 1916 and summer 1917 on the Western Front, which commended him to Hindenburg.[133] Schleicher selected Papen as a candidate precisely because of his political inexperience, which made Schleicher believe he could be even more easily steered. Schleicher himself became Reichswehr minister in the new cabinet, emerging from the shadows for the first time. The former ambassador to London, Konstantin von Neurath, became foreign minister; Gayl, interior minister; and Baron Magnus von Braun, who also came from the old East Prussian landed gentry, minister of food. The Ministry of Finance went to Ministerial Director Count Lutz Schwerin von Krosigk; the Ministry of Post and Transport to Baron Paul von Eltz-Rübenach, previously president of the Reich Rail Directorship in Karlsruhe; and the Ministry of Labor to Hugo Schäffer, a former director of the Krupp factories. Franz Gürtner, who protected Hitler as Bavarian

minister of justice, took over the Ministry of Justice. Hermann Warmbold returned to the cabinet as economics minister.

"Accompanying the birth of the new government are the East Prussian landowners who want to hold on to their over-indebted farms at all
costs, even that of abandoning the nation," noted the *Vossische Zeitung*.[134]
Reactionary East Elbe estate owners, or *Junker*, indeed made up the
majority of the new cabinet. *Vorwärts* aptly dubbed it a "cabinet of barons." The political basis of the new government was just as narrow as the
social origins of its members. Not only did the SPD and KPD declare
war on it, but the Center Party also refused to support Papen for betraying Brüning. The chancellor-designate had resigned from the party on
May 31.[135]

On July 4, Hindenburg dissolved the Reichstag as agreed. July 31 was
set as the date for the new election. On July 16, the ban on the SA and
SS was lifted. This fulfilled Hitler's second condition. The July 31 election brought the expected resounding victory for the National Socialists,
who achieved 37.8 percent of the vote—an increase of 19 percentage
points. With 230 seats, they were the strongest parliamentary group in
the Reichstag. The SPD fell from 24.5 to 21.6 percent. Even together
with the KPD, which increased its support slightly to 14.5 percent, the
two left-wing parties held fewer seats than the Nazi Party. The Catholic
parties remained stable, with the Center improving its showing from 11.8
to 12.5 percent; the BVP, from 3.0 to 3.2 percent. The DNVP continued
to decline, with its support falling from 7.0 to 5.9 percent. The DVP
(with 1.2 percent) and the German State Party (with 1.0 percent) were
completely marginalized.[136] Together, the National Socialists and Communists commanded an absolute majority in the Reichstag and could
exercise their destructive role even more effectively.

These developments weren't inevitable. The struggle for Weimar
democracy, despite all of the system's structural shortcomings, had
always revolved around individual decisions in specific situations, and
they determined how history would unfold. The leaders involved had
the ability to decide one way or the other, right up to the end of Weimar
democracy. If Hindenburg's advisers had not persuaded him to dismiss
Brüning, Reichstag elections would not have had to be held until the

end of the legislative period in September 1934, by which time the economy was likely to have recovered, and the appeal of the radical parties would have waned. Instead, Hitler was able to score another triumph and add further support to his claim on the chancellorship, while Schleicher and the chancellor by his grace, Papen, were weaker than before. The Nazi leader immediately reneged on his promise to tolerate Papen's cabinet. "Now we must come to power and eradicate Marxism," Goebbels commented. "One way or another. Something has to happen. The time for opposition is over. We need deeds now!" [137]

On July 14, two weeks before the Reichstag election, Klaus Mann had the chance to observe Hitler with his entourage in the café of the Hotel Carlton in Munich. He noted in his diary: "Right at the next table: Adolf Hitler, in the most stupid of company. A man of positively conspicuous inferiority. Extremely untalented, the fascination he exerts, the greatest embarrassment in history." [138] Thomas Mann's eldest son thought it impossible that such a repulsive figure could become German chancellor. Like so many others, he was thoroughly mistaken.

9

The Hour of the Barons

PAPEN'S PRUSSIAN COUP D'ÉTAT

The "Prussian Coup" of July 20, 1932: Reichswehr troops position themselves in front of the Prussian Ministry of State on Wilhelmstrasse.

On the morning of July 20, 1932, at around a quarter to eleven, an official from the Reich Chancellery rang the doorbell of Prussian State Premier Otto Braun's cottage getaway in Berlin-Zehlendorf. He handed the baffled man of the house a letter with an official seal. It contained a single, explosive sentence: "Now that the Reich president has appointed me Reich commissioner for the state of Prussia by his decree of July 20, 1932, I am relieving you of your office as Prussian state premier." It was signed "v. Papen."[1] Braun decided to have himself driven to the State Ministry immediately, but Ministerial Director Eduard Nobis informed him by telephone that Reichswehr troops had already occupied the building and confiscated Braun's official car. Braun then declared he would take a cab to the office and let himself be arrested there.

This news caused considerable concern in the Reich Chancellery. A legally elected Prussian state premier being arrested by a Reichswehr detachment outside his official residence would make a very poor impression at home and abroad. Thoughts were bandied back and forth about how to dissuade the prominent SPD politician from his plans. But a short time later came the all-clear. Braun had informed his adviser Herbert Weichmann by telephone that he had changed his mind and now wanted to stay in his cottage. His arrest would "perhaps have provided material for a sensational press report," as he wrote to explain his change of heart in his memoirs, *From Weimar to Hitler*, written in exile, but would otherwise have been "useless."[2] It was a retreat with great symbolic import. The once powerful "Red Tsar" of Prussia no longer believed in resistance. Inwardly, he had long since capitulated.

Aside from brief interruptions in 1921 and 1925, Braun had governed Prussia since March 1920. Under his leadership, Germany's largest regional state by far had come to seem like a bulwark of the Weimar Republic. In any case, the political situation there, where the SPD cooperated with the Center Party and the DDP, was far more stable than at the national level, where governments changed more frequently and the parties of the original Weimar Coalition had not mustered a majority since 1920.

Yet when the consequences of the global economic crisis hit Germany with full force in the early 1930s, it became clear that the bulwark was crumbling. The DDP (renamed the German State Party in 1930) declined into a splinter party. The SPD's tolerance of the Brüning cabinets, to which it had no alternative, condemned Braun's government in Prussia to inaction, if it did not want to jeopardize its own coalition with the Center Party. Moreover, Prussia's financial situation was nothing short of dire, forcing it to make ever harsher budget cuts.

It was obvious under these conditions that the Prussian regional election on April 24, 1932, would turn out badly for the governing coalition, but the extent of their defeat surprised even their adversaries. The Nazi Party was able to increase its seats from 9 to 162, making it almost as powerful as the SPD, the Center Party, and the German State Party combined. Those parties achieved only 163 out of 423 seats, far short of a parliamentary majority. Nevertheless, despite the spectacular Nazi gains, the political Right still didn't have enough mandates to form a government, since the DNVP and DVP lost votes, and the KPD significantly increased its share of the ballots. Together, the National Socialists and Communists commanded a negative majority of 219 seats.[3]

As if anticipating the stalemate to come, the governing parties of the old regional parliament pushed through an amendment to procedure on April 12, 1932, requiring state premiers to be elected by absolute majority. The previous rules, according to which a relative majority was sufficient on the second ballot, were abolished. Otto Braun and Prussian Interior Minister Carl Severing opposed this change because they didn't want to give the impression that they were clinging to power by whatever means necessary. Braun suffered a serious emotional breakdown the day before the election, from which he only slowly recovered. "I am pretty much at the end of my tether," he wrote to a friend at the

Prussian state elections, April 24, 1932: Prussian Prime Minister Otto Braun
with his wife on the way to the polling station in Berlin's Zehlendorf district.

beginning of May, "and I long for the day when I can leave office, since I can no longer be of any use under the current circumstances."[4]

Braun's wish would initially remain unfulfilled. The Braun cabinet announced its resignation before the convening of the new regional parliament on May 24, but as there was no absolute majority in parliament to elect a new state premier, the old government had to remain in office as caretaker. By the second legislative session on May 25, scuffles were already breaking out between members of the Nazi Party and the KPD. Braun withdrew to his cottage in disgust. On June 4, he took a leave of absence and handed over the reins to his deputy, Welfare Minister Heinrich Hirtsiefer of the Center Party. Braun obviously intended to quit politics altogether and possibly to leave the country. On May 30, he had already had a passport issued in place of his previous official identity card. It contained the words: "Without profession."[5]

That very day Hindenburg dismissed Brüning. New Reich Chancellor Franz von Papen and new Reichswehr Minister Kurt von Schleicher, the strongman in the cabinet, pursued a common goal of integrating the Nazi Party into an authoritarian, presidentially appointed regime in the hope of dispelling the fascists' captivating aura. The new interior minister, Baron Wilhelm von Gayl, described this task as "liberating Adolf Hitler's young movement, the circles of which are growing ever wider, from the shackles imposed under Brüning and Severing in order to harness the nationalist force alive within it to rebuild the nation."[6]

The prerequisite was that the power of the "black-red Prussian government" had to be broken once and for all. "There was little point in taking steps toward a better order in the Reich if it could not be simultaneously established in Prussia," Papen would write in his 1952 memoirs by way of justifying his policies.[7] Rumors about the appointment of a Reich commissioner to lead Prussia were already rife in early June 1932. Nonetheless, Papen initially favored a different solution. On June 6, he called on the president of the Prussian Parliament, the National Socialist Hanns Kerrl, suggesting that a new government consisting of the NSDAP, DNVP, and Center Party be formed "without delay." This was an affront to the Prussian government still in power, which had not even been informed.[8]

But coalition talks between the Center and the Nazis made no progress, with the National Socialists making clear that they had no intention of sharing authority. "They want to tie us to governmental power in Prussia," Goebbels noted on June 7. "We will remain in the opposition until we get all the power we need to act comprehensively." Three days later, he wrote, "On the Prussian question, we are setting the Center Party unfulfillable conditions—that's good!"[9] One of those conditions was a demand for the offices of both Prussian state premier and Prussian minister of the interior. The Center was at most prepared to accept a German nationalist, but not a National Socialist, as state premier. Moreover, Braun's deputy, Hirtsiefer, was a staunch supporter of the governing coalition with the Social Democrats. It was unthinkable for him to cooperate with the men who had overthrown Brüning. In July 1932, efforts to reach agreement between the Nazi Party and the Center Party were deemed to have failed, and the Prussian parliament adjourned indefinitely.

As a result, focus shifted to the second option of a Reich intervention in Prussia. On June 11, in a meeting with the state premiers of the regional states, Gayl had denied that any such step was under consideration, calling it "the last resort when the life of the nation is at stake." Papen offered a nearly identically worded assurance the following day in a meeting of the state premiers.[10] Still, the Prussian government remained suspicious. Hirtsiefer, together with Prussian Finance Minister Otto Klepper, was able to fend off the Papen government's attempt to tighten the financial thumbscrews by refusing to fulfill the Reich's obligations to its largest regional state. But Hirtsiefer and Klepper succeeded in averting insolvency by issuing a drastic austerity decree on June 8, 1932.[11]

Severing in particular was keen to be on his best behavior so as not to give the Reich government any excuse to intervene. Protests against the lifting of the SA ban on June 16 came mainly from the southern German states, not from the Prussian minister of the interior, although he too must have been aware that the consequence would be increased National Socialist street intimidation. In a meeting with Gayl in mid-June, Severing went so far as to hold out the prospect of pooling the power of Reich and Prussian police in the event of a threat of unrest after the July 31 Reichstag elections. Gayl interpreted this proposal to mean that Severing himself was now in favor of appointing a Reich commissioner, something he in fact vehemently resisted. Nonetheless, the "cabinet of barons" concluded from Severing's statements that the current Prussian government in power could not be expected to put up any major resistance to a Reich intervention as long as the new national regime maintained the veneer of legality.[12]

What many had feared came true. With the ban on the SA lifted, the number of politically motivated acts of violence rose sharply. National

Socialists and Communists fought bloody street battles almost daily. "We are now living more or less in a madhouse," wrote Dorothy von Moltke.[13] Count Harry Kessler noted, "It is a Bartholomew Night that continues day after day and Sunday after Sunday."[14] The escalation of violence played into the Papen government's hands, since it seemed to prove that the Prussian police could not cope with the terror on the streets. On July 8, in a meeting with Reich Chancellery State Secretary Erwin Planck, Hermann Pünder's successor, the chairman of the DNVP parliamentary group, Friedrich von Winterfeld, demanded a "rapid intervention by the Reich" in Prussia, "even before the Reichstag elections because the most dangerous conditions could arise by then." In a letter that same day to Reich Chancellor Papen, he sounded the alarm: "Conditions have now arisen in Prussia that resemble open civil war." To bolster his demand that the Reich intervene, Winterfeld claimed, without a trace of evidence, that Social Democratic police chiefs had "established close ties with the Communists."[15]

Such transparent fictions nonetheless had an impact. In a ministerial meeting on July 11, immediately after Papen's return from the reparations conference in Lausanne, where he had been able to reap the fruits of Brüning's policies, Interior Minister Gayl declared that after "very careful consideration" he had now concluded that "a favorable moment, psychologically, has come for the Reich government to intervene." The Prussian police, he claimed, were concentrating their efforts on fighting the National Socialists, while the defense against the "Communist danger" was completely "inadequate." Schleicher vigorously agreed. He, too, believed that "the authority of the regional government in Prussia had been shaken." As a result of the meeting, Papen went on record saying that the Reich cabinet "agreed on the appointment of a Reich commissioner in Prussia." Papen added, "The justification and formulation of the decree to be issued will be left to the Reich minister of the interior and the Reich minister of justice."[16]

The following day, the cabinet discussed a corresponding ordinance. State Secretary Otto Meissner, who was present, warned that care had to be taken to ensure that the ordinance would stand up before the State Court. "Prussia must be publicly shown to be in the wrong," he said.

Gayl then dropped a bombshell, alleging that the state secretary in the Prussian Ministry of the Interior, Wilhelm Abegg, had conducted nego-tiations "regarding a merger of the SPD and the KPD." In fact, Abegg had only urged the party to renounce violence in a conversation with two KPD deputies at the beginning of June, pointing out that it could not be in their interest for the National Socialists to take the helm or for a Reich commissioner to be appointed in Prussia. Rudolf Diels, the government councillor present at the meeting and later head of the Gestapo, imme-diately informed the Reich minister of the interior, who made up the absurd story of a Communist–Social Democratic conspiracy.[17]

On July 12, the cabinet also debated the question raised by Econom-ics Minister Hermann Warmbold of what should happen "if a general strike is declared as a result of the appointment of a Reich commissioner in Prussia." Gayl stated categorically that a "military state of emergency must be declared." In the end, the cabinet approved the draft emergency decree. On the morning of July 20, the Prussian ministers Hirtsiefer, Severing, and Klepper were to be summoned to the Reich Chancellery and informed of the appointment of the Reich commissioner.[18]

Severing made every effort to stop the impending Reich interven-tion. On July 12, he called on the populace to exercise restraint in political disputes and instructed the police authorities to "carefully review . . . whether sufficient police forces are available to protect par-ticipants when issuing permits for open-air gatherings and processions." If not, the gatherings would have to be banned. As a result, Interior Min-ister Gayl announced to the cabinet on July 13 that Severing had "for the moment removed the ground from the Reich government for the planned action in Prussia." It would be necessary to "wait and see what effect his decree has."[19]

On July 14, Papen, Gayl, and Meissner traveled to Gut Neudeck to obtain authorization from Hindenburg for their planned coup in Prus-sia. The Reich president had no objections, as he saw the eradication of the last Social Democratic bastion of power as a logical extension of the course he had taken by dismissing Brüning. He signed the Decree on the Restoration of Security and Order in the Territory of Prussia without reservation. However, he left the date open, allowing the Reich government to make use of the presidentially granted authority at the appropriate time.[20] Papen and his cohorts now needed only to wait for the right occasion to issue the decree.

That occasion was the "Altona Bloody Sunday" of July 17, 1932, when the president of the regional state of Schleswig—after consulting with Severing—approved the provocative march of seven thousand SA men through the working-class districts of Altona. (The city on the Elbe River is now part of Hamburg but at the time belonged to Prussia.) The result—wild gunfights—was predictable. In the end, eighteen people were killed and many more injured. "The shock over this new bloody Sunday is widespread and great," noted Kessler.[21]

The following day, DNVP chairman Alfred Hugenberg called for the elimination of the "Marxist hobgoblin" in Prussia.[22] Moreover, Nazi politician Hanns Kerrl suggested in a letter to Papen "whether it might not be better for the Reich to take over police power until constitutional conditions are restored in Prussia."[23]

There was no longer any need for such appeals. The Papen government had long since decided to take action. On July 18, Hirtsiefer, Severing, and Klepper were told to report to the Reich chancellor at 10 a.m. on July 20 in accordance with the decision reached eight days previously. As had already been widely reported in the morning newspapers, what awaited them was the appointment of a Reich commissioner in Prussia. In an article with the headline "Hands off Prussia!" *Vorwärts* warned: "A Reich commissioner means not order, but chaos, not less blood, but more—and nobody can say how much more! A Reich commissioner is the name of the instrument used by a violent minority to seize political power."[24]

As it happened, the decisive meeting took place not in the Reich Chancellery but in the Prussian State Ministry, probably to convince the Prussian ministers that their disempowerment was a fait accompli. Without any preamble, Papen told them that public order and security in Prussia were no longer guaranteed and that he had therefore asked the Reich president for special powers, which he had received. He then read out Hindenburg's decree appointing him Reich commissioner and removing Braun and Severing from office. Papen added that he would personally take over the official duties of state premier and that he had entrusted the provisional leadership of the Prussian Ministry of the Interior to the mayor of Essen, Franz Bracht.

Severing protested that the government's measures violated the constitution and vowed not to voluntarily vacate his post, saying he would "yield only to violence." According to the minutes of the meeting, he added: "He who sows the wind will reap the storm. He feared a civil war as a result of the government's actions." Hirtsiefer was equally taken aback. The actions of the Reich government were "so outrageous" that he "knew of no historical precedent," since they were in a sense being ordered "to receive commands" without being given the opportunity to be heard first. Papen was completely unmoved, telling the two men that they were free to appeal to the State Court.[25] Immediately after the meeting, he ordered a state of military emergency imposed on Berlin and the March Brandenburg.

Executive power in Prussia was transferred to Lieutenant General Gerd von Rundstedt, who would go on to become a field marshal in Hitler's Wehrmacht. Around noon on July 20, he declared Berlin police chief Albert Grzesinski deposed and demanded he vacate his position. That afternoon, after Grzesinski refused, Reichswehr soldiers armed with hand grenades appeared at the police presidium and arrested him, deputy police president Bernhard Weiss, and the commander of the Protection Police, Magnus Heimannsberg. "The officers stood crowded around the windows and doors, waving and shouting 'Freedom,' 'Up with the republic,' and 'Up with our bosses,'" Grzesinski recalled in his autobiography, written in exile in 1933. The detainees were taken to the Moabit military detention center and released that evening only after they had given assurances that they would refrain from "any further official action."[26]

In the meantime, in a letter to the Reich chancellor, the deposed Prussian government had lodged an official complaint against the violation

July 20, 1932: The commander of the Berlin police, Magnus Heimannsberg, is led away in front of the police station at Alexanderplatz. His officers salute him, a gesture of solidarity.

of the constitution and announced that it would immediately appeal to the State Court. It also declined Papen's invitation to attend a meeting of the State Ministry under his direction.[27] This made it clear that the resistance to Papen's coup would remain strictly within the bounds of legality, which was tantamount to capitulation. There was also no sign of any fight when trade-union, Social Democratic, and Reich Banner leaders met on the afternoon of July 20. SPD party chairman Otto Wels accurately described the Papen government's actions as a "bald-faced coup d'état," but like everyone else present, he was "at a loss as to what to do." Not a single participant called for a general strike or any other form of conflict. Instead, the overriding concern was to secure a Reichstag election on July 31—although the SPD had little hope of anything positive from its outcome. On the evening of July 20, the SPD party executive called for the "strictest discipline," saying: "We must resist wild slogans from unauthorized quarters! Now more than ever, concentrated strength for the victory of the Social Democratic movement on July 31!"[28]

The leading trade-union associations, too, appealed to their members to stay calm. The "exemplary discipline of German workers, employees, and civil servants" was to be maintained "under all circumstances even in these trying days." Association leaders promised, "We will not allow opponents of the trade unions to dictate when the time for action has come."[29]

That evening, flush with the prospects of certain triumph, Papen addressed the German populace in a speech broadcast on all the country's radio stations. In it, he justified the coup d'état as a response to an alleged Communist threat the Prussian government had not done enough to combat because of its "political and moral equation of Communists and National Socialists." This, Papen claimed, had resulted in "the unnatural formation of a united front of the antistate forces of communism against the rising Nazi movement."[30] The Reich chancellor could hardly have expressed his sympathies for Hitler's battalions of brownshirts more clearly.

The National Socialists were very pleased with how smoothly "Papen's blow" against Prussia had proceeded. "Everything quiet in Berlin," noted Goebbels. "SPD and trade unions completely meek. They won't do anything either. Reichswehr moving in. Bravo. The swine are now out of power."[31]

Was resistance possible? This question has been hotly debated ever since the days of the Social Democratic exile from the Nazi dictatorship, but historians have never reached a consensus. The Reich government would have undoubtedly responded to any mobilization of the Prussian Police Guards (*Schutzpolizei*) by deploying the Reichswehr, and it is beyond question which force would have been stronger. Moreover, some of the Police Guards, especially in the higher ranks, were by no means as loyal to the republic as subsequent self-depictions suggested. In any case, there was no good reason to expect police officers to unite behind the Prussian government. Severing's decision not to test his strength against the national government and the Reichswehr was thus justifiable.[32] The Prussian ministers could also by no means rely fully on the civil service either. Many of them sensed new opportunities and had already begun adapting to their new masters.

The fighting spirit was most evident and strongest among activists in the Reich Banner, and their disappointment at the SPD leadership's passivity was greatest. "I saw Reich Banner people crying back in those days," recalled Otto Buchwitz, the group's Lower Silesian regional secretary. "Old functionaries threw their membership books at us."[33] But such subjective impressions say little about any actual willingness to fight. On sober reflection, it has to be admitted that the Reich Banner was hardly capable of standing up to the National Socialist paramilitary units.

The most effective countermeasure would have been a general strike, a response that inspired the greatest fear in not only the "cabinet of barons" but also Hitler's entourage. "Is a general strike coming?" Goebbels fretted. "I don't believe it. Wait and see. Feverish tension!"[34] The memory of the Kapp–Lüttwitz Putsch, which had been stymied by a general strike, was still alive. But the situation in 1932 was fundamentally different from that in the spring of 1920. Back in 1920, there had been full employment in Germany. Now there were over six million jobless, and all indications were that a call for a strike would fall upon largely deaf ears. "Do we have the masses behind us today with the same unity as in 1920?" asked Wels at the meeting with trade-union and Reich Banner representatives on July 20, immediately answering his own question: "The Communists and National Socialists oppose us. The state power, that is, the Reichswehr, likewise, as well as the civil service and the broadest circles of the bourgeoisie."[35]

Moreover, the unconstitutionality of Papen's "blow" against Prussia was by no means as clear as it had been with the attempted putsch. In the latter, right-wing conspirators had staged a coup against the legitimate state power. Now, the Reich government and the Reich president himself were directing action against a regional government that had lost its parliamentary majority.

Social Democrats and trade unions can hardly be blamed for shying away from the risk of civil war. But they are culpable for doing nothing and letting things take their course, not even securing the seat of the Prussian government in Wilhelmstrasse with reliable units of Police Guards. Perhaps the Papen regime would have abandoned its plan if it had sensed any determined resistance. Instead, the signal was that no such resistance could be expected. The "democratic bulwark" was razed without a fight, and that demoralized the supporters of the Weimar Republic—and encouraged their adversaries.

Immediately after the coup, Papen appointees began to purge the Prussian administrative apparatus. Most civil servants loyal to the Weimar Republic—state secretaries, ministerial directors, district presidents, police presidents—were forced from their posts. Of the four Social Democratic chief presidents, the only one spared was Gustav Noske, as the Right still felt indebted to him for his role in the counterrevolution of 1919–20.[36] Otherwise, the Reich government went about its work so thoroughly that many National Socialists worried whether it was getting too far ahead of them. "Just don't do too much," Goebbels pleaded. "Leave something for us."[37] Historian Karl Dietrich Bracher rightly described the "blow" against Prussia as a "prelude" to the so-called Nazi seizure of power on January 30, 1933.[38]

On July 25, the State Court in Leipzig rejected the deposed Prussian government's request for a temporary injunction to prevent the Reich commissioner from carrying out his official duties. The final judgment was handed down on October 25. It could not have been more contradictory. On the one hand, it affirmed the Reich president's right to appoint a Reich commissioner in Prussia; on the other, it ruled that the Prussian government could not be eliminated. The ruling did nothing at all to halt the shift in power. The Prussian government executive was formally rehabilitated, but in the future, it would merely lead a shadow existence alongside the Reich commissioner's regime.[39] In February 1933, Otto Braun was removed from office. At the beginning of March, following warnings that he was about to be arrested, he fled to Switzerland.

With their bloodless coup d'état, the old Prussian elite regained a hold on the levers of power. "On 20 July 1932, the day of the putsch," historian Christopher Clark has written, "the old Prussia destroyed the new."[40] But that victory came at enormous cost since it removed one of the last pillars of democracy and paved the way for Hitler, whom the camarilla around Hindenburg believed they could harness for their reactionary purposes—and who would push them effortlessly to the sidelines after 1933. Far too late, the East Prussian *Junker* and the Reich's officer corps would realize what they had done. In this context, the assassination attempt on Hitler on July 20, 1944, by Count Claus Schenk von Stauffenberg was, among other things, a desperate attempt by aristocrats to make amends.

The Finish Line

THE TRANSFER OF POWER TO HITLER

January 30, 1933, evening: Hitler celebrates with the masses from the window of the Reich Chancellery on Wilhelmstrasse.

January 30, 1933. That morning Hitler's followers gathered at the Kaiserhof Hotel on Mohrenstrasse, near the Reich Chancellery, where their leader resided when in Berlin. The air crackled with feverish anticipation. At 11 a.m., Reich President Paul von Hindenburg was scheduled to swear in the new "cabinet of national concentration" under the Nazi Party chairman. People waited and waited. Complications seemed to have arisen. Finally, shortly after twelve, Hitler returned to the hotel to his supporters' cheers. "The time has come," noted Joseph Goebbels, the gauleiter of Berlin and Nazi head of propaganda. "Hitler is Reich chancellor. Like a fairy tale! . . . We all have tears in our eyes. We shake Hitler's hand. He deserves it. Great jubilation!"[1]

In the evening, the National Socialists celebrated their triumph with an hour-long torchlight procession. "The mood tonight in Berlin is pure carnival," observed Count Harry Kessler, who was just as surprised as many of his contemporaries at the appointment of the Nazi leader as chancellor. "I hadn't expected this outcome, and certainly not this quickly."[2] Hitler greeted the SA columns marching past from the illuminated window of his new official residence. Hindenburg stood a few windows away, almost immobile, like a statue, receiving the public's adulation. In a radio address, Hermann Göring, who had been made minister without portfolio in the new cabinet, compared the mood to that of August 1914, when "a nation also set out" to "defend everything it possessed."[3] That established the tone for Nazi propaganda, which would soon glorify January 30, 1933, as a "Day of National Uprising."

"Am I dreaming or am I awake?" wrote Rudolf Hess, Hitler's private secretary, to his wife the next morning. "I'm sitting in the chancellor's study in the Reich Chancellery on Wilhelmplatz. Ministerial officials approach noiselessly on soft carpets to bring files 'for the Reich chancellor' who . . . is preparing the first acts of government." A few hours earlier, Hitler had still believed that everything could still fall apart at the last moment. Hess confided in him that it had been "touch-and-go a few times."[4]

Hitler's path to power was in fact anything but the triumphant march into which Goebbels styled it in his 1934 book, *From the Imperial Court to the Reich Chancellery*. It had been a nerve-racking affair with an uncertain outcome. The National Socialists had reached the peak of their meteoric rise since 1929 with the Reichstag election of July 31, 1932. With 37.3 percent of the vote, the NSDAP had become the strongest party. The door to the chancellor's office seemed wide open. But, intoxicated by the election result, Hitler had gone for broke, demanding the chancellorship for himself and the key ministries for his followers. In a secret meeting with Kurt von Schleicher, the strongest figure in the Papen cabinet, on August 5, 1932, he believed he had won over the Reichswehr minister. "Can't believe it yet," Goebbels wrote in his diary after Hitler informed him of the outcome of the meeting. "At the gates of power."[5]

But the final decision rested with the Reich president, and Hindenburg had serious reservations about the "Bohemian private," as he referred to Hitler within his closest circles. "The old man is reluctant," Goebbels was forced to admit on August 12. "Doesn't want Hitler as chancellor. And that is the *conditio sine qua non*."[6] Two days previously, Hindenburg had made it clear to Papen that he wanted to keep the presidentially appointed cabinet under Papen's leadership. As much as he would welcome "the involvement of the National Socialist movement," the president said, he could not justify appointing Hitler as Reich chancellor. "Hitler was a party leader and the cabinet led by him would then also be a party cabinet, which would not be nonpartisan, but one-sided," Hindenburg was recorded as saying. The former field marshal also resented Hitler breaking his promise to tolerate the Papen cabinet. Such bad faith offered no guarantee that, if appointed chancellor, he would "maintain the character of a presidential government" and respect the Reich president's sphere of power.[7]

At the cabinet meeting that same day, a majority of ministers supported giving the Nazi Party a share of government responsibility but not entrusting Hitler with state leadership. Coming negotiations would have to determine, Papen wrote in summarizing the discussion, "to what extent the National Socialists should be allowed to participate in the government in order to prevent them from remaining in opposition."[8] On the morning of August 13, Hitler learned from Schleicher and Papen what he already knew: Hindenburg refused to give him the chancellorship. Papen offered him the post of vice-chancellor, which Hitler categorically refused. As leader of the strongest party, he said, he could not be expected to "subordinate himself to another chancellor." His movement demanded "to see him heading government business."[9] Schleicher and Papen had tried to whisper in Hitler's ears "as though he were a sick horse," as Goebbels put it, to convince him to back off his maximum demands. But Hitler refused to budge.[10]

The Nazi leadership still hoped Hitler could win over Hindenburg in the audience scheduled for that afternoon, but the latter didn't give the Nazi leader any opportunity to flex his rhetorical muscles with lengthy speeches. Right off the bat, he asked the crucial question of whether Hitler was "prepared to be part of the present Papen government." Hitler repeated what he had told Schleicher and Papen. In view of the strength of the National Socialist movement, he had to demand the leadership of the government "in its entirety for himself and his party." The minutes of the meeting continued: "The Reich president declared . . . that he would have to respond to this demand with a clear, definite 'No.' He couldn't answer to God, his conscience, and the fatherland for transferring the entire power of government to one party, especially a party so totally opposed to dissenters." The rebuff was crystal clear, even if Hindenburg struck a conciliatory note at the end of the audience, which lasted just under half an hour: "We are both old comrades in arms and want to remain so, as our paths may cross again later."[11]

The official communiqué issued on the evening of August 13 reproduced the content of the conversation in abbreviated form. It publicly revealed that Hitler had insisted on "the leadership of the Reich government and full state power in its entirety," giving the Reich president no choice but to reject his demands.[12] As Reich Chancellery State Secretary Erwin Planck, the author of the communiqué, confided to his predecessor, Hermann Pünder, a few days later, he had modeled it on the "Ems dispatch" with which Bismarck had provoked Napoleon III into war in 1870.[13]

Hitler's meeting with Hindenburg on August 13, 1932, was a debacle, the most serious defeat for the Nazi leader since his failed putsch of November 1923. He had overplayed his hand and made himself look like someone concerned not with the good of the country but only with seizing total power for himself and his movement. After visiting Elisabeth Förster-Nietzsche, the philosopher Friedrich Nietzsche's sister, in Weimar, Kessler reported, "She's now completely down on him. She can't forgive him for August 13th. He showed that he wasn't a statesman."[14] In a letter, Dorothy von Moltke expressed the "general opinion" of those around her "that Hitler had missed his chance and had passed the peak of his power."[15] "What a leap, what a fall!" commented Julius Elbau in the *Vossische Zeitung*, predicting that the Nazi Party would slip into decline. "This abrupt Icarus ascent, which has flown all too close to the sun, is one of a kind."[16] The SA, which had already begun preparing for a takeover of government, was also sorely disappointed. Keeping his men in check, explained the brownshirts' leader Ernst Röhm, was "now most difficult."[17]

Frustration among the ranks of the SA had already erupted in a series of acts of violence starting in early August, resulting in numerous deaths. In response, the Papen cabinet approved an August 9 emergency decree applying the death penalty to acts of "politically motivated manslaughter."[18] That very night, a particularly despicable murder was committed in the small Upper Silesian town of Potempa, when SA men broke into the home of a KPD supporter and slaughtered him in front of his mother. On August 22, the special court in Beuthen sentenced five of the defendants to death. (The sentences were commuted to life imprisonment on September 2 on the dubious grounds that the defendants had not been aware of the enhanced punishments in the emergency decree when they committed their crime.) In a telegram, Hitler expressed support for the perpetrators. In view of the "monstrous, bloodthirsty sentence," he felt "bound to them in unlimited loyalty."[19]

Hitler had dropped his facade, revealing his promises to stay within the law to be nothing but tactical falsehoods. "Who can understand a leader of a great political movement daring to honor drunken killers so unhesitatingly?" horrified journalist Benno Reifenberg wrote in the *Frankfurter Zeitung*.[20] After Hitler's humiliating rejection of August 13, such radicalism also turned sympathizers away from his movement. In his diary, Kessler wrote of a "demystification" of the Nazi Party: "August 13 and Potempa are acting like poison in their bodies."[21] Under these conditions, the Nazi leadership feared nothing more than new elections to the Reichstag, where they would likely experience a setback.

Unfortunately for them, by the end of August, Papen had already obtained a blanket authorization from Hindenburg to dissolve parliament. And he made use of it after the Reichstag voted no confidence in his cabinet on September 12 by an overwhelming 512 votes to 42. It was clear proof of how little support his government had. A new election was called for November 6.[22]

"Election prospects rather pessimistic," Goebbels noted in late September. "We have to work until we explode. Then things may succeed again."[23] After the grueling campaigns of the previous months and the disappointment of August 13, the party was understandably showing unmistakable signs of election fatigue, and the mood was described as subdued in many parts of Germany.[24] Moreover, the numerous votes had ripped a gaping hole in the party's coffers. Debts and declining income from donations and membership fees forced the Nazis to make significant cuts in their campaign propaganda. "Raising money is very difficult," complained Goebbels. "The fat cats are siding with Papen."[25] The Papen government's business-friendly economic policies had made it very popular with major industrialists, whose donations this time around went almost exclusively to the two parties behind the "cabinet of barons," the DNVP and DVP.[26]

Despite the unfavorable starting point, Hitler still tried to project confidence. He knew how much risk a new election carried. If he failed to at least duplicate the result of July 31, the trend that had thus far carried his movement from success to success might be reversed. Once again, the Nazi leader anticipated a grueling campaign. Every time he spoke, he tried to justify his decision on August 13—a sign of his failed bid for power still gnawing at him. But this time, Hitler combined his fierce attacks on Papen and his reactionary coterie with hateful antisemitic tirades, which he had largely reined in during the previous campaigns to avoid alienating middle-class voters.[27]

The renewed anticapitalist overtones of Nazi Party propaganda also raised some eyebrows. "Now the most radical socialism should be championed," Goebbels demanded in late September.[28] These were not just words. In early November, just a few days before the election, the Nazi Party supported a strike by employees of the Berlin transportation authority Berliner Verkehrs-Gesellschaft. Members of the National Socialist Company Cell Organization joined forces with the Communist-dominated Revolutionary Trade Union Opposition to bring transport in the German capital to a standstill. "Yesterday: all-day strike," Goebbels noted on November 5. "Our people in the lead . . . Revolutionary mood in Berlin. Keep going! . . . I'm in constant contact with Hitler. He approves of my point of view."[29] Hitler and Goebbels hoped to score points with the working class by backing the strike. Any interaction between Communists and National Socialists, however, must have dumbfounded the Nazis' middle-class sympathizers.

"No election has ever filled people's minds with such excitement as this one," noted Hamburg teacher Luise Solmitz on November 6.[30] The result confirmed the worst fears of National Socialists. They lost over two million votes. Their share of the ballots fell by 4.2 points to 33.1 percent, and their Reichstag seats from 230 to 196. The winners in the election were primarily the DNVP, which increased its share of the vote from 5.9 to 8.9 percent, and the KPD, which went from 14.5 to 16.9 percent and now had 100 Reichstag deputies. That closed the gap with the SPD, which suffered a slight decline from 21.6 to 20.4 percent. The

Reichstag election, November 6, 1932: The cheerful Berlin gauleiter and Nazi head of propaganda, Joseph Goebbels, casts his vote. The result of the election was a serious defeat for the NSDAP.

Catholic parties also lost some ground. The Center Party fell from 12.5 to 11.9 percent; the BVP, from 3.2 to 3.1 percent. The DVP registered a minor gain, from 1.2 to 1.9 percent, while the German State Party stagnated at 1 percent. Voter turnout fell from 84.1 to 80.6 percent vis-à-vis July, negatively impacting the Nazi Party in particular.[31]

The National Socialists were devastated by the outcome of the vote. "We have suffered a serious defeat," Goebbels admitted.[32] The pro-democracy camp was delighted. Although the Nazis were still the strongest party in parliament, they were seen to be on the decline. "A party with character and an agenda can bear and repair a defeat and a program, but not a party based solely on demagoguery," wrote the leftist liberal journalist Hellmut von Gerlach in *Die Weltbühne*. "It needs an aura of invincibility. Once that has faded, it succumbs and is consumed."[33] In a similar vein, the *Vossische Zeitung* commented: "The National Socialists did not yet experience their Jena on November 6, but they have suffered their first serious defeat. . . . Faith that National Socialism is on a mission has been shaken, and the belief in its invincibility, its forward momentum, has been broken. . . . Now that the National Socialists are entering the Reichstag in more modest numbers, will they also be more modest in their demands?"[34]

Hitler clearly answered this question a few weeks later. As discussions proceeded with party leaders about forming a new government, Hindenburg received the NSDAP chairman on November 19 and 21, asking him to reconsider his refusal to join a government of "national concentration." Hitler, however, repeated what he had said in August. Participating in government would be an option only if the Reich president gave him the same position he had "so far given to all holders of presidential power." He meant the power of a Reich chancellor in a presidentially appointed cabinet, as Brüning and Papen had enjoyed previously. Hindenburg was not yet ready for such a step. Nevertheless, this time he promised Hitler that he would appoint him chancellor if he could present "a secure, workable majority with a solid, unified working agenda in the Reichstag."[35] But on November 23, Hitler dismissed Hindenburg's call for the Nazis to enter into negotiations with other parties as unfeasible.

One day later, Hindenburg officially rejected Hitler's demand to lead a presidentially appointed cabinet. His reasoning was the same as that of August 13. He could not justify it "to his oath and his conscience," Hindenburg said, to "give his presidential powers to the leader of a party that has repeatedly emphasized its exclusivity and that is predominantly opposed to him personally as well as to the political and economic measures he considers necessary."[36] The Nazi leadership had expected this response and was anything but surprised. "The old man has no confidence in [Hitler]—it's mutual," Goebbels remarked. "The barons have won again. For how long?"[37] Hitler had "lost another battle," commented Hellmut von Gerlach in *Die Weltbühne*, while warning: "We would be guilty of a mistake of our own, if we thought he was finished. His crown may be losing one point after another, but he still poses a very great danger to the republic."[38]

After the failure of his attempt to arrange a cabinet of "national concentration" including the National Socialists, Hindenburg was left with
the alternative of naming as chancellor either Papen or someone else
he trusted. As things stood, that could only be Schleicher, the *spiritus
rector* of presidentially appointed government. The Reichswehr minister was determined to undercut Papen, who had evaded his control and
managed to win Hindenburg's favor. On the evening of December 1, the
Reich president received Papen and Schleicher. Schleicher reported on
the failure of his efforts to persuade Hitler to change his mind while also
speaking out in favor of "waiting for developments in the Nazi camp."
Hindenburg, however, declared that "a further delay in the decision
would be unacceptable" and asked Papen to continue to govern. Papen
agreed to do so, but only if the Reich president was willing to "place all
presidential authorities at his disposal for the inevitable conflict with the
Reichstag." Hindenburg agreed to this condition.[39]

   That was tantamount to deciding on a "cabinet of confrontation,"
which would now implement the state emergency plans that had been
decided in principle back in late August but that the Papen government
had shied away from carrying out at the time. Those plans included dissolving the Reichstag, postponing new elections indefinitely, and, in the
meantime, pushing ahead with the transformation of the republic into
a conservative-authoritarian "new state" with strong corporative, caste-
based elements. That would have blatantly breached the Weimar Constitution and could have prompted unrest, even civil war.[40]

   On the morning of December 2, Papen informed his cabinet of
Hindenburg's decision, and the meeting took a dramatic turn. Except
for Transport Minister Eltz-Rübenach, the ministers all came out
against a "cabinet of confrontation." When Meissner, who was present,
pointed out that Hindenburg would not be dissuaded from his decision, Schleicher played his strongest trump card. The week before,
he had his ministry simulate whether the Reichswehr would be able
to simultaneously put down internal unrest and protect Germany's
external borders. Now he summoned Lieutenant Colonel Eugen Ott

to the cabinet to report on the negative outcome of that simulation. Ott's presentation made a "shattering impression" on all participants, as Finance Minister Schwerin von Krosigk noted in his diary.[41] Papen had no choice but to forego his mandate to preserve his government. "Then, in God's name, we must let Mr. von Schleicher try his luck," Hindenburg said while bidding farewell to his chancellor and personal favorite.[42] "This cabinet is an end and a beginning," commented the *Tägliche Rundschau*, a newspaper with ties to Schleicher, in welcoming the new government. "The older generation has today put forward its strongest and final representative in the form of the general. It has no one else in reserve."[43]

This second failed bid for power tarnished Hitler's prestige, with the party rank and file increasingly unable to understand his uncompromising insistence on becoming chancellor in a presidentially appointed cabinet. For the first time, serious doubts arose about his strategic vision. And things got even worse. In the municipal elections in Thuringia on December 4, the Nazis suffered heavy losses despite Hitler's extensive campaigning. The party's share of the vote declined by 40 percent compared to the Reichstag elections in July. For the *Frankfurter Zeitung*, this was proof that "Mr. Hitler is not more and more, but less and less proving to be entitled to any special claim to be the leader of the nation." The newspaper added, "December 4 has put Mr. Hitler back among the ranks of the other party leaders where he belongs." And the Social Democratic newspaper *Vorwärts* was also certain that "as a political barometer of sentiment, the Thuringian elections reveal the further rapid ebbing of the National Socialist wave, and this in a regional German state where they first 'came to power.'"[44]

The mood within the party deteriorated. The Nazis could, it was feared, fall into an abyss if fresh elections were called. In Munich, the political police observed the first signs of dissolution in December. More and more members resigned, and membership dues were paid only grudgingly. "The view that the peak has been passed and favorable prospects

Conspirators meet: Reich Chancellor Franz von Papen and Reich Minister
of Defense Kurt von Schleicher at the Berlin Grand Prix, July 17, 1932.

probably missed is commonly held among many National Socialists,"
read the police report.[45] If it wasn't finally rewarded with a share of
power, some observers thought, the Nazi Party might disintegrate.

On December 8, Gregor Strasser, the NSDAP's national organizational director and most powerful figure after Hitler, resigned all his
party offices. He had tried in vain to dissuade Hitler from his rigid all-
or-nothing strategy and to convince him to participate in a government
headed by Schleicher. Schleicher thought he had a concept that could
provide his cabinet with greater social and political support by forming
a "common front across the political spectrum" running from the trade
unions to those parts of the Nazi Party willing to cooperate.[46] There is
no truth, however, to the story that immediately after being appointed

as chancellor, Schleicher had offered Strasser the post of vice-chancellor in a bid to split the Nazi Party, as Goebbels later claimed.[47] In his letter informing Hitler of his decision, Strasser assured him that he did not intend to become the focal point of any opposition movement within the Nazi Party, saying he wanted to resign "without personal resentment and rejoin the party rank and file."[48]

When the letter was delivered that morning to the Kaiserhof Hotel, it shocked Hitler and his entourage. The party leader feared that the crisis could escalate into an internal rebellion and took frantic counter-measures. That afternoon, in a melodramatic ceremony, he had the party inspectors in Berlin, to whom Strasser had previously explained his move, swear their loyalty to him. Later that night, Hitler summoned Goebbels, Himmler, and Röhm to the Kaiserhof for an emergency meeting. The *Tägliche Rundschau* had made a great deal of Strasser's resignation, suggesting he was the only one capable of leading the Nazi Party out of its dead end. Hitler saw this as part of what he suspected was a broad conspiracy. "If the party falls apart, I'll put an end to myself in three minutes," Goebbels's diary quoted him as saying.[49] It was not the first and would not be the last time that Hitler threatened to commit suicide. At the end of April 1945, he would in fact take his own life in the bunker of the Reich Chancellery.

Strasser had no intention whatsoever of challenging Hitler. Instead, he took a long vacation, leaving Hitler to run the show. With that, Schleicher's attempt to use Strasser to tie parts of the party to his government failed. On December 9, Hitler summoned first his higher party functionaries, then Nazi parliamentary deputies, and had them swear a personal oath of loyalty. "They wailed with anger and pain," noted Goebbels. "A huge triumph for Hitler. At the end a spontaneous vow of loyalty. They all shook Hitler's hand. Strasser is isolated. A dead man."[50]

But the party crisis was by no means over. Strasser's resignation had unsettled ordinary Nazi Party members and amplified doubts about whether the party chairman was acting wisely. Hitler undertook a nationwide tour of the Nazis' regional associations in mid-December to address the discontent, but without much success. In his diary, Goebbels complained about the bleak financial situation and poor attendance at meetings. "The entire year 1932 is one single bad-luck streak," he concluded on Christmas Eve 1932. "It must be smashed to smithereens."[51] Undeterred by the growing criticism from within the party, Hitler was uncompromising in his New Year's message to the party. He was "determined to the utmost, especially today, not to sell our movement's birthright for the pittance of taking part in a government without any real power." He added that he would fight "to the last breath" to ensure that "the proudest and greatest uprising of the German people" did not "betray its mission for a few ministerial posts."[52] The party's future political isolation seemed a foregone conclusion.

Pro-democracy circles everywhere felt relief around the turn of the year 1932–33. "The massive National Socialist attack on the democratic state has been repelled," announced editor in chief Rudolf Kircher in the New Year's edition of the *Frankfurter Zeitung*. "Today we can be certain: The cart is not stuck in the mud forever."[53] The other major liberal newspapers struck a similar note. A year-in-review article in the *Vossische Zeitung*, entitled "Year of Decision," proclaimed that the Weimar Republic had been saved: "Not because it was defended, but because the attackers finished each other off. It was a journey through the Devil's Gorge that one cannot look back on without shuddering." This raised the question for editorial writer Julius Elbau: "Will Hitler, who in the frenzy of victory wanted to be Caesar and Messiah rolled into one, be sobered by the failure and find a path to responsible cooperation after all?"[54]

In the highbrow Social Democratic journal *Die Gesellschaft*, former Finance Minister Rudolf Hilferding named August 13—the day on which Hindenburg refused to appoint Hitler as Reich chancellor—as the "decisive turning point," adding, "It is the peripeteia of the drama." Since then, there was less danger of Hitler and Schleicher reaching a compromise "because a party in decline has an infinitely smaller chance of seizing total power by ousting its government partners than one in the ascendance."[55] The satirical magazine *Simplicissimus* opened its New Year's issue in 1933 with the verses: "Only one thing can be said for sure

/ And we are happy all around: / Hitler cannot endure. / This 'Führer' has run aground."[56]

Many foreign observers also believed that Hitler's rise had been halted and that his decline would be inevitable. French Ambassador André François-Poncet, who had taken up his post in Berlin in the fall of 1931, stated in a dispatch on December 29 that the disintegration of Hitler's movement had accelerated beyond belief.[57] Harold Laski, the British political scientist and Labour Party politician, wrote at the end of 1932 that Hitler would probably end his career as "an old man in a Bavarian village, spending his evenings in the Biergarten telling his cronies how he once almost overthrew the German Reich."[58]

Some of Hitler's rivals on the political right were also satisfied with the National Socialists' putative decline. At a meeting of the executive committee of the Pan-Germanic League in mid-December 1932, chairman Heinrich Class declared that "the role of the NSDAP has essentially been played out . . . even should it still attract millions of supporters in the coming years."[59] In conversation with Bavarian State Premier Heinrich Held on December 10, Schleicher expressed his confidence that "the National Socialist danger . . . has been overcome." Nonetheless, he had to admit that Strasser giving up without a fight had spoiled his "broad front" idea since he no longer saw "any way to get the National Socialists to cooperate pragmatically."[60]

But other voices cautioned against writing off Hitler's party prematurely. Carl von Ossietzky started his year-in-review in *Die Weltbühne* with the words: "At the beginning of the year 1932, Nazi dictatorship was just around the corner, the air was full of the smell of blood, and the fulfillment of the Boxheim platform seemed only a matter of time. By the end of the year, the Hitler party was shaken by a violent crisis, the long knives were quietly put back in their sheaths, and all the public could see were the Führer's long ears." At the same time, however, the publicist warned against "exaggerated expectations" in an economic situation "still conducive to breeding desperados." Only a rapid economic upturn could help to "thoroughly deflate national fascism, and even the most unconditional optimists do not dare to hold out any hope for that."[61]

Unemployment was still raging at 5.8 million at the end of 1932 and would rise to over 6 million in January 1933. The seasonal increase, though, was lower than the year before. Journalist Leopold Schwarzschild saw a clear turn for the better at the end of 1932. For the first time, he wrote, "the economic curves . . . have lost their prolonged downward bend" and "a crack in the clouds can be seen on the horizon."[62] The economic crisis seemed to have bottomed out. "Land in Sight!" declared the business section of the *Frankfurter Zeitung* in the early days of 1933.[63]

Four weeks later, the unexpected happened. Hitler became Reich chancellor. This surprising turnaround did not result from any ingenious strategy on the Nazi leader's part, notwithstanding his chief propagandist Goebbels's incessant lies to that effect after 1933. Hitler's ascent to power was the product of a sinister game of behind-the-scenes intrigue in which a handful of players pulled the strings. The decisive figure, the one on whom everything still depended, was the eighty-five-year-old Hindenburg. He was by no means the half-demented old man portrayed by apologist historians after 1945. On the contrary, he was astonishingly sharp mentally and remained in control of his decisions at all times.[64] His most important allies were former Reich Chancellor von Papen, State Secretary Otto Meissner, and his son Oskar von Hindenburg.

The overture came with a meeting between Papen and Hitler, which historian Karl Dietrich Bracher has rightly described as "the birth of the 'Third Reich.'"[65] Cologne banker Kurt von Schroeder got the ball rolling. Schroeder was part of a circle around the middle-class businessman Wilhelm Keppler, whom Hitler had made an economic adviser in the spring of 1932. At the instigation of the former Reichsbank president Hjalmar Schacht, who had become an avid Hitler supporter, a "working office" bearing Keppler's name was set up and tasked with reconciling National Socialist economic ideas with those of the private sector.[66] On December 16, 1932, Schroeder had met Papen at a dinner in the exclusive Berlin gentlemen's association, the Herrenklub. The former chancellor suggested arranging a meeting with Hitler in which they could talk things over and clear up their mutual misgivings. Schroeder immediately informed Keppler, who took up the idea as "extremely important." Papen, Keppler thought, was best placed to gauge "what the mood was like with the old man and how best to overcome resistance on that front." However, it was "absolutely necessary that nothing of this meeting should become known to the outside world."[67] On December 19, Keppler contacted Hitler and offered his services as a mediator, suggesting Schroeder's house in Cologne as a possible venue. He could vouch for the banker's "unconditional reliability," he told the Nazi leader.[68] Hitler agreed to the plan, and on December 26, Keppler was able to inform Schroeder that the "Führer" would arrive in Cologne on the morning of January 4. Keppler made no bones about the fact that Hitler still resented Papen's treatment of him on August 13, which he considered a painful defeat. Still, he hoped that the host's skill would succeed in "removing the final stumbling blocks."[69]

The planned meeting allowed both Papen and Hitler to see new possibilities. Papen still had a score to settle with Schleicher after the latter had forced him out of office in early December. He was deeply hurt, sought revenge, and saw a deal with Hitler as an opportunity to topple Schleicher and, even if he failed to regain the chancellorship, become a major player in a new government. Hitler, for his part, regarded an agreement with Papen as a chance to escape the impasse into which he had steered his party and to combat all the signs of internal party crisis. He knew only too well that Hindenburg had been reluctant to part with Papen and had wanted to keep him on as an adviser. If he could negotiate a deal with Papen, the Nazi leader hoped, perhaps Hindenburg's resistance to his chancellorship could be overcome.[70]

Hitler was accompanied by Himmler and Hess, and Keppler traveled from Berlin. Shortly after their arrival, Hitler and Papen retired to Schroeder's study, with the host listening in silently on their two-hour conversation. Schroeder recalled Hitler immediately going on the offensive and once again reproaching Papen for his government's handling of the Potempa case. Papen suggested that the feuds of the past should be put to one side and turned to the question of how to bring down Schleicher's cabinet and find common ground for a new government. In Schroeder's telling, he proposed a kind of *Duumvirat*—a division of power between himself and Hitler—and offered the National Socialists two key portfolios, the Reichswehr and Interior Ministries. Hitler explained at length that he had to insist on his claim to the chancellorship, while declaring himself willing to accept Papen supporters into a cabinet to be led by himself. The two men didn't reach an agreement, but they did part ways with the promise to continue their dialogue.[71]

In a letter dated January 6, Schacht thanked Schroeder for his "courageous initiative" and expressed his hope that the talks in Schroeder's house would "one day be of historical significance."[72] The former Reichsbank president's hope was quickly fulfilled. The Cologne meeting catapulted Hitler, whose movement had seemed to be in inexorable decline in late December, back into the contest for power in one fell swoop. He and Papen had agreed that they would put aside their mutual animosity and work together to overthrow Schleicher. Even though the decisive question of the chancellorship had not yet been resolved, that was an important first step. A few days later, Hitler informed Goebbels: "Papen hostile to Schleicher. Wants to overthrow and eliminate him completely. Still has the old man's ear. Still stays at his house. Arrangement prepared with us. Either chancellorship or ministries of power: defense and interior. That's worth listening to."[73]

It proved impossible to keep the meeting a secret. Word went around, and when Papen got out of a cab in front of Schroeder's villa in Cologne, a reporter took his picture. On January 5, the *Tägliche Rundschau* newspaper ran the headline: "Hitler and Papen Versus Schleicher."[74] The news caused a sensation. For days, the newspapers speculated about what the two men might have been up to. In a statement published on January 5, Papen sought to defuse suspicions that his conversation with Hitler had been "directed against the Reich chancellor or the current government." On the contrary, Papen insisted, the meeting had been about resolving the issue that they had already been grappling with for six months: how to "integrate the Nazi Party into the nationalist front."[75] In a joint statement the following day, Papen and Hitler asserted that they had merely wanted to explore "the possibility of a great national political united front," which had "no ramifications at all for the incumbent cabinet."[76] But critical observers were not fooled. The *Vossische Zeitung* recognized that Hitler was trying to exploit Hindenburg's esteem for Papen: "Papen is supposed to use his considerable influence in the president's house to pave the way for Hitler to become chancellor after all." However, the newspaper was unsure whether Papen had really made himself available for "the role of Hitler's pacemaker."[77]

Initially, Chancellor Schleicher seems not to have been particularly concerned by all the intrigue. At tea with French Ambassador François-Poncet on January 6, he expressed his disdain for his predecessor, saying that the next time they met, he wanted to tell Papen, "My Fränzchen [poor little Franz], you've made another blunder."[78] The two men did in fact encounter each other on January 9, with Papen trying to convince his rival that his sole intention on January 4 had been to persuade Hitler to join Schleicher's cabinet. The general, himself well versed in intrigue, would scarcely have believed this blatant lie, and it is doubtful that he left "entirely satisfied," as Papen claimed in his memoirs. But for appearances' sake, Schleicher played Papen's game. A joint official communiqué announced that their conversation proved "the complete baselessness" of all press reports of a rift between them.[79]

That very day, Papen sought out Hindenburg and, if Meissner's memoirs are to be believed, continued his game of deception. The main result of his January 4 meeting with Hitler, Papen claimed, was that the Nazi leader had backed down from his demand for chancellorship and declared himself willing to enter a coalition with the other right-wing parties. Based on this information, Hindenburg instructed Papen to continue negotiations with Hitler "personally and in strict confidence."[80] In essence, the Reich president used his authority to cover up an intrigue aimed at forming a new government of "national concentration"—Hindenburg's preferred constellation—behind his current Reich chancellor's back.[81]

Schleicher had every reason to fear that the Reich president could withdraw his confidence. On January 10, Goebbels learned that the chancellor had been told he could no longer count on a presidential dissolution order if the Reichstag were to vote no confidence in him after his reconvening. Schleicher was "on the decline."[82] And Schleicher wasn't on secure footing with the business community either. In a government radio address on December 15, 1932, he had presented himself in the unusual role of a "socially responsible general," for whom "the social aspect" would be a decisive factor in all decisions. Schleicher promised not only to come up with "a generous job-creation program" but also to repeal the Papen cabinet's decree of early September 1932 allowing employers to reduce negotiated wages. Moreover, he confided that he was " a supporter of neither capitalism nor socialism" and that he no longer had "any fear of terms such as 'private or planned economy.'"[83] These heretical statements alienated some captains of industry. Paul Reusch, the chairman of the Gutehoffnungshütte mining company, for example, thought that the chancellor was growing dangerously accommodating to the trade unions.[84] As the economic situation had improved since the end of 1932, Reusch feared that the project of eradicating Weimar democracy was endangered. "It is precisely now, during the crisis, that the decisive cuts must be made to the body of state," he warned Schleicher.[85]

At the same time, the Reich Rural League, the powerful lobbying organization of the large East Prussian estate owners, was mobilizing against the Schleicher government, which it accused of not doing enough to protect agriculture against cheap food imports and foreclosures on bankrupt farms. On the morning of January 11, Hindenburg received the league's presidium, which included the National Socialist Werner Willikens. Executive President Count Eberhard von Kalckreuth painted a gloomy picture, saying that the situation of agriculture was "much more catastrophic" than previously assumed. The difficulties were "so great that there is an urgent risk of unrest in the near future." Visibly consternated, Hindenburg called on Schleicher, Minister of Agriculture Baron Magnus von Braun, and Minister of Economics Hermann Warmbold to hear the farmers' complaints at a further meeting in the afternoon and to agree on measures in response.[86] Immediately after that meeting, it became known that the league's executive committee had released a press statement before the Hindenburg reception, in which it sternly attacked the Schleicher cabinet. "The impoverishment of agriculture," the league had written, "has reached an extent not thought possible even under a completely Marxist government and is being tolerated by the current government." Schleicher felt the league had been grossly disloyal to go public in this way and declared himself no longer willing to negotiate with its representatives.[87]

In some respects, the league's agitation was reminiscent of the campaign against Chancellor Heinrich Brüning's alleged "agrarian Bolshevism," which had greatly contributed to his downfall eight months earlier. Hindenburg, who had a soft spot for agrarian interests, always had an open ear for the *Junker*. In any case, Schleicher could no longer be sure of the Reich president's support. Moreover, his friendship with Hindenburg's son Oskar had cooled considerably, although the cause for their estrangement isn't entirely clear. It's possible that Schleicher, who was known for not mincing words, had made some careless remark that had hurt the young Hindenburg's feelings. Whatever the truth may be, the chancellor had lost a valuable asset in securing him access to the Reich president.[88]

The DNVP also distanced itself from Schleicher. On January 13, party chairman Alfred Hugenberg offered to join Schleicher's cabinet as minister of economics and agriculture on the condition that the latter declare his complete independence from the Reichstag. Schleicher rejected the proposal. He had already made it clear in his government declaration of December 15 that "in the long term, you cannot govern without broad popular sentiment behind you."[89] On January 21, the DNVP Reichstag faction declared its most adamant opposition to Schleicher's government, whose policies were accused of tending toward "socialist-internationalist lines of thought" and "pursuing the liquidation of the authoritarian idea the Reich president had established with the appointment of the Papen cabinet."[90] Thus, it was precisely the prospect that Germany's situation might stabilize that inspired the enemies of the Weimar Republic to try to bring Hitler back into the picture. Increasingly they feared that the crisis could pass without a decisive blow being struck against democracy. Schleicher's position was becoming more and more isolated.

His rivals were anything but idle. On the night of January 10–11, Hitler and Papen met in the villa of spirits merchant Joachim von Ribbentrop in Berlin's upper-class Dahlem neighborhood. Ribbentrop, who married into money by wedding the daughter of the Henckell sparkling wine dynasty, had met Hitler in the summer of 1932 and joined the Nazi Party soon afterward. Via his connections as a member of the Herrenklub, he offered to serve as a mediator between conservatives and National Socialists. There are no records of the details of what Hitler and Papen discussed in their second one-on-one encounter, but it seems they made no progress, since Hitler rejected an invitation to continue talks the following afternoon. "Everything is still up in the air," Goebbels noted. "Everything now depends on Lippe."[91]

At the time Hitler's attention was focused on the upcoming regional election in Lippe-Detmold, which he hoped would prove that the Nazi Party had overcome its crisis and regained its strength. The tiny regional state, with a population of just 174,000, including 117,000 eligible voters, was flooded by a wave of propaganda in the first two weeks of January. "There will not be a hut in Lippe where the talk is not about Adolf Hitler and his proud movement," boasted the local Nazi mouthpiece, the *Lippischer Kurier*.[92] Hitler alone spoke at sixteen meetings in ten days, and he was complemented by a strong contingent of other Nazi celebrities, including Göring, Goebbels, and Frick. The *Lippische Landes-Zeitung* newspaper commented that "a significant decay" had to be eating away at the Nazi Party "if the great 'Führer' himself appears in small villages."[93] Ossietzky mocked: "Hitler is now a Cheruscan, albeit it a rather southeastern one, blowing his horn across the 1,215 square kilometers of the Lippe region in a way rarely heard there since the tuba players of the legions."[94]

Hitler did indeed invoke the myth of the Cheruscan prince Arminius in his speeches in the region to bolster his "national ethnic community" propaganda. The Nazi leader spoke reverently of the "historical ground," on which "the German nation had made its first joint, powerful, and successful appearance in Arminius's battle against Roman rule." Hitler added: "Internal fragmentation and waste of strength have always inflicted serious wounds on the German people. The National Socialist racial and national community will put an end to that state of affairs."[95]

When announced on the evening of January 15, the result made the Nazis the strongest party, with 39,064 votes (39.5 percent). That was almost 6,000 votes more than they had gotten in the region in November, but still some 3,500 fewer than in July 1932. For the centrist *Kölnische Volkszeitung*, it was clear that, despite the flood of propaganda, Hitler had lost his personal "Battle of the Teutoburg Forest." The *Vossische Zeitung* saw definitive evidence that Hitler's "100 percent claim to power was an empty pretension . . . consisting of deception and self-deception."[96] The Nazi press, on the other hand, celebrated the election result as a great victory. The Nazi Party had "completely overcome its stagnation," and "a new upward trajectory" had begun, wrote the *Völkischer Beobachter*. This was "the compelling political conclusion from this election, which no one can avoid drawing."[97] Goebbels was also satisfied: "Party on the rise again. It was worth it after all."[98]

Once again, Hitler had risked his entire prestige and consolidated his position. At the meeting of regional Nazi leaders in Weimar on January 16, he pledged "not to let up for a second, but to keep at the enemy and continue the fight with the greatest intensity."[99] The party leader also took the opportunity to settle accounts with Strasser, and not a single voice spoke out in support of the former Reich organization leader. "Hitler has won a complete victory," Goebbels rejoiced. "The Strasser affair has come to an end. This swindler has gotten what he asked for. He'll end up as nothing, just as he deserves."[100] Hitler wouldn't forget the difficulties his former companion had created in early December 1932 and would have him murdered on June 30, 1934, as part of the purge of the SA commonly known as the Night of the Long Knives.

Following the Weimar conference, Hitler returned to Berlin to continue the secret talks, buoyed by what he felt was his triumph in the Lippe election. On January 17, he met with Hugenberg and DNVP parliamentary group leader Otto Schmidt-Hannover. Although the partners in the Harzburg Front in October 1931 had been at loggerheads through-out 1932, their relationship was more relaxed again. In a private letter on December 28, Hugenberg invited Hitler to meet to explore how "unity within the nationalist movement" could be restored.[101] Having been rebuffed by Schleicher on January 13, Hugenberg hoped Hitler would be more receptive. And indeed, the Nazi leader had let the media mogul know that he would give him a major cabinet position if he became chancellor. When Hugenberg pointed out that everything ultimately depended on Hindenburg, Hitler made disparaging remarks about the Reich president, saying that he was "not an independent player," spoke like "a gramophone record," and had a political vocabulary of no more than eighty sentences. Hugenberg seemed to have "pretty much come to terms with Hitler albeit without reaching an understanding," noted DNVP deputy Reinhold Quaatz, after being briefed by his party chair-man on the outcome of the meeting that evening.[102]

At high noon on January 18, Hitler, accompanied by Himmler and Röhm, met again with Papen in Ribbentrop's Dahlem villa. Even more resolutely than in the two previous meetings, he pressed his claim to the chancellorship. According to Ribbentrop's notes, this time Papen came out and admitted that such a deal would be "beyond his influence with Hindenburg." The negotiations appeared to be deadlocked, and the two men parted without setting a new date for further talks. The only hint of a solution was Ribbentrop's suggestion of bringing Oskar von Hindenburg together with Hitler to apply some family pressure on the Reich president and perhaps overcome the blockade.[103] Papen was palpably disappointed. He had "now made efforts in all directions to advance the cause of a concentrated nationalist front," he wrote to Ruhr industrialist Fritz Springorum on January 20, "but as a result of the elec-tions in Lippe, Hitler is very reluctant to join a cabinet as a junior part-ner."[104] Clearly, Papen had not yet given up on the idea of regaining the chancellorship himself.

Despite the strict secrecy, news of yet another meeting between Papen and Hitler leaked. The liberal *Vossische Zeitung* ran a report with the headline "Busy Game Behind the Scenes" but mistakenly wrote of Papen's "efforts to build a bridge between the government and the National Socialists."[105] On the contrary, Papen's obvious aim was to bring down the Schleicher government.

On the evening of January 22, Hitler, this time accompanied by Reichstag President Göring and NSDAP parliamentary leader Frick, drove back out to Dahlem, where Papen was waiting. Taking up Ribbentrop's suggestion of January 20, the former chancellor had persuaded Oskar von Hindenburg and Meissner to appear as well. Shortly after their arrival, Hitler withdrew with the president's son for two hours of private talks. There has been much speculation about what was discussed. Historian Joachim Fest speculated that Hitler threatened to reveal that Hindenburg had transferred the Neudeck estate to his son to evade inheritance tax, but that's not particularly plausible.[106] Hitler may have promised that if he became chancellor, he would see to it that the considerable debts on the estate were canceled.[107] Above all, however, Hitler ran through in detail the reasons why he should be entrusted with the leadership of a new presidentially appointed cabinet. And he evidently succeeded in impressing the young Hindenburg—at least that was the view he expressed to Meissner during the return journey to the center of the city.[108] Hitler was considerably less taken with his interlocutor. "Young Oskar," he remarked to his circle, was "an example of rare stupidity."[109]

The negotiations of January 22 brought major progress in one respect. Following Hitler's face-to-face meeting with the president's son, Papen told Hitler for the first time that he was in favor of the Nazi leader becoming chancellor and would content himself with the post of vice-chancellor.[110] The following morning, Papen went to Hindenburg and suggested precisely that, but the Reich president continued to insist that Papen, not Hitler, succeed Schleicher, if the latter were replaced. Ribbentrop took it upon himself to inform the Nazi leader of Hindenburg's refusal to cooperate.[111] On the evening of January 23, Hitler went to Munich to relax for a few days. The day after, in conversation with Goebbels, he expressed confidence about what would come next: "Terrain leveled. . . . Papen wants to become vice-chancellor. . . . Schleicher's position very much at risk. He doesn't seem to suspect anything yet."[112]

With Hitler away from Berlin, Göring and Frick continued negotiations with Papen in Dahlem. They all agreed that the best way to
overcome Hindenburg's resistance to a Hitler chancellorship was to fulfill his desire for a "cabinet of national concentration" representing the
entire spectrum of the Harzburg Front. "Resolution on a national front
to support Papen with old Hindenburg," Ribbentrop noted on January
24. The following day, after further discussion with Oskar von Hindenburg, Ribbentrop opined: "It appears that the idea of Hitler as chancellor
under the umbrella of a new national front is not entirely hopeless."[113]
On January 21, Meissner had suggested to Hugenberg that Hindenburg
might give Hitler "far-reaching powers" as Reich chancellor, "if he is
constrained by the DNVP and the Center in the cabinet." The president
of the Reich attached particular importance to the DNVP's role in any
new government, and he reserved the right to dole out the Reichswehr
Ministry and the Foreign Ministry himself.[114]

Meanwhile, Schleicher's influence was rapidly waning. On January 22,
the Reichstag's Council of Elders had decided to reconvene on January 31. It looked as though an overwhelming majority of deputies would
censure the Reich chancellor as they had his predecessor. If a vote of no
confidence topped the agenda, Schleicher had already announced to the
cabinet on January 16 that he would "send the Reichstag a written order
of dissolution." In so doing, he was adopting an emergency plan the
Papen cabinet had also considered: postponing the new elections beyond
the constitutional deadline of sixty days, until the autumn of 1933. By
then, Schleicher calculated, his job-creation program would begin showing results and unemployment would have fallen significantly.[115] It was
uncertain, however, whether Hindenburg would go along with such a
violation of the constitution, especially since Schleicher himself had torpedoed Papen's plan in early December 1932, raising the specter of civil
war and engineering Papen's dismissal. Without Schleicher's attempt,
doomed as it probably was from the outset, to create a sizable support
base with his concept of a broad conservative front, Papen would have
confronted the Nazis as Reich chancellor instead of helping them to

power. The result would have likely been a "New State" following the vision of Papen and Interior Minister Gayl, not a "Third Reich." Here, too, we see the fluidity of the situation. At no point was Hitler's chancellorship inevitable.

The Reich president gave Schleicher a clear answer in person on January 23, saying that he would "consider the question of dissolving the Reichstag" but that he could not "justify postponing the election beyond the date provided for in the constitution" because "such a step would be interpreted by all sides as a breach of the constitution." Before reaching that sort of decision, Hindenburg would have to clarify with party leaders whether they would "recognize the state of emergency and would not raise accusations of a constitutional violation." [116]

Schleicher should not have been surprised by Hindenburg's refusal. After all, by resorting to the state emergency plan, he was admitting his failure to create broader social and political support for his cabinet. Hindenburg seems to have already decided to drop him as chancellor at this point. Papen kept the president apprised about the secret negotiations with Hitler, and so Hindenburg knew that an alternative that would suit him better might be in the offing.

Another incident probably influenced Hindenburg's decision. A few days earlier, in the Reichstag budget committee, Center Party deputies had raised the issue of large-scale East Prussian agrarians misusing public funds to pay off debts on their estates. The so-called Eastern Assistance scandal made waves in the press, and revelations about the abuse threatened to besmirch Hindenburg's name, especially as his friend and neighbor, Elard von Oldenburg-Januschau, was among those involved. Conversely, Oldenburg-Januschau and his ilk resented Schleicher's failure to protect them and stepped up their attacks. [117]

Rumors about Schleicher's emergency plans worried the Center Party and the Social Democrats. In a letter to the chancellor dated January 26, Center Party leader Ludwig Kaas warned against postponing elections, calling it "an undeniable breach of the constitution" and vowing that his party would never agree to such a measure. [118] The same day, *Vorwärts* ran a statement by the SPD party executive and the executive of the SPD parliamentary group that lodged the "strongest protest against the plan for a so-called state emergency law," branding it tantamount to a coup d'état.[119] What the Center and SPD failed to realize was that the main danger was not Schleicher but Papen and his efforts to make a government of "national concentration" under Hitler palatable to the Reich president.

At a cabinet meeting on the morning of January 28, Schleicher announced that he would deliver his government statement to the Reichstag on January 31 only if Hindenburg gave him the order to dissolve the parliament. Since this would probably not be the case, he planned to submit his resignation in order to avoid the "the futile spectacle of certain defeat." He feared "the worst for the near future," Schleicher told his ministers. Hindenburg was still not prepared to appoint Hitler as Reich chancellor, but the formation of a presidentially appointed cabinet under Papen and Hugenberg, the only other solution, would soon result in a crisis of state and presidency since "the sentiment of the broad masses would oppose it in the most adamant way possible."[120]

The cabinet members backed Schleicher completely. Shortly after noon, the chancellor adjourned the meeting and sought out Hindenburg. He returned after just twenty minutes, as expected with the news that Hindenburg had rejected his request. The president had acknowledged the chancellor's attempts to "win over the National Socialists and create a Reichstag majority." But, as he had not succeeded, it was now necessary to look for "other possibilities." Before taking his leave, Schleicher had requested that the Reich president "not give the Reichswehr Ministry to a Hitler partisan." Hindenburg had replied that such a thought was "absolutely" far from his mind.[121]

He had the feeling that he was "talking to a wall," Schleicher told his ministers, adding that "the old man didn't take in his arguments at all, but instead delivered a rehearsed spiel." Finance Minister Schwerin von Krosigk noted: "We were all deeply shocked. The Schleicher cabinet was overthrown after two months by the withdrawal of the Reich president's confidence."[122]

Goebbels was ecstatic. "At least we've got rid of Schleicher," he wrote in his diary, and compared the chancellor to a famous French turncoat. "The old man has almost thrown him out. Just desserts for this Fouché."[123]

Under the headline "Camarilla," Ossietzky wrote of Schleicher's fall: "The 'socially conscious general,' who promised to tackle all the toughest tasks at once, has been exposed as a dilettante, beaten even in his favorite discipline—intrigue."[124] In the *Vossische Zeitung*, Julius Elbau expressed regret at the chancellor's resignation: "This almost literal soldier of fortune has been toppled before fighting his first battle. . . . The permanent crisis the government has been in since the fall of Brüning has now taken dimensions that should be a warning to all the forces of our nation to be both extremely vigilant and extremely prudent."[125]

Immediately after Schleicher's resignation, Hindenburg officially instructed Papen to commence negotiations to form a new government. The day before, on January 27, Hitler had returned to Berlin from Munich. Ribbentrop had informed him of the status of the negotiations in Dahlem and persuaded him to seek further talks with Hugenberg. Hitler and Frick met with the DNVP chairman and Schmidt-Hannover that afternoon at Göring's official residence. Göring opened the discussion with the news that Papen now supported Hitler's appointment as chancellor. But Hugenberg was still reluctant, rejecting Hitler's demand that one of his own be appointed to head the provisional Prussian Ministry of the Interior, which would have given the National Socialists control over the police in Germany's largest regional state. Hugenberg also claimed the posts of head of the Reich Chancellery and Reich press spokesman for the DNVP. That, in turn, was unacceptable to Hitler, and the two men parted, as Ribbentrop noted, "with voices raised." Hitler was so annoyed that he wanted to return to Munich straightaway, and it was only with great difficulty that Göring and Ribbentrop were able to prevent him from leaving the capital.[126]

Hitler's distrust was aroused, and his old fear reawakened, that the conservatives could slam the door to power in his face again just before the finish line, as they had the previous August. "Hitler is still very skeptical and suspicious," Goebbels remarked. "And rightly so. A gang of swindlers over there! They fight, then kiss and make up."[127] And the rumors buzzing around Berlin that Papen would be entrusted to lead a "cabinet of confrontation" after Schleicher's fall would only have deepened Hitler's suspicions. On January 27, he canceled another meeting with the former chancellor. Negotiations were once more on the verge of collapse.

In the end, it was Papen himself who resolved the impasse. At a meeting with Ribbentrop in Dahlem on the evening of January 27, he argued that the differences with Hugenberg should not be overestimated. What was more important was that he, Papen, "was now fully committed to Hitler's chancellorship" and would do everything in his power to push it through with Hindenburg.[128] And over the course of January 28, Papen indeed managed to dispel the Reich president's final reservations by promising that a Chancellor Hitler and his movement would be kept in check and would, as Hindenburg demanded, remain within the framework of the German constitution.[129]

Hugenberg, with whom Papen negotiated on the afternoon of January 28, also proved more willing to compromise after Schleicher's resignation, which had by then been made public. The media mogul agreed that if a pact with Hitler was concluded, attempts would have to be undertaken to "limit his powers as much as possible." For his part, Hugenberg demanded the post of minister of economics in both the Reich and Prussia, arguing that both posts had to be united "in one hand to be able to pursue a sensible policy." Hitler told Papen that Hindenburg could "fill all ministries to his liking . . . as long as the ministers considered themselves independent of party ties." His only demands were that the post of Reich interior minister go to a Nazi Party colleague and that, in addition to the Reich Chancellery, he also be made Reich commissioner for Prussia.[130] Finance Minister Krosigk, whom Papen asked to join him that afternoon, declared his willingness to join a Hitler cabinet if he was "allowed to work professionally."[131] Foreign Minister Neurath and Transport Minister Eltz-Rübenach also promised to remain in office.

Late on January 28, Papen informed the Reich president of the outcome of the negotiations. Hindenburg was happy about the apparent moderation shown by Hitler and particularly pleased that most of the conservative ministers he valued, who had already served under Papen and Schleicher, would be part of the new government. He also wanted to fill the post of Reichswehr minister with a man he trusted. Lieutenant General Werner von Blomberg, the commander of Military District 1 in East Prussia, was a member of the German delegation at the disarmament conference in Geneva at the time. The large East Prussian estate owners had spoken positively about him, and he was acceptable to Hitler—two favorable factors in Hindenburg's eyes. But Blomberg would ultimately prove quite a bit too "open to the Right." It was another fatal miscalculation in the error-strewn final phase of Weimar democracy. On the morning of January 29, Hindenburg instructed his son to summon Blomberg to Berlin by telegraph so that he could present him as Schleicher's successor as Reichswehr minister.[132] Nevertheless, despite all the things going in their favor, Hitler's entourage still fretted that Hindenburg would change his mind. "The old man is unpredictable," warned Goebbels. "Be under no illusions."[133]

The final decision was made on January 29. That morning, Papen and Hitler agreed on the composition of the cabinet, and Papen assented to Hitler's proposal to appoint Frick as Reich interior minister and Göring as provisional Prussian interior minister. In return, Hitler accepted the Reich president's wish that Papen, rather than Hitler, be given the office of Reich commissioner for Prussia. "Hitler swallowed this obvious disappointment with barely restrained resentment," Papen wrote in his memoirs. He failed to mention that he had not opposed another of Hitler's conditions, namely the demand for new elections and a subsequent enabling act.[134] Hitler obviously expected that, once in government, he would be able to increase his electoral support and obtain the necessary two-thirds majority for the enabling act in the Reichstag.

That afternoon, Papen managed to dispel the final reservations of the DNVP against a Hitler cabinet, offering Hugenberg the Ministries of Economics and Agriculture, both in the Reich and in Prussia. The prospect of heading such a superministry was too tempting for the DNVP chairman to refuse any longer. Franz Seldte, the leader of the Stahlhelm, also declared his willingness to join the cabinet as minister of labor. Theodor Duesterberg, the deputy leader of that paramilitary organization, whom the Nazi press had fiercely attacked only a few months earlier because of his Jewish grandfather, warned Hugenberg that the National Socialists were utterly unscrupulous. A time would come when Hugenberg would "have to flee from arrest one night in his underpants through the ministerial gardens," Duesterberg told him. But Hugenberg believed that the predominance of conservatives in the cabinet was a sufficient safeguard, predicting, "We have Hitler contained." [135]

After the meeting, Papen informed Göring and Ribbentrop that the final obstacles to a new government had been removed. Göring broke the news to an entourage waiting at the Kaiserhof. But doubts persisted about whether something might still intervene. "They don't dare to believe it yet. Is Papen honest? Who knows?" Goebbels confided in his diary. [136] The rumor mill in Berlin was churning. Hindenburg could, it was speculated, ultimately favor a Papen–Hugenberg "cabinet of confrontation" without the Nazi Party. Some people even thought that the Reichswehr could be planning a coup. [137]

Although it soon became clear that such worries were unfounded, they accelerated the course of events. Late on January 29, Papen presented Hindenburg with the list of Hitler's cabinet. It included four non-party-affiliated ministers from Schleicher's government: Neurath (Foreign Office), Krosigk (Finance), Eltz-Rübenach (Post and Transport), and Günther Gereke as Reich commissioner for job creation. The new additions were Hugenberg (Economy and Agriculture), Seldte (Labor), and Blomberg (Reichswehr). There were only two National Socialists in ministerial posts: Frick (Interior); and Göring as minister without portfolio, Reich commissioner for air transport, and acting Prussian minister of the interior. Only the minister of justice remained open, and Papen lulled Hindenburg into believing that negotiations were still ongoing with the Center Party about joining the government and that a ministry had to be kept vacant for this purpose. The cabinet was to be sworn in the following morning at eleven o'clock. [138]

And so January 30 dawned. When Blomberg arrived at Berlin's Anhalter Bahnhof train station early in the morning, Oskar von Hindenburg was waiting to spirit him away to Wilhelmstrasse, where the Reich president swore him in as the new Reichswehr minister shortly after 9 a.m.

The "Cabinet of National Concentration" immediately being sworn in. Sitting, from left: Hermann Göring, Adolf Hitler, Franz von Papen. Standing, from left: Franz Seldte, Günther Gereke, Lutz Graf Schwerin von Krosigk, Wilhelm Frick, Werner von Blomberg, Alfred Hugenberg. Missing: Paul von Eltz-Rübenach.

Hugenberg, Schmidt-Hannover, and the two national Stahlhelm leaders also arrived that morning at Papen's apartment in the Ministry of the Interior. They found the designated vice-chancellor in a state of great agitation. "If a new government is not formed by 11 o'clock, the Reichswehr will march. A military dictatorship under Schleicher and Hammerstein is imminent," Duesterberg recalled him exclaiming. It is not entirely clear whether Papen truly reckoned with a possible military coup or was merely trying to deflect possible objections to Hitler's immediate appointment. A short time later, Hitler and Göring also arrived. Once again, the NSDAP leader demonstrated his skills at dissimulation, rushing up to Duesterberg and, seemingly deeply moved, with tears in his eyes, declaring his great regret for all the spiteful attacks against him. "I give you my word I did not initiate them," Hitler lied.[139]

Around 10:45 a.m., a quarter of an hour before the planned inauguration ceremony, the assembled politicians walked to Hindenburg's
official residence, where the other designated ministers (except for
Eltz-Rübenach, who was ill) also arrived. Only then did Hitler tell
Hugenberg that he and Papen had agreed to dissolve the Reichstag and
call new elections. The DNVP leader feared that the modest gains his
party had made in November would be lost, so he vigorously objected.
Even when Hitler promised that whatever the outcome of the election, nothing would change in the composition of the cabinet, Hugenberg insisted that no new elections be called. The new government was
in danger of coming unglued at literally the last minute. Meanwhile,
the appointed hour had passed. Meissner rushed in with a watch in his
hand, saying: "It's 11:15. You can't keep the Reich president waiting any
longer." Only then did Hugenberg relent. Hitler had won a tense contest of who would blink first.[140]

Hindenburg welcomed the new cabinet, expressing his "satisfaction
at the agreement finally reached by the nationalist Right." Papen read
out the list of ministers. After the swearing-in, Hitler took the floor for
a short speech in which he sought to elicit the Reich president's confidence in himself and his cabinet, promising that his government would
respect the constitution and the rights of the Reich president and other
state authorities. He hoped, he said, to be able to earn a working majority after the new Reichstag elections in line with Hindenburg's long-
standing wish.[141] The ceremony ended at around twelve noon. At the
end, the Reich president was "quite moved," Goebbels was told. "That's
the right way to end up. Now we have to win him over completely."[142]

Hitler's triumph was by no means an "occupational hazard" of German history, as many observers have regarded it, but neither was it the
inevitable or necessary result of the crisis in the Weimar Republic. Even
in late January 1933, there were still two ways of keeping Hitler from
power. Either Hindenburg could have left Schleicher in office in an acting capacity if the Reichstag voted no confidence in him—or, as he had
already once done in principle with Papen, he could have granted the

chancellor the authority to dissolve the Reichstag and postpone the new elections beyond the constitutionally set period of sixty days. That solution would have meant a barely disguised military dictatorship, but it would have offered a reasonable chance of buying time until Germany's economic situation had noticeably improved.

It's highly doubtful that Hitler would have dared to mobilize the SA and attack the government in these scenarios, which would have involved them in an armed conflict with the Reichswehr. Hindenburg's decision was decisive. Papen and other advisers had persuaded him that a "cabinet of national concentration," in which Hitler could be "constrained" and "tamed" by the preponderance of conservative ministers, was the lesser evil. It was not long before this idea was revealed to be a fatal instance of wishful thinking.

Wait and See

REACTIONS TO JANUARY 30, 1933

*March 21, 1933: Hitler makes a gesture of submission as he
bows to Hindenburg on the "Day of Potsdam."*

Nikolaus Sieveking, an employee at the Global Economic Archive in Hamburg, saw no reason to be overly concerned about a Nazi chancellor. Hitler, he noted in his diary on January 30, 1933, would "have to develop superhuman diplomatic skill if he doesn't want to be pushed into a corner by the traditional nationalist conservatives." Sieveking was sure that the Nazi "Führer" lacked any such quality. At the same time, the only positive thing Sieveking could see about January 30, 1933, was "the fact that the malicious ignorance of a group of political impostors, which for over two years has made Germany the arena and victim of the worst sort of political uncertainty, will now be exposed." He thus concluded, "I consider making a sensation out of Hitler's chancellorship so childish that I'll leave that to his true-believing followers."[1]

Like Sieveking, many Germans did not initially perceive January 30, 1933, as a dramatic turning point. Hardly anyone suspected what Hitler's appointment as chancellor actually meant. Dorothy von Moltke was one of the few. "So Hitler is now Reich chancellor after all," she wrote immediately after the news broke. "The situation is very serious because practically all the new cabinet members want to violate the constitution. They are a terrible bunch. . . . It's very sad. This is where we are 14 years after the revolution."[2] But many of Moltke's contemporaries reacted with astonishing indifference. Germany had changed presidentially appointed chancellors twice in 1932—Franz von Papen had succeeded Heinrich Brüning in early June and Kurt von Schleicher succeeded Papen in early December. Germans had become almost inured to lightning changes of government. Why should Hitler's regime be anything more than a mere episode?

In *Mein Kampf* and in numerous speeches before 1933, Hitler did not hide his intentions once in power. The Nazi leader had vowed to abolish the hated democratic order of the Weimar "system," eradicate Marxism (which meant both Communists and Social Democrats), and "remove" Jews from Germany by whatever methods necessary. Where foreign policy was concerned, Hitler freely admitted that his priority would be a thorough revision of the Treaty of Versailles and that his long-term goal was to conquer "living space in the East."

The camarilla around Reich President Hindenburg that had lifted Hitler to power through their intrigue completely shared his goals of preventing a return to parliamentary democracy, eviscerating the Treaty of Versailles, massively rearming, and making Germany the leading military power in Europe again. Hitler's conservative allies were inclined to dismiss everything he said he intended to do as mere rhetoric. Once in office, they thought, he would behave reasonably. They also believed that they had "constrained" Hitler in a context that would allow them to curb his megalomania and control the destructive dynamics of his movement.

Papen, the true architect of the alliance of January 30, once told an acquaintance who warned him not to underestimate Hitler's lust for power, "You are mistaken, we have gotten him to serve our ends."[3] He also dismissed criticism from Pomeranian estate owner Ewald von Kleist-Schmenzin with the words: "What's your problem? I'm the one who enjoys Hindenburg's trust. In two months, we'll have pushed Hitler so far into a corner he'll squeak."[4]

Germany's governing elites could not have any more negligently underestimated Hitler's craving for power. The eight conservative ministers in the "cabinet of national concentration" might have outnumbered the three National Socialists, but Hitler had ensured that two of his lackeys, Frick with the Reich Interior Ministry and Göring with the Prussian Interior Ministry, had key portfolios. The latter gave the Nazis control over the police in the largest German regional state—a crucial prerequisite for establishing a dictatorship.

Hugenberg, who had assumed economic and agricultural portfolios in both the Reich and Prussia, was considered the real power in Hitler's cabinet, and there is no reason to believe the tale of him confessing to Leipzig Mayor Carl Goerdeler on January 31 that he had committed the "greatest stupidity" of his life by allying himself with the "biggest demagogue in world history."[5] Like Papen and the other traditionally conservative cabinet members, the new superminister was convinced he could keep Hitler in check and steer him wherever he wanted.

He shared this illusion with captains of industry. In an editorial in the business-friendly *Deutsche Allgemeine Zeitung*, editor in chief Fritz Klein expressed his satisfaction that "the reconciliation between Hindenburg and Hitler, between the Stahlhelm and the National Socialists, between all parts of the German right-wing movement . . . has finally been achieved." The new cabinet, Klein added, could "count on an absolutely professional and benevolent attitude" from big business. Nevertheless, Hitler's appointment was a "daring and bold decision." Working with the National Socialists would probably be "difficult and grueling," Klein admitted, but "the leap into the dark had to be taken." The Hitler movement had become "by far the strongest factor in political life" in Germany; it was now up to the Nazi leader to prove "whether he has what it takes to be a statesman."[6] In any case, the stock markets were completely unconcerned. People were content to wait and see.[7]

Hitler's conservative enablers weren't the only ones to misunderstand distribution of power. His pro-democratic detractors did as well. On January 31, Count Harry Kessler reported on a conversation with Hugo Simon, a former associate of ex–Foreign Minister Walther Rathenau, who had been murdered in 1922: "[Simon] sees Hitler as Hugenberg and Papen's captive." Kessler obviously shared this view, because just a few days later he predicted that the new government wouldn't last since all that held it together was "Papen's windbaggery and intrigue." Kessler added: "Hitler must have realized by now that he has been duped like a peasant. He's completely tied to this government and can't move forward or backward. He and Hugenberg will already butt heads during the election, and much more so afterward, when it comes to taking action."[8]

In his German-language memoir of his youth, written in exile in England in 1939 but first published in 2000, journalist Sebastian Haffner recalled the "icy shock" that had overcome him earlier as a trainee lawyer at the Berlin Court of Appeal at the news of Hitler's appointment.

For a moment, he had "almost physically felt the smell of blood and dirt around this man." That evening, though, he discussed the prospects of the new government with his father, a liberal educational reformer, and they had quickly agreed that while the new regime could probably get up to some mischief, it wouldn't remain in office for long. "A traditionally reactionary conservative government as a whole, with Hitler as its mouthpiece," was how Haffner characterized the new cabinet. "Apart from this addition, it differed little from the last two after Brüning. . . . All in all, this government was no cause for alarm."[9]

The tenor of the major liberal papers was also that things wouldn't be so bad. Theodor Wolff, editor in chief of the *Berliner Tageblatt*, saw the new cabinet as the realization of what the united Right had envisaged at Bad Harzburg in October 1931: "It's become reality. Hitler is Reich chancellor, Papen vice-chancellor, Hugenberg economic dictator; the posts have been distributed just as the gentlemen of the 'Harzburg Front' wanted." The new government would stop at nothing "to intimidate and silence its opponents," Wolff warned. A ban on the Communist Party was high on the agenda, and restrictions on press freedom were to be expected. But not even the far-sighted Wolff was able to halfway accurately imagine the horrific possibilities of a totalitarian dictatorship. There was "a limit beyond which violence cannot penetrate," he wrote. A "mental and spiritual resistance" would arise in the German people, who had always been proud of "freedom of thought and speech," and constrain Hitler's desires for absolute power.[10]

Benno Reifenberg, domestic politics editor of the *Frankfurter Zeitung*, expressed doubts about Hitler's "personal qualifications" for the office of chancellor but did not rule out the possibility that he might grow into the post and become a respectable politician. "We shouldn't write him off completely, but neither can we forget as long as we are not convinced by his deeds."[11]

The editor in chief of the *Vossische Zeitung*, Julius Elbau, also expressed concern. "The signs are pointing to a storm," he wrote in his editorial on January 30, 1933. "What guarantees are there that the

National Socialist leader will exercise only the power that has been transferred to him within the framework of the constitution and on the basis of the legal system?" However, the newspaper also sought to reassure its readers, pointing out that Hitler had not been able to ram through his claim to exclusive power. "It is not a Hitler cabinet; it's a Hitler–Papen–Hugenberg government"—a triumvirate that, despite all internal differences, was united in "completely breaking with the past." Against that backdrop, the paper branded the new regime "a dangerous experiment that can only be accompanied by deep concern and the keenest mistrust." [12]

Carl von Ossietzky reached a similar verdict in *Die Weltbühne*. The new government, he wrote, was "the product of ambitious mediations, surprising improvisations, back-stage games" and "full to the brim with social disharmony." Therefore, Ossietzky proposed, it could "pass into the shadows as quickly as the Schleicher cabinet." However, Ossietzky also warned against assumptions that the government would soon have reached the end of its run. If it succeeded in "keeping German misery bearable," it would have every opportunity to "create a system that will last for a proper lifetime." [13]

The Left was alarmed. "In the Hitler–Papen–Hugenberg cabinet, the Harzburg Front has been resurrected," stated an appeal on January 30, in which the SPD executive and the SPD Reichstag parliamentary group cautioned supporters against taking an "undisciplined approach." The SPD leadership wanted to "fight on the basis of the constitution," in which any attempt by the new government to violate the law would "meet with the utmost resistance from the working class and all liberal-minded segments of the population." [14] But by strictly insisting on legality, the SPD overlooked the fact that the previous presidentially appointed governments had already largely undermined the Weimar Republic's democratic constitution, the last remnants of which Hitler would not hesitate to destroy.

In another misjudgment, the Communist KPD called for a "general strike against the fascist dictatorship of Hitler, Hugenberg, and Papen."

In view of Germany's six million unemployed, workers had little appetite to lay down their tools, as they hadn't in July 1932 after Papen's "Prussian strike." Communist appeals to form a common front largely fell on deaf ears among Social Democrats, who could not forget so quickly that the Communists had recently defamed them as "social fascists."[15]

The trade unions also had little stomach for extraparliamentary activism. "Organization—not demonstration: That is the watchword of the hour!" proclaimed the chairman of the General German Trade Union Federation, Theodor Leipart, on January 31. "The trade unions have been acting in this spirit for decades. They will remain true to this slogan in the coming period by stepping up publicity." Peter Grassmann, the organization's vice-chairman, agreed that it should not be guided by "emotional considerations." It was "understandable in human terms but objectively wrong" that the workforce would prefer to defend itself against "this socially reactionary government by taking direct action." Grassmann added: "There can be no doubt that the trade unions would go against the German workforce's interests, if they gave in to these impulses."[16]

Representatives of the Social Democratic labor movement misinterpreted Hitler as a stooge of the old reactionary aristocratic East Prussian landowners and the Rhenish-Westphalian captains of industry. In a speech in Augsburg in early February 1933, SPD Reichstag deputy Kurt Schumacher dismissed the Nazi leader as merely "decorative." Schumacher added: "The cabinet is named after Adolf Hitler, but the cabinet *is* Alfred Hugenberg. Adolf Hitler can talk. Alfred Hugenberg will act."[17] The danger Hitler posed could not have been more grotesquely misapprehended. Most leading Social Democrats and trade unionists had grown up in the old Wilhelmine Empire. Many had been persecuted under Bismarck's Anti-Socialist Law, but that was the only repression they had endured. They couldn't comprehend that National Socialists were serious about annihilating the labor movement.

Jews living in Germany should have worried most about a fanatical antisemite like Hitler coming to power, but even that was by no means the case. "The motto today is wait and see!" was how the board of the Central Association of German Citizens of the Jewish Faith concluded its statement on January 30. "German Jews are looking seriously and anxiously into the future," declared association director Ludwig Holländer in his editorial in the group's newspaper. While acknowledging the danger posed by leaders of an anti-Jewish party now being in government, Holländer also proposed that "even in these times, German Jews will not lose their equanimity, that reminder of their inseparable bond with everything truly German."[18] An editorial in the Jewish newspaper *Jüdische Rundschau* on January 31 reminded readers that the equal rights of Jews as citizens were enshrined in the constitution and that the Reich president who had appointed Hitler was bound by his "constitutional oath, his moral authority, and his international reputation." The paper was thus convinced "that forces within the German people are still awake that will oppose barbaric anti-Jewish policies."[19] It would take only a few weeks for all these assumptions to be utterly disproved.

Foreign diplomats, too, labored under major misconceptions about the change of power in Germany. American Consul General in Berlin George S. Messersmith may have reported on February 3 that it was impossible to make a clear prediction about the future of the Hitler government, but he also suggested that it was only a transitional phase in the development toward more stable political conditions.[20] British Ambassador Horace Rumbold recommended that the Foreign Office also adopt a wait-and-see attitude toward the new government. He saw Hitler in the weaker position and considered Papen the true mastermind of the new regime. "It may be said that the Hitler movement has been saved for the time being, largely owing to the instrumentality of Herr von Papen." Rumbold predicted that conflicts could soon break out between these unequal allies because Papen and Hugenberg's goal of restoring the Hohenzollern monarchy was incompatible with Hitler's plans.[21]

French Ambassador André François-Poncet criticized the Hitler–Papen–Hugenberg cabinet as a "foolhardy experiment" (*une expérience hasardeuse*), but also advised his government to remain calm and wait and see how things developed. When he met Hitler on the evening of February 8 at a reception hosted by the Reich president for the diplomatic corps, he was relieved. He found the new Reich chancellor "dull and mediocre" (*terne et médiocre*), a kind of miniature Mussolini. Similar views probably likewise convinced Hindenburg's advisers that Hitler would be relatively easy to control and steer.[22]

The news of Hitler's appointment reached Swiss envoy Paul Dinichet while he was taking lunch with "high-ranking German personalities." In his report to Bern on February 2 he described: "Much shaking of heads. 'How long might this last?'—'Well, it could have turned out worse.'" Dinichet also recognized that Papen had masterminded the installation of the new cabinet, but like most commentators, he was mistaken about the upshot: "Hitler, who long aspired to unrestricted autocracy, with two of his disciples, pinned, wedged, or sandwiched—however you want to put it—between his colleagues Papen and Hugenberg."[23]

Rarely has the utter hollowness of a political project been so quickly revealed as conservatives' pretense of "taming" the National Socialists. Hitler was far better at power politics than his colleagues-cum-rivals in the cabinet. Within no time, it was he who drove them into a corner, usurping Papen's favored status with Hindenburg and forcing Hugenberg to resign. There was hardly any resistance. On the contrary, almost all of Germany's institutions and social groups proved quite willing to adapt to and support the new regime. "All opposing forces as if vanished from the face of the earth," observed Victor Klemperer as early as March 1933. "It is this utter collapse of a power only recently present, no, its complete disappearance . . . that I find so staggering."[24]

It took Hitler only five months to consolidate complete power. The "Decree for the Protection of the People and the State," issued after the Reichstag fire on February 28, 1933, abolished Germans' most important fundamental rights: personal liberty; freedoms of speech, press, association, and assembly; and postal and telephone secrecy, as well as the inviolability of home and property. Meanwhile, the ground was being laid to bring those regional states not yet governed by the National

Socialists into line. The "Act to Remedy the Distress of the People and the State"—commonly referred to as the Enabling Act—of March 23 finally repealed the Weimar Constitution and made the Hitler government independent of the Reichstag and the Reich president's right to issue emergency decrees. The "Law for the Restoration of the Professional Civil Service" of April 7 abolished the legal equality of Jews. The occupation of the trade union buildings on May 2 was the first step in dismantling the membership of the General German Trade Union Federation. And in a decree to the regional governments on June 21, Minister of the Interior Frick banned the SPD—the KPD had already been de facto banned in late February. The mainstream, middle-of-the-road parties voluntarily dissolved or were made to do so. "Everything that existed in Germany outside the National Socialist Party" has been "destroyed, dispersed, dissolved, incorporated, or absorbed," François-Poncet concluded in early July 1933. Hitler had "won the game with little effort. . . . All he had to do was huff and puff—and the edifice of German politics collapsed like a house of cards."[25]

Afterword and
Acknowledgments

In the winter of 1962–63, my second semester at the University of Hamburg, historian Fritz Fischer gave a lecture in the main auditorium on the dissolution of the Weimar Republic. Fischer's book *Griff nach der Weltmacht* (*Germany's Aims in the First World War*), published a year earlier, had caused a sensation. In it, he had broken with the entire established historical wisdom about the outbreak of the First World War in 1914. The Wilhelmine German Empire, according to the core thesis, did not "slip" into the war like the other combatants but had deliberately brought about the conflict to achieve a final breakthrough in its excessively ambitious quest to achieve European hegemony and establish itself as an unassailable world power. This provocative thesis immediately made the Hamburg scholar internationally famous. In democratic West Germany, his ideas initially came as a shock, reopening an old wound—paragraph 231 of the Treaty of Versailles, which held Germany solely responsible for the First World War. The entire right wing in Weimar Germany, including conservative German historians, had campaigned against this proposition. The revival of the idea kicked off the "Fischer Controversy," the first and most consequential dispute among historians in the history of West Germany.

I was one of a growing number of students who were attracted to this great breaker of taboos and enrolled in his lectures. During them, Fischer repeatedly cited a Bonn political scientist and historian named

Karl Dietrich Bracher. In the mid-1950s, Bracher had published a lengthy postdoctoral thesis entitled *The Dissolution of the Weimar Republic: A Study on the Decline of Power in a Democracy*. I bought the book, which had been republished in a third, revised and expanded, edition in 1960, read it—and was electrified. Alongside Fischer's *Griff nach der Weltmacht*, Bracher's groundbreaking study was the historical work that most influenced me during my studies. His astute analysis of the three successive presidentially appointed governments, from Brüning to Papen to Schleicher, remains unsurpassed to this day, even though decades of subsequent historical research may have corrected some of the details.

In a sense, then, this present book marks a return to my early days as a student of history. I still feel indebted to Bracher, although I do not view the story of the first German democracy exclusively from the perspective of its "power decay." Instead, I ask about alternative possibilities that might have prevented that democracy's demise. In addition, I owe many fundamental insights to the monumental 1993 history of the Weimar Republic by Heinrich August Winkler, which remains among the finest works of German historiography since Bracher.

This book is dedicated to the memory of my wife, Gudrun, my companion of fifty-seven years, who passed away in April 2022. Our life's work was to answer the question of why civilization in Germany broke down between 1933 and 1945, to help prevent something similar from happening again. My wife wrote her second state examination thesis in 1969 on "Right-Wing Radicalism in the Federal Republic of Germany." At that time, in the September 1969 federal elections, the far-right National Democratic Party of Germany (NPD) had only just failed to clear the 5 percent hurdle needed for national parliamentary representation in the Bundestag. And in some regional states, the NPD garnered enough of the vote to qualify it for local political power. (The state of Baden-Württemberg, where the NPD had taken 9.8 percent, was one example.) Since then, right-wing extremism has always been present in Germany. At times, parties like the NPD or Die Republikaner won troubling numbers of votes in regional elections, especially after German reunification. But before the Alternative für Deutschland (AfD), an ultraconservative-to-extremist right-wing party, they never managed to win seats in Germany's national parliament.

Until the federal elections of February 23, 2025, the AfD was one of the smaller parties in Germany's national parliament. A threat, but one that could be kept in check. Today, the situation has changed dramatically. Coming in with 20.8 percent, the AfD won more votes than the NSDAP in the fateful elections of September 14, 1930. It is now the second-largest parliamentary group in the Bundestag and the strongest party in eastern Germany. This success has come despite there being no mass social and economic misery comparable to that of the late Weimar Republic—and despite the party lacking a charismatic leader in the mold of Hitler. In the next election, the AfD could become even stronger. On the other hand, it is encouraging that many citizens demonstrated before, during, and after the vote against the new danger from the Right. By its end, the first German democracy, the Weimar Republic, lacked any such support from civil society. Now the future of liberal democracies worldwide is once more in jeopardy, in the United States but also in Europe and in Germany. There is still time to prevent a slip into darkness. It depends on us, on how we act, how we protest and how we stand up to the authoritarian sirens that try to lure us into the abyss. Our time is now. Let's not be the ones who dropped the ball.

My greatest thanks go to Gudrun and my son Sebastian, who succeeded Detlef Felken as editor in chief at the C. H. Beck publishing house in October 2023. He came up with the idea for this book and contributed significantly to its creation, with his stimulating criticism. His advice was all the more important to me because he himself, with his dissertation on the "Weimar Complex"—supervised by Heinrich August Winkler, the doyen of German Weimar research—has done fundamental historical work on the aftereffects of the Weimar experience in the political culture of the early Federal Republic.

My thanks also go out to Dorothee Mateika from the Hamburg Research Center for Contemporary History and Mirjam Zimmer and her team from the documentation department at *Die Zeit* newspaper for helping me obtain needed literature. Klaus Wernecke provided me with the multivolume edition *Akten der Reichskanzlei* (Files of the Reich

Chancellery), which is indispensable for the study of the Weimar Republic. As always, Jefferson Chase did a great job in translating my book into English. I am very grateful for our many years of wonderful work together. And last but not least, I would like to thank my American publisher, W. W. Norton, and in particular Dan Gerstle and Caroline Adams, for taking such meticulous care of my book.

As in my previous books, I have allowed contemporaries of the events to speak extensively through their diaries, letters, and memoirs. The journals of Count Harry Kessler, which have been available in an excellent edition for only a few years, are a particularly enlightening source, especially for the Weimar years. In addition, I consulted major newspapers and magazines of the day, including the *Berliner Tageblatt*, the *Vossische Zeitung*, and *Die Weltbühne*. Research on the Weimar Republic has still not paid enough attention to the liberal press in the country's capital, Berlin. In terms of both the quality of reporting and the stylistic brilliance of many of its authors, the standards of that time are rarely found among today's media professionals.

For this book, I was able to draw on my own earlier work, including my brief history of the 1918–19 revolution (2009), the first volume of my Hitler biography (2013), and the account *Germany 1923: Hyperinflation, Hitler's Putsch, and Democracy in Crisis* (2023). Chapters 2, 9, and 11 are revised and greatly expanded versions of articles I wrote for the history section of *Die Zeit*.

Volker Ullrich
Hamburg, February 2025

Notes

Preface

1. See Sebastian Ullrich, "Stabilitätsanker oder Hysterisierungsagentur: Der Weimar-Komplex in der Geschichte der Bundesrepublik," in *Weimars Wirkung: Das Nachleben der ersten deutschen Republik*, ed. Hanno Hochmuth et al. (Göttingen, 2020), 182–96 (here 192–93). For more detail, see Sebastian Ullrich, *Der Weimar-Komplex: Das Scheitern der ersten deutschen Demokratie und die politische Kultur der Bundesrepublik* (Göttingen, 2009).
2. See Nadine Rossol and Benjamin Ziemann, eds., *Aufbruch und Abgründe: Das Handbuch der Weimarer Republik* (Darmstadt, 2021); Sabine Becker, *Experiment Weimar: Eine Kulturgeschichte Deutschlands 1918–1933* (Darmstadt, 2018); Anthony McElligott, *Rethinking the Weimar Republic: Authority and Authoritarianism 1916–1936* (London, 2014).
3. Hagen Schulze, "Vom Scheitern einer Republik," in Karl Dietrich Bracher et al., eds., *Die Weimarer Republik 1918–1933: Politik, Wirtschaft, Gesellschaft* (Düsseldorf, 1987), 617–25 (here 617).
4. Cf. Frank Werner, "Wir müssen über Weimar reden," *Die Zeit* 45 (November 3, 2022).

Chapter 1: A Magical Beginning

1. Harry Graf Kessler, *Das Tagebuch*, vol. 6, *1916–1918*, ed. Günter Riederer with Christoph Hilse (Stuttgart, 2006), 613 (November 3, 1918).
2. Theodor Wolff, *Tagebücher 1914–1919*, part 2, introduced and ed. by Bernd Sösemann (Boppard am Rhein, 1984), 647 (November 9, 1918).
3. Prince Max von Baden, *Erinnerungen und Dokumente* (Berlin, 1927), 638.
4. See Manfred Jessen-Klingenberg, "Die Ausrufung der Republik durch Philipp Scheidemann am 9.11.1918," *Geschichte in Wissenschaft und Unterricht* 19 (1968): 649–56.

5. Gerhard Ritter and Susanne Miller, eds., *Die deutsche Revolution 1918–1919: Dokumente* (Hamburg, 1975), 78–79. See Helmut Trotnow, *Karl Liebknecht: Eine politische Biographie* (Cologne, 1980), 256.

6. Gustav Mayer, *Als deutsch-jüdischer Historiker in Krieg und Revolution 1914–1920: Tagebücher, Aufzeichnungen, Briefe*, ed. and introduced by Gottfried Niedhardt (Munich, 2009), 184 (November 9, 1918).

7. "Berlin am Nachmittag des Umschwungs," *Deutsche Zeitung* 574 (November 10, 1918).

8. *Berliner Tageblatt* 576 (November 10, 1918); also in Bernd Sösemann, ed., *Theodor Wolff: Der Journalist; Berichte und Leitartikel* (Düsseldorf, 1993), 127–30 (here 127).

9. Kessler, *Das Tagebuch*, vol. 6, 628 (November 10, 1918). See also *Berliner Morgenpost* 312 (November 10, 1918): "Events are roaring over us like a hurricane. Much lies in ruins that yesterday still rose to proud heights."

10. Volker Ullrich, *Kriegsalltag: Hamburg im Ersten Weltkrieg* (Cologne, 1982), 65.

11. Ullrich, *Kriegsalltag*, 87.

12. See Volker Ullrich, "Der Januarstreik 1918 in Hamburg, Kiel und Bremen: Eine vergleichende Studie zur Geschichte der Streikbewegungen im Ersten Weltkrieg," *Zeitschrift des Vereins für Hamburgische Geschichte* 71 (1985): 45–74.

13. Bernd Ulrich and Benjamin Ziemann, eds., *Frontalltag im Ersten Weltkrieg: Wahn und Wirklichkeit; Quellen und Dokumente* (Frankfurt am Main, 1994), 164.

14. Ulrich and Ziemann, *Frontalltag im Ersten Weltkrieg*, 129.

15. Ulrich and Ziemann, *Frontalltag im Ersten Weltkrieg*, 202.

16. See Volker Ullrich, *Die nervöse Großmacht 1871–1918: Aufstieg und Untergang des deutschen Kaiserreichs*, rev. ed. (Frankfurt am Main, 2013), 566.

17. See Gerhard Ritter, *Staatskunst und Kriegshandwerk: Das Problem des "Militarismus" in Deutschland*, vol. 4, *Die Herrschaft des deutschen Militarismus und die Katastrophe von 1918* (Munich, 1968), 458.

18. Annelise Thimme, ed., *Friedrich Thimme 1868–1938: Ein politischer Historiker, Publizist und Schriftsteller in seinen; Briefen* (Boppard am Rhein, 1994), 177.

19. See Wilhelm Deist, "Die Politik der Seekriegsleitung und die Rebellion der Flotte Ende 1918," *Vierteljahrshefte für Zeitgeschichte* 14 (1968): 341–68.

20. Kessler, *Das Tagebuch*, vol. 6, 619 (November 7, 1918).

21. Max von Baden, *Erinnerung und Dokumente*, 600.

22. Sigurd von Ilsemann, *Der Kaiser in Holland: Aufzeichnungen des letzten Flügeladjutanten Kaiser Wilhelms II aus Amerongen und Doorn 1918–1923* (Munich, 1967), 35 (November 8, 1918). See also John C. G. Röhl, *Wilhelm II: Der Weg in den Abgrund 1900–1941* (Munich, 2008), 1243–44.

23. Eduard Bernstein, *Die deutsche Revolution von 1918/19: Geschichte und Entstehung der ersten Arbeitsperiode der deutschen Republik*, ed. Heinrich August Winkler, annotated by Teresa Löwe (Bonn, 1998), 63.

24. *Die Regierung der Volksbeauftragten 1918/19*, part 1, ed. Susanne Miller with Heinrich Potthoff, introduced by Erich Matthias (Düsseldorf, 1969), no. 3, 20–21.

25. See *Die Regierung der Volksbeauftragten*, part 1, xxxi–xlvii.

26. *Groß-Berliner Arbeiter- und Soldatenräte. Dokumente des Vollzugsrates vom Ausbruch der Revolution bis zum 1. Reichsrätekongress*, ed. Gerhard Engel et al. (Berlin, 1993), doc. 12, 18.

27. See Heinrich August Winkler, *Von der Revolution zur Stabilisierung: Arbeiter und Arbeiterbewegung in der Weimarer Republik, 1918–1924* (Berlin, 1984), 56–57.

28. See Susanne Miller, *Die Bürde der Macht: Die deutsche Sozialdemokratie 1918–1920* (Düsseldorf, 1978), 99.

29. "Das Programm des Rats der Volksbeauftragten, 12.11.1918," *Der Rat der Volksbeauftragten 1918/19*, part 1, no. 9, 37–38.

30. See Joachim Käppner, *1918: Aufstand für die Freiheit; Die Revolution der Besonnenen* (Munich, 2017), 237–38.

31. "Nach dem Neunten," *Berliner Volks-Zeitung* 534 (November 10, 1918).

32. Ernst Troeltsch, *Die Fehlgeburt einer Republik: Spektator in Berlin 1918 bis 1922*, compiled and with an epilogue by Johann Hinrich Claussen (Frankfurt am Main, 1994), 9.

33. Thomas Mann, *Tagebücher 1918–1921*, ed. Peter de Mendelssohn (Frankfurt am Main, 1979), 67 (November 10, 1918).

34. Kessler, *Das Tagebuch*, vol. 6, 632 (November 12, 1918).

35. Dorothy von Moltke, *Ein Leben in Deutschland: Briefe aus Kreisau und Berlin 1907–1934*, introduced, trans., and ed. Beate Ruhm von Oppen (Munich, 1999), 57 (November 19, 1918).

36. Karl Hampe, *Kriegstagebuch 1914–1919*, ed. Folker Reichert and Eike Wolgast (Munich, 2004), 780 (November 14, 1918), 775 (November 10, 1918). See also Hans-Joachim Bieber, *Bürgertum in der Revolution: Bürgerräte und Bürgerstreiks in Deutschland 1918–1920* (Hamburg, 1992).

37. *Die Regierung der Volksbeauftragten*, part 1, no. 30, 153.

38. See Miller, *Die Bürde der Macht*, 107.

39. *Groß-Berliner Arbeiter- und Soldatenräte*, doc. 61, 154.

40. Rosa Luxemburg, "Der Anfang," *Die Rote Fahne* (November 18, 1918); "Die Nationalversammlung," *Rote Fahne* (November 20, 1918); *Gesammelte Werke*, vol. 4, *August 1914 bis Januar 1919* (Berlin, 1974), 397–400, 407–10. See also Ernst Piper, *Rosa Luxemburg: Ein Leben* (Munich, 2018), 626–29.

41. Mayer, *Als deutsch-jüdischer Historiker*, 188 (November 14, 1918).

42. See Mark Jones, *Am Anfang war Gewalt: Die deutsche Revolution 1918/19 und der Beginn der Weimarer Republik*, trans. Karl Heinz Siber (Berlin, 2017), 85–94.

43. Wolff, *Tagebücher 1914–1919*, part 2, 652 (November 12, 1918).

44. Mayer, *Als deutsch-jüdischer Historiker*, 186 (November 11, 1918), 193 (November 22, 1918).

45. *Illustrierte Geschichte der deutschen Revolution* (Berlin, 1929), 241.

46. *Aus den Geburtsstunden der Weimarer Republik: Das Tagebuch des Obersten Ernst van den Bergh*, ed. Wolfram Wette (Düsseldorf, 1991), 61 (December 19, 1918). On the term "anti-chaos reflex," which goes back to political scientist Richard Löwenthal, see Heinrich August Winkler, *Weimar 1918–1933: Die Geschichte der ersten deutschen Demokratie* (Munich, 1993), 14.

47. Wilhelm Groener, *Lebenserinnerungen: Jugend, Generalstab, Weltkrieg* (Göttingen, 1957), 467–68.

48. Ritter and Miller, *Die deutsche Revolution*, 101–2. See Ulrich Kluge, *Soldatenräte und Revolution: Studien zur Militärpolitik in Deutschland 1917/18* (Göttingen, 1975), 140–41; Winkler, *Von der Revolution zur Stabilisierung*, 71.

49. *Die Regierung der Volksbeauftragten*, part 1, no. 18, 111.

50. Kessler, *Das Tagebuch*, vol. 6, 694 (from December 17, 1918).

51. Gerhart Hauptmann, *Diarium 1917–1933*, ed. Martin Machatzke (Frankfurt am Main, 1980), 29–30 (December 12, 1918).

52. Mayer, *Als deutsch-jüdischer Historiker*, 185 (November 11, 1918).

53. See *Die Regierung der Volksbeauftragten*, part 1, lxi–lxxii.

54. *Die Regierung der Volksbeauftragten*, no. 30, 180–81. See also Winkler, *Von der Revolution zur Stabilisierung*, 72–75; Käppner, *1918*, 246ff.

55. Ritter and Miller, *Die deutsche Revolution*, 226–27.

56. See Winkler, *Von der Revolution zur Stabilisierung*, 84–89; Jens Flemming, *Landwirtschaftliche Interessen und Demokratie: Ländliche Gesellschaft, Agrarverbände und Staat 1890–1925* (Bonn, 1978), 252–58.

57. *Die Regierung der Volksbeauftragten*, part 1, no. 16, 104. On the question of socialization, see Winkler, *Von der Revolution zur Stabilisierung*, 81–84.

58. See Hans-Joachim Bieber, *Gewerkschaften in Krieg und Revolution: Arbeiterbewegung, Industrie, Staat und Militär in Deutschland 1914–1920*, part 2 (Hamburg, 1981), 614. On the Stinnes–Legien Agreement, see Bieber, 595ff.; Winkler, *Von der Revolution zur Stabilisierung*, 45–46.

59. *Groß-Berliner Arbeiter- und Soldatenräte*, doc. 53, 105–6.

60. *Allgemeiner Kongreß der Arbeiter- und Soldatenräte Deutschlands: Vom 16. bis 21. Dezember 1918 im Abgeordnetenhause zu Berlin; Stenographische Berichte* (Berlin, 1919), 6.

61. *Allgemeiner Kongreß der Arbeiter- und Soldatenräte*, 141–42.

62. *Allgemeiner Kongreß der Arbeiter- und Soldatenräte*, 114.

63. *Allgemeiner Kongreß der Arbeiter- und Soldatenräte*, 144–51. See Käppner, *1918*, 311–14.

64. *Allgemeiner Kongreß der Arbeiter- und Soldatenräte*, 172.

65. *Allgemeiner Kongreß der Arbeiter- und Soldatenräte*, 64–72, 90–96. For the text of the "seven points," see Ritter and Miller, *Die deutsche Revolution*, 155–56. On the military and political decisions of the congress of councils, see Kluge, *Soldatenräte und Revolution*, 250–60.

66. *Die Regierung der Volksbeauftragten*, part 2, no. 62, 3–15 (here 4–5, 13–14). See also Winkler, *Von der Revolution zur Stabilisierung*, 106–7.

67. Kessler, *Das Tagebuch*, vol. 6, 704 (December 23, 1918).

68. Arthur Rosenberg, *Geschichte der Weimarer Republik*, ed. Kurt Kersten (Frankfurt am Main, 1961), 46. On the Berlin Christmas battles, see Winkler, *Von der Revolution zur Stabilisierung*, 109–10; Käppner, *1918*, 326–51.

69. Kessler, *Das Tagebuch*, vol. 6, 713 (November 29, 1918).

70. *Die Regierung der Volksbeauftragten*, part 2, no. 77, 73–107 (here 95, 101).

71. *Die Regierung der Volksbeauftragten*, part 2, no. 85, 145.

72. *Die Regierung der Volksbeauftragten*, part 2, no. 82, 142. On Noske's role in Kiel, see Wolfram Wette, *Gustav Noske: Eine politische Biographie* (Düsseldorf, 1987), 198ff.

73. *Berliner Tageblatt* 1 (January 1, 1919); also in Ruth Glatzer, *Berlin zur Weimarer Zeit. Panorama einer Metropole 1919–1933* (Berlin, 2000), 21–22.

74. Hampe, *Kriegstagebuch 1914–1919*, 810, 811 (December 31, 1918, January 1, 1919).

75. Kessler, *Das Tagebuch*, vol. 6, 715 (January 31, 1918).

76. Victor Klemperer, *Leben sammeln, nicht fragen wozu und warum: Tagebücher 1918–1924*, ed. Walter Nowojski with Christian Löser (Berlin, 1996), 42 (December 31, 1918).

77. Mayer, *Als deutsch-jüdischer Historiker*, 207.

78. Hedwig Pringsheim, *Tagebücher*, vol. 6, *1917–1922*, ed. Christiana Herbst (Göttingen, 2017), 247 (December 31, 1918).

79. On the Hamburg and Bremen left-wing radicals, see Volker Ullrich, *Die Hamburger Arbeiterbewegung vom Vorabend des Ersten Weltkriegs bis zur Revolution 1918/19*, vol. 1 (Hamburg, 1976), 404–37, 550–66, 604–10.

80. *Der Gründungsparteitag der KPD: Protokoll und Materialien*, ed. and introduced by Hermann Weber (Frankfurt am Main, 1969), 99, 101.

81. *Der Gründungsparteitag der KPD*, 108.

82. Rosa Luxemburg to Clara Zetkin, January 11, 1919, in Rosa Luxemburg, *Gesammelte Briefe*, vol. 5, 2nd ed. (Berlin, 1987), 426. See Annelies Laschitza, *Im Lebensrausch, trotz alledem: Rosa Luxemburg; Eine Biographie* (Berlin, 1996), 615–16.

83. *Der Gründungsparteitag der KPD*, 126.

84. See Winkler, *Von der Revolution zur Stabilisierung*, 120ff.; Jones, *Am Anfang war Gewalt*, 152ff.; Käppner, *1918*, 386ff.

85. *Die Rote Fahne* 6 (January 6, 1919). See also Jones, *Am Anfang war Gewalt*, 154–55.

86. See Ottokar Luban, "Demokratische Sozialistin oder 'blutige Rosa'? Rosa Luxemburg und die KPD-Führung im Berliner Januaraufstand 1919," *Internationale Wissenschaftliche Korrespondenz zur Geschichte der deutschen Arbeiterbewegung* 36 (1999), 176–207; Piper, *Rosa Luxemburg*, 659.

87. See Wette, *Gustav Noske*, 300.

88. *Die Regierung der Volksbeauftragten*, part 2, no. 96, 198.

89. See Jones, *Am Anfang war Gewalt*, 193–200.

90. Kessler, *Das Tagebuch*, vol. 7, *1919–1923*, ed. Angela Rheinthal et al. (Stuttgart, 2007), 90 (January 12, 1919).

91. Luxemburg, *Gesammelte Werke* 4, 533–38 (here 538). See Piper, *Rosa Luxemburg*, 675.

92. See Klaus Gietinger, *Eine Leiche schwimmt im Landwehrkanal: Die Ermordung Rosa Luxemburgs* (Hamburg, 2008), 104–5. On the arrest and murder of Luxemburg and Liebknecht, see Gietinger, 18ff.; Jones, *Am Anfang war Gewalt*, 217–20; Käppner, *1918*, 411–15.

93. See Jones, *Am Anfang war Gewalt*, 221–22.

94. Hermann Müller, *Die November-Revolution: Erinnerungen* (Berlin, 1928). See Walter Mühlhausen, *Friedrich Ebert 1871–1925: Reichspräsident der Weimarer Republik* (Bonn, 2006), 148.

95. *Die Regierung der Volksbeauftragten*, part 2, no. 109, 281.

96. See Gietinger, *Eine Leiche schwimmt im Landwehrkanal*, 38ff.; Jones, *Am Anfang war Gewalt*, 227–29.

97. Käthe Kollwitz, *Die Tagebücher 1908–1945*, ed. and with an afterword by Jutta Bohnke-Kollwitz (Munich, 2007), 402 (January 25, 1919).

98. *Die Freiheit* 601 (December 11, 1919). See Miller, *Die Bürde der Macht*, 235.

99. Kessler, *Das Tagebuch*, vol. 7, 105 (January 19, 1919).

100. See Thomas Mergel, "Wahlen, Wahlkämpfe und Demokratie," in Rossol and Ziemann, *Aufbruch und Abgründe*, 198–222 (here 200–201).

101. See the detailed election analysis in Winkler, *Von der Revolution zur Stabilisierung*, 135–44.

102. *Die Regierung der Volksbeauftragten*, part 2, no. 103a, 225. See Heiko Holste, *Warum Weimar: Wie Deutschlands erste Republik zu ihrem ersten Geburtsort kam* (Vienna, 2017).

103. Excerpts from the Ebert speech of February 6, 1919, in Peter Longerich, ed., *Die Erste Republik: Dokumente zur Geschichte des Weimarer Staates* (Munich, 1992), 99–103 (here 102).

104. *Berliner Tageblatt* 56 (February 7, 1919). See Mühlhausen, *Friedrich Ebert*, 166.

105. Kessler, *Das Tagebuch*, vol. 7, 124 (February 6, 1919).

106. On the formation of the Weimar Coalition and Ebert's election, see Mühlhausen, *Friedrich Ebert*, 171–85.

107. Wette, *Aus den Geburtsstunden der Weimarer Republik*, 88 (February 13, 1919).

108. See Wette, *Gustav Noske*, 399–401.

109. Mark Jones, *Founding Weimar Violence and the German Revolution of 1918–1919* (Cambridge, 2016), 70.

110. *Vorwärts* 126 (March 10, 1919). See also Wette, *Gustav Noske*, 420; Jones, *Am Anfang war Gewalt*, 255.

111. See Wette, *Gustav Noske*, 421; Jones, *Am Anfang war Gewalt*, 254.

112. See Jones, *Am Anfang war Gewalt*, 261–65.

113. See Piper, *Rosa Luxemburg*, 679–80.

114. Kessler, *Das Tagebuch*, vol. 7, 194–95 (March 19, 1919).

115. See Bernhard Grau, *Kurt Eisner 1867–1919: Eine Biographie* (Munich, 2001), 388ff.

116. See Jones, *Am Anfang war Gewalt*, 293ff.

117. Victor Klemperer, *Man möchte immer weinen und lachen in einem: Revolutionstagebuch 1919* (Berlin, 2015), 162–63 (May 2, 1919).

118. Erich Mühsam, *Tagebücher (1910–1924)*, ed. and with an afterword by Chris Hirte (Munich, 1994), 191 (May 7, 1919).

119. Troeltsch, *Die Fehlgeburt einer Republik*, 61–62 (June 26, 1919).

120. Gerhard Ritter to his parents, May 18, 1919; see Christoph Cornelißen, *Gerhard Ritter: Geschichtswissenschaft und Politik im 20. Jahrhundert* (Düsseldorf, 2001), 94.

121. T[heodor] W[olff], "Nein!," *Berliner Tageblatt* 206 (May 8, 1919). See also Jörn Leonhard, *Der überforderte Frieden: Versailles und die Welt 1918–1923* (Munich, 2018), 971ff.

122. See Eberhard Kolb, *Der Frieden von Versailles* (Munich, 2005), 58–69; Winkler, *Weimar*, 90–91.

123. See Winkler, *Weimar*, 87–89.

124. See Winkler, *Weimar*, 91–92; Wette, *Gustav Noske*, 463–64.

125. See Mühlhausen, *Friedrich Ebert*, 258.

126. See Wette, *Gustav Noske*, 466–67.

127. On the "war of notes," see Leonhard, *Der überforderte Frieden*, 993–1008; Eckart Conze, *Die große Illusion: Versailles und die Neuordnung der Welt* (Munich, 2018), 359–62.

128. Kessler, *Das Tagebuch*, vol. 7, 245 (June 17, 1919).

129. See Winkler, *Weimar*, 92–94; Kolb, *Der Frieden von Versailles*, 80–82.

130. See Winkler, *Weimar*, 94–95; Kolb, *Der Frieden von Versailles*, 82–85. On the ceremony in Versailles on June 28, 1919, see Leonhard, *Der überforderte Frieden*, 1024–31; Conze, *Die große Illusion*, 372–77.

131. *Berliner Tageblatt* 289 (June 28, 1919), reprinted in Sösemann, *Theodor Wolff*, 139–42 (here 141).

132. Pringsheim, *Tagebücher*, vol. 6, 298 (June 30, 1919).

133. See Winkler, *Weimar*, 99; Heiko Bollmeyer, *Der steinige Weg zur Demokratie: Die Weimarer Nationalversammlung zwischen Kaiserreich und Republik* (Frankfurt am Main, 2007), 219–20.

134. See Bollmeyer, *Der steinige Weg zur Demokratie*, 221–28.

135. *Die Regierung der Volksbeauftragten*, part 2, nos. 104, 105, 237–66.

136. See Bollmeyer, *Der steinige Weg zur Demokratie*, 318.

137. See Winkler, *Weimar*, 99–100.

138. See Bollmeyer, *Der steinige Weg zur Demokratie*, 340–44, on the disputes over the office of Reich president.

139. Oliver F. R. Haardt and Christopher Clark, "Die Weimarer Reichsverfassung als Moment der Geschichte," in *Das Wagnis der Demokratie: Eine Anatomie der Weimarer Reichsverfassung*, ed. Horst Dreier and Christian Waldhoff (Munich, 2018), 9–44 (here 29).

140. See Michael Stolleis, "Die soziale Problematik der Weimarer Reichsverfassung," in Dreier and Waldhoff, *Das Wagnis der Demokratie*, 195–218.

141. See Winkler, *Weimar*, 103–4; Nadine Rossol, "Republikanische Gruppen, Ideen und Identitäten," in Rossol and Ziemann, *Aufbruch und Abgründe*, 326.

142. See Bollmeyer, *Der steinige Weg zur Demokratie*, 363–64.

143. Kessler, *Das Tagebuch*, vol. 7, 265 (August 21, 1919). See Mühlhausen, *Friedrich Ebert*, 203–4.

144. See Haardt and Clark, "Die Weimarer Reichsverfassung," 29.

145. Wilhelm Dittmann, *Erinnerungen*, vol. 2, ed. and introduced by Jürgen Rojahn (Frankfurt am Main, 1995), 631.

146. Heinrich August Winkler, *Die Deutschen und die Revolution: Eine Geschichte von 1848 bis 1989* (Munich, 2023), 67.

147. Alexander Gallus, "Die umkämpfte Revolution," *Zeit-Geschichte* 6 (2018): 14–20 (here 15).

148. *Berliner Tageblatt* 534 (November 10, 1919). Excerpts reprinted in Sösemann, *Theodor Wolff*, 247–49.

Chapter 2: Marching on Berlin

1. On the course of the meeting, see Johannes Erger, *Der Kapp-Lüttwitz-Putsch: Ein Beitrag zur deutschen Innenpolitik 1919/20* (Düsseldorf, 1967), 141–46 (here 143, 146); Wette, *Gustav Noske*, 637–39; Winkler, *Weimar*, 121–22.

2. See Reinhardt's report on the course of the cabinet meeting, March 15, 1920, *Akten der Reichskanzler [AdR]: Das Kabinett Bauer 21. Juni 1919 bis 27. März 1920*, ed. Anton Golecki (Boppard am Rhein, 1980), no. 188, 672–76; notes by Koch-Weser, March 13, 1920, in Erwin Könnemann and Gerhard Schulze, eds., *Der Kapp-Lüttwitz-Ludendorff-Putsch* (Munich, 2002), no. 91, 137–38; Erger, *Der Kapp-Lüttwitz-Putsch*, 146–48; Wette, *Gustav Noske*, 640–42; Winkler, *Weimar*, 122.

3. Otto Meissner, *Staatssekretär unter Ebert-Hindenburg-Hitler* (Hamburg, 1950), 89.

4. Koch-Weser's notes, March 13, 1920; Könnemann and Schulze, *Der Kapp-Lüttwitz-Ludendorff-Putsch*, 138.

5. Kessler, *Das Tagebuch*, vol. 7, 269 (September 2, 1919).

6. Troeltsch, *Die Fehlgeburt einer Republik*, 101 (December 19, 1919).

7. Könnemann and Schulze, *Der Kapp-Lüttwitz-Ludendorff Putsch*, 19.

8. Minutes of Ebert's meeting with Generals Lüttwitz and Maercker, August 19, 1919, in Könnemann and Schulze, *Der Kapp-Lüttwitz-Ludendorff Putsch*, 23.

9. On the question of troop reduction, see Wette, *Gustav Noske*, 544–51.

10. See Gabriele Krüger, *Die Brigade Ehrhardt* (Hamburg, 1971), 11ff. On the "Baltic men," see Wette, *Gustav Noske*, 561–76; Winkler, *Weimar*, 114–15.

11. See Könnemann and Schulze, *Der Kapp-Lüttwitz-Ludendorff-Putsch*, xix, xv–xvi; Gerald D. Feldman, *Hugo Stinnes: Biographie eines Industriellen 1870–1924* (Munich, 1998), 601.

12. Kapp to Colonel Heye, July 5, 1919; Könnemann and Schulze, *Der Kapp-Lüttwitz-Ludendorff-Putsch*, 11–13.

13. Margarethe Ludendorff, *Als ich Ludendorffs Frau war*, ed. Walther Ziersch (Munich, 1929), 209. See Manfred Nebelin, *Ludendorff: Diktator im Ersten Weltkrieg* (Munich, 2010), 508.

14. Below's record of the meeting on July 8, 1919, in Könnemann and Schulze, *Der Kapp-Lüttwitz-Ludendorff-Putsch*, 13–14.

15. Kapp's memorandum, September 18, 1919, in Könnemann and Schulze, *Der Kapp-Lüttwitz-Ludendorff-Putsch*, 28–35 (here 28).

16. See Wette, *Gustav Noske*, 508–14; Klaus Gietinger, *Der Konterrevolutionär: Waldemar Pabst—eine deutsche Karriere* (Hamburg, 2008), 198–94.

17. Hopman's diary entry of August 14, 1919, in Feldman, *Hugo Stinnes*, 601. On the financing of the National Association, see Feldman, 601–2; Könnemann and Schulze, *Der Kapp-Lüttwitz-Ludendorff Putsch*, xvi.

18. See Erger, *Der Kapp-Lüttwitz-Putsch*, 90–92; Gietinger, *Der Konterrevolutionär*, 199–200.

19. See Erger, *Der Kapp-Lüttwitz-Putsch*, 115–16; Wette, *Gustav Noske*, 627–28.

20. See Erger, *Der Kapp-Lüttwitz Putsch*, 116–21; Wette, *Gustav Noske*, 629–31.

21. See Gustav Noske, *Von Kiel bis Kapp: Zur Geschichte der deutschen Revolution* (Berlin, 1920), 207; Erger, *Der Kapp-Lüttwitz-Putsch*, 121–22, 317–18 (doc. 20); Wette, *Gustav Noske*, 631–32; Mühlhausen, *Friedrich Ebert*, 316–17.

22. See Erger, *Der Kapp-Lüttwitz Putsch*, 125.

23. See Erger, *Der Kapp-Lüttwitz Putsch*, 318–19 (doc. 21); Kapp's letter to an East Prussian friend, September 22, 1920, in Könnemann and Schulze, *Der Kapp-Lüttwitz-Ludendorff-Putsch*, 523.

24. Report of State Commissioner von Berger, March 8, 1920, in *AdR: Das Kabinett Bauer*, no. 183, 653–56 (here 653, 656). Noske did not read the report until March 10, 1920; Noske, *Von Kiel bis Kapp*, 204.

25. See Erger, *Der Kapp-Lüttwitz-Putsch*, 124; Könnemann and Schulze, *Der Kapp-Lüttwitz-Ludendorff-Putsch*, 132 (note 2).

26. Cabinet meeting, March 12, 1920, in *AdR: Das Kabinett Bauer*, no. 186, 667–68.

27. See Erger, *Der Kapp-Lüttwitz-Putsch*, 133; Wette, *Gustav Noske*, 635–36.

28. Trotha's report on his inspection of the Döberitz camp, March 12, 1920, in *AdR: Das Kabinett Bauer*, no. 187, 670–72; see Erger, *Der Kapp-Lüttwitz-Putsch*, 136–37; Wette, *Gustav Noske*, 634–35; Krüger, *Die Brigade Ehrhardt*, 50–51.

29. Reinhardt's report on the events in Berlin on the night of March 12–13, 1920, in Könnemann and Schulze, *Der Kapp-Lüttwitz-Ludendorff-Putsch*, 213–17 (here 214–15). See Erger, *Der Kapp-Lüttwitz-Putsch*, 139–40; Wette, *Gustav Noske*, 637–38; Krüger, *Die Brigade Ehrhardt*, 51–52.

30. Glatzer, *Berlin zur Weimarer Zeit*, 67, 65–66. See also Erger, *Der Kapp-Lüttwitz-Putsch*, 161–62.

31. Kollwitz, *Die Tagebücher*, 457 (March 13, 1920).

32. Krüger, *Die Brigade Ehrhardt*, 55; see Gietinger, *Der Konterrevolutionär*, 215; Könnemann and Schulze, *Der Kapp-Lüttwitz-Ludendorff-Putsch*, xxiii.

33. Report by Undersecretary of State Albert, *AdR: Das Kabinett Bauer*, no. 189, 677–79; report by a ministry official, in Könnemann and Schulze, *Der Kapp-Lüttwitz-Ludendorff-Putsch*, 136–37; Schiffer's report, in Könnemann and Schulze, 140–41.

34. Colonel von Heyes to Friedrich von Rabenau, March 27, 1940, in Könnemann and Schulze, *Der Kapp-Lüttwitz-Ludendorff-Putsch*, xxiii, 603.

35. Könnemann and Schulze, *Der Kapp-Lüttwitz-Ludendorff-Putsch*, 142–44.

36. Könnemann and Schulze, *Der Kapp-Lüttwitz-Ludendorff-Putsch*, 148–50.

37. Report on the press conference, in Könnemann and Schulze, *Der Kapp-Lüttwitz-Ludendorff-Putsch*, 167–68; statement by Undersecretary of State von Falkenhausen, Leipzig, March 27–28, 1920, in Könnemann and Schulze, 420–28 (here 421, 425).

38. See Erger, *Der Kapp-Lüttwitz Putsch*, 167–68.

39. Erger, *Der Kapp-Lüttwitz Putsch*, 151.

40. Kapp to Count Westarp, August 20, 1920, in Könnemann and Schulze, *Der Kapp-Lüttwitz-Ludendorff-Putsch*, 517–19 (here 518).

41. Kessler, *Das Tagebuch*, vol. 7, 291 (March 15, 1920).

42. Könnemann and Schulze, *Der Kapp-Lüttwitz-Ludendorff-Putsch*, 780. See Wilhelm Ribhegge, *August Winnig: Eine historische Persönlichkeitsanalyse* (Bonn, 1973), 226–27.

43. See Könnemann and Schulze, *Der Kapp-Lüttwitz-Ludendorff-Putsch*, vii–ix, 950–53; Diethard Hennig, *Johannes Hoffmann: Sozialdemokrat und Bayerischer Ministerpräsident* (Munich, 1990), 428–35.

44. Könnemann and Schulze, *Der Kapp-Lüttwitz-Ludendorff Putsch*, 146–48.

45. Könnemann and Schulze, *Der Kapp-Lüttwitz-Ludendorff Putsch*, 196–97 (here 197). See Hans Meier-Welcker, *Seeckt* (Frankfurt am Main, 1967), 263–64.

46. Wolfram Pyta, *Hindenburg: Herrschaft zwischen Hohenzollern und Hitler* (Munich, 2007), 451.

47. See Feldman, *Hugo Stinnes*, 602–4; Winkler, *Von der Revolution zur Stabilisierung*, 306.

48. Könnemann and Schulze, *Der Kapp-Lüttwitz-Ludendorff-Putsch*, 211–13 (here 212).

49. Erwin Könnemann and Hans-Joachim Krusch, *Aktionseinheit contra Kapp-Putsch: Der Kapp-Putsch im März 1920 und der Kampf der deutschen Arbeiterklasse sowie anderer Werktätiger gegen die Errichtung der Militärdiktatur und für demokratische Verhältnisse* (East Berlin, 1972), 283–84.

50. See Erger, *Der Kapp-Lüttwitz Putsch*, 206–19; AdR: *Das Kabinett Bauer*, no. 218, 771–72.

51. Könnemann and Schulze, *Der Kapp-Lüttwitz-Ludendorff Putsch*, 176–77.

52. Könnemann and Schulze, *Der Kapp-Lüttwitz-Ludendorff Putsch*, 151–55. See also Ludwig Richter, *Die Deutsche Volkspartei 1918–1933* (Düsseldorf, 2002), 90–94.

53. Könnemann and Schulze, *Der Kapp-Lüttwitz-Ludendorff Putsch*, 157–58.

54. Könnemann and Schulze, *Der Kapp-Lüttwitz-Ludendorff Putsch*, 145.

55. See Miller, *Die Bürde der Macht*, 378–79; Wette, *Gustav Noske*, 650–52.

56. Könnemann and Schulze, *Der Kapp-Lüttwitz-Ludendorff Putsch*, 180–81.

57. Könnemann and Schulze, *Der Kapp-Lüttwitz-Ludendorff Putsch*, 155–56. See Erger, *Der Kapp-Lüttwitz-Putsch*, 195–97; Winkler, *Von der Revolution zur Stabilisierung*, 302–3.

58. Könnemann and Schulze, *Der Kapp-Lüttwitz-Ludendorff-Putsch*, 158–60 (here 159), 169–71. See Erger, *Der Kapp-Lüttwitz-Putsch*, 200–202; Winkler, *Von der Revolution zur Stabilisierung*, 303–4.

59. Mayer, *Als deutsch-jüdischer Historiker*, no. 99, 444.

60. Alfred Kerr, *Berlin wird Berlin: Briefe aus der Reichshauptstadt 1897–1922*, ed. Deborah Vietor-Engländer, vol. 4, *1917–1922* (Göttingen, 2021), 208–9 (March 31, 1920).

61. Wette, *Aus den Geburtsstunden der Weimarer Republik*, 130 (March 17, 1920).

62. See Könnemann and Krusch, *Aktionseinheit contra Kapp-Putsch*, 187; Erger, *Der Kapp-Lüttwitz-Putsch*, 203.

63. Könnemann and Schulze, *Der Kapp-Lüttwitz-Ludendorff Putsch*, 190–93.

64. Könnemann and Schulze, *Der Kapp-Lüttwitz-Ludendorff Putsch*, no. 157, 221, 237; see also Krüger, *Die Brigade Ehrhardt*, 57–59; Feldman, *Hugo Stinnes*, 604.

65. Notes by Koch-Weser, March 13, 1920, in Könnemann and Schulze, *Der Kapp-Lüttwitz-Ludendorff-Putsch*, 139.

66. See Mühlhausen, *Friedrich Ebert*, 322–23; Wette, *Gustav Noske*, 643–45;

notes by Government Councillor Doehle about his trip to Dresden March 13–14, 1920, in *AdR: Das Kabinett Bauer*, 679–81; report by the government councillor Otto Meissner, April 14, 1920, in Könnemann and Schulze, *Der Kapp-Lüttwitz-Ludendorff-Putsch*, 444–47.

67. Joint meeting of the Württemberg State Ministry and the Reich cabinet, March 15, 1920 (4 p.m.), in *AdR: Das Kabinett Bauer*, no. 193, 685.

68. Notes by Koch-Weser, March 15–16, 1920, in Könnemann and Schulze, *Der Kapp-Lüttwitz-Ludendorff Putsch*, 221.

69. Koch-Weser to Schiffer, March 15, 1920, in *AdR: Das Kabinett Bauer*, no. 194, 686–87.

70. Notes by Koch-Weser on the cabinet meeting of March 16, 1920, in *AdR: Das Kabinett Bauer*, no. 198, 695–99. See Erger, *Der Kapp-Lüttwitz-Putsch*, 244–48; Mühlhausen, *Friedrich Ebert*, 326–27; Wette, *Gustav Noske*, 647–48.

71. See Erger, *Der Kapp-Lüttwitz-Putsch*, 252–60 (here 260); Richter, *Die Deutsche Volkspartei*, 99–101.

72. Kapp to Schiffer, March 17, 1920, in *AdR: Das Kabinett Bauer*, no. 200, 701–2. Kapp's official resignation of March 17, 1920, was similarly worded. See Erger, *Der Kapp-Lüttwitz-Putsch*, 266.

73. Heye to Friedrich von Rabenau, March 27, 1940, in Könnemann and Schulze, *Der Kapp-Lüttwitz-Ludendorff-Putsch*, 604. On the resignation of Lüttwitz, see Erger, *Der Kapp-Lüttwitz-Putsch*, 273–78.

74. Notes by Schiffer, March 17, 1920, in Könnemann and Schulze, *Der Kapp-Lüttwitz-Ludendorff-Putsch*, 258. See Meier-Welcker, *Seeckt*, 268–69.

75. See Krüger, *Die Ehrhardt-Brigade*, 62.

76. Carl von Ossietzky, "Die demokratische Parole," in *Sämtliche Schriften*, vol. 1, *1911–1921*, ed. Mathias Bertram et al. (Reinbek bei Hamburg, 1994), 191 (April 1, 1920).

77. T[heodor] W[olff], "Nach dem Sieg des Volkes," *Berliner Tageblatt* 135 (March 24, 1920).

78. Könnemann and Schulze, *Der Kapp-Lüttwitz-Ludendorff-Putsch*, 270–71. See Winkler, *Von der Revolution zur Stabilisierung*, 309–10.

79. Könnemann and Schulze, *Der Kapp-Lüttwitz-Ludendorff Putsch*, 139.

80. Wette, *Aus den Geburtsstunden der Weimarer Republik*, 134 (March 17, 1920).

81. Wette, *Gustav Noske*, 657–58; notes by Koch-Weser, March 18, 1920, in Könnemann and Schulze, *Der Kapp Lüttwitz-Ludendorff-Putsch*, 276. Noske was also unapologetic in his memoirs, claiming that he had been made a "scapegoat for the mistakes of others": Noske, *Von Kiel bis Kapp*, 210.

82. Cabinet meeting, March 20, 1920, in *AdR: Das Kabinett Bauer*, no. 206, 728–32; see Wette, *Gustav Noske*, 662–63.

83. See Wette, *Gustav Noske*, 663–64; Mühlhausen, *Friedrich Ebert*, 335–36.

84. See Winkler, *Von der Revolution zur Stabilisierung*, 310–14.

85. See Winkler, *Weimar*, 128–29; Wette, *Gustav Noske*, 665–75; Miller, *Die Bürde der Macht*, 395–96, 398–99.

86. See Hagen Schulze, *Otto Braun oder Preußens demokratische Sendung* (Frankfurt, 1977), 297–303; Winkler, *Weimar*, 129–31; Miller, *Die Bürde der Macht*, 399–401.

87. Hedwig Pringsheim, *Meine Manns: Briefe an Maximilian Harden 1900–1922*, ed. Helga and Manfred Neumann (Berlin, 2006), 244 (May 2, 1920).

88. Ignaz Wrobel (Kurt Tucholsky), "Kapp-Lüttwitz," *Die Weltbühne* 16, no. 12–14, 363 (March 25, 1920).

89. See Wette, *Gustav Noske*, 685–86.

90. Carl von Ossietzky, "Die demokratische Parole," in *Sämtliche Schriften*, vol. 1, 192 (April 1, 1920). On the "Red Ruhr Army," see the seminal work by Erhard Lucas, *Märzrevolution 1920*, 3 vols. (Frankfurt am Main, 1970–1978). Summarized by Winkler, *Weimar*, 131–35.

91. See Könnemann and Schulze, *Der Kapp-Lüttwitz-Ludendorff-Putsch*, 381–82, note 2; Feldman, *Hugo Stinnes*, 606; Gietinger, *Der Konterrevolutionär*, 220–23.

92. Gietinger, *Der Konterrevolutionär*, 220.

93. See Winkler, *Weimar*, 138–39, 140; Ursula Büttner, *Weimar: Die überforderte Republik 1918–1933* (Stuttgart, 2008), 147–48.

94. Rosenberg, *Geschichte der Weimarer Republik*, 99.

Chapter 3: "The Enemy Is on the Right"

1. *Vossische Zeitung* 297 (June 25, 1922). See Martin Sabrow, *Die verdrängte Verschwörung: Der Rathenau-Mord und die deutsche Gegenrevolution* (Frankfurt am Main, 1999), 82.

2. See Martin Sabrow, *Der Rathenaumord: Rekonstruktion einer Verschwörung gegen die Republik von Weimar* (Munich, 1994), 88.

3. See Christian Schölzel, *Walther Rathenau: Eine Biographie* (Paderborn, 2006), 373.

4. See Lothar Gall, *Walther Rathenau: Portrait einer Epoche* (Munich, 2009), 243.

5. See Winkler, *Weimar*, 173.

6. See Harry Graf Kessler, *Walther Rathenau: Sein Leben und Werk* ([Wiesbaden, 1928] Berlin, n.d.), 365.

7. Kessler, *Das Tagebuch*, vol. 7, 312 (from May 25, 1920). See Hans Paasche, *"Ändert Euren Sinn!" Schriften eines Revolutionärs*, ed. Helmut Donat and Helga Paasche (Bremen, 1992).

8. Theobald Tiger (Kurt Tucholsky), "Paasche," *Die Weltbühne* 16/23 (June 3, 1920), 659.

9. See also Sabrow, *Der Rathenaumord*, 27–44 (here 34).

10. See Sabrow, *Der Rathenaumord*, 17–27, 49–56.

11. See Sabrow, *Der Rathenaumord*, 56–68.

12. Kessler, *Das Tagebuch*, vol. 7, 425 (March 20, 1922).

13. See Ernst Schulin, *Walther Rathenau: Repräsentant, Kritiker und Opfer seiner Zeit* (Göttingen, 1979), 133.

14. Walther Rathenau, *Briefe*, part 2, *1914–1922*, ed. Alexander Jaser et al. (Düsseldorf, 2006), 2602.

15. Regina Scheer, *"Wir sind die Liebermanns": Die Geschichte einer Familie* (Berlin, 2006), 391.

16. Alfred Kerr, *Walther Rathenau: Erinnerungen eines Freundes* (Amsterdam, 1935), 11. See Schölzel, *Walther Rathenau*, 370.

17. Kessler, *Das Tagebuch*, vol. 7, 524 (June 24, 1922).

18. Erich Marcks to Heinrich Wölfflin, June 30, 1922, in Jens Nordalm, *Erich Marcks (1861–1938) in der deutschen Geschichtswissenschaft* (Berlin, 2003), 344.

19. Peter-André Alt, *Franz Kafka: Der ewige Sohn; Eine Biographie* (Munich, 2005), 628.

20. Mühlhausen, *Friedrich Ebert*, 514.

21. *Berliner Tageblatt* 294 (June 24, 1922). Excerpts also in Sösemann, *Theodor Wolff*, 178–80.

22. Stefan Zweig to Romain Rolland, June 25, 1922, in Stefan Zweig, *Briefe 1920–1931*, ed. Knut Beck and Jeffrey B. Berlin (Frankfurt am Main, 2000), 68–70, 408–9 (here 70 [French version], 408 [German translation]).

23. Georg Bernhard, "Wer schützt die Republik?," *Vossische Zeitung* 296 (June 24, 1922).

24. Erich Dombrowski, "Die gestrige Reichstagssitzungen," *Vossische Zeitung* 295 (June 25, 1922).

25. Kessler, *Das Tagebuch*, vol. 7, 525 (June 24, 1922).

26. See Sabrow, *Der Rathenaumord*, 161.

27. Kessler, *Das Tagebuch*, vol. 7, 526 (June 25, 1922).

28. See Heinrich Küppers, *Joseph Wirth: Parlamentarier, Minister und Kanzler der Weimarer Republik* (Stuttgart, 1997), 189–90.

29. Georg Bernhard, "Die Verteidigung der Republik," *Vossische Zeitung* 298 (June 26, 1922).

30. Kessler, *Das Tagebuch*, vol. 7, 528 (June 27, 1922).

31. See Mühlhausen, *Friedrich Ebert*, 515.

32. Kessler, *Das Tagebuch*, vol. 7, 529 (June 27, 1922).

33. Friedrich Stampfer, *Die ersten 14 Jahre der Deutschen Republik* (Offenbach, 1947), 186–87.

34. Klemperer, *Tagebücher 1918–1924*, 598 (June 28, 1922).

35. Thomas Mann, "Von deutscher Republik," in *Essays II 1914–1926*, ed. and critically reviewed by Hermann Kurzke (Frankfurt am Main, 2002), 514–59. See also Klaus Harpprecht, *Thomas Mann: Eine Biographie* (Reinbek bei Hamburg, 1995), 503–11.

36. Pringsheim, *Tagebücher*, vol. 6, 505 (June 26, 1922).

37. See Gerhard Hecker, *Walther Rathenau und sein Verhältnis zu Militär und Krieg* (Boppard am Rhein, 1983), 499–500.

38. See Richard Albrecht, *Der militante Sozialdemokrat: Carlo Mierendorff 1897 bis 1943; Eine Biographie* (Berlin, 1987), 53ff.

39. See Dietz Bering, *Kampf um Namen: Bernhard Weiß gegen Joseph Goebbels* (Stuttgart, 1991), 43ff.

40. See Sabrow, *Der Rathenaumord*, 89–103; Wolfgang Brenner, *Walther Rathenau: Deutscher und Jude* (Munich, 2005), 478–99.

41. See Schulin, *Walther Rathenau*, 138; Ernst Schulin and Wolfgang Michalka, *Walther Rathenau im Spiegel seines Moskauer Nachlasses* (Heidelberg, 1993), 12.

42. See Wilhelm von Sternburg, *Joseph Roth: Eine Biographie* (Cologne, 2009), 261. On the trial before the State Court, see Sabrow, *Der Rathenaumord*, 103–14.

43. See Heinrich Hannover and Elisabeth Hannover-Drück, *Politische Justiz 1918–1933* (Frankfurt am Main, 1966), 123.

44. See Sabrow, *Der Rathenaumord*, 206–15 (here 213).

45. Theobald Tiger (Kurt Tucholsky), "Rathenau," *Die Weltbühne* 18/26 (June 29, 1922), 653.

46. See Sabrow, *Die verdrängte Verschwörung*, 143.

Chapter 4: Madhouse

1. "Die Besetzung Essens," *Berliner Tageblatt* 19 (January 12, 1923).

2. Klemperer, *Tagebücher 1918–1924*, 650 (January 5, 1923).

3. Ebert to Walther Reinhardt, February 8, 1921, in Mühlhausen, *Friedrich Ebert*, 442. See also Gerd Meyer, "Die Reparationspolitik: Die Reparationspolitik; Ihre außen- und innenpolitische Rückwirkungen," in *Die Weimarer Republik 1918–1933: Politik-Wirtschaft-Gesellschaft*, ed. Karl Dietrich Bracher et al. (Düsseldorf, 1987), 327–42.

4. Edgar Vincent D'Abernon, *An Ambassador of Peace*, vol. 2, *The Years of Crisis, June 1922–December 1923* (London, 1929), 159.

5. "Katastrophenstimmung im Ruhrgebiet," *Vossische Zeitung* 27 (January 17, 1923).

6. Hauptmann, *Diarium*, 83 (February 1, 1923).

7. See Volker Ullrich, *Deutschland 1923: Das Jahr am Abgrund* (Munich, 2022), 41ff.; Peter Longerich, *Außer Kontrolle: Deutschland 1923* (Vienna, 1922), 32ff.

8. Friedrich Stampfer, "Einen Monat Ruhrkrieg," *Vorwärts* 71 (February 12, 1923).

9. Klaus Wisotzky, "Der 'blutige Karsamstag' 1923 bei Krupp," in *Der Schatten des Weltkriegs: Die Ruhrbesetzung 1923*, ed. Gerd Krumeich and Joachim Schröder (Essen, 2004), 265–87 (here 277).

10. See Hans Hecker, "Karl Radeks Werben um die deutsche Rechte. Die Sowjetunion und der Ruhrkampf," in Krumeich and Schröder, *Der Schatten des Weltkriegs*, 187–205; Winkler, *Weimar*, 195–96.

11. See Gerald D. Feldman, *The Great Disorder: Politics, Economics, and Society in the German Inflation, 1914–1924* (Oxford, 1997).

12. Kessler, *Das Tagebuch*, vol. 7, 567 (November 7, 1922).

13. See the table in Feldman, *Great Disorder*, 643.

14. See Ron Chernow, *The Warburgs: The Twentieth-Century Odyssey of a Remarkable Jewish Family* (London, 1993), 231.

15. Klemperer, *Tagebücher 1918–1924*, 725 (August 2/3, 1923).

16. See Frederick Taylor, *Inflation: Der Untergang des Geldes in der Weimarer Republik und die Geburt eines deutschen Traumas* (Munich, 2013), 211ff.

17. Frank Fassland, "Wirtschaftsführer: Hugo Stinnes," *Die Weltbühne*, 18/11 (March 16, 1922). See also Feldmann, *Hugo Stinnes*, 759ff; and Ullrich, *Deutschland 1923*, 80–85.

18. See Wolfgang Martynkewicz, *1920: Am Nullpunkt des Sinns* (Berlin, 2019), 76.

19. "Die Auslandsmissionen in Berlin: Von einem Deutschen," *Die Weltbühne*, 18/48 (November 30, 1922), 566.

20. Sebastian Haffner, *Defying Hitler: A Memoir*, trans. Oliver Pretzel (New York, 2000), 53. On the social effects of hyperinflation, see Ullrich, *Deutschland 1923*, 87–104; Longerich, *Außer Kontrolle*, 122–63.

21. Klaus Mann, *Der Wendepunkt: Ein Lebensbericht* (Frankfurt am Main, 1963), 108.

22. See Ulrich Linse, *Barfüßige Propheten: Erlöser der zwanziger Jahre* (Berlin, 1983), 34.

23. Walter Benjamin, *Gesammelte Schriften*, vol. 4, part 1, ed. Tilman Rexroth (Frankfurt am Main, 1991), 98.

24. Georg Bernhard, "Der Leidensweg der Mark," *Vossische Zeitung* 348 (July 22, 1923).

25. Morus (Richard Lewinsohn), "Hochbetrieb," *Die Weltbühne* 18/44, 478 (November 2, 1922).

26. Klemperer, *Tagebücher 1918–1924*, 697 (May 27, 1923).

27. Haffner, *Defying Hitler*, 56.

28. George Grosz, *Ein kleines Ja und ein großes Nein: Sein Leben von ihm selbst erzählt* (Reinbek bei Hamburg, 1974), 120.

29. Klaus Mann, *The Turning Point* (New York, 1942), 86–87.

30. See Lothar Fischer, *Anita Berber: Ein getanztes Leben* (Berlin, 2014).

31. Carl Zuckmayer, *Als wär's ein Stück von mir: Horen der Freundschaft* (Stuttgart, 1966), 305.

32. Friedrich Kroner, "Überreizte Nerven," *Berliner Illustrierte Zeitung* 34 (August 26, 1923); also in Hans Ostwald, *Sittengeschichte der Inflation: Ein Kulturdokument aus den Jahren des Marksturzes* (Berlin, 1931), 74.

33. Jens Bisky, *Biographie einer großen Stadt* (Berlin, 2019), 467.

34. Memorandum by Hamm dated June 16, 1923, in *Akten der Reichskanzlei (AdR): Weimarer Republik—Das Kabinett Cuno; 22. November 1922 bis 12. August 1923*, ed. Karl-Heinz Harbeck (Boppard am Rhein, 1968), no. 192, 575–77 (here 575).

35. *Germania* 205 (July 27, 1923); also in *AdR: Weimarer Republik—Das Kabinett Cuno*, no. 233, 695, note 1.

36. See Eberhard Kolb, *Gustav Stresemann* (Munich, 2003), 76.

37. See Kurt Koszyk, *Gustav Stresemann: Der kaisertreue Demokrat; Eine Biographie* (Cologne, 1989), 262.

38. See Jonathan Wright, *Gustav Stresemann 1878–1929: Weimars größter Staatsmann* (Munich, 2006), 225; Ullrich, *Deutschland 1923*, 120–22.

39. See Bernhard H. Bayerlein et al., eds., *Deutscher Oktober 1923: Ein Revolutionsplan und sein Scheitern* (Berlin, 2003).

40. Larissa Reissner, *Hamburg auf den Barrikaden: Erlebes und Erhörtes aus dem Hamburger Aufstand* (Berlin, 1925), 33. See Heinz Habedank, *Zur Geschichte des Hamburger Aufstands 1923* (East Berlin, 1958).

41. Thea Sternheim, *Tagebücher 1903–1971*, vol. 1, *1903–1925*, ed. Thomas Ehrmann and Regula Wyss (Göttingen, 2002), 672 (October 23, 1923).

42. See Ullrich, *Deutschland 1923*, 157–68.

43. See Ullrich, *Deutschland 1923*, 176–80; Longerich, *Außer Kontrolle*, 177–81.

44. See Ambassador Houghton to Foreign Secretary Hughes, September 23, 1923, in George W. F. Hallgarten, *Hitler, Reichswehr und Industrie: Zur Geschichte 1918–1933* (Frankfurt am Main, 1955), 67–68.

45. See Felix Kellerhoff, *Die NSDAP: Eine Partei und ihre Mitglieder* (Stuttgart, 2017), 172.

46. Stefan Grossmann, "Die Hitlerei," *Das Tage-Buch* 16/4 (April 21, 1923), 550–54 (here 552). On Hitler's rhetoric, see Volker Ullrich, *Adolf Hitler: Biographie*, vol. 1, *Die Jahre des Aufstiegs 1889–1939* (Frankfurt am Main, 2013; trans. Jefferson Chase as *Hitler: Ascent 1889–1939*, New York, 2016), 113–22.

47. *Hitler: Sämtliche Aufzeichnungen 1905–1924*, ed. Eberhard Jäckel with Axel Kuhn (Stuttgart, 1980), no. 592, 1049–50. On the prehistory of the Hitler Putsch, see Ullrich, *Adolf Hitler*, vol. 1, 162–69; Sven Felix Kellerhoff, *Der Putsch: Hitlers erster Griff nach der Macht* (Stuttgart, 2023), 115ff.

48. Ernst Deuerlein, ed., *Der Hitler-Putsch: Bayerische Dokumente zum 8./9. November 1923* (Stuttgart, 1962), doc. 86, 310.

49. On the course of the putsch, see Ullrich, *Adolf Hitler*, vol. 1, 170–79; Kellerhoff, *Der Putsch*, 215ff.

50. See Dirk Walter, *Antisemitische Kriminalität und Gewalt: Judenfeindschaft in der Weimarer Republik* (Bonn, 1999), 119–36.

51. On the "Scheunenviertel" riots, see also Traude Maurer, *Ostjuden in Deutschland 1918–1933* (Hamburg, 1986), 329–38.

52. Ernst Feder, "Das Ende der Hanswurstiade," *Berliner Tageblatt* 529 (November 10, 1923).

53. See David Clay Large, *Hitlers München: Aufstieg und Fall der Hauptstadt der Bewegung*, trans. Karl Heinz Siber (Munich, 1998), 242.

54. On the trial and its aftermath, see Wolfgang Niess, *Der Hitlerputsch 1923: Geschichte eines Hochverrats* (Munich, 2023), 239–67.

55. See Ullrich, *Deutschland 1923*, 211–12.

56. Moltke, *Ein Leben in Deutschland*, 80 (dated November 2, 1923).

57. See the table in Feldman, *Great Disorder*, 782.

58. See Feldman, *Great Disorder*, 795.

59. Klemperer, *Tagebücher 1918–1924*, 761 (December 4, 1923).

60. Moltke, *Ein Leben in Deutschland*, 86 (December 26, 1923).

61. Kessler, *Das Tagebuch*, vol. 8, *1923–1926*, ed. Angela Reinthal et al. (Stuttgart, 2009), 167 (December 4, 1923).

62. Gustav Stresemann, *Vermächtnis: Der Nachlass in drei Bänden*, vol. 1, ed. Henry Bernhard (Berlin, 1932), 245.

63. See Ullrich, *Deutschland 1923*, 264–68.

64. D'Abernon, *Ambassador of Peace* 2, 290.

65. Stefan Zweig, *The World of Yesterday*, trans. Anthea Bell (London, 1943), 238, 240.

66. Haffner, *Defying Hitler*, 53.

67. See Hermann Kurzke, *Thomas Mann: Das Leben als Kunstwerk* (Munich, 1999), 353.

68. Rosenberg, *Geschichte der Weimarer Republik*, 129.

Chapter 5: The Turn to the Right

1. On Ebert's illness and death, see Mühlhausen, *Friedrich Ebert*, 967–74.

2. On the smear campaign against Ebert, see Mühlhausen, *Friedrich Ebert*, 911–36.

3. See Mühlhausen, *Friedrich Ebert*, 936–39 (here 939).

4. On the Magdeburg trial, see Mühlhausen, *Friedrich Ebert*, 936–53 (here 939, 952).

5. See Mühlhausen, *Friedrich Ebert*, 956–66.

6. Stresemann, *Vermächtnis*, vol. 2, 37–41 (here, 37, 39). See Richter, *Die Deutsche Volkspartei*, 370; Wright, *Gustav Stresemann*, 309.

7. Georg Bernhard, "Der Retter," *Vossische Zeitung* 102 (March 1, 1925).

8. Erich Dombrowski, "Friedrich Ebert," *Berliner Tageblatt* 101 (February 28, 1925).

9. See Heinrich August Winkler, *Der Schein der Normalität: Arbeiter und Arbeiterbewegung in der Weimarer Republik 1924 bis 1930* (Berlin, 1985), 231–32.

10. Katia Mann to Thomas Mann, March 4, 1925, in Tilman Lahme, *Die Manns: Geschichte einer Familie* (Frankfurt am Main, 2015), 30–31.

11. See Mühlhausen, *Friedrich Ebert*, 975–79. Excerpt from Luther's speech in Hans Luther, *Politiker ohne Partei: Erinnerungen* (Stuttgart, 1960), 328–29.

12. See files of the Reich Chancellery, *AdR: Die Kabinette Luther I und II*, ed. Karl-Heinz Minuth (Boppard am Rhein, 1977), no. 36, 137 (March 3, 1925).

13. See Pyta, *Hindenburg*, 462–63; Ulrich von Hehl, *Wilhelm Marx 1863–1946: Eine politische Biographie* (Mainz, 1987), 335–36; Meier-Welcker, *Seeckt*, 463–65; Richter, *Die Deutsche Volkspartei*, 368–69, 370–71. On the "Reich Citizens' Council" founded at the beginning of January 1919, see Bieber, *Bürgertum in der Revolution*, 78–81.

14. See Schulze, *Otto Braun*, 471; on the Prussian government crisis, Schulze, 467–70; Richter, *Die Deutsche Volkspartei*, 363–64; Stampfer, *Die ersten 14 Jahre*, 442–43.

15. *Vossische Zeitung* 114 (March 8, 1925).

16. See Hehl, *Wilhelm Marx*, 336–37.

17. See Hehl, *Wilhelm Marx*, 337; Pyta, *Hindenburg*, 463–64; Richter, *Die Deutsche Volkspartei*, 371–72.

18. Stresemann to Gessler, March 11, 1925, in Stresemann, *Vermächtnis*, vol. 2, 44–45. On Stresemann's rejection of Gessler's candidacy, see Richter, *Die Deutsche Volkspartei*, 372–74; Pyta, *Hindenburg*, 464; Wright, *Gustav Stresemann*, 309–10.

19. Theodor Wolff, "Hellpach," in Sösemann, *Theodor Wolff*, 202–4 (here 202).

20. See Ullrich, *Adolf Hitler*, vol. 1, 213–14, 216.

21. See Authors' Collective, *Ernst Thälmann: Eine Biographie*, 3rd ed. (East Berlin, 1980), 222.

22. See the election analysis in Winkler, *Der Schein der Normalität*, 235–36.

23. See Ullrich, *Adolf Hitler*, vol. 1, 217.

24. See Hehl, *Wilhelm Marx*, 339–40; Schulze, *Otto Braun*, 473–74; Winkler, *Weimar*, 279–80.

25. Hehl, *Wilhelm Marx*, 340–41. See also "Der Volksblock," *Vossische Zeitung* 160 (April 4, 1925). Chancellor Luther's attempt to put forward the president of the Reich Court and deputy Reich president, Walter Simon, as the candidate of all parliamentary groups failed due to the objections of the SPD and the Center

Party, who declared that they had already decided on Marx's candidacy. See *AdR: Die Kabinette Luther I und II*, vol. 1, no. 64/65, 231–36 (April 3, 1925).

26. See Pyta, *Hindenburg*, 465–66; Winkler, *Weimar*, 280.

27. See Pyta, *Hindenburg*, 443–51.

28. Hindenburg to Ludendorff, March 21, 1925, in Walther Hubatsch, *Hindenburg und der Staat: Aus den Papieren des Generalfeldmarschalls und Reichspräsidenten von 1878 bis 1934* (Göttingen, 1966), 69.

29. See Richter, *Die Deutsche Volkspartei*, 379–80.

30. Richter, *Die Deutsche Volkspartei*, 380 and note 68 for the wording of the Hindenburg telegram. See also Pyta, *Hindenburg*, 467–68.

31. See Richter, *Die Deutsche Volkspartei*, 381–83; Pyta, *Hindenburg*, 486–87.

32. See Hehl, *Wilhelm Marx*, 342.

33. See Winkler, *Der Schein der Normalität*, 239. See Authors' Collective, *Ernst Thälmann*, 227.

34. See "Warnende Stimmen," *Vossische Zeitung* 164 (April 9, 1925); and "Ruinöse Wirkung," *Vossische Zeitung* 179 (April 16, 1925).

35. Winkler, *Der Schein der Normalität*, 239.

36. Mann, *Essays II*, 978.

37. "Das Opfer," *Vossische Zeitung* 167 (April 8, 1925).

38. Kessler, *Das Tagebuch*, vol. 8, 670–71 (April 19, 1925).

39. Stresemann, *Vermächtnis*, vol. 2, 50 (April 19, 1925).

40. Stresemann, *Vermächtnis*, vol. 2, 50–52 (here 52).

41. Max von Stockhausen, *Sechs Jahre Reichskanzlei: Von Rapallo bis Locarno; Erinnerungen und Tagebuchnotizen 1922–1927*, ed. Walter Görlitz (Bonn, 1954), 155 (April 15, 1925).

42. See Hehl, *Wilhelm Marx*, 344–45.

43. "Der Retter," *Vossische Zeitung* 187 (April 21, 1925).

44. Pyta, *Hindenburg*, 474–75.

45. See Hehl, *Wilhelm Marx*, 346–47; Pyta, *Hindenburg*, 475; "Wilhelm Marx in Ostpreussen," *Vossische Zeitung* 176 (April 15, 1925); "Marx vor den Republikanern Berlins," *Vossische Zeitung* 182 (April 18, 1925); "Wilhelm Marx in Stuttgart," *Berliner Tageblatt* 192 (April 24, 1925).

46. Itta Shedletzky, ed., *Betty Scholem–Gershom Scholem: Mutter und Sohn im Briefwechsel 1917–1946* (Munich, 1989), 129 (April 26, 1925). See "An Alle!! Die Rundfunk-Ansprachen," *Vossische Zeitung* 194 (April 25, 1925).

47. Theodor Lessing, *"Wir machen nicht mit!" Schriften gegen den Nationalismus und zur Judenfrage*, ed. Jörg Wollenberg with Helmut Donat (Bremen, 1997), 87–91 (here 91). On the "Lessing case," see also Jörg Wollenberg, afterword to Lessing, 252ff.; Rainer Marwedel, *Theodor Lessing: Eine Biographie* (Darmstadt, 1987), 258ff.

48. Kessler, *Das Tagebuch*, vol. 8, 680 (April 26, 1925).

49. See Winkler, *Der Schein der Normalität*, 240.

50. Winkler, *Weimar*, 281; Hehl, *Wilhelm Marx*, 348.

51. See the election analysis in Winkler, *Der Schein der Normalität*, 240–43; Hehl, *Wilhelm Marx*, 348–49; Pyta, *Hindenburg*, 475–76.

52. See Ullrich, *Adolf Hitler*, vol. 1, 217.

53. *Berliner Börsen-Zeitung* 194 (April 27, 1925).

54. Stresemann, *Vermächnis*, vol. 2, 56 (April 27, 1925).

55. *Berliner Tageblatt* 197 (April 27, 1925); Winkler, *Weimar*, 282.

56. Kessler, *Das Tagebuch*, vol. 8, 681 (April 26, 1925).

57. Sternheim, *Tagebücher*, vol. 1, 722 (April 28, 1923).

58. Klemperer, *Tagebücher 1925–1932*, 49 (April 27, 1925).

59. Ignaz Wrobel (Kurt Tucholsky), "Was nun . . . ?," *Die Weltbühne*, 21/18 (May 5, 1925), 645–48 (here 648, 646).

60. See Hagen Schulze, *Weimar: Deutschland 1917–1933* (Berlin, 1982), 296–97.

61. Stockhausen, *Sechs Jahre Reichskanzlei*, 158 (April 28, 1925).

62. Stresemann, *Vermächnis*, vol. 2, 56 (April 28, 1925). See also ministerial meeting of April 28, 1925, in *AdR: Die Kabinette Luther I und II*, vol. 1, no. 77, 260–61.

63. See Pyta, *Hindenburg*, 484–85; Stockhausen, *Sechs Jahre Reichskanzlei*, 161; Hubatsch, *Hindenburg und der Staat*, 76.

64. Kessler, *Das Tagebuch*, vol. 8, 685 (May 12, 1925).

65. Hubatsch, *Hindenburg und der Staat*, 77.

66. Kessler, *Das Tagebuch*, vol. 8, 685–86 (May 12, 1925).

67. Stresemann, *Vermächtnis*, vol. 2, 59 (dated May 12, 1925).

68. Luther, *Politiker ohne Partei*, 337. See Meissner, *Staatssekretär unter Ebert-Hindenburg-Hitler*, 148.

69. Stresemann, *Vermächtnis*, vol. 2, 60–61 (May 19 and June 9, 1925). See Wright, *Gustav Stresemann*, 311.

70. See Ulrich Herbert, *Geschichte Deutschlands im 20. Jahrhundert* (Munich, 2014), 221–22.

71. See Pyta, *Hindenburg*, 486.

72. Winkler, *Weimar*, 284; see also Pyta, *Hindenburg*, 461, 486; Kolb, *Die Weimarer Republik*, 81–82.

Chapter 6: A Dark Day

1. See Heinrich Brüning, *Memoiren 1918–1934* (Stuttgart, 1970), 150–52; Johannes Hürter, *Wilhelm Groener: Reichswehrminister am Ende der Weimarer Republik (1928–1932)* (Munich, 1993), 242–43; Herbert Hömig, *Brüning: Kanzler in der Krise; Eine Weimarer Biographie* (Paderborn, 2000), 134–35.

2. See Brüning, *Memoiren*, 158–61 (here 160); Hürter, *Wilhelm Groener*, 243–44; Hömig, *Brüning*, 135.

3. Brüning's transcript of a conversation with Hindenburg, March 1, 1930, *Politik und Wirtschaft in der Krise 1930–1932: Quellen zur Ära Brüning*, part 1, ed. Ilse Maurer et al., introduced by Gerhard Schulz (Düsseldorf, 1980), no. 24, 61–62.

4. See the election analysis in Winkler, *Der Schein der Normalität*, 521–27.

5. Ernst Feder, "Der Zusammenbruch der Rechtskoalition," *Berliner Tageblatt* 237 (May 21, 1928).

6. Victor Klemperer, *Tagebücher 1925–1932* (Berlin, 1996), 434 (May 25, 1928).

7. See Schulze, *Otto Braun*, 539–41; Winkler, *Weimar*, 335.

8. *AdR: Weimarer Republik; Das Kabinett Müller II; 28. Juni 1928 bis 27. März 1930*, vol. I, *Juni 1928 bis Juli 1929*, ed. Martin Vogt (Boppard am Rhein, 1970), no. 1, 1, note 2. See also Peter Reichel, *Der tragische Kanzler: Hermann Müller und die SPD in der Weimarer Republik* (Munich, 2018), 256–57; Winkler, *Weimar*, 335.

9. See Schulze, *Otto Braun*, 542–44; Richter, *Die Deutsche Volkspartei*, 486–88.

10. See Winkler, *Weimar*, 336; Richter, *Die Deutsche Volkspartei*, 491.

11. Stresemann, *Vermächtnis*, vol. 2, 298–99.

12. See Richter, *Die Deutsche Volkspartei*, 494–97; Winkler, *Der Schein der Normalität*, 536.

13. See Winkler, *Weimar*, 337.

14. On the appointment of the cabinet, see *AdR: Das Kabinett Müller II*, vol. I, ix–xv.

15. See Winkler, *Weimar*, 338. The *Berliner Tageblatt* (no. 294, June 26, 1928) spoke of a "cabinet with a built-in permanent crisis."

16. See ministerial meeting of July 3, 1928, in *AdR: Das Kabinett Müller II*, vol. I, no. 5, 13; Winkler, *Weimar*, 338–39.

17. See Wolfgang Wacker, *Der Bau des Panzerschiffs "A" und der Reichstag* (Tübingen, 1959), 90ff; Winkler, *Der Schein der Normalität*, 533–34, 541–55; Reichel, *Der tragische Kanzler*, 264–75.

18. *AdR: Das Kabinett Müller II*, vol. I, no. 15, 61–64.

19. Ministerial meeting, November 14, 1928, in *AdR: Das Kabinett Müller II*, vol. I, no. 64, 225.

20. Ministerial meeting, January 15, 1928, in *AdR: Das Kabinett Müller II*, vol. I, no. 65, 227.

21. Winkler, *Weimar*, 340.

22. Stresemann, *Vermächtnis*, vol. 2, 428–33 (here 432).

23. See Heinrich August Winkler, *Musste Weimar scheitern? Das Ende der ersten: Deutschen Republik und die Kontinuität der deutschen Geschichte* (Munich, 1991), 15; Büttner, *Weimar*, 499–500.

24. See also Bernd Weisbrod, *Schwerindustrie in der Weimarer Republik: Interessenpolitik zwischen Stabilisierung und Krise* (Wuppertal, 1978), 415–56; Winkler, *Der Schein der Normalität*, 557–72.

25. See Weisbrod, *Schwerindustrie in der Weimarer Republik*, 420–21.

26. Cabinet meeting with subsequent ministerial meeting, November 28, 1928, in *AdR: Das Kabinett Müller II*, vol. I, no. 73, 250–57 (here 254).

27. See Herbert, *Geschichte Deutschlands im 20. Jahrhundert*, 260.

28. See Klaus Wernecke, *Der vergessene Führer: Alfred Hugenberg; Pressemacht und Nationalsozialismus* (Hamburg, 1982), 146. On the Hugenberg group, see Wernecke, 67ff; Heidrun Holzbach, *Das "System" Hugenberg: Die Organisation bürgerlicher Sammlungspolitik vor dem Aufstieg der NSDAP* (Stuttgart, 1981), 259ff.; Hans Mommsen, *Die verspielte Freiheit: Der Weg der Republik von Weimar in den Untergang 1918 bis 1933* (Berlin, 1989), 261–64.

29. See Rudolf Morsey, "Die Deutsche Zentrumspartei," in *Das Ende der Parteien 1933*, ed. Erich Matthias and Rudolf Morsey (Düsseldorf, 1960), 283ff. (here 291).

See Winkler, *Weimar*, 343–44; Mommsen, *Die verspielte Freiheit*, 268–69; Büttner, *Weimar*, 387.

30. See Winkler, *Der Schein der Normalität*, 662; see also Winkler, 661–97; Winkler, *Weimar*, 349–52; Büttner, *Weimar*, 385–86.

31. See Hermann Weber and Bernhard H. Bayerlein, eds., *Der Thälmann-Skandal: Geheime Korrespondenzen mit Stalin* (Berlin, 2003).

32. See Thomas Kurz, *Blutmai: Sozialdemokraten und Kommunisten im Brennpunkt der Berliner Ereignisse von 1929* (Berlin, 1986).

33. Hermann Müller to Otto Wels, February 12, 1929, in Winkler, *Der Schein der Normalität*, 576.

34. Cabinet meeting, April 10, 1929, in *AdR: Das Kabinett Müller II*, vol. 1, no. 168, 542–43. On the reconstitution of the government, see *Das Kabinett Müller II*, vol. 1, no. 168, xv–xvii; Winkler, *Weimar*, 344–46; Reichel, *Der tragische Kanzler*, 282–87.

35. Julius Curtius, *Der Young-Plan: Entstehung und Wahrheit* (Stuttgart, 1970), 17. On the prehistory of the Young Plan, see Peter Krüger, *Die Außenpolitik der Republik von Weimar*, 2nd ed. (Darmstadt, 1993), 428ff.; Winkler, *Weimar*, 342–43; Büttner, *Weimar*, 353–54; Longerich, *Deutschland 1918–1933*, 251–52.

36. See Christopher Kopper, *Hjalmar Schacht: Aufstieg und Fall von Hitlers mächtigstem Bankier* (Munich, 2006), 133–34, 137–38, 141–42.

37. On the Paris negotiations and Schacht's role in them, see Kopper, *Hjalmar Schacht*, 144–55; Winkler, *Weimar*, 346–47. On the Müller cabinet's reaction to Schacht's behavior, see Reichel, *Der tragische Kanzler*, 304–9.

38. See Winkler, *Weimar*, 347–48; Büttner, *Weimar*, 355–56; Longerich, *Deutschland 1918–1933*, 252.

39. *AdR: Das Kabinett Müller II*, vol. 1, no. 226, 738.

40. Stresemann to Löbe, September 19, 1929, in Stresemann, *Vermächtnis*, vol. 3, 568. See also Wright, *Gustav Stresemann*, 480.

41. See Volker R. Berghahn, *Der Stahlhelm: Bund der Frontsoldaten 1918–1935* (Düsseldorf, 1966), 115ff.; Wernecke, *Der vergessene Führer*, 148–49; Ullrich, *Adolf Hitler*, vol. 1, 247–48.

42. For the wording of the draft law, see Stampfer, *Die ersten 14 Jahre*, 547; see also Berghahn, *Der Stahlhelm*, 124–25; Winkler, *Weimar*, 354–55; Kolb, *Die Weimarer Republik*, 116.

43. Ministerial meeting, October 18, 1929, in *AdR: Die Regierung Müller II*, vol. 2, no. 323, 1046.

44. See Karl Dietrich Bracher, *Die Auflösung der Weimarer Republik: Eine Studie zum Problem des Machtverfalls in der Demokratie*, 3rd ed. (Villingen, 1960), 318–22; Friedrich Freiherr Hiller von Gaertringen, "Die Deutschnationale Volkspartei," in Matthias and Morsey, *Das Ende der Parteien*, 544ff.

45. Hermann Pünder, *Politik in der Reichskanzlei: Aufzeichnungen aus den Jahren 1929–1932*, ed. Thilo Vogelsang (Stuttgart, 1961), 25 (December 2, 1929). See Winkler, *Weimar*, 356; Kolb, *Die Weimarer Republik*, 136.

46. See Wernecke, *Der vergessene Führer*, 153; Ullrich, *Adolf Hitler*, vol. 1, 248.

47. See Ullrich, *Adolf Hitler*, vol. 1, 248, 253.

48. Kessler, *Das Tagebuch*, vol. 9, *1926–1932*, ed. Sabine Gruber et al. (Stuttgart, 2010), 264–65 (October 3 and 4, 1929).

49. Sösemann, *Theodor Wolff*, 262–66 (here 264).

50. Carl von Ossietzky, "Abschied on Stresemann," in *Sämtliche Schriften*, vol. 5, *1929–1930*, ed. Bärbel Boldt et al. (Reinbek bei Hamburg, 1994), 208–12 (here 209).

51. Shedletzky, *Betty Scholem–Gershom Scholem*, 207 (October 9, 1929).

52. See Richter, *Die Deutsche Volkspartei*, 585–94; AdR: *Das Kabinett Müller II*, vol. 1, xvii.

53. See Büttner, *Weimar*, 388; Longerich, *Deutschland 1918–1933*, 254.

54. See Helga Timm, *Die deutsche Sozialpolitik und der Bruch der Großen Koalition im März 1930* (Düsseldorf, 1952), 23–25; Kolb, *Die Weimarer Republik*, 89; Büttner, *Weimar*, 373–74; Karl Christian Führer, "Die Sozialpolitik der Weimarer Republik," in Rossol and Ziemann, *Aufbruch und Abgründe*, 338–63 (here 364).

55. See Timm, *Die deutsche Sozialpolitik*, 124–26; Winkler, *Weimar*, 352–53.

56. Cabinet meeting, May 6, 1929, in *AdR: Das Kabinett Müller II*, vol. 1, no. 196, 638–42 (here 639, 641).

57. *AdR: Das Kabinett Müller II*, vol. 2, no. 278, 895; no. 302, 963.

58. See Timm, *Die deutsche Sozialpolitik*, 132–39; Richter, *Die Deutsche Volkspartei*, 578–82.

59. See Winkler, *Der Schein der Normalität*, 738–39.

60. Pünder, *Politik in der Reichskanzlei*, 26 (November 29, 1929). See also Kopper, *Hjalmar Schacht*, 159–61.

61. *AdR: Das Kabinett Müller II*, vol. 2, 1210–15 (here 1212–13).

62. Schacht to Reich Chancellor Müller, December 5, 1929, with attached memorandum, in *AdR: Das Kabinett Müller II*, no. 369, 1219–29. See also Kopper, *Hjalmar Schacht*, 162–63.

63. Carl von Ossietzky, "Der Schacht-Putsch," in *Sämtliche Schriften*, vol. 5, 252–54 (here 252).

64. Pünder, *Politik in der Reichskanzlei*, 28 (December 6, 1929).

65. See ministerial discussions, December 6, 1929, in *AdR: Das Kabinett Müller II*, vol. 2, no. 371/372, 1231–35. Text of the declaration in *Das Kabinett Müller II*, vol. 2, no. 371/372, 1235, note 2.

66. Meeting of parliamentary party leaders, December 11, 1929; *Das Kabinett Müller II*, vol. 2, no. 376, 1246–47; see also Richter, *Die Deutsche Volkspartei*, 596; Winkler, *Der Schein der Normalität*, 741–45.

67. Meeting of parliamentary party leaders, December 14, 1929, in *AdR: Das Kabinett Müller II*, vol. 2, no. 383, 1260–62 (for the exact wording see 1262, note 6). See also Pünder, *Politik in der Reichskanzlei*, 29–32 (December 15, 1929); Winkler, *Der Schein der Normalität*, 745–46; Richter, *Die Deutsche Volkspartei*, 597–99.

68. See Meissner on the conversation between Schacht and Hindenburg and the ministerial meeting on December 16, 1929, in *AdR: Das Kabinett Müller II*, vol. 2, nos. 387 and 389, 1266–67, 1270–72.

69. See Winkler, *Der Schein der Normalität*, 747–50.

70. Pünder, *Politik in der Reichskanzlei*, 32 (December 20, 1929).

71. Hilferding to Müller, December 20, 1929, in *AdR: Das Kabinett Müller II*, vol. 2, no. 397, 1297.

72. See *Das Kabinett Müller II*, vol. 1, xviii.

73. See Werner Plumpe, *Carl Duisberg 1861–1935: Anatomie eines Industriellen* (Munich, 2016), 750–53; Winkler, *Der Schein der Normalität*, 759–60; Richter, *Die Deutsche Volkspartei*, 603.

74. See Plumpe, *Carl Duisberg*, 755.

75. Gilsa to Reusch, January 25 and 29, 1930, in *Politik und Wirtschaft*, part 1, no. 9, 23–24, no. 11a/b, 32, 34 (here 23, 34). See Winkler, *Der Schein der Normalität*, 783; Richter, *Die Deutsche Volkspartei*, 605–6; Weisbrod, *Schwerindustrie in der Weimarer Republik*, 471.

76. Gilsa to Reusch, February 5, 1930, in *Politik und Wirtschaft*, part 1, no. 14, 41–43 (here 41–42).

77. See Kolb, *Die Weimarer Republik*, 83.

78. On the plans of the Reichswehr and Hindenburg's entourage for a presidential cabinet, see Winkler, *Der Schein der Normalität*, 761–62; Hürter, *Wilhelm Groener*, 241–43; Pyta, *Hindenburg*, 558–67; Hömig, *Brüning*, 132–33.

79. Meissner, *Staatssekretär unter Ebert-Hindenburg-Hitler*, 188.

80. See Hürter, *Wilhelm Groener*, 243.

81. Westarp's notes on his conversation with Hindenburg, January 15, 1930, in *Politik und Wirtschaft*, part 1, no. 7, 15–18.

82. On the Hague Conference, see Curtius, *Der Young-Plan*, 94–95; Timm, *Die deutsche Sozialpolitik*, 163–66; Winkler, *Der Schein der Normalität*, 767–68.

83. *Die Protokolle der Reichstagsfraktion und des Fraktionsvorstands der Deutschen Zentrumspartei 1926–1933*, ed. Rudolf Morsey (Mainz, 1969), no. 503, 376–78 (for the exact wording, see 377).

84. Winkler, *Der Schein der Normalität*, 776.

85. Ministerial meeting, January 30, 1930, in *AdR: Das Kabinett Müller II*, vol. 2, no. 426, 1402–6 (here 1403).

86. Party leaders' meeting, Feburary 7, 1930, in *Das Kabinett Müller II*, vol. 2, no. 437, 1438.

87. See Timm, *Die deutsche Sozialpolitik*, 168–71; Richter, *Die Deutsche Volkspartei*, 609–15.

88. Pünder, *Politik in der Reichskanzlei*, 41 (March 3, 1930).

89. *AdR: Das Kabinett Müller II*, vol. 2, no. 462, 1535–39 (here 1538). See Winkler, *Der Schein der Normalität*, 787–88.

90. See Timm, *Die deutsche Sozialpolitik*, 172, notes 315, 316.

91. *Politik und Wirtschaft*, part 1, no. 30, 76, note 1. See Winkler, *Der Schein der Normalität*, 788–89; Richter, *Die Deutsche Volkspartei*, 616–17.

92. Duisberg to Moldenhauer, March 14, 1930, *Politik und Wirtschaft*, part 1, no. 34, 86.

93. Pünder, *Politik in der Reichskanzlei*, 42 (March 9, 1930); ministerial conference, March 7, 1930, in *AdR: Das Kabinett Müller II*, vol. 2, no. 468, 1550–54. See also Kopper, *Hjalmar Schacht*, 173–75.

94. *Die Protokolle der Reichstagsfraktion*, no. 542, 413. On the morning of March 11,

Hindenburg also gave Hermann Müller the same assurance he gave the chancellor in the party leaders' meeting on March 11, 1930. *AdR: Das Kabinett Müller II*, vol. 2, no. 471, 1565.

95. Astrid von Pufendorf, *Die Plancks: Eine Familie zwischen Patriotismus und Widerstand* (Berlin, 2006), 232.

96. Gilsa to Reusch, March 18, 1930, in *Politik und Wirtschaft*, part 1, no. 36, 87–88. See also Winkler, *Weimar*, 368.

97. Hindenburg to Müller, March 18, 1930, in *Das Kabinett Müller II*, vol. 2, no. 480, 1580–82.

98. Meissner to Schleicher, March 19, 1930, in *Politik und Wirtschaft*, part 1, no. 38c, 94.

99. Redlhammer to Curtius, March 20, 1930, in *Politik und Wirtschaft*, no. 39, 95.

100. Pufendorf, *Die Plancks*, 233.

101. See Richter, *Die Deutsche Volkspartei*, 622, 620–21; Winkler, *Weimar*, 369.

102. Party leaders' meeting, March 25, 1930, in *AdR: Das Kabinett Müller II*, no. 484, 1594–98 (here 1597).

103. *Die Protokolle der Reichstagsfraktion*, no. 552, 423.

104. Party leaders' meeting, March 26, 1930, in *AdR: Das Kabinett Müller II*, vol. 2, no. 486, 1600–2 (here 1601).

105. See *AdR: Das Kabinett Müller II*, vol. 2, no. 487, 1602–5; no. 488, 1605–7.

106. See Richter, *Die Deutsche Volkspartei*, 624; Winkler, *Der Schein der Normalität*, 805–7.

107. Ministerial meeting, March 27, 1930, 5 and 7 p.m., in *AdR: Das Kabinett Müller II*, vol. 2, no. 489, 1608–10.

108. F[ritz] K[lein], "Wendepunkt," *Deutsche Allgemeine Zeitung* 147 (March 28, 1930).

109. "Eine unheilvolle Entscheidung," *Frankfurter Zeitung* 234 (March 28, 1930).

110. *Berliner Tageblatt* (March 28, 1930), cited in Reichel, *Der tragische Kanzler*, 340.

111. "Wissell besiegt Müller," *Vossische Zeitung* 148 (March 28, 1930).

112. See Schulze, *Otto Braun*, 625.

113. Rudolf Hilferding, "Der Austritt aus der Regierung," *Die Gesellschaft* 7 (1930/31): 385–92; See also Winkler, *Der Schein der Normalität*, 812–13.

114. Bracher, *Die Auflösung der Weimarer Republik*, 331ff.

115. See Richter, *Die Deutsche Volkspartei*, 627–28; Winkler, *Weimar*, 373–74.

116. See Hürter, *Wilhelm Groener*, 248–49.

117. See Winkler, *Weimar*, 376–77.

118. Pünder, *Politik in der Reichskanzlei* 46 (March 30, 1930).

119. See Winkler, *Weimar*, 377.

120. See Heinrich August Winkler, *Der Weg in die Katastrophe: Arbeiter und Arbeiterbewegung in der Weimarer Republik 1930 bis 1933* (Berlin, 1987), 189–94.

121. *Vossische Zeitung* 435 (September 15, 1930). See also J[ulius] E[lbau], "Zeit der Gärung," *Vossische Zeitung* 436 (September 16, 1930): "The center, fractured and worn down, faces the question of what it can do to alleviate the dramatic consequences of this grave day, to counter further radicalization and to get the state through the serious crisis of the winter."

122. Klemperer, *Tagebücher 1925–1932*, 659 (September 15, 1930).

123. Kessler, *Das Tagebuch*, vol. 9, 375, 377 (September 15, 1930).

124. Rosenberg, *Geschichte der Weimarer Republik*, 211.
125. See Larry Eugene Jones, "Von der Demokratie zur Diktatur: Das Ende der Weimarer Republik und der Aufstieg des Nationalsozialismus," in Rossol and Ziemann, *Aufbruch und Abgründe*, 120–41 (here 120–21).

Chapter 7: The Thuringia Model

1. Klaus Schönhoven and Hans Jochen Vogel, eds., *Frühe Warnungen vor dem Nationalsozialismus: Ein historisches Lesebuch* (Bonn, 1998), 81–92.
2. Georg Witzmann, *Thüringen von 1918–1933: Erinnerungen eines Politikers* (Meisenheim am Glan, 1958), 157; "Frick tritt sein Amt an," *Vossische Zeitung* 40 (January 24, 1930).
3. See Donald R. Tracey, "Der Aufstieg der NSDAP bis 1930," in *Nationalsozialismus in Thüringen*, ed. Detlev Heiden and Gunther Mai (Weimar, 1995), 49–72 (here 52–53); Peter Merseburger, *Mythos Weimar: Zwischen Geist und Macht* (Stuttgart, 1998), 312.
4. See Merseburger, *Mythos Weimar*, 308; Volker Mauersberger, *Hitler in Weimar: Der Fall einer deutschen Kulturstadt* (Berlin, 1999), 154.
5. Karsten Rudolph, "Untergang auf Raten: Die Auflösung und Zerstörung der demokratischen Kultur in Thüringen 1930 im regionalen Vergleich," in *Weimar 1930: Politik und Kultur im Vorfeld der NS-Diktatur*, ed. Lothar Ehrlich and Jürgen John (Cologne, 1998), 15–29 (here 16).
6. See *Hitler: Reden Schriften Anordnungen; Februar 1925 bis Januar 1933*, vol. 1, *Die Wiederbegründung der NSDAP: Februar 1925–Juni 1926*, ed. and annotated by Clemens Vollnhals (Munich, 1992), doc. 17/18, 48–51; doc. 78, 184–205.
7. See Mauersberger, *Hitler in Weimar*, 224. Cf. *Hitler: Reden Schriften Anordnungen*, vol. 2, part 1, *Juli 1926–Juli 1927*, ed. and annotated by Bärbel Dusik (Munich, 1992), doc. 6/7, 15–25.
8. See Tracey, *Der Aufstieg der NSDAP bis 1930*, 67–68; Merseburger: *Mythos Weimar*, 337–38.
9. See Jochen Lang, "Martin Bormann—Hitlers Sekretär," in *Die braune Elite: 22 biographische Skizzen*, ed. Ronald Smelser and Rainer Zitelmann (Darmstadt, 1989), 1–14 (here 3–4).
10. Mauersberger, *Hitler in Weimar*, 211–12.
11. Cf. Tracey, "Der Aufstieg der NSDAP bis 1930," 69–70.
12. *Berliner Tageblatt* 580 (December 9, 1929).
13. Fritz Dickmann, "Die Regierungsbildung in Thüringen als Modell der Machtergreifung: Ein Brief Hitlers aus dem Jahre 1930," *Vierteljahrshefte für Zeitgeschichte* 14 (1966): 454–64 (here 461).
14. *Die Tagebücher von Joseph Goebbels* (hereafter Goebbels, *Die Tagebücher*), vol. 1, part 2/1, *Dezember 1929–Mai 1931*, ed. Elke Fröhlich (Munich, 2005), 58 (January 8, 1930).
15. Dickmann, *Die Regierungsbildung in Thüringen*, 461.
16. Dickmann, *Die Regierungsbildung in Thüringen*, 462.
17. Goebbels, *Die Tagebücher*, vol. 1, part 2/1, 60 (from January 11, 1930).

18. Goebbels, *Die Tagebücher*, vol. 1, part 2/1, 71 (January 24, 1930).

19. See Witzmann, *Thüringen von 1918–1933*, 154.

20. See Richter, *Die Deutsche Volkspartei*, 607; Winkler, *Der Schein der Normalität*, 767.

21. See Günter Neliba, "Wilhelm Frick und Thüringen als Experimentierfeld für die nationalsozialistische Machtergreifung," in Heiden and Mai, *Nationalsozialismus in Thüringen*, 75–94 (here 78–79); Witzmann, *Thüringen von 1918–1933*, 159.

22. Dickmann, *Die Regierungsbildung in Thüringen*, 462–63.

23. Mauersberger, *Hitler in Weimar*, 264. See Goebbels, *Tagebücher*, vol. 1, part 2/1, 73 (January 28, 1930): "Frick . . . held a first speech to the civil servants in his ministry that was truly barnstorming. The Jews are crying bloody murder in the papers."

24. See Neliba, "Wilhelm Frick und Thüringen als Experimentierfeld," 79–80.

25. Neliba, "Wilhelm Frick und Thüringen als Experimentierfeld," 87; cf. Winkler, *Der Schein der Normalität*, 797.

26. Note by Pünder on December 18, 1930, and draft of suggested agreement between the Reich and Thuringia, in *Staat und NSDAP 1930–1932: Quellen zur Ära Brüning*, introduced by Gerhard Schulz, ed. Ilse Maurer and Udo Wengst (Düsseldorf, 1977), nos. 21a, 21b, 172–74. See also Neliba, "Wilhelm Frick und Thüringen als Experimentierfeld," 81–83; Witzmann, *Thüringen 1918–1933*, 167–68; Gerhard Schulz, *Von Brüning zu Hitler: Der Wandel des politischen Systems in Deutschland 1930–1933* (Berlin, 1992), 143–45.

27. Goebbels, *Die Tagebücher*, vol. 1, part 2/1, 172 (June 7, 1930).

28. See Neliba, "Wilhelm Frick und Thüringen als Experimentierfeld," 84–85; Mauersberger, *Hitler in Weimar*, 264–65.

29. Decree by Frick April 16, 1930, in Detlev Heiden and Gunther Mai, eds., *Thüringen auf dem Weg ins "Dritte Reich"* (Erfurt, 1996), no. 19a, 225–27; see also Witzmann, *Thüringen 1918–1933*, 168–72.

30. See Merseburger, *Mythos Weimar*, 330.

31. Heiden and Mai, *Thüringen auf dem Weg*, no. 19b, 227. See also Mauersberger, *Hitler in Weimar*, 271–72; Witzmann, *Thüringen 1918–1933*, 172.

32. See Neliba, "Wilhelm Frick und Thüringen als Experimentierfeld," 87; Mauersberger, *Hitler in Weimar*, 266–67.

33. Goebbels, *Die Tagebücher*, vol. 1, part 2/1, 301 (December 10, 1930).

34. Decree by Frick April 5, 1930, in Heiden and Mai, *Thüringen auf dem Weg*, no. 18, 223–24; see also Neliba, "Wilhelm Frick und Thüringen als Experimentierfeld," 87–88.

35. See Merseburger, *Mythos Weimar*, 326.

36. Schönhoven and Vogel, *Frühe Warnungen vor dem Nationalsozialismus*, 93–107 (here 94, 97, 107).

37. Goebbels, *Die Tagebücher*, vol. 1, part 2/1, 175 (June 11, 1930). See also Merseburger, *Mythos Weimar*, 326–27; Neliba, "Wilhelm Frick und Thüringen als Experimentierfeld," 89–90.

38. Heiden and Mai, *Thüringen auf dem Weg*, no. 21, 228–30 (here 229, 230).

39. Neliba, "Wilhelm Frick und Thüringen als Experimentierfeld," 88–89; see also Mauersberger, *Hitler in Weimar*, 274–76.

40. See Merseburger, *Mythos Weimar*, 329.

41. Dickmann, *Die Regierungsbildung in Thüringen*, 465.

42. See Neliba, "Wilhelm Frick und Thüringen als Experimentierfeld," 90; Merseburger, *Mythos Weimar*, 327–28.

43. Witzmann, *Thüringen 1918–1933*, 175–76. See also Bernhard Post, "Vorgezogene Machtübernahme 1932: Die Regierung Sauckel," in Heiden and Mai, *Thüringen auf dem Weg*, 147–81 (here 150–51).

44. "Fricks letzte Versuche gescheitert: Volkspartei bleibt fest," *Vossische Zeitung* 154 (April 1, 1931).

45. Schönhoven and Vogel, *Frühe Warnungen vor dem Nationalsozialismus*, 107–12 (here 111, 112).

46. See Hermann Brill, *Gegen den Strom* (Offenbach, 1946), 8–14; Rudolf Morsey, "Hitler als Braunschweigischer Regierungsrat," *Vierteljahrshefte für Zeitgeschichte* 8 (1960): 419–48 (here 420, 422–28); Neliba, "Wilhelm Frick und Thüringen als Experimentierfeld," 91–92; Merseburger, *Mythos Weimar*, 330–31.

47. Goebbels, *Die Tagebücher*, vol. 1, *Aufzeichnungen 1923–1941*, part 2/2, *Juni 1931–September 1932*, ed. Elke Fröhlich (Munich, 2004), 212 (February 5, 1932).

48. "Fricks missglückte Schiebung," *Vossische Zeitung* 58 (February 4, 1932).

49. See Post, *Vorgezogene Machtübernahme 1932*, 156.

50. Brill, *Gegen den Strom*, 8.

51. *Hitler: Reden Schriften Anordnungen*, vol. 4, *Von der Reichstagswahl bis zur Reichspräsidentenwahl Oktober 1930—März 1932*, part 1, *Oktober 1930—Juni 1931*, ed. and commentated by Constantin Goschler (Munich, 1994), doc. 78, 245–46.

Chapter 8: The Beginning of the End

1. Pünder, *Politik in der Reichskanzlei*, 127 (May 29, 1932).

2. On the course of the conversation on May 29, 1932, see Brüning, *Memoiren*, 597–600, notes by Otto Meissner, June 10, 1932; Hubatsch, *Hindenburg und der Staat*, 329–30; Winkler, *Weimar*, 470–71; Pyta, *Hindenburg*, 696–98.

3. See Pyta, *Hindenburg*, 592.

4. See Büttner, *Weimar*, 423–24; Longerich, *Deutschland 1918–1933*, 283–84.

5. See Bracher, *Die Auflösung der Weimarer Republik*, 405–6. On Brüning's foreign policy priorities, see Winkler, *Weimar*, 404, 411, 420–21; Longerich, *Deutschland 1918–1933*, 279–80; Kolb, *Die Weimarer Republik*, 128–29.

6. See Winkler, *Der Weg in die Katastrophe*, 23–24; Longerich, *Deutschland 1918–1933*, 303.

7. See Winkler, *Der Weg in die Katastrophe*, 24–55; Longerich, *Deutschland 1918–1933*, 303–5; Büttner, *Weimar*, 436–41; Detlev J. K. Peukert, *Wie Weimarer Republik: Krisenjahre der klassischen Moderne* (Frankfurt am Main, 1987), 247–48.

8. See Glatzer, *Berlin zur Weimarer Zeit*, 395–96.

9. See Winkler, *Weimar*, 421, 439, 441; Longerich, *Deutschland 1918–1933*, 314–16; Büttner, *Weimar*, 425, 451–53; Hans-Ulrich Wehler, *Deutsche Gesellschaftsgeschichte*, vol. 4 (Munich, 2003), 526–28.

10. Pünder, *Politik in der Reichskanzlei*, 62 (September 30, 1930).

11. Pünder, *Politik in der Reichskanzlei*, 76 (November 23, 1930). On the SPD's policy of tolerance, see Bracher, *Die Auflösung der Weimarer Republik*, 371–72; Winkler, *Weimar*, 394–96; Schulze, *Otto Braun*, 640–41, 646.

12. *AdR: Die Kabinette Brüning I und II; 30. März 1930 bis 10. Oktober 1931; 10. Oktober 1931 bis 1. Juni 1932*, vol. 1, *30. März 1930 bis 28. Februar 1931*, ed. Tilman Koops (Boppard am Rhein, 1982), no. 183, 667.

13. See Pyta, *Hindenburg*, 589.

14. Brüning, *Memoiren*, 378–79.

15. See Longerich, *Deutschland 1918–1933*, 278; Büttner, *Weimar*, 422.

16. See Philipp Austermann, *Der Weimarer Reichstag: Die schleichende Ausschaltung, Entmachtung und Zerstörung eines Parlaments* (Vienna, 2020), 150–51; Mommsen, *Die verspielte Freiheit*, 365–66; Pyta, *Hindenburg*, 599.

17. See Winkler, *Der Weg in die Katastrophe*, 247.

18. See Winkler, *Weimar*, 400, 407, 425–26; Büttner, *Weimar*, 421–22; Schulze, *Otto Braun*, 651–53.

19. See Winkler, *Musste Weimar scheitern?*, 20. See also Heinrich August Winkler, "Von Weimar zu Hitler: Die gespaltene Arbeiterbewegung und das Scheitern der ersten deutschen Demokratie," in Winkler, *Streitfragen der deutschen Geschichte: Essays zum 19. und 20. Jahrhundert* (Munich, 1997), 71–92 (here 83–86).

20. See Winkler, *Der Weg in die Katastrophe*, 387, 305ff., 385ff.; Ossip K. Flechtheim, *Die KPD in der Weimarer Republik* (Frankfurt am Main, 1969), 263ff.

21. Rudolf Hess to Fritz Hess, October 24, 1930, in Rudolf Hess, *Briefe 1908–1933*, ed. Wolf Rüdiger Hess (Munich, 1987), 405–6.

22. Figures from Ernst Deuerlein, ed., *Der Aufstieg der NSDAP in Augenzeugenberichten* (Munich, 1974), 345, 366. On the problems with the numbers, see Kellerhoff, *Die NSDAP*, 171–73.

23. See Andreas Heusler, *Das braune Haus: Wie München "Hauptstadt der Bewegung" wurde* (Munich, 2008), 127ff.; Ullrich, *Adolf Hitler*, vol. 1, 277–81.

24. See Henry A. Turner, *Die Großunternehmer und der Aufstieg Hitlers* (Berlin, 1985), 125ff.; Ullrich, *Adolf Hitler*, vol. 1, 282–83.

25. Werner Jochmann, *Nationalsozialismus und Revolution: Ursprung und Geschichte der NSDAP in Hamburg 1922–1933; Dokumente* (Frankfurt am Main, 1968), 405 (April 23, 1932).

26. See Büttner, *Weimar*, 444.

27. *Hitler: Reden Schriften Anordnungen*, vol. 3, part 3, *Januar 1930–September 1930*, ed. and commentated by Christian Hartmann (Munich, 1995), doc. 123, 434–51 (here 440, 445, 441). See also Ullrich, *Adolf Hitler*, vol. 1, 270–71.

28. See Martin Döring, *"Parlamentarischer Arm der Bewegung": Die Nationalsozialisten im Reichstag der Weimarer Republik* (Düsseldorf, 2001), 268–79; Ullrich, *Adolf Hitler*, part 1, 272–74.

29. Carl von Ossietzky, "Winterkönig," *Die Weltbühne* 27/7 (February 17, 1931), 235–37 (here 235); Ossietzky, "Brutus schläft," *Die Weltbühne* 5 (February 3, 1931), 157–60 (here 157). See also Alexander Gallus, *Heimat "Weltbühne": Eine Intellektuellengeschichte im 20. Jahrhundert* (Göttingen, 2012), 55.

30. See Peter Longerich, *Die braunen Bataillone: Geschichte der SA* (Munich, 1989), 81ff., 111 (membership numbers in 1931), 115ff.

31. Longerich, *Die braunen Bataillone*, 120ff.

32. *Hitler: Reden Schriften Anordnungen; Februar 1925 bis Januar 1933*, vol. 4, part 1, doc. 67, 200–201.

33. See Ullrich, *Adolf Hitler*, vol. 1, 274–75, 276–77.

34. See Winkler, *Weimar*, 408.

35. Winkler, *Weimar*, 415. On Hoover's initiative, see Schulz, *Von Brüning zu Hitler*, 410–20.

36. Sternheim, *Tagebücher*, vol. 2, 362 (July 13, 1931). On the banking crisis, see Winkler, *Weimar*, 416–17; Büttner, *Weimar*, 431–32; Hömig, *Brüning*, 345–46.

37. Shedletzky, *Betty Scholem–Gershom Scholem*, 243 (August 4, 1931).

38. Goebbels, *Die Tagebücher*, vol. 1, part 2/2, 56 (July 14, 1931).

39. Klemperer, *Tagebücher 1925–1932*, 370 (September 2, 1931). See also Winkler, *Weimar*, 419–20; Büttner, *Weimar*, 434–35; Hömig, *Brüning*, 350–53.

40. Reichslandbund to Hindenburg, July 22, 1931, in *AdR: Die Kabinette Brüning I und II*, vol. 2, no. 404, 1411–12 (here 1412).

41. Reusch to Kastl, September 6, 1931, and Kastl to Reusch, September 11, 1931, in *Politik und Wirtschaft*, part 2, no. 303, 944, and no. 307, 950.

42. Protocol of Brüning's meeting with representatives of the Reich Industrial Association, September 18, 1931, in *Politik und Wirtschaft*, part 2, no. 317, 967–75 (here 968, 971). See also Plumpe, *Carl Duisberg*, 773.

43. *AdR: Die Kabinette Brüning I und II*, vol. 2, no. 496, 1764–1469 (here 1467, 1469).

44. Gilsa to Reusch, October 9, 1931, in *Politik und Wirtschaft*, part 2, no. 337, 1031. See Richter, *Die Deutsche Volkspartei*, 720–21.

45. Brüning, *Memoiren*, 385–86, 417. On the anti-Brüning campaign in the fall of 1931, see Pyta, *Hindenburg*, 632.

46. See Hürter, *Wilhelm Groener*, 276, 288–91; Schulz, *Von Brüning zu Hitler*, 159–60.

47. Hess, *Briefe 1908–1933*, 414 (September 9, 1931). On Schleicher's notion of taming Hitler, see Bracher, *Die Auflösung der Weimarer Republik*, 425–26; Hürter, *Wilhelm Groener*, 292; Larry Eugene Jones, "Taming the Nazi-Beast: Kurt von Schleicher and the End of the Weimar Republic," in *From Weimar to Hitler: Studies in the Dissolution of the Weimar Republic and the Establishment of the Third Reich, 1932–1934*, ed. Hermann Beck and Larry Eugene Jones (New York, 2019), 23–52.

48. Goebbels, *Die Tagebücher*, vol. 1, part 2/2, 116 (October 5, 1931).

49. See Deuerlein, *Der Aufstieg der NSDAP*, 355. On the contact between Schleicher and Hitler, see Thilo Vogelsang, *Reichswehr, Staat und NSDAP: Beiträge zur deutschen Geschichte 1930–1932* (Stuttgart, 1962), 135–37.

50. Pünder's note, October 9, 1931, in *AdR: Die Kabinette Brüning I und II*, vol. 2, no. 512, 1817–18 (here 1817).

51. Ministerial meeting, October 7, 1931, in *Die Kabinette Brüning I und II*, vol. 2, no. 511, 1815–16 (here 1816). On the German-Austrian customs union project, see Schulz, *Von Brüning zu Hitler*, 298–316.

52. See Bracher, *Die Auflösung der Weimarer Republik*, 416–18; Winkler, *Weimar*, 429–30; Büttner, *Weimar*, 449–50.

53. Schäffer's notes about the second Brüning cabinet, in *Politik und Wirtschaft*, part 2, no. 338, 1032. See also Pünder, *Politik in der Reichskanzlei*, 106 (November 1, 1931): "The re-formation did not bring about the success we hoped for." At an evening social event hosted by Meissner, Schleicher said, "Hindenburg is dissatisfied that Brüning hasn't arranged a right-wing cabinet." See *Die Deutschnationalen und die Zerstörung der Weimarer Republik: Aus dem Tagebuch von Reinhold Quaatz 1928–1933*, ed. Hermann Weiß and Paul Hoser (Munich, 1989), 158 (October 20, 1931).

54. Goebbels, *Die Tagebücher*, vol. 1, part 2/2, 127 (October 17, 1931). See Winkler, *Weimar*, 432.

55. Brüning, *Memoiren*, 391.

56. See Pyta, *Hindenburg*, 1014, note 43. See also Pyta, 635–37. On the allegedly "extremely poor impression Hitler made on Hindenburg," see Hömig, *Brüning*, 398.

57. Goebbels, *Die Tagebücher*, vol. 1, part 2/2, 121 (October 12, 1931).

58. Hans Brosius, "Der Aufmarsch in Harzburg," *Unsere Partei* 20 (October 17, 1931). See also Volker Ullrich, "Das Signal zum Angriff," *Die Zeit* 41 (October 6, 2011); Ullrich, *Adolf Hitler*, vol. 1, 291–93; Schulz, *Von Brüning zu Hitler*, 554–59.

59. Gilsa to Reusch, October 13, 1931, in *Politik und Wirtschaft*, part 2, no. 342, 1044.

60. *Hitler: Reden Schriften Anordnungen*, vol. 4, part 2, *Juli 1931–Dezember 1931*, ed. and commentated by Christian Hartmann (Munich, 1996), docs. 43 and 44, 123–32.

61. See Willibald Gutsche, *Ein Kaiser im Exil: Der letzte deutsche Kaiser Wilhelm II in Holland* (Marburg, 1991), 136.

62. Goebbels, *Die Tagebücher*, vol. 1, part 2/2, 123 (October 12, 1931).

63. See Ulrich Herbert, *Best: Biographische Studien über Radikalismus, Weltanschauung und Vernunft 1903–1999* (Bonn, 1999), 112–15.

64. Meissner's note about Hindenburg's reception of Göring, December 11, 1931, in *AdR: Die Kabinette Brüning I und II*, vol. 3, *10. Oktober 1931 bis 30. Mai 1932*, no. 599, 2091–93 (here 2091).

65. See *Die Kabinette Brüning I und II*, vol. 3, 116–18; Winkler, *Weimar*, 433–35.

66. *Chronik eines Untergangs: Deutschland 1924–39; Die Beiträge Leopold Schwarzschilds in den Zeitschriften "Das Tage-Buch" und "Das Neue Tage-Buch,"* ed. Andreas P. Wesemann (Vienna, 2005), 177 (December 26, 1931).

67. Kessler, *Das Tagebuch*, vol. 9, 400 (December 31, 1931).

68. Erich Krämer, "Jahr des Unheils," *Vossische Zeitung* 1 (January 1, 1932).

69. Klemperer, *Tagebücher 1925–1932*, 739 (December 25, 1931).

70. Goebbels, *Die Tagebücher*, vol. 1, part 2/2, 186 (January 1, 1932).

71. Pünder's note about Hindenburg's meeting with Brüning, January 5, 1932, in *AdR: Die Kabinette Brüning I und II*, vol. 3, no. 617, 2139–40.

72. See Brüning, *Memoiren*, 451; Winkler, *Weimar*, 444; Pyta, *Hindenburg*, 645–50. On the overall situation, see Larry Eugene Jones, *Hitler Versus Hindenburg: The 1932 Presidential Elections and the End of the Weimar Republic* (Cambridge, 2016), 141ff.

73. See Hürter, *Wilhelm Groener*, 322–23.

74. *Hitler: Reden Schriften Anordnungen*, vol. 4, part 3, *Januar 1932–März 1932*, ed.

and commentated by Christian Hartmann (Munich, 1997), doc. 6, 27–28; doc. 8, 34–44. See Pünder's notes on negotiations over Hindenburg's reelection, January 8–13, 1932, in *Politik und Wirtschaft*, part 2, no. 401a, 1208–15; Ullrich, *Adolf Hitler*, vol. 1, 328–29.

75. See Hugenberg to Brüning, January 12, 1932, in *AdR: Die Kabinette Brüning I und II*, vol. 3, no. 622, 2153–54.

76. Brüning, *Memoiren*, 518–19.

77. Pünder, *Politik in der Reichskanzlei*, 114 (February 15, 1932); Pünder's notes about the presidential election, February 15, 1932, in *AdR: Die Kabinette Brüning I und II*, vol. 3, no. 673, 2293–95. See Winkler, *Weimar*, 444–45; Pyta, *Hindenburg*, 659–63; Jones, *Hitler Versus Hindenburg*, 154–73.

78. Hindenburg to Oldenburg-Januschau, February 17, 1932, in Vogelsang, *Reichswehr, Staat und NSDAP*, no. 18, 442.

79. Goebbels, *Die Tagebücher*, vol. 1, part 2/2, 207 (January 30, 1932).

80. See Ullrich, *Adolf Hitler*, vol. 1, 329–31.

81. Goebbels, *Die Tagebücher*, vol. 1, part 2/2, 228 (February 26, 1932). See Morsey, *Hitler als Braunschweigischer Regierungsrat*, 419–48.

82. See Schönhoven and Vogel, *Frühe Warnungen vor dem Nationalsozialismus*, 245–46; see Winkler, *Weimar*, 446.

83. See Winkler, *Weimar*, 446; Hömig, *Brüning*, 511.

84. Brüning, *Memoiren*, 529.

85. See Winkler, *Der Weg in die Katastrophe*, 512–13.

86. See Winkler, *Der Weg in die Katastrophe*, 513.

87. See Hömig, *Brüning*, 518.

88. Hömig, *Brüning*, 516–17. On Brüning's campaign, see Jones, *Hitler Versus Hindenburg*, 206–8.

89. See Goebbels, *Die Tagebücher*, vol. 1, part 2/2, 230–31 (March 1, 1932); Gerhard Paul, *Aufstand der Bilder: Die NS-Propaganda vor 1933* (Bonn, 1990), 95–96; Jones, *Hitler Versus Hindenburg*, 250–59.

90. *Hitler: Reden Schriften Anordnungen*, vol. 4, part 3, doc. 39, 191.

91. Goebbels, *Die Tagebücher*, vol. 1, part 2/2, 237 (March 9, 1932).

92. *Vossische Zeitung* 125 (March 14, 1932).

93. Goebbels, *Die Tagebücher*, vol. 1, part 2/2, 241–42 (March 14, 1932). On the election results, see Winkler, *Weimar*, 448–49; Jones, *Hitler Versus Hindenburg*, 274–77.

94. Veit Valentin, "Gegen-Angriff," *Vossische Zeitung* 126 (March 15, 1932).

95. Brüning, *Memoiren*, 533; see also Pyta, *Hindenburg*, 681.

96. See Stephan Malinowski, *Die Hohenzollern und die Nazis: Geschichte einer Kollaboration* (Berlin, 2021), 125–29, 247–49; Pyta, *Hindenburg*, 674–77.

97. Goebbels, *Die Tagebücher*, vol. 1, part 2/2, 243 (March 16, 1932).

98. See Ullrich, *Adolf Hitler*, vol. 1, 336–37; Jones, *Hitler Versus Hindenburg*, 293–94.

99. See Winkler, *Weimar*, 453; Jones, *Hitler Versus Hindenburg*, 308–12.

100. Pyta, *Hindenburg*, 683.

101. Pünder, *Politik in der Reichskanzlei*, 118 (April 11, 1932). See also Brüning, *Memoiren*, 541; Winkler, *Weimar*, 414; Pyta, *Hindenburg*, 685.

102. Groener to Brüning, April 10, 1932, in *AdR: Die Kabinette Brüning I und II*, vol. 3, no. 714, 2426–29 (here 2428).

103. Pünder, *Politik in der Reichskanzlei*, 118 (April 11, 1932). See also Hürter, *Wilhelm Groener*, 332–44; Winkler, *Weimar*, 449–51; Hömig, *Brüning*, 525–30.

104. *Hitler: Reden Schriften Anordnungen*, vol. 5, part 1, *April 1932–September 1932*, ed. and commentated by Klaus A. Lankheit (Munich, 1996), doc. 36, 54–56 (here 56).

105. See Dagmar Bussiek, *Benno Reifenberg 1892–1970: Eine Biographie* (Göttingen, 2011), 232.

106. See Winkler, *Weimar*, 454–55; Hömig, *Brüning*, 533. Goebbels noted: "Marvelous press for us on the issue of the SA ban." *Die Tagebücher*, vol. 1, part 2/2, 261 (April 15, 1932).

107. Hindenburg to Groener, April 15, 1932, in *Politik und Wirtschaft*, part 2, no. 467, 1383. See Hürter, *Wilhelm Groener*, 346.

108. Carl von Ossietzky, "Dank vom Hause Hindenburg," *Die Weltbühne* (April 26, 1932); also in Ossietzky, *Sämtliche Schriften*, vol. 6, *1931–1933*, ed. Gerhard Kraiker et al. (Reinbek bei Hamburg, 1994), 359–61 (here 360).

109. Groener to Generalmajor (ret.) von Gleich (April 25, 1932), *Politik und Wirtschaft*, part 2, no. 477, 1408.

110. Ministerial meeting, May 3, 1932, in *AdR: Die Kabinette Brüning I und II*, vol. 3, no. 733, 2483–85. See Hürter, *Wilhelm Groener*, 347.

111. Heuss to Reinhold Maier, May 14, 1932, in Theodor Heuss, *Bürger der Weimarer Republik: Briefe 1918–1933*, ed. Michael Dorrmann (Munich, 2008), 465. See also Pünder, *Politik in der Reichskanzlei*, 120 (April 10, 1932): "The catastrophic impression from the speech was generally shared."

112. Brüning, *Memoiren*, 587.

113. Pünder, *Politik in der Reichskanzlei*, 121 (May 11, 1932).

114. See Hürter, *Wilhelm Groener*, 350–51; Winkler, Weimar, 464–65.

115. Pünder, *Politik in der Reichskanzlei*, 122–23 (May 13, 1932).

116. See Warmbold to Hindenburg, April 28, 1932, in *Politik und Wirtschaft*, part 2, no. 485, 1423–24; Büttner, *Weimar*, 459.

117. Goebbels, *Die Tagebücher*, vol. 1, part 2/2, 271 (April 29, 1932), 274 (May 5, 1932), 276 (May 9, 1932).

118. See Brüning, *Memoiren*, 586.

119. Goebbels, *Die Tagebücher*, vol. 1, part 2/2, 281 (May 14, 1932), 283 (May 18, 1932), 284 (May 19, 1932), 285 (May 20, 1932), 288 (May 25, 1932).

120. Von Gayl to Hindenburg, May 24, 1932, in *Politik und Wirtschaft*, part 2, no. 512b, 1486–87. On the disagreement about the settlement issue, see Schulz, *Von Brüning zu Hitler*, 843–57.

121. Kalckreuth to Hindenburg, May 24, 1932, in Schulz, *Von Brüning zu Hitler*, no. 513, 1496.

122. Meissner's notes, June 14, 1932, in Hubatsch, *Hindenburg und der Staat*, 327–28; Pünder, *Politik in der Reichskanzlei*, 126 (May 26, 1932).

123. Meissner's notes, June 14, 1932, in Hubatsch, *Hindenburg und der Staat*, 329; Brüning, *Memoiren*, 601; Pünder, *Politik in der Reichskanzlei*, 129 (May 29, 1932).

124. Pünder's notes of the ministerial meeting, May 30, 1932, in *AdR: Die Kabinette Brüning I und II*, vol. 3, no. 773, 2585–87; Hömig, *Brüning*, 568.

125. Brüning, *Memoiren*, 601–2; see also Pyta, *Hindenburg*, 698.

126. Goebbels, *Die Tagebücher*, vol. 1, part 2/2, 293 (May 30, 1932).

127. Sternheim, *Tagebücher*, vol. 2, 409 (May 31, 1932).

128. Kessler, *Das Tagebuch*, vol. 9, 427 (May 30, 1932).

129. Hanns-Erich Kaminski, "Brüning," *Die Weltbühne* 28/23 (June 7, 1932), 844–47 (here 846).

130. Winkler, *Weimar*, 472.

131. See Winkler, *Musste Weimar scheitern?*, 22–23.

132. Goebbels, *Die Tagebücher*, vol. 1, part 2/2, 293 (May 30, 1932). See also Meissner's note, May 30, 1932, in Vogelsang, *Reichswehr, Staat und NSDAP*, 458–59.

133. See Joachim Petzold, *Franz von Papen: Ein deutsches Verhängnis* (Munich, 1995), 15ff.; Winkler, *Weimar*, 477–78.

134. J[ulius] E[lbau], "Der Stein im Rollen," *Vossische Zeitung* 262 (June 1, 1932).

135. See Winkler, *Weimar*, 478–80.

136. See Winkler, *Weimar*, 505–6.

137. Goebbels, *Die Tagebücher*, vol. 1, part 2/2, 330 (August 1, 1932).

138. Klaus Mann, *Tagebücher 1931 bis 1933*, ed. Joachim Heimannsberg et al. (Munich, 1989), 64 (July 14, 1932).

Chapter 9: The Hour of the Barons

1. Schulze, *Otto Braun*, 745.

2. Schulze, *Otto Braun*, 746.

3. See Winkler, *Weimar*, 457–58.

4. Schulze, *Otto Braun*, 729.

5. Schulze, *Otto Braun*, 733.

6. Schulze, *Otto Braun*, 736.

7. Franz von Papen, *Der Wahrheit eine Gasse* (Munich, 1952), 215.

8. Papen to Kerrl, June 6, 1932, in *AdR: Das Kabinett von Papen; 1. Juni bis 3. Dezember 1932*, vol. 1, *Juni bis September 1932*, ed. Karl-Heinz Minuth (Boppard am Rhein, 1989), no. 10, 22–23.

9. Goebbels, *Die Tagebücher*, vol. 1, part 2/2, 298 (June 7, 1932), 300 (June 10, 1932).

10. *AdR: Das Kabinett von Papen*, vol. 1, no. 18, 57; no. 21, 66.

11. See Winkler, *Weimar*, 486.

12. See Winkler, *Weimar*, 486–87.

13. Moltke, *Ein Leben in Deutschland*, 205 (July 14, 1932).

14. Kessler, *Das Tagebuch*, vol. 9, 461–62 (July 12, 1932).

15. *AdR: Das Kabinett von Papen*, vol. 1, no. 53, 190–91; no. 54, 192–93.

16. *AdR: Das Kabinett von Papen*, vol. 1, no. 57, 204–8.

17. See Winkler, *Weimar*, 491; Thomas Alexander, *Carl Severing: Sozialdemokrat aus Westfalen mit preußischen Tugenden* (Bielefeld, 1992), 199–200.

18. *AdR: Das Kabinett von Papen*, vol. 1, no. 59, 211–12.

19. *AdR: Das Kabinett von Papen*, vol. 1, no. 60, 217; 217, note 17 (Severing's decree of July 2, 1932).

20. See ministerial meeting, July 16, 1932, in *AdR: Das Kabinett von Papen*, vol. 1, no. 63, 240 (Gayl's report on his meeting with Hindenburg on July 14, 1932). On Hindenburg's perspective, see Pyta, *Hindenburg*, 712–13.

21. Kessler, *Das Tagebuch*, vol. 9, 465 (July 18, 1932). On the Altona Bloody Sunday, see Winkler, *Der Weg in die Katastrophe*, 650–52.

22. Bracher, *Die Auflösung der Weimarer Republik*, 581.

23. Kerrl to Papen, June 18, 1932, in *AdR: Das Kabinett von Papen*, vol. 1, no. 64, 241–5 (here 244–45).

24. Winkler, *Der Weg in die Katastrophe*, 656.

25. Conference with the Prussian state ministers, July 20, 1932, in *AdR: Das Kabinett von Papen*, vol. 1, no. 69a, 257–59; no. 69b, 259–62 (Hirtsiefer's and Severing's notes).

26. Albert Grzesinski, *Im Kampf um die Republik: Erinnerungen eines Sozialdemokraten*, ed. Eberhard Kolb (Munich, 2001), 271–73.

27. Preußische Staatsregierung to Papen, July 20, 1932, in *AdR: Das Kabinett Papen*, vol. 1, no. 71, 263–64.

28. Winkler, *Der Weg in die Katastrophe*, 660–61, 662.

29. *Quellen zur Geschichte der deutschen Gewerkschaftsbewegung im 20. Jahrhundert*, vol. 4, *Die Gewerkschaften in der Endphase der Republik 1930–1933*, ed. Peter Jahn with Detlev Brunner (Cologne, 1988), doc. 110, 625–26.

30. See Winkler, *Weimar*, 500.

31. Goebbels, *Die Tagebücher*, vol. 1, part 2/2, 324 (July 21, 1932).

32. See Peter Lessmann, *Die preußische Schutzpolizei in der Weimarer Republik: Streifendienst und Strassenkampf* (Düsseldorf, 1989), 366–70.

33. See Winkler, *Der Weg in die Katastrophe*, 671.

34. Goebbels, *Die Tagebücher*, vol. 1, part 2/2, 324 (July 20, 1932).

35. Winkler, *Weimar*, 498.

36. Winkler, *Weimar*, 503.

37. Goebbels, *Die Tagebücher*, vol. 1, part 2/2, 325 (July 23, 1932).

38. Bracher, *Die Auflösung der Weimarer Republik*, 590.

39. See Winkler, *Weimar*, 504, 530–31.

40. Christopher Clark, *The Iron Kingdom: The Rise and Downfall of Prussia 1600–1947* (Cambridge, MA, 2006), 652.

Chapter 10: The Finish Line

1. Goebbels, *Die Tagebücher*, vol. 1, part 2/3, *Oktober 1932–März 1933*, ed. Elke Fröhlich and Angela Hermann (Munich, 2000), 120 (January 31, 1933).

2. Kessler, *Das Tagebuch*, vol. 9, 536–37 (January 30, 1933).

3. See Lothar Machtan, *Der Kaisersohn bei Hitler* (Hamburg, 2006), 279.

4. Hess, *Briefe 1908–1933*, 424–25 (January 31, 1933).

5. Goebbels, *Die Tagebücher*, vol. 1, part 2/2, 334 (August 7, 1932).

6. Goebbels, *Die Tagebücher*, vol. 1, part 2/2, 338 (August 12, 1932).

7. Meissner's notes, August 11, 1932, Hubatsch, *Hindenburg und der Staat*, 335–38 (here 336).

8. Ministerial meeting, August 10, 1932, in *AdR: Das Kabinett von Papen*, vol. 1, no. 99, 378–86 (here 385).

9. Papen, *Der Wahrheit eine Gasse*, 222–23.

10. Goebbels, *Die Tagebücher*, vol. 1, part 2/2, 340 (August 14, 1932).

11. Meissner's notes, August 13, 1932, in *AdR: Das Kabinett von Papen*, vol. 1, no. 101, 391–92.

12. *AdR: Das Kabinett von Papen*, vol. 1, no. 101, 392, note 5.

13. Pünder, *Politik in der Reichskanzlei*, 141 (August 18, 1932). See Schulz, *Von Brüning zu Hitler*, 964.

14. Kessler, *Das Tagebuch*, vol. 9, 519 (October 24, 1932).

15. Moltke, *Ein Leben in Deutschland*, 209 (September 3, 1932).

16. Julius Elbau, "Das Wort hat der Reichstag," *Vossische Zeitung* 389 (August 14, 1932).

17. Goebbels, *Die Tagebücher*, vol. 1, part 2/2, 341 (August 14, 1932).

18. Ministerial meeting, August 9, 1932, in *AdR: Das Kabinett von Papen*, vol. 1, no. 98, 374–77.

19. *Hitler: Reden Schriften Anordnungen*, vol. 5, part 1, doc. 174, 317. See also Paul Kluke, "Der Fall Potempa," *Vierteljahrshefte für Zeitgeschichte* 5 (1957): 279–97.

20. See Bussiek, *Benno Reifenberg*, 237.

21. Kessler, *Das Tagebuch*, vol. 9, 496 (August 28, 1932).

22. See Winkler, *Weimar*, 523–24, 528.

23. Goebbels, *Die Tagebücher*, vol. 1, part 2/2, 372 (September 28, 1932), 373 (September 29, 1932).

24. See Wolfgang Horn, *Der Marsch zur Machtergreifung: Die NSDAP bis 1933* (Königstein, 1980), 357; Mathias Rösch, *Die Münchner NSDAP 1925–1933: Eine Untersuchung zur inneren Struktur der NSDAP in der Weimarer Republik* (Munich, 2002), 365–66; Goebbels, *Die Tagebücher*, vol. 1, part 2/3, 38 (November 16, 1932).

25. Goebbels, *Die Tagebücher*, vol. 1, part 2/3, 38 (November 16, 1932).

26. See Turner, *Die Großindustrie und der Aufstieg Hitlers*, 358.

27. See Ullrich, *Adolf Hitler*, vol. 1, 366–68.

28. Goebbels, *Die Tagebücher*, vol. 1, part 2/2, 370 (September 25, 1932).

29. Goebbels, *Die Tagebücher*, vol. 1, part 2/2, 51 (November 5, 1932). On the Berlin transport strike, see Winkler, *Der Weg in die Katastrophe*, 765–63.

30. See Werner Jochmann, *Nationalsozialismus und Revolution: Ursprung du Geschichte der NSDAP in Hamburg 1922–1933; Dokumente* (Frankfurt, 1968), 416.

31. See Winkler, *Weimar*, 535–36.

32. Goebbels, *Die Tagebücher*, vol. 1, part 2/3, 53 (November 7, 1932).

33. Hellmut von Gerlach, "Der neue Reichstag," *Die Weltbühne* 18/45 (November 8, 1932), 672.

34. "Ohne Mehrheit," *Vossische Zeitung* 534 (November 7, 1932).

35. See Meissner's notes on Hindenburg's meetings with Hitler, November 19 and

21, 1932, in *AdR: Das Kabinett von Papen*, vol. 2, no. 222, 984–86; no. 224, 968–92 (here 990, 988).

36. Meissner to Hitler, November 24, 1932, in *AdR: Das Kabinett von Papen*, vol. 2, no. 227, 998–1000.

37. Goebbels, *Die Tagebücher*, vol. 1, part 2/3, 67 (November 25, 1932), 68 (November 26, 1932).

38. Hellmut von Gerlach, "Talmudist Hitler," *Die Weltbühne* 18/48 (November 29, 1932), 783–86 (here 785).

39. See Meissner's notes on meetings with Hindenburg, December 1 and 2, 1932, in Hubatsch, *Hindenburg und der Staat*, no. 103, 366–67. See also Pyta, *Hindenburg*, 759–66; Ullrich, *Adolf Hitler*, vol. 1, 374–78.

40. See Eberhard Kolb, "Die Staatsnotstandsplanung unter den Regierungen Papen und Schleicher," in *Umbrüche deutscher Geschichte 1866/71, 1918/19, 1929/33: Ausgewählte Aufsätze*, ed. Dieter Langewiesche and Klaus Schönhoven (Munich, 1993), 331–58. On Papen's concept of a "new state," see Bracher, *Die Auflösung der Weimarer Republik*, 536–45; Mommsen, *Die verspielte Freiheit*, 483–85.

41. See Schwerin von Krosigk's diary entry about the ministerial meeting on December 2, 1932, in *AdR: Das Kabinett von Papen*, vol. 2, no. 2396, 1036–38.

42. Papen, *Der Wahrheit eine Gasse*, 250.

43. *Tägliche Rundschau* 286 (December 4, 1932).

44. See Eberhard Kolb, "Die Weimarer Republik und das Problem der Kontinuität vom Kaiserreich zum 'Dritten Reich,'" in *Umbrüche deutscher Geschichte*, 367.

45. Henry A. Turner, *Hitler's Thirty Days to Power: January 1933* (Reading, MA, 1996), 58. See also Rösch, *Die Münchner NSDAP 1925–1933*, 370–71.

46. On Schleicher's plans for a united front, see Axel Schildt, *Militärdiktatur auf Massenbasis? Die Querfrontkonzeption der Reichswehrführung um General Schleicher am Ende der Weimarer Republik* (Frankfurt, 1981); Benjamin Carter Hett, *The Death of Democracy: Hitler's Rise to Power and the Downfall of the Weimar Republic* (New York, 2018), 164–66.

47. See Peter Longerich, *Hitler: Biographie* (Munich, 2015), 279.

48. See Udo Kissenkötter, *Gregor Straßer und die NSDAP* (Stuttgart, 1978), 172.

49. Goebbels, *Die Tagebücher*, vol. 1, part 2/3, 78 (December 9, 1932). See also Ullrich, *Adolf Hitler*, vol. 1, 381–83.

50. Goebbels, *Die Tagebücher*, vol. 1, part 2/3, 79 (December 10, 1932).

51. Goebbels, *Die Tagebücher*, vol. 1, part 2/3, 89 (December 24, 1932).

52. *Hitler: Reden Schriften Anordnungen*, vol. 5, part 2, *Oktober 1932–Januar 1933*, ed. and commentated by Christian Hartmann and Klaus A. Lankheit (Munich, 1998), doc. 107, 297–311 (here 310–11).

53. See Günther Gillessen, *Auf verlorenem Posten: Die Frankfurter Zeitung im Dritten Reich* (Berlin, 1986), 86.

54. Julius Elbau, "Jahr der Entscheidung," *Vossische Zeitung* 1 (January 1, 1933).

55. See Kolb, *Umbrüche deutscher Geschichte*, 368.

56. See Schulze, *Weimar*, 393.

57. Claus W. Schäfer, *André François-Poncet als Botschafter in Berlin (1931–1938)* (Munich, 2004), 160.

58. See Joachim Fest, *Hitler: A Biography*, trans. Richard and Clara Winston (London, 2000), 356.

59. See Rainer Hering, *Konstruierte Nation: Der Alldeutsche Verband 1890–1939* (Hamburg, 2003), 484–85.

60. *AdR: Das Kabinett von Schleicher; 3. Dezember 1932 bis 30. Januar 1933*, ed. Anton Golecki (Boppard am Rhein, 1986), no. 16, 57.

61. Carl von Ossietzky, "Wintermärchen," *Die Weltbühne* 29/1 (January 3, 1933), 1–6 (here 1, 3); also in Ossietzky, *Sämtliche Schriften*, vol. 6, 437–43.

62. *Chronik eines Untergangs*, 232 (December 31, 1932).

63. Quoted from Turner, *Hitler's Thirty Days*, 46.

64. Pyta, *Hindenburg*, 791.

65. Karl Dietrich Bracher, *Die Auflösung der Weimarer Republik*, 691.

66. Turner, *Die Großunternehmer und der Aufstieg Hitlers*, 293–301.

67. Keppler to Schroeder, December 19, 1932, in Eberhard Czichon, *Wer verhalf Hitler zur Macht? Zum Anteil der deutschen Industrie an der Zerstörung der Weimarer Republik* (Cologne, 1967), no. 18, 74–76.

68. See Heinrich Muth, "Das 'Kölner Gespräch' am 4. Januar 1933. Teil 2," *Geschichte in Wissenschaft und Unterricht* 37 (1986): 531.

69. Keppler to Schroeder, December 26, 1932, in Czichon, *Wer verhalf Hitler zur Macht?*, no. 19, 76–77.

70. See Turner, *Hitlers Weg zur Macht: Der Januar 1933*, trans. Enrico Heinemann and Thomas Pfeiffer (Munich, 1996), 60–62.

71. On the course and content of the conversation, see Kurt von Schroeder's affidavit of July 21, 1947, in Czichon, *Wer verhalf Hitler zur Macht?*, no. 21, 77–79; Turner, *Hitlers Weg zur Macht*, 63–64; Muth, "Das 'Kölner Gespräch,'" 533–36.

72. Schacht to Schroeder, January 6, 1933, in Czichon, *Wer verhalf Hitler zur Macht?*, no. 22, 79.

73. Goebbels, *Die Tagebücher*, vol. 1, part 2/3, 103 (January 10, 1933).

74. Turner, *Hitler's Thirty Days*, 29.

75. "Eine Erklärung Papens," *Vossische Zeitung* 9 (January 6, 1933).

76. *Hitler: Reden Schriften Anordnungen*, vol. 5, part 2, no. 116, 332.

77. "Hitler und Papen," *Vossische Zeitung* 8 (January 5, 1933).

78. Turner, *Hitler's Thirty Days*, 50; cf. Hett, *Death of Democracy*, 171–72.

79. Papen, *Der Wahrheit eine Gasse*, 260–61. On January 13, 1933, Schleicher learned via Crown Prince Wilhelm, who had installed an informant in the "Brown House" in Munich, that Hitler's aim at the meeting on January 4 had been "to persuade the Reich president, through Papen's mediation, to withdraw confidence from the chancellor before the new elections and to replace him with some other constellation." Wilhelm of Prussia to Schleicher, January 13, 1933, in *AdR: Das Kabinett von Schleicher*, no. 54, 220–24 (here 222).

80. Meissner, *Staatssekretär unter Ebert-Hindenburg-Hitler*, 261.

81. Pyta, *Hindenburg*, 780.

82. Goebbels, *Die Tagebücher*, vol. 1, part 2/3, 103 (January 10, 1933).

83. Schleicher's radio speech, December 15, 1932, in *AdR: Das Kabinett von Schleicher*, no. 25, 101–17 (here 109, 103, 106).

84. See Turner, *Die Großindustrie und der Aufstieg Hitlers*, 370–71.

85. See Reinhard Neebe, *Großindustrie, Staat und NSDAP 1930–1933: Paul Silverberg und der Reichsverband der Deutschen Industrie in der Krise der Weimarer Republik* (Marburg, 1979), 144. See also Herbert, *Geschichte Deutschlands im 20. Jahrhundert*, 297.

86. *AdR: Das Kabinett von Schleicher*, no. 50, 206–8 (here 207), no. 51, 208–14.

87. *AdR: Das Kabinett von Schleicher*, no. 51, 214, note 16.

88. Turner, *Hitlers Weg zur Macht*, 152–53; Pyta, *Hindenburg*, 770.

89. *AdR: Das Kabinett von Schleicher*, no. 56, 324, note 15 (here no. 23, 103).

90. Resolution of the Reichstag faction of the DNVP, January 21, 1933, in *AdR: Das Kabinett von Schleicher*, no. 64, 283.

91. Goebbels: *Die Tagebücher*, vol. 1, part 2/3, 105 (January 13, 1933). See also Wolfgang Michalka, "Joachim von Ribbentrop—Vom Spirituosenhändler zum Außenminister," in *Die braune Elite: 22 biographische Skizzen*, ed. Ronald Smelser and Rainer Zitelmann (Darmstadt, 1989), 201–11 (here 202–3); Joachim von Ribbentrop, *Zwischen London und Moskau: Erinnerungen und letzte Aufzeichnungen; Aus dem Nachlass*, ed. Annelies Ribbentrop (Leoni am Starnberger See, 1961), 36–38.

92. Jutta Ciolek-Kümper, *Wahlkampf in Lippe: Die Wahlkampfpropaganda der NSDAP zur Landtagswahl am 15. Januar 1933* (Munich, 1976), 144.

93. Ciolek-Kümper, *Wahlkampf in Lippe*, 147.

94. Carl von Ossietzky, "Bankrott der Autorität," *Die Weltbühne* 29/3 (January 17, 1933), 81–85 (here 83); also in Ossietzky, *Sämtliche Schriften*, vol. 6, 449–55 (here 452).

95. *Hitler: Reden Schriften Anordnungen*, vol. 5, part 2, doc. 117, 333.

96. See Ciolek-Kümper, *Wahlkampf in Lippe*, 271, 272. On the election result, see Turner, *Hitlers Weg zur Macht*, 89–90.

97. Ciolek-Kümper, *Wahlkampf in Lippe*, 279–80.

98. Goebbels, *Die Tagebücher*, vol. 1, part 2/3, 107 (from January 16, 1933).

99. *Hitler: Reden Schrift Anordnungen*, vol. 5, part 2, doc. 140, 370.

100. Goebbels, *Die Tagebücher*, vol. 1, part 2/3, 108 (January 17, 1933).

101. Hugenberg to Hitler, December 28, 1932, in *AdR: Das Kabinett von Schleicher*, no. 56, 232, note 9. See also Larry Eugene Jones, "The Greatest Stupidity of My Life: Alfred Hugenberg and the Formation of the Hitler Cabinet, January 1933," *Journal of Contemporary History* 27 (1992): 63–87 (here 70).

102. *Die Deutschnationalen und die Zerstörung*, 223 (January 17, 1933).

103. Ribbentrop, *Zwischen London und Moskau*, 39 (January 18, 1933).

104. Papen to Springorum, January 20, 1933, in Muth, "Das 'Kölner Gespräch,'" 538.

105. "Papen-Hitler-Schleicher, Geschäftiges Spiel hinter den Kulissen," *Vossische Zeitung* 30 (January 18, 1933).

106. Fest, *Hitler*, 501.

107. Pyta, *Hindenburg*, 787.

108. Papen, *Der Wahrheit eine Gasse*, 265; see also Meissner, *Staatssekretär unter Ebert-Hindenburg-Hitler*, 263.

109. Goebbels, *Die Tagebücher*, vol. 1, part 2/3, 114 (January 25, 1933). On the negotiations on January 22, 1933, see Turner, *Hitlers Weg zur Macht*, 154–56.

110. Ribbentrop, *Zwischen London und Moskau*, 39 (January 22, 1933)

111. Ribbentrop, *Zwischen London und Moskau*, 39 (January 23, 1933). See also Turner, *Hitlers Weg zur Macht*, 157–58.

112. Goebbels, *Die Tagebücher*, vol. 1, part 2/3, 114 (January 25, 1933).

113. Ribbentrop, *Zwischen London und Moskau*, 39–40. See also Goebbels, *Die Tagebücher*, vol. 1, part 2/3, 116 (January 26, 1933): "Harzburg front reappears. Frick and Goering negotiate."

114. *Die Deutschnationalen und die Zerstörung*, 224 (January 21, 1933).

115. Ministerial meeting, January 16, 1933, in *AdR: Das Kabinett von Schleicher*, no. 56, 230–38 (here 231).

116. Meissner's notes on Schleicher's reception by Hindenburg, January 23, 1933, in *AdR: Das Kabinett von Schleicher*, no. 65, 284–85.

117. See Dieter Hoffmann, *Der Skandal: Hindenburgs Entscheidung für Hitler* (Bremen, 2020), 38ff.; Winkler, *Weimar*, 578–81.

118. Kaas to Schleicher, January 26, 1933, in *AdR: Das Kabinett von Schleicher*, no. 70, 304–5.

119. Winkler, *Weimar*, 582.

120. Ministerial meeting, January 28, 1933, in *AdR: Das Kabinett von Schleicher*, no. 71, 306–9 (here 307).

121. Meissner's notes on the conversation between Schleicher and Hindenburg, January 28, 1933, in *AdR: Das Kabinett von Schleicher*, no. 72, 310–11.

122. Schwerin von Krosigk's diary entry on the events in Berlin between January 23 and 28, 1933, in *AdR: Das Kabinett von Schleicher*, no. 77, 316–19 (here 317).

123. Goebbels, *Die Tagebücher*, vol. 1, part 2/3, 118 (January 29, 1933).

124. Carl von Ossietzky, "Kamarilla," *Die Weltbühne* 29/5 (January 31, 1933), 153–55 (here 153); also in Ossietzky, *Sämtliche Schriften*, part 6, 459–62 (here 459).

125. Julius Elbau, "Kanzlersturz—und was dann?," *Vossische Zeitung* 39 (January 29, 1933).

126. See Ribbentrop, *Zwischen London und Moskau*, 40 (January 27, 1933); Turner, *Hitlers Weg zur Macht*, 182–83; Jones, "Greatest Stupidity of My Life," 73.

127. Goebbels, *Die Tagebücher*, vol. 1, part 2/3, 118 (January 29, 1933).

128. Ribbentrop, *Zwischen London und Moskau*, 41 (January 27, 1933).

129. Papen, *Der Wahrheit eine Gasse*, 269; Meissner, *Staatssekretär unter Ebert-Hitler-Hindenburg*, 266.

130. Papen, *Der Wahrheit eine Gasse*, 269–70. Cf. Turner, *Hitlers Weg zur Macht*, 185.

131. Schwerin von Krosigk's diary entries, in *AdR: Das Kabinett von Schleicher*, no. 77, 318.

132. Papen, *Der Wahrheit eine Gasse*, 271; Turner, *Hitlers Weg zur Macht*, 191–92; Kirsten A. Schäfer, *Werner von Blomberg: Hitlers erster Feldmarschall; Eine Biographie* (Paderborn, 2006), 97–100.

133. Papen, *Der Wahrheit eine Gasse*, 271; Turner, *Hitlers Weg zur Macht*, 191–92; Schäfer, *Werner von Blomberg*, 97–100.

134. Papen, *Der Wahrheit eine Gasse*, 271–72; Ribbentrop, *Zwischen London und Moskau*, 42 (January 29, 1933). Cf. Turner, *Hitlers Weg zur Macht*, 192–93.

135. Theodor Duesterberg, *Der Stahlhelm und Hitler* (Wolfenbüttel, 1949), 38–39. See Turner, *Hitlers Weg zur Macht*, 193–95.

136. Goebbels, *Die Tagebücher*, vol. 1, part 2/3, 119 (January 30, 1933).

137. On the coup rumors, see Turner, *Hitlers Weg zur Macht*, 197–98; Ullrich, *Adolf Hitler*, vol. 1, 407–8.

138. See Turner, *Hitlers Weg zur Macht*, 198–201; Meissner, *Staatssekretär unter Ebert-Hindenburg-Hitler*, 268–69.

139. Duesterberg, *Der Stahlhelm und Hitler*, 39–40; see Turner, *Hitlers Weg zur Macht*, 205–6.

140. Duesterberg, *Der Stahlhelm und Hitler*, 40–41; cf. Turner, *Hitlers Weg zur Macht*, 206–7.

141. See Schwerin von Krosigk's diary entries on the formation of Hitler's cabinet, January 29 and 30, 1933, in *AdR: Das Kabinett von Schleicher*, no. 79, 320–23 (here 323); Meissner, *Staatssekretär unter Ebert-Hindenburg-Hitler*, 270.

142. Goebbels, *Die Tagebücher*, vol. 1, part 2/3, 120 (January 31, 1933).

Chapter 11: Wait and See

1. Frank Bajohr et al., eds., *Bedrohung, Hoffnung, Skepsis: Vier Tagebücher des Jahres 1933* (Göttingen, 2013), 407.

2. Moltke, *Ein Leben in Deutschland*, 223 (January 30, 1933).

3. Lutz Graf Schwerin von Krosigk, *Es geschah in Deutschland: Menschenbilder unseres Jahrhunderts* (Tübingen, 1951), 147.

4. Ewald von Kleist-Schmenzin, "Die letzte Möglichkeit: Zur Ernennung Hitlers zum Reichskanzler am 30. Januar 1933," *Politische Studien* 10 (1959): 92. See also Turner, *Hitlers Weg zur Macht*, 196.

5. See Gerhard Ritter, *Carl Goerdeler und die deutsche Widerstandsbewegung* (Munich, 1954), 65–66. See also Jones, "Greatest Stupidity of My Life," 63.

6. F[ritz] K[lein], "An der Macht," *Deutsche Allgemeine Zeitung* 50 (January 30, 1933). See also Turner, *Die Großunternehmer und der Aufstieg Hitlers*, 391.

7. See Wieland Eschenhagen, ed., *Die "Machtergreifung": Tagebuch einer Wende nach Presseberichten vom 1. Januar bis 6. März 1933* (Darmstadt, 1982), 125, 142.

8. Kessler, *Das Tagebuch*, vol. 9, 538 (January 31, 1933), 539 (February 6, 1933).

9. Haffner, *Geschichte eines Deutschen*, 104–5, 106.

10. Sösemann, *Theodor Wolff*, 351–53.

11. See Gillessen, *Auf verlorenem Posten*, 92; Bussiek, *Benno Reifenberg*, 249.

12. "Der Sprung," *Vossische Zeitung* 50 (January 30, 1933). See also Dirk Blasius, "January 30, 1933: Tag der Machtergreifung," in *Tage deutscher Geschichte im 20. Jahrhundert*, ed. Dirk Blasius and Wilfried Loth (Göttingen, 2006), 43–58 (here 49–51).

13. Carl von Ossietzky, "Kavaliere und Rundköpfe," *Die Weltbühne* 29/6 (February 7, 1933), 193–95; also in Ossietzky, *Sämtliche Schriften*, vol. 6, 466–70.

14. See Josef Becker and Ruth Becker, eds., *Hitlers Machtergreifung: Vom Machtantritt Hitlers 30. Januar 1933 bis zur Besiegelung des Einparteienstaates 14. Juli 1933* (Munich, 1983), 34. See Winkler, *Der Weg in die Katastrophe*, 867.

15. Winkler, *Der Weg in die Katastrophe*, 867–68.

16. Peter Jahn, ed., *Die Gewerkschaften in der Endphase der Weimarer Republik 1930–1933* (Cologne, 1988), doc. 170, 830–32 (here 331, 832).

17. Becker and Becker, *Hitlers Machtergreifung*, 45.

18. See Wolfgang Benz, ed., *Die Juden in Deutschland 1933–1945: Leben unter nationalsozialistischer Herrschaft* (Munich, 1999), 17. See also Saul Friedländer, *Das Dritte Reich und die Juden*, vol. 1, *Die Jahre der Verfolgung 1933–1939* (Munich, 1998), 27.

19. *Die Verfolgung und Ermordung der europäischen Juden durch das nationalsozialistische Deutschland 1933–1945*, vol. 1, *Deutsches Reich 1933–1937*, ed. Wolf Gruner (Munich, 2008), doc. 1, 65–67 (here 66).

20. Frank Bajohr and Christoph Strupp, eds., *Fremde Blicke auf das "Dritte Reich": Berichte ausländischer Diplomaten über Herrschaft und Gesellschaft in Deutschland 1933–1945* (Göttingen, 2011), 356–57.

21. Cf. Detlev Clemens, *Herr Hitler in Germany: Wahrnehmung und Deutungen des Nationalsozialismus in Großbritannien 1920 bis 1939* (Göttingen, 1996), 252–55 (here 254).

22. Cf. Schäfer, *André François-Poncet als Botschafter in Berlin*, 163–68, 327–29.

23. Bajohr and Strupp, *Fremde Blicke auf das "Dritte Reich,"* 354–56 (here 355).

24. Klemperer, *I Shall Bear Witness: The Diaries of Victor Klemperer 1933–41*, trans. Martin Chalmers (London, 1999), 5–6.

25. See Becker and Becker, *Hitlers Machtergreifung*, 365–66.

Bibliography

Primary Sources

Akten der Reichskanzlei: Das Kabinett Bauer; 21. Juni 1919 bis 27. März 1920. Edited by Anton Golecki. Boppard am Rhein, 1980.

Akten der Reichskanzlei: Das Kabinett Cuno; 22. November 1922 bis 12. August 1923. Edited by Karl-Heinz Harbeck. Boppard am Rhein, 1968.

Akten der Reichskanzlei: Die Kabinette Luther I und II. Edited by Karl-Heinz Minuth. Boppard am Rhein, 1977.

Akten der Reichskanzlei: Das Kabinett Müller II; 28. Juni 1928 bis 27. März 1930. Vol. 1, *Juni 1928 bis Juli 1929*; Vol. 2, *August 1929 bis März 1930.* Edited by Martin Vogt. Boppard am Rhein, 1970.

Akten der Reichskanzlei: Die Kabinette Brüning I und II; Vol. 1, *30. März 1930 bis 28. Februar 1931*; Vol. 2, *1. März 1931 bis 10. Oktober 1931*; Vol. 3, *10. Oktober 1931 bis 30. Mai 1932.* Edited by Tilman Koops. Boppard am Rhein, 1982, 1990.

Akten der Reichskanzlei: Das Kabinett von Papen; 1. Juni bis 3. Dezember 1932. Vol. 1, *Juni bis September 1932*; Vol. 2, *September bis Dezember 1932.* Edited by Karl-Heinz Minuth. Boppard am Rhein, 1989.

Akten der Reichskanzlei: Das Kabinett von Schleicher; 3. Dezember 1932 bis 30. Januar 1933. Edited by Anton Golecki. Boppard am Rhein, 1986.

Allgemeiner Kongress der Arbeiter- und Soldatenräte Deutschlands: Vom 16. bis 21. Dezember 1918 im Abgeordnetenhause zu Berlin; Stenographische Berichte. Berlin, 1919.

Bajohr, Frank, and Christoph Strupp, eds. *Fremde Blicke auf das "Dritte Reich": Berichte ausländischer Diplomaten über Herrschaft und Gesellschaft in Deutschland 1933–1945.* Göttingen, 2011.

Bayerlein, Bernhard H., Leonid Babicenko, Fridrich I. Firsov, et al., eds. *Deutscher Oktober 1923: Ein Revolutionsplan und sein Scheitern.* Berlin, 2003.

Becker, Josef, and Ruth Becker, eds. *Hitlers Machtergreifung: Vom Machtantritt Hitlers 30. Januar 1933 bis zur Besiegelung des Einparteienstaates 14. Juli 1933.* Munich, 1983.

Benjamin, Walter. *Gesammelte Schriften*. Vol. 4, Part 1, edited by Tilman Rexroth. Frankfurt am Main, 1991.

Chronik eines Untergangs: Deutschland 1924–39; Die Beiträge Leopold Schwarzschilds in den Zeitschriften "Das Tage-Buch" und "Das Neue Tage-Buch." Edited by Andreas P. Wesemann. Vienna, 2005.

Czichon, Eberhard. *Wer verhalf Hitler zur Macht? Zum Anteil der deutschen Industrie an der Zerstörung der Weimarer Republik*. Cologne, 1967.

Der Gründungsparteitag der KPD: Protokoll und Materialien. Edited and with an introduction by Hermann Weber. Frankfurt am Main, 1969.

Deuerlein, Ernst, ed. *Der Aufstieg der NSDAP in Augenzeugenberichten*. Munich, 1974.

Deuerlein, Ernst, ed. *Der Hitler-Putsch: Bayerische Dokumente zum 8./9. November 1923*. Stuttgart, 1962.

Die Regierung der Volksbeauftragten 1918/19: Erster und Zweiter Teil. Edited by Susanne Miller with Heinrich Potthoff, introduction by Erich Matthias. Düsseldorf, 1969.

Die Protokolle der Reichstagsfraktion und des Fraktionsvorstands der Deutschen Zentrumspartei 1926–1933. Edited by Rudolf Morsey. Mainz, 1969.

Die Verfolgung und Ermordung der europäischen Juden durch das nationalsozialistische Deutschland 1933–1945. Vol. 1, *Deutsches Reich 1933–1937*, edited by Wolf Gruner. Munich, 2008.

Eschenhagen, Wieland, ed. *Die "Machtergreifung": Tagebuch einer Wende nach Presseberichten vom 1. Januar bis 6. März 1933*. Darmstadt, 1982.

Glatzer, Ruth. *Berlin zur Weimarer Zeit: Panorama einer Metropole 1919–1933*. Berlin, 2000.

Groß-Berliner Arbeiter- und Soldatenräte in der Revolution 1918/19: Dokumente des Vollzugsrates vom Ausbruch der Revolution bis zum 1. Reichsrätekongress. Edited by Gerhard Engel, Bärbel Holtz, and Ingo Materna. Berlin, 1993.

Hitler: Reden Schriften Anordnungen; Februar 1925 bis Januar 1933. Vol. 1, *Die Wiederbegründung der NSDAP: Februar 1925–Juni 1926*, edited by Clemens Vollnhals. Munich, 1992.

Hitler: Reden Schriften Anordnungen. Vol. 2, Part 1, *Juli 1926–Juli 1927*, edited by Bärbel Dusik. Munich, 1992.

Hitler: Reden Schriften Anordnungen. Vol. 3, Part 3, *Januar 1930–September 1930*, edited by Christian Hartmann. Munich, 1995.

Hitler: Reden Schriften Anordnungen. Vol. 4, Part 1, *Oktober 1930–Juni 1931*, edited by Constantin Goschler. Munich, 1994.

Hitler: Reden Schriften Anordnungen. Vol. 4, Part 2, *Juli 1931–Dezember 1931*, edited by Christian Hartmann. Munich, 1996.

Hitler: Reden Schriften Anordnungen. Vol. 4, Part 3, *Januar 1932–März 1932*, edited by Christian Hartmann. Munich, 1997.

Hitler: Reden Schriften Anordnungen. Vol. 5, Part 1, *April 1932–September 1932*, edited by Klaus A. Lankheit. Munich, 1996.

Hitler: Reden Schriften Anordnungen. Vol. 5, Part 2, *Oktober 1932–Januar 1933*, edited by Christian Hartmann and Klaus A. Lankheit. Munich, 1998.

Hitler: Sämtliche Aufzeichnungen 1905–1924. Edited by Eberhard Jäckel with Axel Kuhn. Stuttgart, 1980.

Hubatsch, Walther. *Hindenburg und der Staat: Aus den Papieren des Generalfeldmarschalls und Reichspräsidenten von 1878 bis 1934.* Göttingen, 1966.

Jochmann, Werner. *Nationalsozialismus und Revolution: Ursprung und Geschichte der NSDAP in Hamburg 1922–1933; Dokumente.* Frankfurt am Main, 1968.

Könnemann, Erwin, and Gerhard Schulz, eds. *Der Kapp-Lüttwitz-Ludendorff-Putsch: Dokumente.* Munich, 2002.

Lessing, Theodor. *"Wir machen nicht mit!" Schriften gegen den Nationalismus und zur Judenfrage.* Edited by Jörg Wollenberg with Helmut Donat. Bremen, 1997.

Longerich, Peter, ed. *Die Erste Republik: Dokumente zur Geschichte des Weimarer Staates.* Munich, 1992.

Luxemburg, Rosa. *Gesammelte Werke.* Vol. 4, *August 1914 bis Januar 1919.* Berlin, 1974.

Mann, Thomas. *Essays II: 1914–1926.* Edited by Hermann Kurzke. Frankfurt am Main, 2002.

Ossietzky, Carl von. *Sämtliche Schriften.* Vol. 1, *1911–1921,* edited by Mathias Bertram, Ute Maak, and Christoph Schottes. Reinbek bei Hamburg, 1994.

Ossietzky, Carl von. *Sämtliche Schriften.* Vol. 5, *1929–1930,* edited by Bärbel Boldt, Ute Maak, and Günther Nickel. Reinbek bei Hamburg, 1994.

Ossietzky, Carl von. *Sämtliche Schriften.* Vol. 6, *1931–1933,* edited by Gerhard Kraiker, Günther Nickel, Renke Siems, and Elke Suhr. Reinbek bei Hamburg, 1994.

Paasche, Hans. *"Ändert Euren Sinn!" Schriften eines Revolutionärs.* Edited by Helmut Donat and Helga Paasche. Bremen, 1992.

Politik und Wirtschaft in der Krise 1930–1932: Quellen zur Ära Brüning. Edited by Ilse Maurer and Udo Wengst with Jürgen Heideking, introduction by Gerhard Schulz. Düsseldorf, 1980.

Quellen zur Geschichte der deutschen Gewerkschaftsbewegung im 20. Jahrhundert. Vol. 4, *Die Gewerkschaften in der Endphase der Republik 1930–1933,* edited by Peter Jahn with Detlev Brunner. Cologne, 1988.

Ritter, Gerhard, and Susanne Miller, eds. *Die deutsche Revolution 1918–1919: Dokumente.* Hamburg, 1975.

Schönhoven, Klaus, and Hans Jochen Vogel, eds. *Frühe Warnungen vor dem Nationalsozialismus: Ein historisches Lesebuch.* Bonn, 1998.

Staat und NSDAP: Quellen zur Ära Brüning. Edited by Ilse Maurer and Udo Wengst, introduction by Gerhard Schulz. Düsseldorf, 1977.

Ulrich, Bernd, and Benjamin Ziemann, eds. *Frontalltag im Ersten Weltkrieg: Wahn und Wirklichkeit; Quellen und Dokumente.* Frankfurt am Main, 1994.

Weber, Hermann, and Bernhard H. Bayerlein, eds. *Der Thälmann-Skandal: Geheime Korrespondenzen mit Stalin.* Berlin, 2003.

Diaries, Correspondence, and Memoirs

Aus den Geburtsstunden der Weimarer Republik: Das Tagebuch des Obersten Ernst van den Bergh. Edited by Wolfram Wette. Düsseldorf, 1991.

Baden, Prinz Max von. *Erinnerungen und Dokumente.* Berlin, 1927.

Bajohr, Frank, Beate Meyer, and Joachim Szodrzynski, eds. *Bedrohung, Hoffnung, Skepsis: Vier Tagebücher des Jahres 1933*. Göttingen, 2013.

Brill, Hermann. *Gegen den Strom*. Offenbach, 1946.

Brüning, Heinrich. *Memoiren 1918–1934*. Stuttgart, 1970.

D'Abernon, Viscount Edgar Vincent. *Amabassador of Peace*. London, 1930.

Die Deutschnationalen und die Zerstörung der Weimarer Republik: Aus dem Tagebuch von Reinhold Quaatz 1928–1933. Edited by Hermann Weiß and Paul Hoser. Munich, 1989.

Die Tagebücher von Joseph Goebbels. Part 1, *Aufzeichnungen 1923–1941*, Vol. 2/Part 1, *Dezember 1929–Mai 1931*, edited by Elke Fröhlich. Munich, 2005.

Die Tagebücher von Joseph Goebbels. Part 1, Vol. 2/Part 2, *Juni 1931–September 1932*, edited by Elke Fröhlich. Munich, 2004.

Die Tagebücher von Joseph Goebbels. Part 1, Vol. 2/Part 3, *Oktober 1932–März 1934*, edited by Elke Fröhlich and Angela Hermann. Munich, 2000.

Dittmann, Wilhelm. *Erinnerungen*. Vol. 2, introduction by Jürgen Rojahn. Frankfurt am Main, 1995.

Duesterberg, Theodor. *Der Stahlhelm und Hitler*. Wolfenbüttel, 1949.

Groener, Wilhelm. *Lebenserinnerungen: Jugend, Generalstab, Weltkrieg*. Göttingen, 1957.

Grosz, George. *Ein kleines und ein großes Nein: Sein Leben erzählt von ihm selbst*. Reinbek bei Hamburg, 1974.

Grzesinski, Albert. *Im Kampf um die Republik: Erinnerungen eines Sozialdemokraten*. Edited by Eberhard Kolb. Munich, 2001.

Haffner, Sebastian. *Geschichte eines Deutschen: Die Erinnerungen 1914–1933*. Stuttgart, 2000.

Hampe, Karl. *Kriegstagebuch 1914–1919*. Edited by Folker Reichert and Eike Wolgast. Munich, 2004.

Hauptmann, Gerhard. *Diarium 1917–1933*. Edited by Martin Machatzke. Frankfurt am Main, 1980.

Hess, Rudolf. *Briefe 1908–1933*. Edited by Wolf Rüdiger Hess. Munich, 1987.

Heuss, Theodor. *Bürger der Weimarer Republik: Briefe 1918–1933*. Edited by Michael Dorrmann. Munich, 2008.

Ilsemann, Sigurd von. *Der Kaiser in Holland: Aufzeichnungen des letzten Flügeladjutanten Kaiser Wilhelms II aus Amerongen und Doorn 1918–1923*. Munich, 1967.

Kerr, Alfred. *Berlin wird Berlin: Briefe aus der Reichshauptstadt 1897–1922*. Vol. 4, *1917–1922*, edited by Deborah Vietor-Engländer. Göttingen, 2021.

Kerr, Alfred. *Walther Rathenau: Erinnerungen eines Freundes*. Amsterdam, 1935.

Kessler, Harry Graf. *Das Tagebuch*. Vol. 6, *1916–1918*, edited by Günther Riederer with Christoph Hilse. Stuttgart, 2006.

Kessler, Harry Graf. *Das Tagebuch*. Vol. 7, *1919–1923*, edited by Angela Rheinthal with Janna Brechmacher and Christoph Hilse. Stuttgart, 2007.

Kessler, Harry Graf. *Das Tagebuch*. Vol. 8, *1923–1926*, edited by Angela Reinthal, Günter Riederer, and Jörg Schuster. Stuttgart, 2009.

Kessler, Harry Graf. *Das Tagebuch*. Vol. 9, *1926–1932*, edited by Sabine Gruber and Ulrich Ott with Christoph Hilse and Nadin Weiss. Stuttgart, 2010.

Klemperer, Victor. *Ich will Zeugnis ablegen bis zum letzten: Tagebücher 1933–1945*. Edited by Walter Nowojski with Hadwig Klemperer. Berlin, 1995.

Klemperer, Victor. *Leben sammeln, nicht fragen wozu und warum: Tagebücher 1918–1924.* Edited by Walter Nowojski with Christian Löser. Berlin, 1996.

Klemperer, Victor. *Leben sammeln, nicht fragen wozu und warum: Tagebücher 1925–1932.* Edited by Walter Nowojski with Christian Löser. Berlin, 1996.

Klemperer, Victor. *Man möchte immer weinen und lachen in einem: Revolutionstagebuch 1919.* Berlin, 2015.

Kollwitz, Käthe. *Die Tagebücher 1908–1945.* Edited and with an epilogue by Jutta Bohnke-Kollwitz. Munich, 2007.

Ludendorff, Margarethe. *Als ich Ludendorffs Frau war.* Edited by Walther Ziersch. Munich, 1929.

Luther, Hans. *Politiker ohne Partei: Erinnerungen.* Stuttgart, 1960.

Luxemburg, Rosa. *Gesammelte Briefe.* Vol. 5. Berlin 1987.

Mann, Klaus. *Der Wendepunkt: Ein Lebensbericht.* Frankfurt am Main, 1963.

Mann, Klaus. *Tagebücher 1931 bis 1933.* Edited by Joachim Heimannsberg, Peter Laemmle, and Wilfried F. Schoeller. Munich, 1989.

Mann, Thomas. *Tagebücher 1918–1921.* Edited by Peter de Mendelssohn. Frankfurt am Main, 1979.

Mayer, Gustav. *Als deutsch-jüdischer Historiker in Krieg und Revolution 1914–1920: Tage-bücher, Aufzeichnungen, Briefe.* Edited and with an introduction by Gottfried Nied-hardt. Munich, 2009.

Meissner, Otto. *Staatssekretär unter Ebert-Hindenburg-Hitler.* Hamburg, 1950.

Moltke, Dorothy von. *Ein Leben in Deutschland: Briefe aus Kreisau und Berlin 1907–1934.* Edited by Beate Ruhm von Oppen. Munich, 1999.

Mühsam, Erich. *Tagebücher (1910–1924).* Edited and with an epilogue by Chris Hirte. Munich, 1994.

Müller, Hermann. *Die November-Revolution: Erinnerungen.* Berlin, 1928.

Noske, Gustav. *Von Kiel bis Kapp: Zur Geschichte der deutschen Revolution.* Berlin, 1920.

Papen, Franz von. *Der Wahrheit eine Gasse.* Munich, 1952.

Pringsheim, Hedwig. *Meine Manns: Briefe an Maximilian Harden 1900–1922.* Edited by Helga and Manfred Neumann. Berlin, 2006.

Pringsheim, Hedwig. *Tagebücher.* Vol. 6, *1917–1922,* edited by Christina Herbst. Göttingen, 2017.

Pünder, Hermann. *Politik in der Reichskanzlei: Aufzeichnungen aus den Jahren 1929–1932.* Edited by Thilo Vogelsang. Stuttgart, 1961.

Rathenau, Walther. *Briefe.* Part 2, *1914–1922,* edited by Alexander Jaser, Clemens Picht, and Ernst Schulin. Düsseldorf, 2006.

Reissner, Larissa. *Hamburg auf den Barrikaden: Erlebtes und Erhörtes aus dem Hamburger Aufstand.* Berlin, 1925.

Ribbentrop, Joachim. *Zwischen London und Moskau: Erinnerungen und letzte Aufzeichnungen; Aus dem Nachlass.* Edited by Annelies Ribbentrop. Leoni am Starnberger See, 1961.

Schwerin von Krosigk, Lutz Graf. *Es geschah in Deutschland: Menschenbilder unseres Jahrhunderts.* Tübingen, 1951.

Shedletzky, Itta, ed. *Betty Scholem–Gershom Scholem: Mutter und Sohn im Briefwechsel 1917–1946.* Munich, 1989.

Sösemann, Bernd, ed. *Theodor Wolff: Der Journalist; Berichte und Leitartikel.* Düsseldorf, 1993.

Stampfer, Friedrich. *Die ersten 14 Jahre der Deutschen Republik.* Offenbach, 1947.

Sternheim, Thea. *Tagebücher 1903–1971.* Vol. 1, *1903–1925*; Vol. 2, *1925–1936.* Edited by Thomas Ehrmann and Regula Wyss. Göttingen, 2002.

Stockhausen, Max von. *Sechs Jahre Reichskanzlei: Von Rapallo bis Locarno; Erinnerungen und Tagebuchnotizen 1922–1927.* Edited by Walter Görlitz. Bonn, 1954.

Stresemann, Gustav. *Vermächtnis: Der Nachlass in drei Bänden.* Edited by Henry Bernhard. Berlin, 1932.

Thimme, Annelise, ed. *Friedrich Thimme 1868–1938: Ein politischer Historiker, Publizist und Schriftsteller in seinen Briefen.* Boppard am Rhein, 1994.

Troeltsch, Ernst. *Die Fehlgeburt einer Republik: Spektator in Berlin 1918 bis 1922.* Collected and with an epilogue by Johann Hinrich Claussen. Frankfurt am Main, 1994.

Witzmann, Georg. *Thüringen von 1918–1933: Erinnerungen eines Politikers.* Meisenheim am Glan, 1958.

Wolff, Theodor. *Tagebücher 1914–1919.* Part 2, edited and with an introduction by Bernd Sösemann. Boppard am Rhein, 1984.

Zuckmayer, Carl. *Als wär's ein Stück von mir: Horen der Freundschaft.* Stuttgart-Hamburg, 1966.

Zweig, Stefan. *Briefe 1920–1931.* Edited by Knut Beck and Jeffrey B. Berlin. Frankfurt am Main, 2000.

Zweig, Stefan. *Die Welt von Gestern: Erinnerungen eines Europäers.* Stuttgart, n.d.

Secondary Literature

Albrecht, Richard. *Der militante Sozialdemokrat: Carlo Mierendorff 1897 bis 1943; Eine Biographie.* Berlin, 1987.

Alexander, Thomas. *Carl Severing: Sozialdemokrat aus Westfalen mit preussischen Tugenden.* Bielefeld, 1992.

Alt, Peter-André. *Franz Kafka: Der ewige Sohn; Eine Biographie.* Munich, 2005.

Austermann, Philipp. *Der Weimarer Reichstag: Die schleichende Ausschaltung, Entmachtung und Zerstörung eines Parlaments.* Vienna, 2020.

Authors' collective. *Ernst Thälmann: Eine Biographie.* East Berlin, 1980.

Becker, Sabine. *Experiment Weimar: Eine Kulturgeschichte Deutschlands 1918–1933.* Darmstadt, 2021.

Berghahn, Volker. *Der Stahlhelm: Bund der Frontsoldaten 1918–1935.* Düsseldorf, 1966.

Bering, Dietz. *Kampf um Namen: Bernhard Weiß gegen Joseph Goebbels.* Stuttgart, 1991.

Bernstein, Eduard. *Die deutsche Revolution von 1918/19: Geschichte und Entstehung der ersten Arbeitsperiode der deutschen Republik.* Edited and with an introduction by Heinrich August Winkler. Annotated by Teresa Löwe. Bonn, 1998.

Bieber, Hans-Joachim. *Bürgertum in der Revolution: Bürgerräte und Bürgerstreiks in Deutschland 1918–1920.* Hamburg, 1992.

Bieber, Hans-Joachim. *Gewerkschaften in Krieg und Revolution: Arbeiterbewegung, Industrie, Staat und Militär in Deutschland 1914–1920.* Part 2. Hamburg, 1981.

Bisky, Jens. *Berlin: Biographie einer großen Stadt*. Berlin, 2019.

Blasius, Dirk. "30. Januar 1933: Tag der Machtergreifung." In *Tage deutscher Geschichte im 20. Jahrhundert*, edited by Dirk Blasius and Wilfried Loth. Göttingen, 2006.

Bollmeyer, Heiko. *Der steinige Weg zur Demokratie: Die Weimarer Nationalversammlung zwischen Kaiserreich und Republik*. Frankfurt am Main, 2007.

Bracher, Karl Dietrich. *Die Auflösung der Weimarer Republik: Eine Studie zum Problem des Machtverfalls in der Demokratie*. Villingen, 1960.

Brenner, Wolfgang. *Walther Rathenau: Deutscher und Jude*. Munich, 2005.

Büttner, Ursula. *Weimar: Die überforderte Republik 1918–1933*. Stuttgart, 2008.

Bussiek, Dagmar. *Benno Reifenberg 1892–1970: Eine Biographie*. Göttingen, 2011.

Chernow, Ron. *The Warburgs: The Twentieth-Century Odyssey of a Remarkable Jewish Family*. London, 1993.

Ciolek-Kümper, Jutta. *Wahlkampf in Lippe: Die Wahlkampfpropaganda der NSDAP zur Landtagswahl am 15. Januar 1933*. Munich, 1976.

Clark, Christopher. *The Iron Kingdom: The Rise and Downfall of Prussia, 1600–1947*. New York, 2007.

Clemens, Detlev. *Herr Hitler in Germany: Wahrnehmung und Deutungen des Nationalsozialismus in Großbritannien 1920 bis 1939*. Göttingen, 1996.

Conze, Eckart. *Die große Illusion: Versailles 1919 und die Neuordnung der Welt*. Munich, 2018.

Cornelißen, Christoph. *Gerhard Ritter: Geschichtswissenschaft und Politik im 20. Jahrhundert*, Düsseldorf, 2001.

Curtius, Julius. *Der Young-Plan: Entstehung und Wahrheit*. Stuttgart, 1970.

Deist, Wilhelm. "Die Politik der Seekriegsleitung und die Rebellion der Flotte Ende 1918." *Vierteljahrshefte für Zeitgeschichte* 16 (1968): 341–68.

Dickmann, Fritz. "Die Regierungsbildung in Thüringen als Modell der Machtergreifung: Ein Brief Hitlers aus dem Jahre 1930." *Vierteljahrshefte für Zeitgeschichte* 14 (1966): 454–64.

Döring, Martin. *"Parlamentarischer Arm der Bewegung": Die Nationalsozialisten im Reichstag der Weimarer Republik*. Düsseldorf, 2001.

Erdmann, Karl Dietrich, and Hagen Schulze. *Weimar: Selbstpreisgabe einer Demokratie; Eine Bilanz heute*. Düsseldorf, 1984.

Erger, Johannes. *Der Kapp-Lüttwitz-Putsch: Ein Beitrag zur deutschen Innenpolitik 1919/20*. Düsseldorf, 1967.

Eschenburg, Theodor. *Die improvisierte Demokratie: Gesammelte Aufsätze zur Weimarer Republik*. Munich, 1964.

Falter, Jürgen. *Thomas Lindenberger und Siegfried Schumann: Wahlen und Abstimmungen in der Weimarer Republik; Materialien zum Wahlverhalten 1919–1933*. Munich, 1986.

Feldman, Gerald D. *The Great Disorder: Politics, Economics, and Society in the German Inflation, 1914–1924*. Oxford, 1997.

Feldman, Gerald D. *Hugo Stinnes: Biographie eines Industriellen 1870–1924*. Munich, 1998.

Fest, Joachim. *Hitler: Eine Biographie*. Frankfurt am Main, 1973.

Flechtheim, Ossip K. *Die KPD in der Weimarer Republik*. Frankfurt am Main, 1969.

Flemming, Jens. *Landwirtschaftliche Interessen und Demokratie: Ländliche Gesellschaft, Agrarverbände und Staat 1890–1925*. Bonn, 1978.

Friedländer, Saul. *Das Dritte Reich und die Juden.* Vol. 1, *Die Jahre der Verfolgung 1933–1939.* Munich, 1998.

Führer, Karl Christian. "Die Sozialpolitik der Weimarer Republik." In *Aufbruch und Abbrüche: Das Handbuch der Weimarer Republik,* edited by Nadine Rossol and Benjamin Ziemann. Darmstadt, 2021.

Gaertringen, Friedrich Freiherr Hiller von. "Die Deutschnationale Volkspartei." In *Das Ende der Parteien 1933,* edited by Erich Matthias and Rudolf Morsey. Düsseldorf, 1960.

Gall, Lothar. *Walther Rathenau: Portrait einer Epoche.* Munich, 2009.

Gallus, Alexander. "Die umkämpfte Revolution." *Zeit-Geschichte* 6 (2018): 14–20.

Gallus, Alexander, ed. *Die vergessene Revolution 1918/19.* Göttingen, 2010.

Gallus, Alexander. *Heimat "Weltbühne": Eine Intellektuellengeschichte im 20. Jahrhundert.* Göttingen, 2012.

Gallus, Alexander, and Ernst Piper, eds. *Die Weimarer Republik als Ort der Demokratiegeschichte: Eine kritische Bestandsaufnahme.* Bonn, 2023.

Gietinger, Klaus. *Der Konterevolutionär: Waldemar Pabst—eine deutsche Karriere.* Hamburg, 2008.

Gietinger, Klaus. *Eine Leiche schwimmt im Landwehrkanal: Die Ermordung Rosa Luxemburgs.* Hamburg, 2008.

Gillessen, Günther. *Auf verlorenem Posten: Die Frankfurter Zeitung im Dritten Reich.* Berlin, 1986.

Grau, Bernhard. *Kurt Eisner 1867–1919: Eine Biographie.* Munich, 2001.

Gutsche, Willibald. *Ein Kaiser im Exil: Der letzte deutsche Kaiser Wilhelm II in Holland.* Marburg, 1991.

Haardt, Oliver F. Ra, and Christopher Clark. "Die Weimarer Reichsverfassung als Moment der Geschichte." In *Das Wagnis der Demokratie: Eine Anatomie der Weimarer Reichsverfassung,* edited by Horst Dreier and Christian Waldhoff. Munich, 2018.

Hallgarten, George W. F. *Hitler, Reichswehr und Industrie: Zur Geschichte 1918–1933.* Frankfurt am Main, 1955.

Hannover, Heinrich, and Elisabeth Hannover-Drück. *Politische Justiz 1918–1933.* Frankfurt am Main, 1966.

Harpprecht, Klaus. *Thomas Mann: Eine Biographie.* Reinbek bei Hamburg, 1995.

Hecker, Hans. "Karl Radeks Werben um die deutsche Rechte: Die Sowjetunion und der Ruhrkampf." In *Der Schatten des Weltkriegs: Die Ruhrbesetzung 1923,* edited by Gerd Krumeich and Joachim Schröder. Essen, 2004.

Hehl, Ulrich von. *Wilhelm Marx 1863–1946: Eine politische Biographie.* Mainz, 1987.

Hennig, Diethard. *Johannes Hoffmann: Sozialdemokrat und Bayerischer Ministerpräsident.* Munich, 1990.

Herbert, Ulrich. *Best: Biographische Studien über Radikalismus, Weltanschauung und Vernunft 1903–1999.* Bonn, 1999.

Herbert, Ulrich. *Geschichte Deutschlands im 20. Jahrhundert.* Munich, 2014.

Hering, Rainer. *Konstruierte Nation: Der Alldeutsche Verband 1890–1939.* Hamburg, 2003.

Hett, Benjamin Carter. *The Death of Democracy: Hitler's Rise to Power and the Downfall of the Weimar Republic.* New York, 2018.

Heusler, Andreas. *Das Braune Haus: Wie Munich "Hauptstadt der Bewegung" wurde.* Munich, 2008.

Hömig, Herbert. *Brüning: Kanzler in der Krise; Eine Weimarer Biographie.* Paderborn, 2000.

Hoffmann, Dieter. *Der Skandal: Hindenburgs Entscheidung für Hitler.* Bremen, 2020.

Holste, Heiko. *Warum Weimar: Wie Deutschlands erste Republik zu ihrem ersten Geburtsort kam.* Vienna, 2017.

Holzbach, Heidrun. *Das "System" Hugenberg: Die Organisation bürgerlicher Sammlungspolitik vor dem Aufstieg der NSDAP.* Stuttgart, 1981.

Horn, Wolfgang. *Der Marsch zur Machtergreifung: Die NSDAP bis 1933.* Königstein, 1980.

Hürter, Johannes. *Wilhelm Groener: Reichswehrminister am Ende der Weimarer Republik (1928–1932).* Munich, 1993.

Jessen-Klingenberg, Manfred. "Die Ausrufung der Republik durch Philipp Scheidemann am 9.11.1918." *Geschichte in Wissenschaft und Unterricht* 19 (1968): 649–56.

Jones, Larry Eugene. "The Greatest Stupidity of My Life: Alfred Hugenberg and the Formation of the Hitler Cabinet, January 1933." *Journal of Contemporary History* 27 (1992): 63–87.

Jones, Larry Eugene. *Hitler Versus Hindenburg: The 1932 Presidential Elections and the End of the Weimar Republic.* Cambridge, 2016.

Jones, Larry Eugene. "Taming the Nazi Beast: Kurt von Schleicher and the End of the Weimar Republic." In *From Weimar to Hitler: Studies in the Dissolution of the Weimar Republic and the Establishment of the Third Reich, 1932–1934*, edited by Hermann Beck and Larry Eugene Jones. New York, 2019.

Jones, Larry Eugene. "Von der Demokratie zur Diktatur: Das Ende der Weimarer Republik und der Aufstieg des Nationalsozialismus." In *Aufbruch und Abgründe: Das Handbuch der Weimarer Republik*, edited by Nadine Rossol and Benjamin Ziemann. Darmstadt, 2021.

Jones, Mark. *Am Anfang war Gewalt: Die deutsche Revolution 1918/19 und der Beginn der Weimarer Republik.* Translated by Karl Heinz Siber. Berlin, 2017.

Käppner, Joachim. *1918: Aufstand für die Freiheit; Die Revolution der Besonnenen.* Munich, 2017.

Kellerhoff, Sven Felix. *Der Putsch: Hitlers erster Griff nach der Macht.* Stuttgart, 2023.

Kellerhoff, Sven Felix. *Die NSDAP: Eine Partei und ihre Mitglieder.* Stuttgart, 2017.

Kershaw, Ian. *Hitler 1889–1936: Hubris.* London, 1998.

Kessler, Harry Graf. *Walther Rathenau: Sein Leben und Werk.* Berlin, n.d. Originally published in Wiesbaden, 1928.

Kissenkötter, Udo. *Gregor Straßer und die NSDAP.* Stuttgart, 1978.

Kluge, Ulrich. *Soldatenräte und Revolution: Studien zur Militärpolitik in Deutschland 1917/18.* Göttingen, 1975.

Kluke, Paul. "Der Fall Potempa." *Vierteljahrshefte für Zeitgeschichte* 5 (1957): 279–97.

Könnemann, Erwin, and Hans-Joachim Krusch. *Aktionseinheit contra Kapp-Putsch im März 1920 und der Kampf der deutschen Arbeiterklasse sowie anderer Werktätiger gegen die Errichtung der Militärdiktatur und für demokratische Verhältnisse.* East Berlin, 1972.

Kolb, Eberhard. *Der Frieden von Versailles*. Munich, 2005.

Kolb, Eberhard. *Die Weimarer Republik*. Munich, 1988.

Kolb, Eberhard. *Gustav Stresemann*. Munich, 2003.

Kolb, Eberhard. *Umbrüche deutscher Geschichte 1866/71, 1918/19, 1929/33: Ausgewählte Aufsätze*. Edited by Dieter Langewiesche and Klaus Schönhoven. Munich, 1993.

Kopper, Christopher. *Hjalmar Schacht: Aufstieg und Fall von Hitlers mächtigstem Bankier*. Munich, 2006.

Koszyk, Kurt. *Gustav Stresemann: Der kaisertreue Demokrat; Eine Biographie*. Cologne, 1989.

Krüger, Gabriele. *Die Brigade Ehrhardt*. Hamburg, 1971.

Krüger, Peter. *Die Außenpolitik der Republik von Weimar*. Darmstadt, 1993.

Küppers, Heinrich. *Joseph Wirth: Parlamentarier, Minister und Kanzler der Weimarer Republik*. Stuttgart, 1997.

Kurz, Thomas. *Blutmai: Sozialdemokraten und Kommunisten im Brennpunkt der Berliner Ereignisse von 1929*. Berlin, 1986.

Kurzke, Hermann. *Thomas Mann: Das Leben als Kunstwerk*. Munich, 1999.

Lahme, Tilmann. *Die Manns: Geschichte einer Familie*. Frankfurt am Main, 2015.

Lang, Jochen. "Martin Bormann—Hitlers Sekretär." In *Die braune Elite: 22 biographische Skizzen*, edited by Ronald Smelser and Rainer Zitelmann. Darmstadt, 1989.

Large, David Clay. *Where Ghosts Walked: Munich's Road to the Third Reich*. New York, 1997.

Laschitza, Annelies. *Im Lebensrausch, trotz alledem: Rosa Luxemburg; Eine Biographie*. Berlin, 1996.

Leonhard, Jörn. *Der überforderte Frieden: Versailles und die Welt 1918–1923*. Munich, 2018.

Leßmann, Peter. *Die preußische Schutzpolizei in der Weimarer Republik: Streifendienst und Straßenkampf*. Düsseldorf, 1989.

Linse, Ulrich. *Barfüßige Propheten: Erlöser der zwanziger Jahre*. Berlin, 1983.

Longerich, Peter. *Außer Kontrolle: Deutschland 1923*. Vienna, 2022.

Longerich, Peter. *Deutschland 1918–1933: Die Weimarer Republik; Handbuch zur Geschichte*. Hanover, 1995.

Longerich, Peter. *Die braunen Bataillone: Geschichte der SA*. Munich, 1989.

Longerich, Peter. *Hitler: Biographie*. Munich, 2015.

Luban, Ottokar. "Demokratische Sozialistin oder 'blutige Rosa'? Rosa Luxemburg und die KPD-Führung im Berliner Januaraufstand 1919." *Internationale Wissenschaftliche Korrespondenz zur Geschichte der deutschen Arbeiterbewegung* 36 (1999): 176–207.

Lucas, Erhard. *Märzrevolution 1920*. 3 vols. Frankfurt am Main, 1970–78.

Machtan, Lothar. *Der Kaisersohn bei Hitler*. Hamburg, 2006.

Malinowski, Stephan. *Die Hohenzollern und die Nazis: Geschichte einer Kollaboration*. Berlin, 2021.

Martynkewicz, Wolfgang. *1920: Am Nullpunkt des Sinns*. Berlin, 2019.

Marwedel, Rainer. *Theodor Lessing: Eine Biographie*. Darmstadt, 1987.

Mauersberger, Volker. *Hitler in Weimar: Der Fall einer deutschen Kulturhauptstadt*. Berlin, 1999.

Maurer, Traude. *Ostjuden in Deutschland 1918–1933*. Hamburg, 1986.

McElligott, Anthony. *Rethinking the Weimar Republic: Authority and Authoritarianism 1916–1936*. London, 2014.

Meier-Welcker, Hans. *Seeckt*. Frankfurt am Main, 1967.

Mergel, Thomas. "Wahlen, Wahlkämpfe und Demokratie." In *Aufbruch und Abgründe: Das Handbuch der Weimarer Republik*, edited by Nadine Rossol and Benjamin Ziemann. Darmstadt, 2021.

Merseburger, Peter. *Mythos Weimar: Zwischen Geist und Macht*. Stuttgart, 1998.

Meyer, Gerd. "Die Reparationspolitik: Ihre außen- und innenpolitischen Rückwirkungen." In *Die Weimarer Republik 1918–1933: Politik-Wirtschaft-Gesellschaft*, edited by Karl Dietrich Bracher, Manfred Funke, and Hans-Adolf Jacobsen. Düsseldorf, 1987.

Michalka, Wolfgang. "Joachim von Ribbentrop—Vom Spirituosenhändler zum Außenminister." In *Die braune Elite: 22 biographische Skizzen*, edited by Ronald Smelser and Rainer Zitelmann. Darmstadt, 1989.

Miller, Susanne. *Die Bürde der Macht: Die deutsche Sozialdemokratie 1918–1920*. Düsseldorf, 1978.

Möller, Horst. *Die Weimarer Republik: Demokratie in der Krise*. Munich, 2018.

Mommsen, Hans. *Die verspielte Freiheit: Der Weg der Republik von Weimar in den Untergang 1918 bis 1933*. Berlin, 1989.

Morsey, Rudolf. "Die Deutsche Zentrumspartei." In *Das Ende der Parteien 1933*, edited by Erich Matthias and Rudolf Morsey. Düsseldorf, 1960.

Morsey, Rudolf. "Hitler als Braunschweigischer Regierungsrat." *Vierteljahrshefte für Zeitgeschichte* 8 (1960): 419–48.

Mühlhausen, Walter. *Friedrich Ebert 1871–1925: Reichspräsident der Weimarer Republik*. Bonn, 2006.

Muth, Heinrich. "Das 'Kölner Gespräch' am 4. Januar 1933." *Geschichte in Wissenschaft und Unterricht* 37 (1986): Part 1, 463–80; Part 2, 529–41.

Nebelin, Manfred. *Ludendorff: Diktator im Ersten Weltkrieg*. Munich, 2010.

Neebe, Reinhard. *Großindustrie, Staat und NSDAP 1930–1933: Paul Silverberg und der Reichsverband der Deutschen Industrie in der Krise der Weimarer Republik*. Marburg, 1979.

Neliba, Günter. "Wilhelm Frick und Thüringen als Experimentierfeld für die nationalsozialistische Machtergreifung." In *Nationalsozialismus in Thüringen*, edited by Detlev Heiden and Gunther Mai. Weimar, 1995.

Niess, Wolfgang. *Der Hitlerputsch 1923: Geschichte eines Hochverrats*. Munich, 2023.

Nordalm, Jens. *Erich Marcks (1861–1938) in der deutschen Geschichtswissenschaft*. Berlin, 2003.

Ostwald, Hans. *Sittengeschichte der Inflation: Ein Kulturdokument aus den Jahren des Marksturzes*. Berlin, 1931.

Petzold, Joachim. *Franz von Papen: Ein deutsches Verhängnis*. Munich, 1995.

Peukert, Detlev J. K. *Die Weimarer Republik: Krisenjahre der klassischen Moderne*. Frankfurt am Main, 1987.

Piper, Ernst. *Rosa Luxemburg: Ein Leben*. Munich, 2018.

Plumpe, Werner. *Carl Duisberg 1861–1935: Anatomie eines Industriellen*. Munich, 2016.

Post, Bernhard. "Vorgezogene Machtübernahme 1932: Die Regierung Sauckel." In

Nationalsozialismus in Thüringen, edited by Detlev Heiden and Gunther Mai. Weimar, 1995.

Pufendorf, Astrid von. *Die Plancks: Eine Familie zwischen Patriotismus und Widerstand*. Berlin, 2006.

Pyta, Wolfram. *Hindenburg: Herrschaft zwischen Hohenzollern und Hitler*. Munich, 2007.

Reichel, Peter. *Der tragische Kanzler: Hermann Müller und die SPD in der Weimarer Republik*. Munich, 2018.

Ribhegge, Wilhelm. *August Winnig: Eine historische Persönlichkeitsanalyse*. Bonn, 1973.

Richter, Ludwig. *Die Deutsche Volkspartei 1918–1933*. Düsseldorf, 2002.

Ritter, Gerhard. *Carl Goedeler und die deutsche Widerstandsbewegung*. Munich, 1954.

Ritter, Gerhard. *Staatskunst und Kriegshandwerk: Das Problem des "Militarismus" in Deutschland*. Vol. 4, *Die Herrschaft des deutschen Militarismus und die Katastrophe von 1918*. Munich, 1968.

Röhl, John C. G. *Wilhelm II: Der Weg in den Abgrund 1900–1941*. Munich, 2008.

Rösch, Matthias. *Die Münchner NSDAP 1925–1933: Eine Untersuchung zur inneren Struktur der NSDAP in der Weimarer Republik*. Munich, 2002.

Rosenberg, Arthur. *Geschichte der Weimarer Republik*. Edited by Kurt Kersten. Frankfurt am Main, 1961.

Rossol, Nadine, and Benjamin Ziemann, eds. *Aufbruch und Abgründe: Das Handbuch der Weimarer Republik*. Darmstadt, 2021.

Rudolph, Karsten. "Untergang auf Raten: Die Auflösung und Zerstörung der demokratischen Kultur in Thüringen 1930 im regionalen Vergleich." In *Weimar 1930: Politik und Kultur im Vorfeld der NS-Diktatur*, edited by Lothar Ehrlich and Jürgen John. Cologne, 1998.

Sabrow, Martin. *Der Rathenaumord: Rekonstruktion einer Verschwörung gegen die Republik von Weimar*. Munich, 1994.

Sabrow, Martin. *Die verdrängte Verschwörung: Der Rathenau-Mord und die deutsche Gegenrevolution*. Frankfurt am Main, 1999.

Schäfer, Claus W. *André François-Poncet als Botschafter in Berlin (1931–1938)*. Munich, 2004.

Schäfer, Kirsten A. *Werner von Blomberg: Hitlers erster Feldmarschall; Eine Biographie*. Paderborn, 2006.

Scheer, Regina. *"Wir sind die Liebermanns": Die Geschichte einer Familie*. Berlin, 2006.

Schildt, Axel. *Militärdiktatur auf Massenbasis? Die Querfrontkonzeption der Reichswehrführung um General Schleicher am Ende der Weimarer Republik*. Frankfurt am Main, 1981.

Schölzel, Christian. *Walther Rathenau: Eine Biographie*. Paderborn, 2006.

Schulin, Ernst. *Walther Rathenau: Repräsentant, Kritiker und Opfer seiner Zeit*. Göttingen, 1979.

Schulin, Ernst, and Wolfgang Michalka. *Walther Rathenau im Spiegel seines Moskauer Nachlasses*. Heidelberg, 1993.

Schulz, Gerhard. *Von Brüning zu Hitler: Der Wandel des politischen Systems in Deutschland 1930–1933*. Berlin, 1992.

Schulze, Hagen. *Otto Braun oder Preußens demokratische Sendung*. Frankfurt am Main, 1977.

Schulze, Hagen. "Vom Scheitern einer Republik." In *Die Weimarer Republik 1918–1933: Politik, Wirtschaft, Gesellschaft*, edited by Karl Dietrich Bracher, Manfred Funke, and Hans-Adolf Jacobsen. Düsseldorf, 1987.

Schulze, Hagen. *Weimar: Deutschland 1917–1933*. Berlin, 1982.

Sternburg, Wilhelm von. *Joseph Roth: Eine Biographie*. Cologne, 2009.

Stolleis, Michael. "Die soziale Problematik der Weimarer Reichsverfassung." In *Das Wagnis der Demokratie: Eine Anatomie der Weimarer Reichsverfassung*, edited by Horst Dreier and Christian Waldhoff. Munich, 2018.

Taylor, Frederick. *Inflation: Der Untergang des Geldes in der Weimarer Republik und die Geburt eines deutschen Traumas*. Munich, 2013.

Timm, Helga. *Die deutsche Sozialpolitik und der Bruch der Großen Koalition im März 1930*. Düsseldorf, 1952.

Tracy, Donald R. "Der Aufstieg der NSDAP bis 1930." In *Nationalsozialismus in Thüringen*, edited by Detlev Heiden and Gunther Mai. Weimar, 1995.

Trotnow, Helmut. *Karl Liebknecht: Eine politische Biographie*. Cologne, 1980.

Turner, Henry A. *Die Großunternehmer und der Aufstieg Hitlers*. Berlin, 1985.

Turner, Henry A. *Hitlers Weg zur Macht: Der Januar 1933*. Munich, 1996.

Ullrich, Sebastian. *Der Weimar-Komplex: Das Scheitern der ersten deutschen Demokratie und die politische Kultur der Bundesrepublik*. Göttingen, 2009.

Ullrich, Sebastian. "Stabilitätsanker oder Hysterisierungsagentur: Der Weimar-Komplex in der Geschichte der Bundesrepublik." In *Weimars Wirkung: Das Nachleben der ersten deutschen Republik*, edited by Hanno Hochmuth, Martin Sabrow, and Tilmann Siebeneichner. Göttingen, 2020.

Ullrich, Volker. *Adolf Hitler: Biographie*. Vol. 1, *Die Jahre des Aufstiegs 1889–1939*. Frankfurt am Main, 2013. Translated by Jefferson Chase as *Hitler: Ascent 1889–1939* (New York, 2016).

Ullrich, Volker. *Deutschland 1923: Das Jahr am Abgrund*. Munich, 2022. Translated by Jefferson Chase as *Germany 1923: Hyperinflation, Hitler's Putsch, and Democracy in Crisis* (New York, 2023).

Ullrich, Volker. *Die Hamburger Arbeiterbewegung vom Vorabend des Ersten Weltkriegs bis zur Revolution 1918/19*. Hamburg, 1976.

Ullrich, Volker. *Die nervöse Großmacht 1871–1918: Aufstieg und Untergang des deutschen Kaiserreichs*. Rev. ed. Frankfurt am Main, 2013.

Ullrich, Volker. *Die Revolution von 1918/19*. Munich, 2009.

Ullrich, Volker. *Kriegsalltag: Hamburg im Ersten Weltkrieg*. Cologne, 1982.

Vogelsang, Thilo. *Reichswehr, Staat und NSDAP: Beiträge zur deutschen Geschichte 1930–1932*. Stuttgart, 1962.

Wacker, Wolfgang. *Der Bau des Panzerschiffs "A" und der Reichstag*. Tübingen, 1959.

Walter, Dirk. *Antisemitische Kriminalität und Gewalt: Judenfeindschaft in der Weimarer Republik*. Bonn, 1999.

Wehler, Hans-Ulrich. *Deutsche Gesellschaftsgeschichte*. Vol. 4, *Vom Beginn des Ersten Weltkriegs bis zur Gründung der beiden deutschen Staaten 1914–1949*. Munich, 2003.

Weisbrod, Bernd. *Schwerindustrie in der Weimarer Republik: Interessenpolitik zwischen Stabilisierung und Krise*. Wuppertal, 1978.

Wernecke, Klaus. *Der vergessene Führer Alfred Hugenberg: Pressemacht und Nationalsozial-ismus.* Hamburg, 1982.

Werner, Frank. "Wir müssen über Weimar reden." *Die Zeit* 45 (November 3, 2022).

Wette, Wolfram. *Gustav Noske: Eine politische Biographie.* Düsseldorf, 1987.

Winkler, Heinrich August. *Der Schein der Normalität: Arbeiter und Arbeiterbewegung in der Weimarer Republik 1924 bis 1930.* Berlin, 1985.

Winkler, Heinrich August. *Der Weg in die Katastrophe: Arbeiter und Arbeiterbewegung 1930 bis 1933.* Berlin, 1987.

Winkler, Heinrich August. *Die Deutschen und die Revolution: Eine Geschichte von 1848 bis 1989.* Munich, 2023.

Winkler, Heinrich August. *Musste Weimar scheitern? Das Ende der ersten deutschen Republik und die Kontinuität der deutschen Geschichte.* Munich, 1991.

Winkler, Heinrich August. *Streitfragen der deutschen Geschichte: Essays zum 19. und 20. Jahrhundert.* Munich, 1997.

Winkler, Heinrich August. *Von der Revolution zur Stabilisierung: Arbeiter und Arbeiterbe-wegung in der Weimarer Republik 1918–1924.* Berlin, 1984.

Winkler, Heinrich August, ed. *Weimar im Widerstreit: Deutungen der ersten deutschen Republik im geteilten Deutschland.* Munich, 2002.

Winkler, Heinrich August. *Weimar 1918–1933: Die Geschichte der ersten deutschen Demokratie.* Munich, 1993.

Wisotzky, Klaus. "Der 'blutige Karsamstag' 1923 bei Krupp." In *Der Schatten des Welt-kriegs: Die Ruhrbesetzung 1923*, edited by Gerd Krumeich and Joachim Schröder. Essen, 2004.

Wright, Jonathan. *Gustav Stresemann 1878–1929: Weimars größter Staatsmann.* Munich, 2006.

Zerback, Ralf. *Triumph der Gewalt: Drei deutsche Jahre 1932 bis 1934.* Stuttgart, 2022.

Illustration Credits

Index

Page numbers in *italic* refer to illustrations.

AVAILABLE AND COMING SOON
FROM PUSHKIN PRESS

Pushkin Press was founded in 1997, and publishes novels, essays, memoirs, children's books—everything from timeless classics to the urgent and contemporary.

Our books represent exciting, high-quality writing from around the world: we publish some of the twentieth century's most widely acclaimed, brilliant authors such as Stefan Zweig, Yasushi Inoue, Teffi, Antal Szerb, Gerard Reve and Elsa Morante, as well as compelling and award-winning contemporary writers, including Dorthe Nors, Edith Pearlman, Perumal Murugan, Ayelet Gundar-Goshen and Chigozie Obioma.

Pushkin Press publishes the world's best stories, to be read and read again. To discover more, visit www.pushkinpress.com.

I LIVE A LIFE LIKE YOURS
JAN GRUE

A LINE IN THE WORLD
DORTHE NORS

STALKING THE ATOMIC CITY
MARKIYAN KAMYSH

CLOUDS OVER PARIS
FELIX HARTLAUB

THE WOLF AGE
TORE SKEIE

A WOMAN IN THE POLAR NIGHT
CHRISTIANE RITTER

A LIFE IN THE MAKING
FRANZ MICHAEL FELDER